THE CONNECTED
CARIBBEAN

Sidestone Press

THE CONNECTED
CARIBBEAN

A socio-material network approach
to patterns of homogeneity and
diversity in the pre-colonial period

Proefschrift

ter verkrijging van
de graad van Doctor aan de Universiteit Leiden,
op gezag van Rector Magnificus prof. mr. C.J.J.M. Stolker,
volgens besluit van het College voor Promoties
te verdedigen op 13 mei 2014
klokke 13:45 uur

door

Angenitus Arie Andries Mol

geboren te Rotterdam
in 1984

Promotor:

Prof. dr. C.L. Hofman (Universiteit Leiden)

Co-promotor:

Prof. dr. R.H.A. Corbey (Universiteit Leiden)

Overige leden:

Prof. dr. J.E. Terrell (Field Museum of Natural History, Chicago)
Prof. dr. U. Brandes (Universität Konstanz)
Dr. D.R. Fontijn (Universiteit Leiden)

Published by Sidestone Press, Leiden
www.sidestone.com

ISBN 978-90-8890-259-8

Lay-out & cover design: Sidestone Press

De totstandkoming van dit proefschrift werd financieel mogelijk gemaakt
door de Nederlandse Organisatie voor Wetenschappelijk Onderzoek (NWO);
projectnummer 277-62-001.

La mer, la mer, toujours recommencée

Paul Valéry, 1920

Voor André

Contents

List of figures

List of Tables

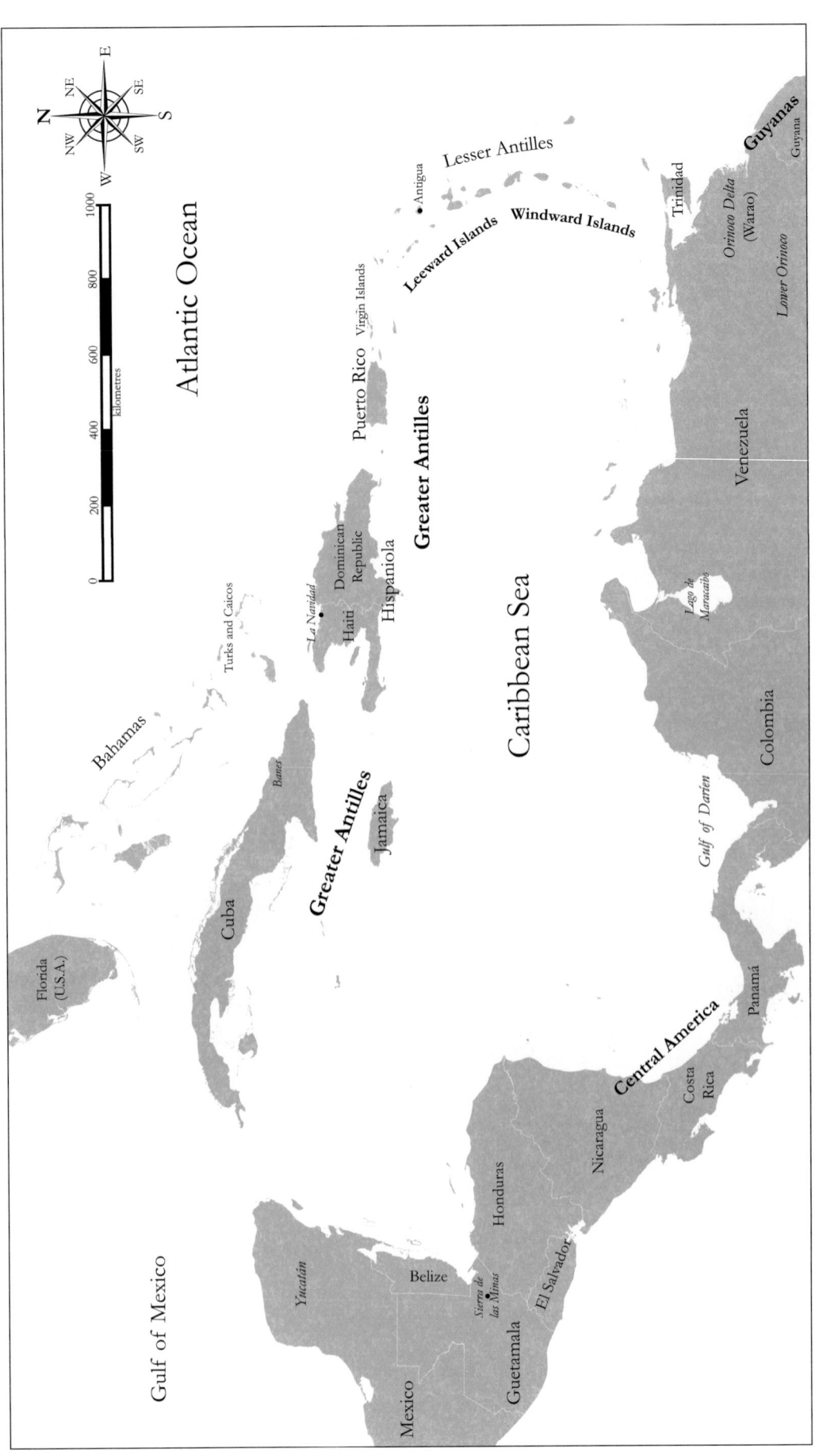

N

NW · NE

W · E

SW · SE

S

Atlantic Ocean

0   200   400   600   800   1000
kilometres

Gulf of Mexico

Florida (U.S.A.)

Bahamas

Turks and Caicos

Cuba

Greater Antilles

Jamaica

Banes

La Navidad

Haiti

Dominican Republic

Hispaniola

Greater Antilles

Puerto Rico

Virgin Islands

Leeward Islands

Windward Islands

Antigua

Lesser Antilles

Guyanas

Guyana

Trinidad

Orinoco Delta (Warao)

Lower Orinoco

Caribbean Sea

Venezuela

Lago de Maracaibo

Colombia

Gulf of Darién

Panamá

Costa Rica

Central America

Nicaragua

Honduras

El Salvador

Belize

Sierra de las Minas

Guatamala

Yucatán

Mexico

Chapter 1

Introduction: Homogeneity and Diversity in the Pre-colonial Caribbean

Ever since the entry of man into the Caribbean region, there have been two contradictory patterns at work. One trend has been toward homogeneity, the other toward diversity

Foreword to the *Caribbean* by Franklin W. Knight (2011: xv)

This work seeks to study the patterns of homogeneity and diversity that characterize the societal and cultural history of the pre-colonial Caribbean through an archaeological network approach. In the Caribbean islands, this history began when settlers colonized Trinidad from the Venezuelan coast around 6000 BC and Cuba from the Yucatán peninsula around 5000 BC. These first voyages into this pristine island world were the beginning of innumerable long-, middle-, and micro-distance movements of people, ideas, and goods. These movements and interactions shaped the Caribbean into what it is today: a stunningly diverse but also intricately interconnected geo-cultural region (Hofman and Hoogland 2011; Wilson 2007).

To the outside world, the Caribbean is perhaps most famous for the stereotypical image sold to its many tourist visitors depicting it as endless palm-dotted, white beaches bordered by a warm, bright blue sea (Sheller 2003). Although beaches and sea can certainly be found aplenty, this is only one of the Caribbean's many faces. For those who have the privilege to spend some time travelling in the region it soon becomes clear that there is not one Caribbean. Every Caribbean island nation has a different character and takes pride in their unique heritage. This is the result of the particular social, political and cultural historical trajectories and the often singular assets of Caribbean islands and peoples. What is more, the many smaller communities within these larger territories also each have their own "personality", based on distinctly local histories, ecologies, cultural practices, moral, political and legal systems, languages, and economies.

Nonetheless, wherever one travels along these dissimilar coasts of the Caribbean Sea there will always be a lingering feeling that individual island and mainland scenes are in some inexplicable way connected. The result is that the region's unity in diversity is unmatched by many of today's nation states or other political unions

(Knight 2011). This almost rhythmic pattern of homogeneity and diversity moved the literary scholar Antonio Benítez-Rojo to designate the Caribbean as a place that is different from most other regions on earth, labelling it a "meta-archipelago" (Benítez Rojo 1998; Figure 1.1). This metaphor is fitting as it underlines that the Caribbean is a space in which landmasses are separated and connected by water. On the other hand the Caribbean as a "meta-place" is something diverse yet connected, transcending the physical space itself.

The current political, cultural and social layout of this "meta-archipelagic" Caribbean is not only a result of shared colonial histories or of the region's globalizing economy and many interisland itinerants. For one, the contemporary Caribbean has been decidedly impacted by the Columbian Exchange (Crosby 2003). As a result of this a mass-movement of living beings, goods and ideas took place between the New and the Old world, two previously unconnected parts of the globe. The fact that the Caribbean was the nexus of this "exchange" had tremendous impact on the diversity of cultural, social, biological and political features found in the Caribbean today. Yet even long before one of history's major encounters had taken place, the societies and cultures of the pre-colonial Caribbean were already highly diverse yet intricately interconnected.

This is clear to scholars who are specialized in the study of the pre-colonial period of the Caribbean. When they compare the archaeological record from various periods and places they perceive a similar sort of immanent pattern of homogeneity and diversity that can be found in the contemporary Caribbean. In the archaeological record this pattern takes the shape of material cultural repertoires and practices that display overarching similarities overlying a bewildering local variety of material cultural assemblages. In the literature this aspect of the pre-colonial Caribbean is referred to under various headers: Chaos (Keegan 2004, 2007), veneer (*ibid.*), cultural mosaic (Wilson 1993), diffuse unity (Hoopes and Fonseca 2003; Rodríguez Ramos 2010b), Greater Caribbean culture (Rodríguez Ramos 2010a), multi-vectorality (Rodríguez Ramos and Pagán Jiménez 2006), (interlocked) interaction spheres (Boomert 2000; Mol 2011a), island rhythms (Hofman, Bright, *et al.* 2007), kaleidoscope (Siegel, *et al.* 2013) or webs (Oliver 2009).

The pan-Caribbean theory

The last decade and a half has seen a renewed interest in the question of how movements and interactions of people, goods and ideas defined this complex and chaotic pre-colonial Caribbean. This is correlated with new ways of thinking about the main lines of cultural history in the Caribbean (Curet and Hauser 2011; Fitzpatrick and Ross 2010; Hofman and van Duijvenbode 2011; Keegan, *et al.* 2013: Part III; Mol 2013; Rodríguez Ramos 2010a). Both these developments are prominently reflected in the formulation of a pan-Caribbean theory, which seeks to undo the disjoined perspective of Pre-Colombian Caribbean culture history, partitioned into islands and mainlands (Hofman and Bright 2010; Rodríguez Ramos 2010b). A pan-Caribbean theory opposes the idea of the Caribbean islands as a closed cultural area in which interactions within the region were stronger than interactions with other regions, restricted to East Venezuela and the Guianas (Curet 2011; cf. Rouse 1977; Rouse 1992). At the time it was introduced, it presented:

> "a broad, regional take on the prehistory of the wider Caribbean[, which] should not only provide a holistic view of the patterns of material interaction in the area, but, by expanding the scale of analysis, [open] the door to exploring hitherto un(der)considered long-distance, inter-societal engagements between the inhabitants of the islands and those of the surrounding continental regions" (Hofman and Bright 2010: i).

Although versions of the pan-Caribbean theory had been around for some time (Geurds and van Broekhoven 2010), it is not much of an exaggeration to say that the recent interest was sparked off by the ground-breaking results of a study on greenstone axes from Antigua (Harlow, et al. 2006). These axes were collected by Reg Murphy at the Royall's site (dated to around AD 250-750) and their geochemical composition was analysed by the research group of George Harlow at the American Museum of Natural History. The results showed that the green stone of which the axes were made was jadeitite with a strong similarity to Guatemalan sources in the Sierra de las Minas, a distance of a little under 3000 kilometres across the expanse of the Caribbean Sea. This was evidence of movement of materials over distances that, before the results of this study were made public, no one really expected to have existed in the pre-colonial Caribbean. If these Antiguan jades and others that have been found since then indeed originate from Guatemala, they suggested the existence of a sprawling distribution network that in terms of pure geographic distance is matched by only a few other non-state, non-modern cases – e.g. the well-known Polynesian or Viking Age exchange networks (Brink and Price 2008: part II; Kirch 1997).[1] It is therefore understandable that these jades and the possible ties that underlie their movement across the Caribbean had an enormous impact on the archaeology of the wider region, especially the Antillean islands.

The impact of these finds was heightened by the notion, held by some, that Caribbean archaeology at the beginning of the new millennium suffered an existential crisis (Fitzpatrick 2004; Keegan and Rodríguez Ramos 2004). It was felt that many post-1940 archaeological studies had placed the Caribbean at a dead-end street of migration and cultural diffusion, connected only to the rest of the world through the island bridge of the Lesser Antilles. The realization that the archaeological record of the pre-colonial Antilles possibly held hitherto unrecognized clues about interactions with cultures from regions other than Eastern Venezuela and the Guinanas therefore rapidly took hold. Growing evidence of the possible mobility of people, goods and ideas across the Caribbean readied the way for an approach in which the Caribbean Sea is seen to connect rather than separate landmasses and the people living on them. The result was a new pan-Caribbean

---

1   Since then two other jade sources have been found in the Antilles: on Hispaniola and Cuba. Petrographic characterization on these sources is not fully conclusive and more research is currently pending (Garcia-Casco, et al. 2013).

perspective stressing both the connections and diversity in the cultural histories of the islands (Hofman and Bright 2010; Hofman and Hoogland 2011).

Another field in which connections, rather than boundaries, have become increasingly important is in space-time systematics (Fitzpatrick 2006; Pestle, et al. 2013; Rodríguez Ramos, et al. 2010). Integration of C14 data sets, botanical studies and cultural stratigraphies with existing data sets has led to new understandings of ways in which space-time-cultural processes in the Caribbean may be linked. One of the results is a new picture of the interregional spread of "Neolithic" technologies, which goes far deeper back in time than previously recognized. It places the introduction of such innovations well into the "Archaic Age", a period previously considered to have a strictly "Meso-Indian" way of life, e.g. no larger and long-time settlements, no ceramics, no horticulture, no forms of social organisation beyond kinship ties, very little evidence for ritual activities or personal ornaments, and no cross-regional interactions or diffusion of ideas. Yet, more and more archaeologists have shown that many of these traits did already occur in the "Archaic Age" and have furthermore uncovered a deep history of cross-cultural interactions and varied cultural identities (Hofman, Boomert, et al. 2011; Pagán Jiménez 2011; Pagán Jiménez and Ramos 2007).

On the other side of the pre-historical spectrum, the Late Ceramic Age, the perceived unity of space-time-culture units is also under pressure. The validity of umbrella-terms like "the Taíno" and "chiefdom society" are put into doubt and in some cases abandoned altogether (Curet 2003; Rodríguez Ramos 2010a; Torres 2005, 2010). This has made room for new studies and ideas that take account of the various social, cultural and political connections underlying such questionable catch-all concepts.

The promises of ever-growing local data sets combined with hitherto unrecognized geographical and temporal connections defines the mind-set of the present period, characterized by some as a sort of regional disciplinal paradigm shift (cf. Kuhn 1962; Pestle, et al. 2013).[2] At the turn of the millennium the slow accretion of contra-theoretic findings had created a growing sense of crisis. Various landmark discoveries, among which the identification of possible Guatemalan jade in Antigua and other places in the eastern Caribbean, represented the tipping point in which the veracity of many longstanding, core theories were put into doubt. In addition, this period marked the final end of the reign of site assemblage-based, culture historical approaches, which had been steadily declining for some decades (Agorsah 1993; Curet 2005, 2011; Siegel 1996a; Trigger 2006: Chapter 7). In the wake of the perceived systemic failure of old theories and methodologies, many new, not necessarily mutually supportive, models and approaches now exist alongside each other. This means that for the moment pre-colonial Caribbean archaeology has become as diverse as its subject matter.

---

2   There is no clear starting point for this unease. It perhaps began somewhere in the eighties or nineties of the previous century with theories that went contrary to established ideas (Chanlatte Baik 1984; Chanlatte Baik and Narganes Storde 1990; Zucchi 1984, 1991).

Problems with categorization

It seems self-defeating to start off with a discussion of the pre-colonial Caribbean as a connected yet divided "meta-place", since it does not seem to offer much leeway for a systematic study of how society and culture in the region developed over time. Defining the Caribbean in this way is not the solution to understanding its local and regional histories, it is the starting point. Ultimately these metaphors, even as evocative as the "meta-archipelago" of Benítez-Rojo (1995) or the "cultural mosaic" of Samuel Wilson (1993), fail to capture the complexity of the Caribbean. Expanding the list of concepts as short-hands for describing what the Caribbean is will also not bring resolution. As can be seen from the "word clouds" on the cover or the one below of the first chapter of Benítez-Rojo's *La Isla que se repite* (Figure 1.1), adding descriptive concepts does not necessarily increase our understanding of what kind of thing "the Caribbean" is. Other ways of definition are required in order to come to grips with the patterns of homogeneity and diversity in the Caribbean.

Figure 1.1: A "word cloud" of the first chapter of La Isla que se repite *(Benítez-Rojo 1998). Word clouds are a visual presentation of the most frequently used words in a text. In this particular cloud many of the words can be seen as central concepts for discussions of the identity of place and culture in the post-colonial Caribbean. Nevertheless, although these concepts and their intuitive presentation provide a first approximation of the fluidity of recent Caribbean cultures and societies, "textual" and "metaphorical" approaches such as these do not allow for a deeper exploration of the millennia old patterns of connectivity in the region.*

In pre-colonial archaeology one of the solutions has been to divide the record into discrete entities that can be categorized and ordered, a way of working that is often referred to as the "culture historical project". The prevalent "modes of categorization" of this project lies at the heart of a long history of research on the origins and relations between pre-colonial cultures and societies, already going back to the first beginnings of Caribbean archaeology as a coherent scientific discipline (Ulloa Hung 2013: 21-25). The American anthropologist Jesse W. Fewkes, for instance, begins his conclusions on one of the first regional surveys with the following remark:

> "In the preceding account of archeological material from different islands the plan has been to group them as far as possible on a geographical basis. It is evident that there are great differences in the remains from different islands, and it is sought to account for these differences by minor variations in culture. A distinction in variety of cultures, probably in the beginning more marked, was more or less broken down by interchange of material cult objects before the advent of the Europeans, [but] the problem is a very complex one" (Fewkes 1912/1913: 259).

As this shows, Fewkes' solution was to divide the Caribbean into categories based on geographic proximity and material culture similarity – in this case the Greater Antilles, the Lesser Antilles and the Bahamas (*ibid.*: 266). Even if new studies proposed alternative divisions based on new lines of evidence and different categorizations, this has been the standard approach for over a century (e.g. Allaire 1977; Bullen and Bullen 1975; Keegan 1995; Lovén 1935; Petersen, *et al.* 2004; Rainey 1935; Rouse 1939, 1992).

In their most basic form these categorizations are based on a "binary" division that strongly focuses on the presence or absence of one trait or aspect of material culture assemblages. Based on this a period, region, site, or artefact will be put into a category for which a range of other cultural aspects are an implicit part. For instance, a temporal, spatial, cultural and societal boundary has traditionally been drawn between a-ceramic and ceramic material culture assemblages (cf. Rouse 1992). This means that if a site record contains ceramics it is understood to be part of a group of Ceramic Age sites. This is thought of as one category that includes other societal or cultural traits, such as horticulture, clearly articulated religious and ceremonial life, *etc.* The problem with theories based on one "binary" categorization is that they are much too inclusive to explain the complex nature of the archaeological record. When this was recognized the boundaries of dichotomous categories were often shifted or abandoned altogether, such as has happened with the infamous identification of "Crab and Shell peoples" in Puerto Rico (e.g. Rainey 1935, 1952).

As a result more binary subdivisions of primary binary categories were often added later. This resulted in "two-stepped binary" models. Examples of such two-stepped binary classifications systems in the Caribbean are the early archaeological writings on the Arawaks, peaceful with fine material culture, and Caribs, warlike with cruder material culture (e.g. Pinchon 1961; Rouse 1948a, 1948b). The *modos de vida* approach of the Latin American Social Archaeology is another two-stepped classification system and is sometimes still used today. Here a division is made based on subsistence techniques and socio-political ideology and structure, e.g. egalitarian hunter-gatherers and hierarchical agriculturalists (Vargas Arenas 1985). Another prevalent stepped binary mode of categorization is applied in order to divide the Archaic, Early and Late Ceramic Age cultures on the basis of their material culture assemblages and their status as a tribe or chiefdom society (Curet 1992, 2003; Siegel 1992). Often a third step category is added to this which is based on region. This differentiates between an Archaic, Early and Late Ceramic Age that have specific Greater and Lesser Antillean components – such as in the horizon approach adopted by Jacques and Henry Petit-Jean Roget (Bright 2011: 68-70).

The result of this way of categorizing assemblages was that, when more detailed data became available, this often falsified the original mode of categorization. This then necessitated a differentiation into ever smaller regional, temporal or cultural scales.[3] The one thing all the different categorizations have in common is that, based on presence and absence of certain material cultural traits, smaller categories are ordered into larger sets of categories. Often the vertical and horizontal ordering relate to temporal and geographic association. In the Caribbean, the modal approach by Rouse and the type-variety approach used by Bullen and Bullen, are examples of these more sophisticated modes of categorization.[4] They are essentially stepped binary models but due to their scope can hardly be recognized as such. In for example the modal approach, a style, comprised of a collection of assemblages, is part of a subseries (ending with the suffix –an) and multiple subseries are grouped into a series (ending with the suffix –oid): e.g. a sherd from components of the Maisabel site displays a Hacienda Grande style that is part of the Cedrosan Saladoid subseries, which is part of the Saladoid series that is imbedded in Ceramic Age culture (Figure 1.2, Rouse 1992; Siegel 1992). This mode of categorization can be referred to as "nested". The result of this has been a sophisticated "splitting or lumping project" (Siegel 1996a) and the creation of an expansive spatial-temporal-cultural model.

The beauty of such categorizations is that they can provide locally detailed groupings and order these as larger supra-categories. This provides relatively clear models of (material) cultural history and geography. Yet, what researchers studying diachronic and interregional patterns of mobility and exchange have found is that nested categories do not adequately reflect the transitivity and interrelatedness of Caribbean social histories and material cultural repertoires. The problem with these models is that even the most sophisticated nested categories necessitate a hard break that eventually has to be drawn between different groups (Petersen,

---

3   Sometimes this results into the recognition of overlap between categories, such as the Cuban *proto-agricolas*. Thought to represent a *modos de vida* that was partly agricultural but lacking a clear hierarchical society and culture (Ulloa Hung and Valcárcel Rojas 2002).

4   Although Rouse and Bullen and Bullen were the main proponents of their theories and method, many others took similar or closely related routes of approach to this problem (e.g. Allaire 1977; Chanlatte Baik and Narganes Storde 1990; Pinchon 1961; Veloz Maggiolo 1972).

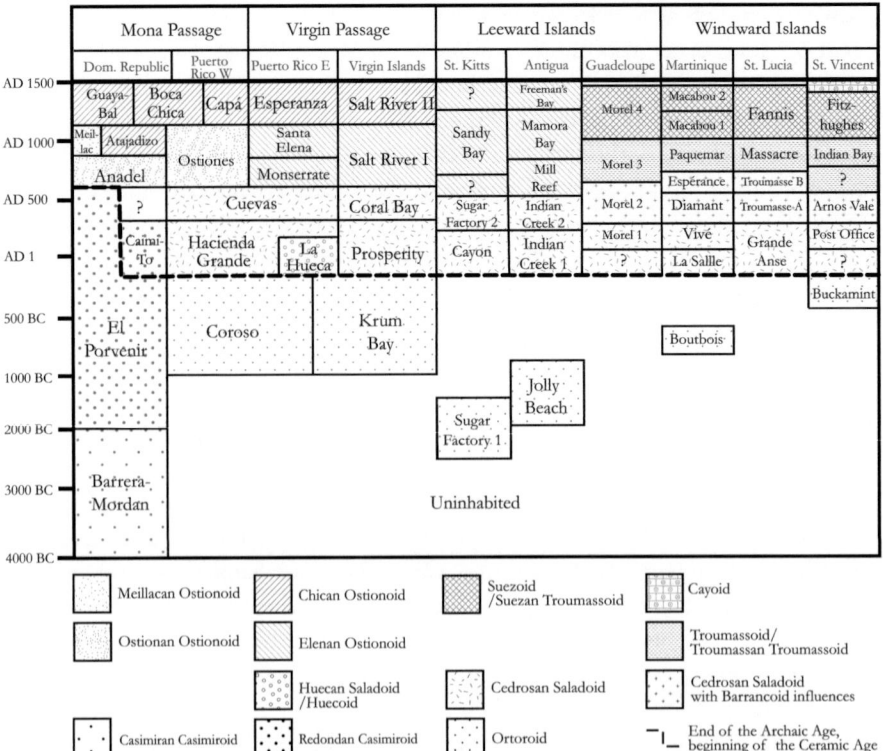

Figure 1.2: The culture history of the Northeastern Caribbean based on a categorization following the modal approach (cf. Rouse 1992).

et al. 2004).[5] So, while (nested) models are highly advanced, particularly in the Caribbean, it is now often felt that they fail to capture the social and cultural intricacies of pre-colonial history (Curet 2005: 57-58; Hofman and Hoogland 2011; Keegan and Rodríguez Ramos 2004).

The result is a growing incompatibility between the increasingly complex nature of the pre-colonial Caribbean archaeological record and prevalent categorizations that stress bounded groups of material culture and monolithic historical processes. It has thus become apparent that the Caribbean cannot only be understood in terms of categories of material cultures reflecting histories of bounded groups or islands (Rodríguez Ramos and Pagán Jiménez 2006). I will expand upon this insight by showing that the societies and histories of the indigenous peoples of the Caribbean can in fact best be studied through the complex and multi-faceted connections that make up its archaeological record. I will argue that we can use the information gained from studying site assemblages, object categories, and other material culture practices and repertoires to form or "abstract" networks, which

---

5   In Rouse (1986: 7)'s words: "[T]he areal and temporal divisions of a chronological chart are made culturally as homogeneous as possible, each combination of the two of them [...] ought to contain a different people and culture."

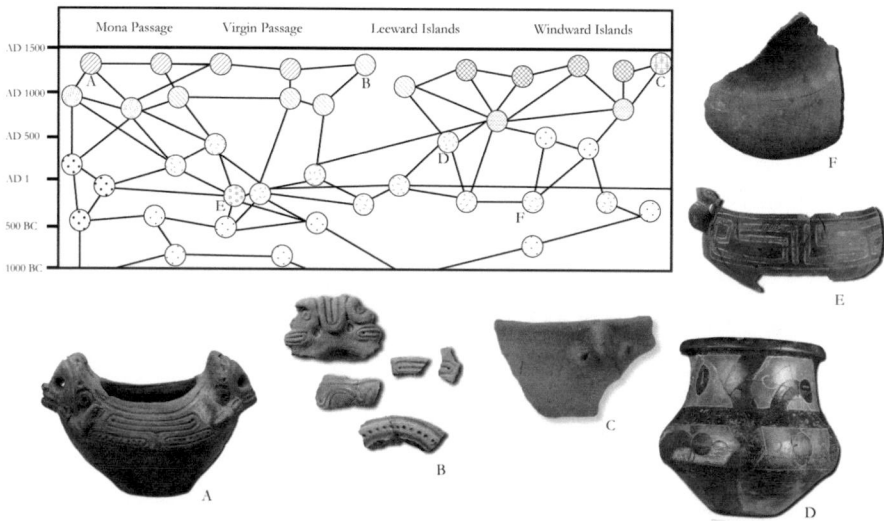

Figure 1.3: A network of the connections between ceramic assemblages and their spatial and temporal distribution. It is based on Rouse's culture historical scheme (Figure 1.2), but it shows how the homogeneity and diversity of (ceramic) assemblages could be adapted to be visualized as a network. A node represents the ceramic assemblage of one site and the node's colour is based on the identification of the dominant (sub)series according to Rouse (see Figure 1.2 for key). The lettered nodes correspond to the illustrated ceramics from actual site ceramic assemblages (not to scale). Node A: Boca Chica style vessel from Boca Chica (Dominican Republic). Node B: Boca Chica style sherds from Kelbey's Ridge 2 (Saba). Node C: Cayo rim sherd from Argyle 2 (St. Vincent, photograph courtesy of Arie Boomert). Node D: (Insular) Saladoid vessel from Golden Rock (St. Eustatius). Node E: Huecoid vessel from La Hueca (Vieques, Puerto Rico). Node F: Badly eroded Early Saladoid vessel wall from Brighton Beach (St. Vincent). Photo B courtesy of Menno Hoogland and Corinne L. Hofman and photo C, D, E courtesy of Arie Boomert.

can be explored, analysed and interpreted by adopting a network approach (Figure 1.3).

Network concepts and network models

Networks consist of nodes and ties, represented by dots and lines in most popular network visualizations. The networks and the nodes therein are defined by their dependencies, or the relations between the nodes. This is in contrast to (statistical) groupings into categories, in which the idea is to separate individual "entities" – sites, artefacts or archaeological cultures – into more or less homogenous collectives. As discussed above, these entities are defined by their structural boundaries. Network approaches on the other hand place most emphasis on dependencies within (data)sets (Borgatti, *et al.* 2009; Brandes, *et al.* 2013; Newman 2010; Scott 2000). To further study and analyse such networks in archaeological assemblages this study will utilize basic concepts and measures from graph theory. Matrix calculations are used to measure the structural properties of nodes and networks, in which rows and columns are nodes and their intersections are ties (Chapter 3).

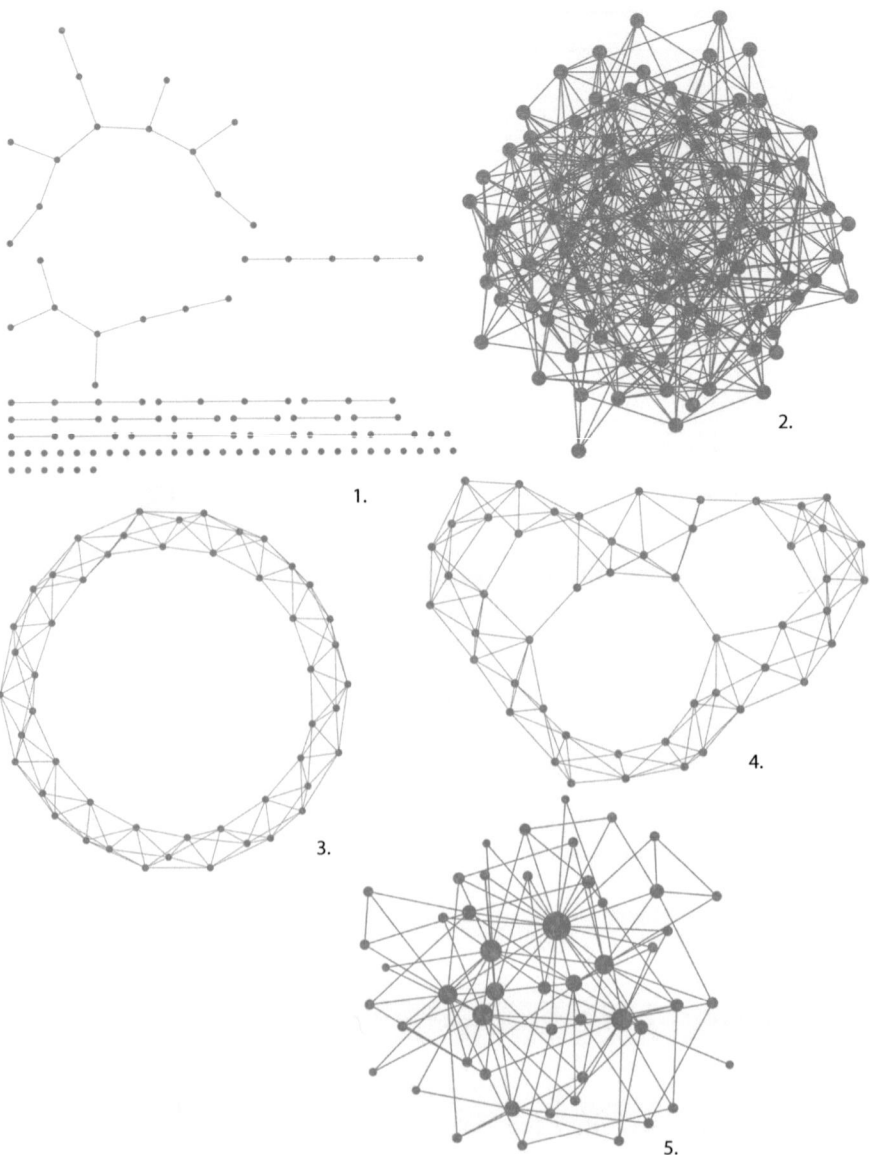

Figure 1.4: Five examples of network models: 1. Sparse random network (p = 0.01); 2. Dense random network (p = 0.1); 3. Lattice network (neighbourhood = 3); 4. Small world network (neighbourhood = 3, edge re-wiring p = 0.1); 5 Scale-free network (node size relative to node degree).

A network approach is built on the premise that it is insightful to study how individual "entities" in a data set are differentially connected to other "entities". At the outset it is important to note that basically anything can constitute a node and the ties connecting it can be any sort of "relation", which allows for a variety of network approaches that will be expanded upon in later chapters. A node can have as many ties as there are nodes in the network which it is a part of – or even more if nodes can be connected by more than one type of tie. What is especially interesting for the purposes of this study is that in networks there is differential grouping of nodes and ties. Yet, because a network approach focuses on connections not boundaries, the composition of groups is based on ties between nodes and not on group boundaries (Figure 1.3). This also means that, while a node can be connected to one group, it can also have ties that make it part of a different group. In a Caribbean network such groupings can be contrasted with some of the traditionally recognized (material culture) categories.

It is important to note that the networks that can be abstracted in this way function not as direct reflections of reality but as models that should be used to test hypotheses with. In the network sciences one avenue of approach is to test hypotheses on the formational and developmental dynamics that drive a real world network model by contrasting them to other possible network models guided by (slightly) different dynamics and parameters. Although numerous models and theories can account for network formation and change, I will briefly illustrate how certain dynamics can act upon networks by discussing random, (ring) lattice, small-world and scale-free networks (Figure 1.6). These are just a selection from many possible models. The reason for choosing these models is that they are the most widely known and have already been applied in the archaeological network literature.

A random graph is a model network in which specific parameters have fixed values, but the network is random in other respects. Usually these parameters define the chance that a tie connects one node to another node.[6] The $G(n,p)$ model assigns the same possibility for every tie to be included. If a random network contains a hundred nodes and the probability that a node connects to another node is 0.01 it is likely to have only a few larger components, many pairs of nodes and many nodes that have no ties to others (Figure 1.4.1). On the other hand if a network contains one hundred nodes and $p = 0.1$ all the nodes in the network are likely to be connected to at least a few other nodes, creating one large component in which it is difficult to visually distinguish individual nodes and ties from each other (Figure 1.4.2).

Structures abstracted from real networks generally display traits that are highly unlikely to occur in simple random networks such as the $G(n,p)$ model. For example, in the case of any given person it is extremely improbable that his or her social network will be structured according to the parameters of the $G(n,p)$ model, so different rules must be structuring social networks as well. An example of such a rule is how classic and modern, cross-cultural research on the extents of people's social network time and again yields the same result: the vast majority of people can be connected with any random individual through a small number of steps from one node to another. These steps, representing all sorts of social interactions from sexual encounters to handshakes, are also known as "degrees of separation" (Watts 2003).

---

6   More than being an actual model in itself, random networks more often serve as a substrate to test the possibility of a process taking place on another network (Newman 2010: Chapter 12).

Six is the magic number of degrees – pointing to the concept that six social interactions separate two random individuals on average. This network distance is often referred to in fictional and popular scientific accounts of network structures, but is, depending on the setting of the network under study, a little on the low side. It is nevertheless true that random nodes in many real-life networks can be connected by means of a surprisingly short path. This has become known as the "small-world phenomenon" (Watts 1999; Figure 2.6.4). So-called "weak ties" play a pivotal part in small-world networks because they allow an individual to reach out beyond his or her local group of "strong" ties.[7] The idea of "weak ties" is conceptually close to the importance archaeologists lend to exotic objects in site assemblages: serving to connect the local people originally living at the site to other's beyond the immediate region. The function of weak ties in (social) networks is clear, but how do certain networks form "small-worlds"?

The physicists Watts and Strogatz modelled how such small-worlds depended on tie attachment and a clustering co-efficient. In their random α-model they first abstracted to two extremes, one was called the "cavemen" and the other the "Solaria" network.[8] Watts and Strogatz realized, however, that between these extremes there were very large clustering co-efficient ranges and that propensity for clustering was already dependent on a substrate of node and tie-relations. In their β-model they started out from a ring-lattice network. This is a perfectly circular graph in which n nodes are related to K other nodes, $K/2$ on each side (Figure 1.4.3). From this perfect ring-lattice an iterated, random tie-rewiring would be undertaken with probability β. What will follow for most values of β is a network of locally dense clusters linked to other clusters by means of a small number of ties (Watts 1999).

Overall, small-worlds seem to be an attractive model to explain features of the connected past. For example, in his study on the connected world of the Vikings, Sindbaek constructs two networks that provide a good example of a historically and archaeologically attested small-world (Sindbaek 2007). One network is based on site assemblages, while the other is an affiliation network of locations and individuals mentioned in the *Vita Anskarii*, an account of the life and times of the missionary Bishop Anskar. What is interesting is that, as a network model, the textual study and the network based on co-occurrence of artefact types present

---

7 Note that the connotation "weak" is slightly misleading. Being weak does not mean that the tie itself is doubtful or not of high value: e.g. when, in an archaeological case, we see little evidence for a connection or that the amount of exotic material is only very small compared to the amount of local material. The "weakness" of a tie is relative to the composition of a node's dominant subgraphs. In fact, because of their connective potential, one could say that the impact of such exotic ties for the overall network is greater than those of "strong" ties. The centrality of weak ties is thus essentially a network operationalization of the (in the Caribbean) well-known work of Mary Helms on the "power of the exotic" (Helms 1988).

8 In a cavemen network if a node is connected to another node it is also highly likely that it will connect to a node that the other node is already connected to. The result is a large number of mutual contacts – mimicking the popular cliché that our Palaeolithic ancestors were part of small, localized cave-groups. This is good for local cohesion, but detrimental for connections between groups. Solaria was a fictional human-inhabited planet in Isaac Asimov's *Foundation* and *Robot* series. This planet was only sparsely inhabited by extreme isolationists who only randomly paired up to mate. Nodes in the Solaria model will have no propensity to interact with anyone in particular, so it is highly unlikely that local clustering will evolve.

comparable results. Both indicate that the Viking network was held together by a small number of weak ties between (geographically) local clusters. Therefore, even if they were spread all over Europe and beyond, some Viking Age communities were part of a small-world.

Sindbaek's case-study also showed that weak ties tended to cluster at specific nodes. According to the *Vita Anskarii* it was Bishop Anskar and other clergymen but not laity who did most of the travelling between villages and towns. Higher-ranking members of the Church therefore created the small network distances between the widely dispersed locations mentioned in the text. The same can be said for Viking Age sites. Viking trading towns or *emporia*, such as Hedeby and Ribe in Denmark, held the majority of the ties within the model. Trading towns thus lay at the basis of the small-world of the Vikings and were responsible for holding it together. This shows that, aside from weak ties, connectivity in the wider network can also depend on the central position of certain nodes.

The idea of powerful or central nodes is closely allied to the dynamic and complex structure of a network. These network hubs can be conceptualized as "ports of trade", because they are the start- or endpoint of numerous routes (Polanyi 1963). Due to the sheer quantity of ties that go to or away from them, they are the centre of otherwise less-connected network components (Figure 1.4.5). Yet even though such hubs are a frequent occurring feature of real life networks, their emergence is not a probability whenever network ties follow a simple random model such as $G(n,p)$ or even that of a small-world (Watts 2003: 104). Although weak ties can explain how real life networks can form small-worlds structures they cannot explain why some real life networks contain hubs with an extremely high degree of ties.

Studies dating to the late 1990s carried out by the physicist Barabasí and his research group on the structure of the worldwide web show how unlikely hubs really are in random networks. At that time the worldwide web was thought to contain around a billion (10^9) webpages. The chance of a website having an indegree of 500 – 500 incoming links from other webpages – in a randomly linked worldwide web was calculated to be 10^{-99}. Nonetheless, a survey of less than 20% of the real worldwide web found over four hundred of such highly connected pages, a small number of which had an even higher indegree. Based on this and similar studies Barabasí and colleagues found that node degrees in networks such as the worldwide web had the fat-tailed distribution indicative of a power law (Albert, *et al.* 1999; Barabasí, *et al.* 1999). A power law, made well known by studies of self-organizing systems, is defined by the exponential relation of the frequency of an occurrence to another trait of that occurrence (Barabasí 2003). One trait of a power law is that it is scale-free: the introduction of a constant factor results in a proportionate scaling of the original power-law relation (Newman 2004).

The first surprising result of their studies of the web prompted Barabasí and his research group to look for power laws in other networks, too. This quest for power law distributions is described in his publication *Linked*. It hammered home the importance of (scale-free) networks to a wide audience, including several archaeologists (Brughmans 2013), by claiming to have located them in an astounding range of real life networks: from co-starring Hollywood actors to the metabolic system of the human cell. Something all such networks share is that they follow a form of Pareto's principle in which the majority of the ties point to a minority of the nodes (Figure 1.4.5).[9] Barabasí proposes that there are two general dynamic processes responsible for this. The first is sequential network growth. This process has a network evolving on a step by step basis. During every step a new node and n ties are added to the network that wire to a random node. In this way nodes that are the first on the scene have the largest aggregate chance of receiving incoming ties. Latecomers should therefore always be less connected than the "early birds". It is not difficult to imagine that this might work in a real world scenario.[10] In fact, it seems archaeological network studies are pre-eminently suited for studying this type of sequential network growth. It is, for example, a feature of Sindbaek (2007)'s Viking network: Ribe, the oldest emporium, is also one of the most central nodes in the network. A similar feature high degree coupled to node and tie persistence can be found in the multi-scalar data sets of Southwest U.S.A. networks (Mills, *et al.* 2013).

The second process acting on the formation of large hubs in scale-free networks is preferential attachment. This is in effect a "rich get richer" measure in which new nodes in the network will preferentially tie themselves to those nodes that already have many ties. This too seems to be part of real life network dynamics: a popular song will be played more often on the radio and becomes more popular; an academic paper that is often cited will be widely known and will therefore be cited even more often; and an artefact style or form found in many locations is more likely to diffuse to even more places (Bentley and Shennan 2003; Kandler and Laland 2009). Together sequential growth and preferential attachment hold the key to creating hubs of truly epic proportions.

In the wake of the discoveries made by Barabasí and his team, the scale-free network model has become immensely popular across different disciplines, including archaeology. A plethora of researchers have since tried to argue for the presence of power laws in their own data sets (Stumpf and Porter 2012). However, power laws are in the end statistical distributions that depend upon large relational data sets that need to be rigorously tested with the right statistical tools before they can be called significant. In most cases, archaeological relational data sets will lack the parameters to truly prove whether they form scale-free networks or not. In some cases this can perhaps be done (Grove 2011; Mills, *et al.* 2013), but these should be seen as the exception rather than the norm. Ironically, the substantiation of the hypothesis that sequential network growth and preferential attachment dynamics

---

9   This rule holds that the majority (80%) of effects is correlated with a minimum (20%) of the causes. Pareto's principle is just a rule of thumb, but it is remarkable how applicable it is with regard to many areas of life. My personal experience during archaeological fieldwork is that 80% of the most interesting finds take place in 20% of the excavation time – Murphy's law then ensures that these are often the final 20% of the days of the excavation campaign.

10   Although it is not always true that what has been around the longest is also the most popular. In a separate case-study Barabasí factors in the possibility of successful newcomers and tie rewiring that allows for a rearrangement of sequential growth networks (see Chapter 5).

underlie several or many real networks may benefit from the type of evolutionary study offered by archaeology.

In theory, the hypothesis that pre-colonial interaction networks take the shape and follow the dynamics of one or more of the models discussed above can be verified against archaeology reality. For example, with a stretch of the imagination, it could be claimed that diachronic continuity and change in the Caribbean archaeological record were "random" processes. In this case we would see patterns of homogeneity and diversity that are unchecked by any other types of processes, but for the p that a node is related to a random other node. This is perhaps closest to the undifferentiated view held by Benítez-Rojo that envisions the Caribbean as a space of chaos, although it should be noted that Keegan has pointed out that this "chaotic" Caribbean is itself a complex adaptive system (Keegan 2004). In contrast to this, patterns of homogeneity and diversity may be regularly structured, e.g. following a lattice layout. For example, communities would connect to only a few of their closest neighbours, for whatever measure of distance one takes (Keegan 2010). This view comes close to Rouse's (1992) migration and cultural diffusion model. In this model the network is initially based on large-scale migrations within a geographically constrained but interlocked archipelagic world. Then again, as has been discussed above, recent evidence suggests that the Caribbean was rather more like a small world, with various and sustained long-distance weak ties connecting its various coastal and island communities (Hofman and Hoogland 2011). It is also possible that certain places and (material) cultural repertoires, practices and identities developed to become so central in the networks of people, goods and ideas that they started acting as hubs, giving (parts of) the network a free-scale character. Such hubs could have formed the basis of a robustly connected yet slightly less diverse network. It is this type of model that seems to be proposed in recent archaeological theories focusing on one island region or type of material culture as the spoke in the wheel of interregional interactions (e.g. Heckenberger 2013; Rodríguez Ramos 2010a, 2010b, 2011).

Even if the adaptation of specific network science models and theories into archaeology has been productive, here I consider whatever network model or theory best characterizes or explains the structure of a (number of) pre-colonial network(s) to be of secondary importance. The reason for this is that these networks first need to be abstracted and explored from the available data, before we can start to formulate systemic theories or models that can explain for them. In addition, a number of concepts and methods that will be employed are new to (Caribbean) archaeology. Similar network data-sets from which general dynamics can be hypothesized and contrasted are thus not readily available. The result of this is that the networks that will be explored in Chapters 5 to 8 have no directly compatible models to which they can comfortably be compared to at this moment. Aside from this is the fact that identifying the network dynamics at play in the pre-colonial Caribbean will not suffice to understand them as networks of a particular kind, embedded within actual historical and local contexts. Because of this, at this point in time I consider it most fruitful to integrate and check theories and hypotheses that may be drafted from the existing body of Caribbean archaeological theories.

Hidden network models in Caribbean archaeology

This new approach to the indigenous past of the region has already been foreshadowed by one and a half decade of studies that have addressed a myriad of "network" interactions in the form of mobility and exchange studies of people, goods and ideas (e.g. Boomert 2000; Bright 2011; Cooper, *et al.* 2008; Crock 2000; Curet 2005; Curet and Hauser 2011; de Waal 2006; Delpuech and Hofman 2004; Fitzpatrick 2013a; Fitzpatrick, *et al.* 2008; Hofman and Bright 2010; Hofman, Bright, *et al.* 2008; Hofman, Bright, *et al.* 2007; Hofman and Hoogland 2003; Hofman, Mol, *et al.* 2011; Hofman and van Duijvenbode 2011; Isendoorn, *et al.* 2008; Keegan 2007; Knippenberg 2007; Laffoon 2012; Mol 2007, 2008, 2010, 2011a, b, 2013; Mol and Mans 2013; Morsink 2012; Pagán Jiménez and Ramos 2007; Rodríguez Ramos 2010a, 2011; Rodríguez Ramos, *et al.* 2008; Rodríguez Ramos and Pagán Jiménez 2006; Ulloa Hung 2013; Valcárcel Rojas 2012).[11] In fact, several of the network explorations in this work could not have been undertaken without some of the wide-ranging and breakthrough studies of recent years.

An asset of these new approaches to mobility and interaction in the pre-colonial Caribbean is that they depart more and more from a multi-scalar approach (Heckenberger 2011; Hofman and Hoogland 2011). How movements of material culture and people at the site level are mediated and how this can be correlated with interactions at other scales of analysis is actively being investigated by a number of researchers (Curet 2005; Hofman and Hoogland 2011; Keegan 2007; Mans 2011; Mol 2011a; Samson 2010; Ulloa Hung 2013). Another strength of a majority of these works is that they are emphatically multi-disciplinary and (cross-)regionally

---

11   The popularity of archaeological studies of pre-colonial interaction is also visible when one views the number of symposia dealing with the subject. The first of an ongoing series titled "Leiden in the Caribbean" was held in 2002 and chaired by Corinne Hofman and André Delpuech. The symposium "Late Ceramic Age Societies in the Eastern Caribbean", brought together a large group of scholars to rethink the connections between Eastern Caribbean communities (published as Delpuech and Hofman 2004). This symposium was the kickoff point for a wave of symposia and workshops on interactions in the pre-colonial Caribbean. Papers presented at other "Leiden in the Caribbean" symposia, of which five to date have been organised, often take the study of Pre-Columbian patterns of mobility and exchange as their point of departure. Moreover, several SAA symposia, among which the opening session "Islands in the Stream" chaired by Curet at the 2006 71st annual meeting (published as Curet and Hauser 2011), the "Mobility and Exchange from a Pan-Caribbean Perspective" symposium chaired by Hofman and Bright at the 2008 (published as Hofman and Bright 2011) 73rd annual meeting were the platforms for breakthrough studies. In 2009, "The Caribbean Basin before Columbus" a one-day symposium chaired by Keegan and sponsored by the Pre-Columbian Society in Washington, D.C. also had mobility and exchange as its central themes. The "Rethinking Precolonial Socialities in the Ancient Caribbean" symposium chaired by Rodríguez Ramos and Torres at the 2010 75th annual meeting advanced the concept of methodological relationalism. Recently, at the 2013 SAA, a session was organized by Corinne Hofman and Ian Lilley that focused on the analogous histories of cultural encounters in the Pacific and the Caribbean. Last, but not least, this decade has also seen a sharp incline in papers dealing with topics of mobility and exchange on all levels and in all periods in the Proceedings of the (bi-annual) Congress of the International Association for Caribbean Archaeology.

focused. Particularly archaeometrical analysis has yielded much new information on pre-colonial patterns of interaction (Hofman, Hoogland, *et al.* 2008). The broadening of the field of Caribbean archaeology proper to include Caribbean coastal regions of the South American and Central American mainland has also been influential in widening the scope of pre-colonial patterns of interactions (Harlow, *et al.* 2006; Hofman and Bright 2010; Rodríguez Ramos 2010b; Wilson 1993). Comparable research in other island regions has also stressed the importance of interaction networks for the archaeology of islands and archipelagoes on a global scale (e.g. Terrell 2008).

As Rouse predicted over a quarter of a century ago (Rouse 1986: 172-175), thanks to methodological and theoretical advances it seems the time is ripe to further explore the social (network) history of the Caribbean. On the other hand, while there are now more studies that focus on relations between communities, individuals and groups of material culture, the supposed dynamics underlying these connections have not been addressed from a systemic or network point of view. It is safe to say that there exists a general unawareness of the hidden assumptions about the structure of networks that come with specific past and present theoretical viewpoints. This is not surprising considering the fact that the data sets on which these new approaches were built were also still framed in the previously discussed traditional categorizations.

With the risk of oversimplifying a decidedly multi-theoretical field, it can be said that the types of Caribbean archaeological theories of immediate interest for this study fall within two groups: (1) theories of culture historical continuity and change and (2) theories of socio-political organization and its relations to material culture. Both these themes present their own quite specific perspectives on social interaction and the wider networks resulting from them. For example, as can be seen from the quote by Fewkes above it has been established early on that the quantity and direction of human mobility and interactions is a shaping factor for cultural change in the region (Fewkes 1912/1913; Rouse 1986). Similar broadly shared notions apply to socio-political developments, such as the idea that systems of relations between items of material culture influence and are impacted by socio-political organization and ideology (Boomert 2001a; Curet 1996; Oliver 2009; Walker 1993).

To give more specific examples: the various cultural historical theories bring with them their own ideas on the structure and dynamics of relations. These can be "translated" into specific types of network models (Figure 1.5). For instance, the migration theories of Rouse (1986, 1992) present a particular network structure and dynamic in which a network is taken over by new and different nodes (the migrants) who do not seek to interact with nodes that were already present in the network (the original inhabitants). In contrast, a network based on the idea of "interaction spheres", another prevalent Caribbean theory (Allaire 1991; Boomert 2000; Caldwell 1964; Haviser 1991), consists of cliques or completely connected groups of nodes because they are at least joined by one type of interaction (religious, economic, political, *etc.*). Similarly, world-systems theory presents a view of interacting cores and peripheral nodes (Hardy 2008). Recent theories on

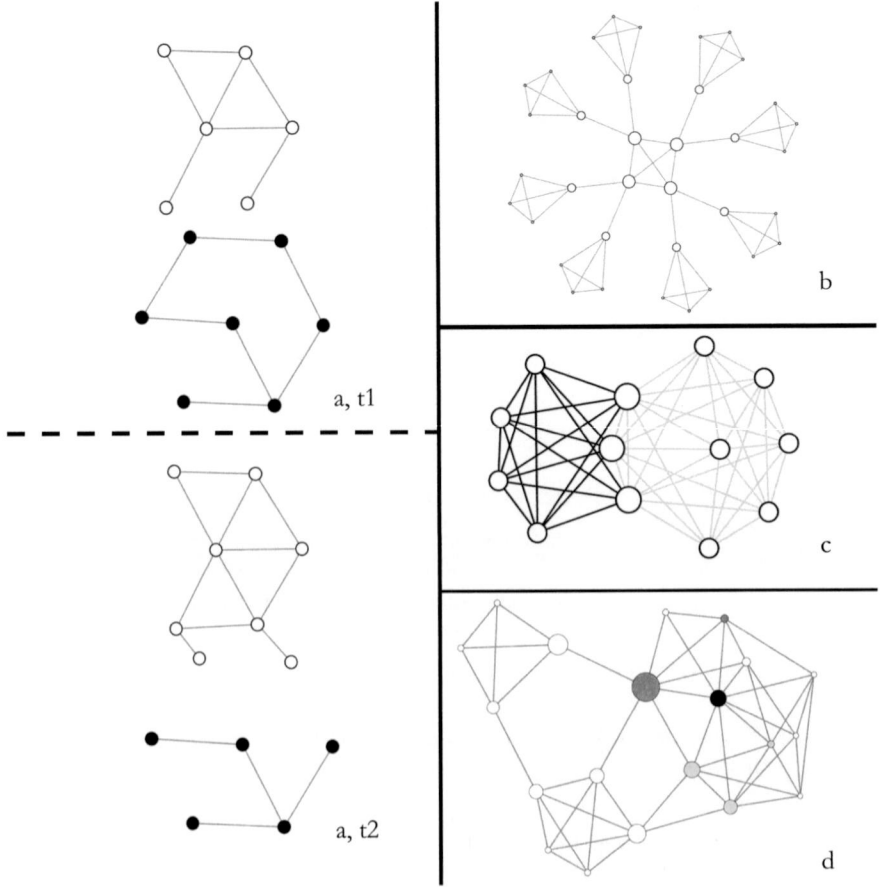

Figure 1.5: Four "hidden" network models in Caribbean archaeological theory. A: t1 to
t2 shows a model of migration that replaces previous cultural practices (cf. Rouse 1992).
B: World-systems theory, node size correlates to status centrality (Hardy 2008; for an
explanation of "status centrality" see Chapter 3). C: Two interlocked interaction spheres, for
example a religious network (grey ties) and a trade network (black ties), node size correlates to
betweenness centrality and following Caldwell (1964) the node size is indicative of the measure
of innovation at the location of the node (e.g. Allaire 1990; Boomert 2000; Haviser 1991; for
an explanation of "betweenness centrality" see Chapter 3). D: Dual-Processual model (cf.
Blanton, et al. 1996), node size is based on betweenness centrality (representing nodes most
successful in "network" strategies) and node colour from black to white represents status
centrality (representing nodes most successful at "corporate" strategies). Note that this model
shows that it is most advantageous to mix both strategies (see Chapter 7).

the spread of Arawakan languages and material culture repertoires are based on
the idea of cultural assimilation (Heckenberger 2013). This can be transposed to a
network that shows a clique, of "cultural infiltrators", that is embedded in a larger
network of culturally "autochthonous" people.

Socio-political evolutionary theories often present their own views on the
longitudinal development of societal and material cultural systems. So-called cultural
evolutionary theories provide models of political organization that emphasized

how certain types of group structures, inter-personal hierarchies, and material culture belonged together (e.g. Siegel 1992). This often goes in conjunction with an ecological perspective (e.g Steward 1948; Service 1962). In the school of Latin American Social Archaeology, a variant of historical materialist Marxism (McGuire 2002; McGuire and Navarrete 2005), evidence for certain subsistence strategies are considered to be indicative of how socio-political networks were formed and maintained (e.g. Sanoja 2007; Vargas Arenas 1985, 1989; Veloz Maggiolo *et al.* 1981). More recent works on socio-political complexity have a more flexible understanding of the flow of power in networks. Yet here assumptions are also made on how the formation and development of the networks in question is structured. Corporate and network strategies of the Dual-Processual theory (Blanton *et al.* 1996; Siegel 2004), for instance, suggest the existence of two types of political network strategies, one in which there are strong interactions in communities versus political networks that are built on the creation and maintenance of inter-group ties.

What these "hidden" network structures and dynamics in Caribbean archaeological theories tell us is that the problem is not that it is difficult to formulate and apply (social) network theories in Caribbean archaeology, as some would content (Keegan 2007; Oliver 2009). On the contrary, "hidden" network theory formulation and application has already been undertaken on a large scale. This has led to a discrepancy between the extent that theories of (social) networks have been employed and the awareness that these models presuppose specific (social) network structures and dynamics. The result hereof is that these systems are often interpreted from the top down based on the specific theoretic perspectives that have been used to understand them. In the case studies I will use existing theories and explicitly draft and discuss them as networks. These "standard networks" will then be contrasted to network explorations based on archaeological and ethnohistorical sources in order to check their original hypotheses.

Networks of "people" and networks of "pots"

Although the prefix "social" is almost instinctively put before any type of network study, there is nothing inherently social about networks (Brandes, *et al.* 2013). It is rather the other way around: there is something inherently networked about societies, communities, families and other human relations. Moreover, there is something inherently networked about material culture, which is of course the premise of archaeological inquiry – i.e. uncovering the pattern of relations between things, based on shape, material, decoration, context, *etc*. So, while the ties in archaeological data can be conceptualized as "social" and originally were part of flows of goods, services, respect, leadership, alliances, conflicts, marriage partners, friendship, information and advice *etc*. (e.g. Borgatti *et al.* 2009; Prell 2011; Scott 2012), the networks themselves are not directly representative of this. Any inferences on the structure and dynamic of past social networks is not based on data from the direct observation or investigation of human interaction, as is generally the case in social network studies – with the exception of archaeological studies of the present (e.g. Mans 2011; Mol and Mans 2013; Mol, in press). This is a basic but important divergence between social network approaches and archaeological network approaches.

Even if they are not abstractions of social but of material ties, the Caribbean archaeological record can be explored as a network. However, when we directly conceptualize the kinds of material systems based on archaeological study as social networks we run the risk of perceiving "pots as peoples", without taking into account how networks of "pots" are actually reflective of networks of "people". Hence, what is needed is a specific understanding that does not focus exclusively on these systems being either social or material, but rather perceives of them as being "interdependent". From this point of view the Caribbean archaeological record was shaped by "ties that matter" and "matter that ties".[12] The fact that these two phrases chase each other's tail, illustrates that the connections between social and material networks are intricate and many-sided. As we will see, it is often impossible to understand social and material ties as separate phenomena. Furthermore, it also shows the potentially close overlaps between the two central approaches of this study. The question of how "matter" —objects, things, artefacts, *etc.* – created by people ties together people and other materials is the domain of material culture studies, based in anthropology and archaeology (e.g. Tilley, *et al.* 2006). The study of the influence of (social) relations, or "ties that matter", is based in the broad disciplinary field of (social) network science (Borgatti, *et al.* 2009; Brandes, *et al.* 2013).

In the context of an archaeological network study, these disciplines are not only commensurable but unavoidably constitutive of each other. Network science theories and methods present models of network phenomena or representations, not on the social or material factors that cause these phenomena or representations. This is why "applied" network science needs to be amended with further relational theories that form the interpretational basis for the exploration and analysis of a network. In other words, a framework of theories is required in order to explain how social and material networks in the Caribbean or other places are "interdependent". Network approaches will be applied in conjunction with more substantive theories of forms of social relations, exchange and values (e.g.; Graeber 2001; Mauss 1990). One of the more important of these reference theories is provided by Alan Fiske's "relational models theory" (Fiske 1991).

In his *Structures of Social Life* Fiske proposes that there are four elementary forms of human relations. These four models are Communal Sharing, Authoritative Ranking, Equality Matching, and Market Pricing. Communal Sharing (*ibid.*: 13, 211-213) is a relation of equivalence, characterized by a complete emphasis on group identity and equality. To put it bluntly: in a Communal Sharing model

---

12 The phrases "matter that ties" and "ties that matter" are not my invention. The first time I heard them being applied in conjunction was by Pieter ter Keurs (at the time of writing employed at the Rijksmuseum van Oudheden and Leiden University) who acted as discussant at a small symposium (*Material Interactions*) held in Leiden in 2011. Keurs has not published these phrases or has any current plans to use them in publication, but I have re-used them with his permission (Keurs, personal communication 2013).

of relations you are either in the group or you are out. If you are in the group there is no differentiation of who does or gets and thus should do or get what.[13] Secondly, Authority Ranking models (Fiske 1991: 14, 213-215) produce relations characterized by means of a transitive inequality. Such relations are part of social hierarchies in which people think of themselves and others as differing in status. Higher-ranking individuals have more relations and the benefits and responsibilities flowing forth from these than lower-ranking peoples. The third model is Equality Matching (Fiske 1991: 14, 215-216). In Equality Matching "everyone is equal and things come out even." It is thus a balanced relation between equivalent but potentially distinct partners, which is different from a Communal Sharing in which the relation does not need to be balanced and partners are thought of as dissimilar. It differs from an Authority Ranking model since in that model not everyone is equal. Presenting gifts as discussed by Mauss (1990) might be the most distinct example of this type of reciprocity (see Chapter 4).[14] Fourthly, Market Pricing (Fiske 1991: 15, 217-219), is the model in which relations are valued by reference to an external pricing mechanism. Although in Market Pricing the participants are still interested in the relation itself, this has nothing to do with their exchange partners and the intrinsic value of what he or she has to offer, but with the proportionality of the exchange on offer (see also Bloch and Parry 1989).

I have opted to employ Fiskes's theory because his models provide a good baseline for defining and discussing different types of social relations in the pre-colonial Caribbean as well as cross-culturally (Haslam 2004; Pinker 2011). His proposed models furthermore suffer less from the conceptual confusion surrounding social strategies found in similar universally applicable (evolutionary) models of social strategies (West, *et al.* 2007). Finally, I have discussed in other publications how the type of social strategies that are represented by Communal Sharing, Authority Ranking, Equality Matching and Market Pricing models of relations can be related to different applications of material culture (Mol 2007; Mol 2010; Mol 2011a).

With the combination of these more substantive social and material culture theories as well as network science concepts this work situates itself as part of a larger movement that stresses social, material *and* relational thinking in anthropology and archaeology (e.g. Henare, *et al.* 2007; Hodder 2012; Ingold 2007a, 2007b; Knappett 2005, 2011; Knappett and Malafouris 2008). However, it differentiates

---

13 In evolutionary strategic terms this sort of social behaviour is much debated and has been suggested to be correlated with a variety of indirect reciprocal evolutionary strategies: altruism (Sober and Wilson 1998), mutual aid (Kropotkin 1907), cooperation (Axelrod and Hamilton 1981; Hamilton 1964b), reciprocal altruism (Trivers 1971), group selection theory (Richerson and Boyd 2004), strong reciprocity (Gintis 2000), generalized reciprocity (Pfeiffer, *et al.* 2005). These various theories are both conflicting and difficult to distinguish from one another (West, *et al.* 2007), but their underlying connection is that close contacts – either based on genetic social closeness – are the key to a social relations in which there is no form of accounting between individuals.

14 Such an exchange is most synonymous with the concept of "direct reciprocity" (Trivers 1971), in which there is a tit-for-tat situation (Axelrod 1981). This reciprocity might be immediate or delayed and it might be an exchange of different things as long as the relation is constructed as being the same in kind. It is not entirely clear from Fiske's discussion whether consciously indirect or networked reciprocity – e.g. cyclic relations in social networks (Lieberman, et al. 2005) – constitute an Equality Matching relation.

itself by the adoption of an explorative network approach. Moreover, as will be discussed in the following chapters, the archaeological and ethnohistoric record of the Caribbean shows clear evidence for a deep-historic ontology in which objects were part of a wider socio-cosmic network of relations between humans, animals, spirits and other subjective beings. As such this works seeks to employ network science concepts to integrate perspectives on how interactions between humans, humans and things, and things themselves take place in (1) heterogeneous, (2) multi-levelled, and (3) temporally transitive, (4) interdependent systems:

Heterogeneity: Networks are in a sense always heterogeneous since they consist of different nodes that are related not through their essential characteristics but through the incidences of their ties with other nodes. Social network analysts recognize the need to include more or less the same types of social actors in their networks (Prell 2012). Archaeological networks are built from relations between material culture and archaeological histories are based on inferences of socio-cultural continuity and change in these material networks. As discussed above, this is the point where archaeological network studies divert from traditional network studies in the humanities. However, another disconnect may arise when the results of these studies need to be placed in an interpretation that tries to take account of the past ontologies of the indigenous people of the Caribbean. As we shall see it is and will remain a challenge to meaningfully interpret these "etic" models from an "emic" point of view.

Multi-scalarity: Networks are multi-levelled because interactions on one archaeological scale of analysis reciprocally impact and are impacted by other levels of the network (Heckenberger 2011). The data sets on which various levels of the network are built are often methodologically varied and archaeologists have traditionally collected and presented their data in terms of various scales: intra-site relational data for interactions on the local scale, relational data on the interaction between sites in one region as the intermediate scale, and evidence for long distance movement of raw materials and goods as the interregional scale.

Temporality: Human social and cultural structures are rarely stagnant for extended periods, undergoing many transformations through time. While it is true that most network models are somewhat at odds with approaches that take an extreme "*panta rhei*'" view of structure, a network can be modelled and understood as a dynamic but diachronically contingent entity. Like birds in a group fleeing for a predator whose current movement is a contingency of all the previous movements of all the group's members, the transitive contingency of networks is distributed across the individual nodes and ties of the network. In addition, one of the ways in which social networks can function as relatively stable system is because the social "memory" of the network is itself distributed through intangible and tangible links with other humans (Dunbar 2003; Dunbar, *et al.* 2010a; Gamble, *et al.* 2011).

Interdependency: At the heart of this work is the idea that the networks that archaeologists construct are not just of one type, but rather consist of multiple, interdependent systems. In network interdependencies one system acts on another and vice versa, thereby changing the structures and dynamics of both networks (Padgett and Powell 2012). The idea of (inter)dependency has deep roots in network science (Brandes *et al.* 2013). An analogous theoretical concept involving material culture has recently been put forward by Ian Hodder (2012), who speaks of "human-thing entanglements". Although there are many ways that humans are dependent on objects and vice versa (see also Knappett 2005), the foremost of the interdependencies that will be looked at in this work are those that occur in what have been called "socio-material networks" (cf. Knappett 2011).

Aims and questions

One aim of this work is to provide proof of concept for an archaeological network approach that bases itself on diversity and homogeneity in material culture systems to understand networks between humans (see also Terrell 2008, 2010; Knappett 2011, 2013). It is important to emphasize that network approaches in general have been relatively underutilized in archaeology and are completely new for Caribbean archaeology (Brughmans 2013). This work thus represents the first steps in the integration of network science methods and techniques in Caribbean archaeology and there is still a lot of ground to cover. It is therefore necessary to place a small cave-at with my discussion and utilization of network science. Network science consists of a constellation of often highly specialized theories, methods and techniques and I am not a network science specialist. So, for readers from outside this discipline this study should not be taken as a definitive "litmus test" for what the wider field has to offer. Similarly, from the perspective of a reader from the network sciences it may be that this study falls short in some areas, because it remains on the level of network exploration and does not implement full-fledged network modelling or analyses.

The above is related to the fact that the focus here lies on archaeological questions and data sets from the Caribbean. In some ways, the pre-colonial Caribbean is an excellent period and region to explore the usefulness of an archaeological network approach, because its record boasts a relatively high density of direct and indirect evidence for the exchange of various forms of material culture, mobility of people, and concomitant social practices. Additionally, its social and physical geography, logistical challenges and potentials, and cultural history make it a stimulating context for such a study (see Chapter 2). On the other hand, for a variety of reasons, Caribbean archaeology lacks the integrated and larger databases present in the archaeologies of some other regions. Although this situation is being remedied, it has had an effect on the breadth and type of network analyses that could be undertaken.

This has as additional benefit that the discussions and case studies are quite representative for many other types of and regions in archaeology, because they use lines of evidence that are generally available, e.g. provenance based on macroscopic analyses and iconographic studies. In some cases archaeological perspectives have been further enhanced by the use of more advanced archaeometrical studies or by substantive lines of evidence based on historic sources and (ethnographic) analogies. However, the greatest recursive benefit of testing an archaeological network approach in the Caribbean is that it will provide new views on old questions concerning aspects of the pre-colonial connectivity in this region.

Together with providing a proof of concept for an archaeological socio-material network approach, this aim shapes the main question of this work: how can we explain the patterns of homogeneity and diversity in the pre-colonial Caribbean as the result of socio-material networks, based on evidence from material culture practices and repertoires? This will be done by answering a range of more specific questions: what are the correlations between the hypotheses of "hidden" network models and observed network relations; what are the network interdependencies of material culture practices and social interactions; which social strategies were possibly used in the creation of ties on the local, regional and interregional scale; how were network types and levels integrated; how were networks temporally and cross-culturally transitive?

Outline

This introductory chapter identified several themes of importance. The first hereof was the realization that the pre-colonial Caribbean archaeological record is not only the outcome of social networks, but can itself also be understood as consisting of "networks" or systems of material culture. These systems can be understood by combining two disciplines, material culture studies and network science. The latter presents a view of relations between entities, rather than their inherent qualities, while material culture studies focuses on relations between humans and material culture. It is profitable to combine the two, because they can reveal the interdependencies between social interaction and material culture or, on a larger scale, societal histories and systems of material cultural practices and repertoires. This will contribute to a disciplinary movement away from essentialist classifications of bounded or nested sets of material culture assemblages and, by extension, monolithic theories on the histories of pre-colonial cultures and societies. The idea is to explore some of these more traditional theories with network approaches. These more traditional archaeological theories already contain ideas on the dynamics and structure of past (social) networks of which the hypotheses will be tested in reference to the network case studies.

Chapter 2 will provide an overview of the current understanding of pre-colonial mobility and interaction in its geographic, ecological and historical contexts. This will provide the necessary context for the network case studies as well as pinpoint some of the parameters and dynamics that shaped pre-colonial networks. Chapter 3 serves as an introductory chapter into the network science concepts and measures employed in the case studies. Chapter 4 will provide a conceptual framework to discuss the specific interdependencies of social and material relations by drawing on theories from Maussian and Lowland South American ethnographic perspectives. Chapters 5, 6, 7 and 8 trace, analyse and interpret a diverse set of networks from the pre-colonial and proto-colonial period and contrast these to existing theories and hypotheses, particularly as they deal with the themes of cultural diversity and socio-political organization. Rather than provide a synthesis of these case studies, the final chapter will discuss how they can be seen as first steps in a new, "networked" understanding that combines network science methods and techniques with substantive lines of evidence, anthropological viewpoints on exchange, material culture theories, and indigenous ontologies. This joint approach is critical for understanding the networks taken from the archaeological record in terms of the societal and cultural histories of the indigenous people of the Caribbean (Chapter 9).

Chapter 2

A Dynamic Island World: The Northeastern Caribbean

A dynamic pan-Caribbean web of social relationships and interlocking networks would likely have resulted from the continuous coming and going of individuals and groups of people with a range of motives (environmental, socio-political, economic, ideological) between various parts of the continent and islands.

Corinne Hofman and Menno Hoogland (2011: 17)

This chapter will start out with a discussion of Caribbean geography, geology and ecology. Subsequently I will highlight some of the logistics of pre-colonial interaction, in other words the routes, means, and other factors involved in moving people and goods around in this island world. After this a broad overview of the social and cultural historical trajectories of pre-colonial networks will be presented. In the historic overview I will focus on the origins of and interactions between culturally diverse peoples and the development of group and political structures, in particular that of the *cacicazgo*. These particular issues will be picked up in later chapters. This chapter will conclude with a small review of current ideas on indigenous ethnic, cultural and linguistic groups followed by a discussion on the prominent characteristics of indigenous ontologies in the region that also affected past interactions. The intent is not to provide the reader with an in-depth regional introduction or a full overview of the state of the field (see e.g. Keegan, *et al.* 2013; Wilson 2007), but to frame the discussion directly within a perspective that focuses on some of the factors that impacted pre-colonial social and material systems.

The reason for this extensive background into the Caribbean setting of this study is that context is all-important for framing and interpreting networks. As we shall see, networks can be abstracted from many kinds of real-world phenomena, but it is through their structural properties that they can be explored and eventually compared. For example, a model resulting from a study of the nodes and ties between stations in a subway network or the nutrition network of *Physarum polycephalum* – a brainless, amoeba-like slime mould – may be indistinguishable from that of a given social network (Tero, *et al.* 2010). Still, in terms of what these networks do, other than connect nodes in a structurally similar manner, they are not identical.

In other words, if I understand how a mould looks for its nutrition, this does not automatically give me the capability to effortlessly navigate the Tokyo subway. What is more, the context of a network is not only of interpretive significance but will also have been a shaping factor in the formation and development of the network in the first place. Consequently, networks of whatever kind are generally not studied as systems that exist and function *sui generis*. This is definitely the case for archaeological networks which cannot be understood without a clear grasp of the setting in which they were embedded.

Geography

One way to define the Caribbean as a region is by its most prominent geographical and ecological feature: the Caribbean Sea. Together with the Gulf of Mexico, it can technically be considered as a mediterranean sea – a sea that is semi-isolated from an adjacent ocean (Sverdrup, *et al.* 1942) – and is the second largest non-oceanic body of water, comprising an area of *c.*2,754,000 km². The Caribbean Sea proper is bordered by the Greater Antilles to the north, Lesser Antilles to the east, the South American mainland to the south and Central America to the west. It connects to the Gulf of Mexico at its western extents and the Atlantic Ocean to the north and east. In the south it connects to two other bodies of water: the Lago de Maracaibo in Venezuela and the Gulf of Paria. Through the latter and the Columbus Passage between Trinidad and the mainland, one can gain access to the delta of the Orinoco River (International Hydrographic Organization 1953).

Today the Caribbean consists of thirty island and twelve mainland territories – including sovereign states, dependencies, and overseas departments – the combined territory of which comprises over seven thousand islands. These islands vary hugely in size: from Cuba, the largest island in the Caribbean, to isles that are hardly more than a rock surfacing above sea level. Cuba, Hispaniola (nowadays Haiti and Dominican Republic), Puerto Rico, and Jamaica together form the Greater Antilles. The many islands making up the Bahamas and Turks and Caicos lie to the north thereof. Another archipelago, collectively known as the (U.S. and British) Virgin Islands lie to the east of Puerto Rico. In the East, the Lesser Antilles consist of a collection of island archipelagoes that are often subdivided into the Leeward and Windward islands (with the division at the Dominica channel, south of Guadeloupe and Marie-Galante). The islands of Trinidad and Tobago, officially not part of the Windward Island group, are located close to the South American mainland divided by means of the Gulf of Paria and the Colombus passage from the Venezuelan mainland and Orinoco delta. There are also island archipelagoes off the coast of Venezuela, such as Isla Margarita, Los Roques, Aruba,Curaçao, and Bonaire with similar small archipelagoes positioned off Yucatán and the Central American mainland (see the Map on p.14).

The list above also contains territories that often feature in Caribbean archaeological publications but do not strictly border the Caribbean Sea, such as the Bahamas and the coasts of the Guianas. Actually, most of the major islands in the Caribbean do not only have a Caribbean but also an Atlantic coast. Others, such as Barbados, are completely surrounded by the Atlantic Ocean. Furthermore, some if not most archaeological studies carried out in Caribbean mainland settings have often left out any form of discussion or perspective on the Caribbean islands and vice versa (Rodríguez Ramos 2010b). In short, defining the Caribbean by means of its main body of water does not seem to work out in practice.

Another alternative would be to define the Caribbean through emic means. On the other hand while it is possible to distinguish the vague cultural or geo-political outlines of the contemporary Caribbean, this is not so easy when referring to pre-colonial times. It is nevertheless a valid question whether there would have been an indigenous concept that is analogous to our concept of the Caribbean. Even if indigenous notions of natural and cultural geographies have not been preserved directly, there is some understanding of them through other sources. Numerous names given to individual islands and their locations by the indigenous inhabitants are known today. They come to us through the contemporary use of originally indigenous names for places. The meaning of these names can sometimes be found by studying linguistic and ethnohistoric records or folk etymologies (Boomert 2001b; Ulloa Hung and Corbea Calzado 2011).

Historic documents shed some light on indigenous perceptions of travel distances, mutual intelligibility and political boundaries. These may serve to establish a first, crude reconstruction of the way in which indigenous (cultural) geographies mapped out (Mol 2011a). Geographies were furthermore projected into indigenous histories of the deep past of the region (Keegan 2007; Oliver 2000). Such (de)ontological narrative maps included actual but also "before-time" places and peoples. In these narratives travel over or through water was one of the central elements shaping local identities and the interactions with others. Even in the case that islands contained large inland regions, the oral history of these places seems to be partly defined in the relation to the sea and other lands.[1]

Even if many indigenous cosmographies include concepts of space and dimension that are unparalleled by most Western cartographies, none of those I am familiar with present a scope of place even remotely akin to the geographic or cultural area we refer to today as the Caribbean. Furthermore, as far as we know, no predominant institutes – central authorities, affiliated polities, organized religions, trade specialists, *etc.* – were by themselves capable of creating pan-Caribbean territories, or of seeking to control larger portions of it. In other words, it is highly unlikely that *the* Caribbean existed as a geographic, cultural or political body before European contact. Instead, Caribbean networks were mostly created and maintained from the bottom-up, by the movements and interactions of individuals and groups interacting with others. The conceptualization of the Caribbean as a

---

1   This is clear from the role the sea or sea travel plays in Hispaniolan narratives on the origin of various cultural and societal traits (Pané 1999 [1571]). The Lesser Antillean Kalinago also had a similar importance of actual and "before-time" oversea relations. These shaped the identities of local communities as well as their alliances and conflicts with others (Boomert 1986; Breton 1999 [1665]). This is analogous to narratives from contemporary indigenous peoples of the Guianas and Orinoquia, in which the world is essentially water locked (Roe 1982). The Warao of the Orinoco delta, for example, conceive of their actual and primordial world as surrounded by a sea in which actual islands, such as Trinidad, lie at the fringes of cosmographic maps (Boomert 2009; Wilbert 1993).

cultural or geographic place is thus first and foremost a post-contact phenomenon, initially arising with the establishment of the Spanish Main as a political and economic region (Sauer 1966).

On the other hand the interlocked movement of people, goods and ideas could have created social networks that covered the expanse of what is now recognized as the Caribbean. Would this not have created a region in all but name? There is a catch to taking this approach. Because such an inclusive network is an open entity, there is no reason to stop tracing its outlines at the borders of the Caribbean Sea. Even when taking a minimalist view to the idea of diffusion and interaction there is always some evidence to be found for (interregional) ties. Indeed, based on current lines of evidence, the concept that many social networks are "small worlds" – networks that consist of nodal clusters that are only connected by a few ties – can be extrapolated to the pre-colonial Caribbean (see Chapter 3). In other words, local island communities could be connected by means of surprisingly few intermediate ties to communities far beyond Caribbean shores.

For instance, as I shall discuss below, at certain moments in time the Orinoco Delta and Lower Orinoco was as much part of a Caribbean interaction sphere as were the coasts and islands – or part of a Lower Orinoco interaction sphere, depending on one's perspective (Boomert 2000). Communities from these regions were in turn interacting, either directly or through the coast of the Guianas and the Middle and Upper Orinoco, with the Amazon region and beyond (Heckenberger 2005; Hornborg, *et al.* 2005; Hornborg 2005). The same can be said with regard to connections between the Colombian and Venezuelan coast and the Andes region or Central America and Mexico (Hoopes and Fonseca 2003; Rouse and Cruxent 1963). By means of this route or perhaps even Floridian connections, the Caribbean was probably connected to the North American Southwest and Southeast, and so forth.

The catch is that a network perspective, being based on connectivity, does not lend itself readily for delineating regional or cultural boundaries and is in fact in complete contrast to it (Malkin 2011). Even when acknowledging that everything is (potentially) connected, one cannot meaningfully discuss pre-colonial systems of interaction that could stretch from Alaska to Cape Horn. The remedy to this problem is to simply cut off the areal of the research at a predefined border. Where to draw the line then depends on the theme, scale of analysis and the period under study, more than on the potential for wider connections. The network case studies here will remain centred on a single geographic zone: the area consisting of the eastern Greater Antilles (Hispaniola and Puerto Rico), the Virgin Islands and the northern Lesser Antilles (Leeward Islands). This region will be referred to as the Northeastern Caribbean (Figure 2.1).

It has long been known that the geographic layout of this region was instrumental in shaping the archaeologically visible patterns of human mobility and interaction. Due to specific geological processes (see below), the Greater and Lesser Antilles geography takes the shape of an arc. Within this arc almost all islands are intervisible

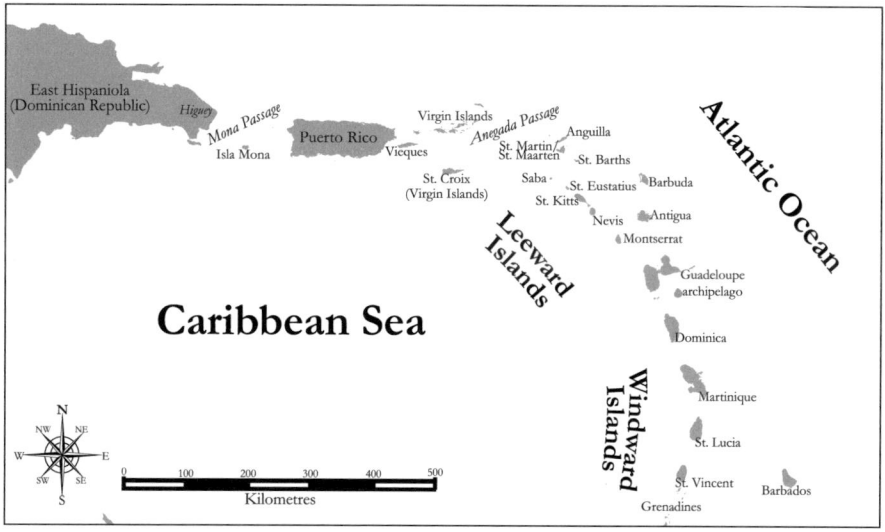

Figure 2.1: Map of the Northeastern Caribbean.

and connected by means of relatively narrow sea-passages.[2] The relatively short distances between landmasses presented pre-colonial mariners with excellent navigational landmarks. Other than the stretches of water located between Trinidad and Grenada and the Anegada Passage, there are no other stretches from which someone could not see from one end to the other on a clear day. The intervisibility of islands could have been even further enhanced by being in higher elevations or in the case of certain atmospheric effects, further enabling intervisibility. When certain atmospheric conditions are met, several other mainland to island stretches of water, not traditionally perceived as passages, perhaps did not even represent large navigational obstacles (Torres and Rodríguez Ramos 2008).

Viewed from large cultural scales it is clear that geography is partly responsible for the patterns of mobility and exchange in the region (Siegel 1992; Watters 1982, 1997). Shifts in material cultural repertoires, specifically ceramic styles, line up with the idea of a chained island world to a certain extent. For instance, research carried out by Rouse (1986, 1992) that has been re-confirmed by Bright (2011), indicates that the ceramic assemblages from the extremities of two opposing islands often share more traits than ceramic assemblages between the north and south side of one island (see also Figure 1.2). Distribution of raw materials also primarily takes

---

2   As may be expected, the average width of channels between the islands depends on which region of the map one looks at. In the southern Windward islands, many isles could have served as stepping stones, here the distance between land masses is often no larger than 10-20 km The same situation can be found in the Virgin Islands and Puerto Rico, where Anegada Island in the East is laced to Puerto Rico by means of a succession of small islands. The Leewards and northern Windwards have somewhat larger stretches of water measuring 20-50 km The Mona Passage between Puerto Rico and Hispaniola is much wider (c.130-140 km), but Mona Island is located at its half-way point. The large, unbroken stretches are located between Trinidad and Grenada in the south (130-140 km) as well as between St. Vincent or St. Lucia and Barbados (150-160 km/140-150 km) The Anegada Passage (c.130 km) lies between the islands of Anegada and Sombrero (Anguilla).

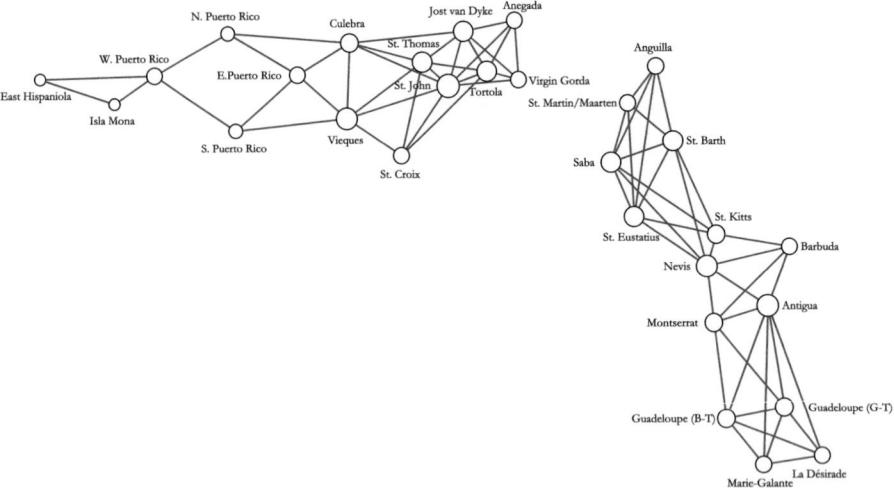

Figure 2.2: PPA-network of the Northeastern Caribbean islands (neighbourhood number = 4), illustrating the ties between the islands that are each other's nearest neighbour. The geographical layout of the region causes the network to fall apart into two network components (the network has been layouted to mimic the real geography). It also shows that in each component the islands are more or less equally connected. Because of this the network has the appearance of two quarters of a ring-lattice model.

place within smaller regions. A sharp quantitative fall-off of a certain raw material can often be seen outside its immediate area of procurement (e.g. Isendoorn, *et al.* 2008; Knippenberg 2007).

A Proximal Point Analysis (or PPA) of landmasses is illustrative of the geographic dynamics of North-Eastern Caribbean networks (Broodbank 2000: 180-210; Terrell 1977).[3] PPA is a type of geographical network analysis based on a fixed neighbourhood number for nodes. The underlying idea is that those places that are geographically closest would have had the most interactions. The neighbourhood number can theoretically be set at anything, but is normally 3 or 4. For the model in Figure 2.2 it has been set at 4. In order to create a PPA model ties are drawn from one node to its closest neighbours. Once this has been carried out with the entire set of nodes, unreciprocated ties are removed from the model.

In the case of the Northeastern Caribbean the result hereof is a model that strongly resembles two broken up quarters of a type of network called a "ring-lattice" (Figure 2.2; further discussed in Chapter 3). Certain areas, like the Virgin Islands with their many small islands located close to each other, have higher clustering than other regions (see also Chapter 6). Together with the larger distance between Anguilla and Anegada this causes the network to break down into two components. Nevertheless, even if the real geography of the Caribbean is not a perfect ring-lattice, it comes quite close to the shape of such a network. In other words, the geographic substrate of a North-Eastern Caribbean closest neighbour

---

3 A node is established by identifying an island (region) measuring between 10 km² and 1000 km². Distances between islands are based on straight travel across open sea from the closest headlands.

network would steer regional interaction networks into the direction of a ring-lattice shape, favouring down-the-line interaction.

A diverse geology and ecology

The Caribbean islands, with the exception of Cuba, lie on the Caribbean plate, the geological history of which is still heavily debated (Jackson 2002; Pindell and Barrett 1990). The northern extremity of this plate is a transform vault, running along the southern coasts of Cuba and the northern coast of Hispaniola and Puerto Rico. These islands were presumably formed during the Upper Cretaceous, undergoing volcanic, marine sedimentation and meta-morphic processes in the course of their formation (Draper, *et al.* 1994). Nowadays the tectonics are relatively tranquil compared to its early history and the fault line does not generate any active volcanism. However, due to the proximity of the Hispaniola and Puerto Rican trenches, the area can be subject to destructive quakes, for example the ones that struck Port Royal, Jamaica (1692) or Haiti (2010). A complex combination of lithospheric processes, including subduction at an early stage with subsequent high pressures but low temperatures and slow lithospheric movement, is the reason why this area of the Caribbean has unique metamorphic formations containing stones such as jadeitite and serpentinite, semi-precious stones which were also exploited by the indigenous peoples (see Chapter 5).

The Lesser Antilles are much younger, presumably dating to the Early or Middle Eocene. These islands were created by the lithospheric movements of the eastern extents of the Caribbean tectonic plate. This active subduction zone runs from Puerto Rico to the South American Plate in the south, creating an area of intense volcanic activity that formed the majority of the Lesser Antillean islands. Shifts in the location of the subduction zone have created a younger inner arc (running from Saba to Grenada) and an older outer arc (from Anguilla to Marie Galante). The inner arc represents the current location of the converging Atlantic and Caribbean Plate fault line, creating an area with much volcanism. The older arc represents an older and more varied geology, in which volcanic but also other formations can be found. In the outer arc a rise of the seabed has created the low-lying limestone (parts of) islands in the region, which have a different geology and altitude and, as a result of this, a much different weather system than the higher volcanic islands. All in all, the geology of the Caribbean is varied with numerous local formations, such as the Blue Mountain belt of Jamaica, and phenomena – seventeen volcanoes and other unique features such as the boiling lake in Dominica – with particular geological contexts (Draper, *et al.* 1994).

Aside from giving the region its arc-shape when looked at on a map, these processes produced a diverse geological landscape. The geology and shape of an island was and is an important factor that influenced the choices and practices of daily human life. High areas were strategically advantageous, while flat surfaces were suited for building larger villages, for example. Settling inland would have brought communities relative seclusion, while rivers and bays presented logistical opportunities (Cooper 2007). Volcanic eruptions were infrequent but calamitous.

Flat, limestone islands on the other hand would provide few areas with wind shade in case of a tropical storm or hurricane. Most importantly, its varied geology also implied that the region was dotted with lithic resources, such as various types of cherts and semi-precious stones (see Chapter 5).

The Caribbean islands and coasts (except for the Bahamas north of Rum Cay) are all located in the tropical belt between the Tropic of Cancer and 8° north, providing the entire region with a tropical marine climate. Nonetheless, across the region and during the year we see a relatively large variation in average low and high temperatures and in the average rainfall per month, ranging between 22° (average low January) and 33° C. (average high July) and 76 mm (March, Aruba) to a torrential 3788 mm. (November, windward Dominica) of rainfall. These fluctuations in temperature and precipitation depend on factors such as season, geographic longitude, elevation, location in relation to the main bodies of water (windward, leeward and central parts of the islands), and (trade) winds. In fact, even the same temperature and rainfall might be experienced differently on a day-to-day basis, depending on cloud patterns, sun intensity, wind speeds and general humidity (see also Cooper 2013).

These weather fluctuations and micro-climates from temperate to hot and dry to extremely wet lead to a considerable variety in ecology. As part of the larger Neotropical ecozone, the Caribbean is one of the most ecologically diverse regions in the world, containing eight out of fourteen major terrestrial habitat zones – comprised of many types of biotopes (Olson, *et al.* 2001). It also sports a large variety of marine habitats with various littoral, pelagic and deep sea-zones dotted with shallows, banks and (coral) reefs. The natural richness of the Caribbean is also one of the aspects most commented upon by chroniclers of the early contact period. They took careful note of how indigenous peoples utilised a diverse range of flora for food, decoration, tool-making, medicine and numerous other purposes (e.g. de Oviedo y Valdés 1851).

Archaeobotanical research has shown that (semi-)management of a diversity of plant species probably goes back to the earliest period of human occupation. The first settlers introduced a variety of fruit bearing trees and smaller seed bearing herbs into the archipelago. They included wild avocado and yellow zapote (eggfruit), that originated from Mesoamerica or Central America, where they are associated with home garden cultivation. Species of timber were also exploited during this period, for construction, fuel, and wooden tools and other objects (Newsom and Wing 2004). Starch grains analysis carried out on tools from Puerto Rico, Vieques and Cuba indicate that maize (*Zea mays*), beans (*Fabaceae, Phaseolus* sp.), sweet potato (*Ipomoea batatas*), manioc (*Manihot esculenta*), and other (wild) tubers were cultivated as early as 3000 B.C. (Pagán Jiménez 2011, 2013; Pagán Jiménez and Ramos 2007).

Paleobotanical evidence from sites dating to the period 400-200 BC indicates a huge growth in the cultivation of fruit trees and crops. New species of fruits were consumed, of which some, such as papaya (*Carica papaya*) and genip (*Melicoccus bijugatus*), were introduced into the Caribbean islands from the mainland. Between 600 and 1492 AD the Greater Antilles is characterized by a huge variety of plants that were cultivated in home gardens. Staple foods included a mix of various tubers – such as the cultivated manioc (*Manihot esculenta*) and sweet potato (*Ipomoea batatas*) and the wild marunguey or zamia (*Zamia* sp.) – beans (Leguminosae) and corn (*Zea mays*). Gourds (*Cucurbita* sp.) served both as food and containers (Mickleburgh and Pagán-Jiménez 2012; Newsom 1993; Newsom and Wing 2004). Alongside these food crops the indigenous peoples cultivated cotton, various hallucinogenic and medicinal plants, and spices. In addition, (hardwood) trees were utilized for hafting tools and manufacturing statues, ornaments, amulets and in construction (Ostapkowicz 1998). Plant use in the Lesser Antilles during the Ceramic Age is also characterized by home gardening and the cultivation of a variety of fruits and staple crops. From 600 AD onwards, subtle changes with regard to the composition of the floral assemblage indicate increased pressure on the local environment (Blancaneaux 2009; Newsom and Pearsall 2003).

Exploitation of faunal resources was influenced by the differential access to specific terrestrial and maritime zones (DeFrance 2013). In particular, the accessibility to coastal and maritime resources, such as reefs and mangroves was of key importance to the initial colonization of the islands and would continue to play an important role in later periods. Relatively large-scale of off-shore fishing at places such as Saba, Île à Rat on the north coast of Haiti, the Turks and Caicos and the Bahamian islands has been documented (Hoogland and Hofman 1999; Keegan 2009; Keegan, *et al.* 2008; Morsink 2012). Other seafood like shellfish were a large part of many diets. Refuse middens containing crab remains and (sea) shells have been found on every island and have even been at the basis of a cultural taxonomy (Rainey 1952). Shell was also an important raw material with regard to tools and valuables (Carlson 1993; Lammers-Keijsers 2007; Mol 2007; Ortega 2005). Other larger marine animals, such as sea-turtles (Cheloniidae) and manatees (*Trichechus manatus*) also had an important dual role to play as foodstuff and raw material for the manufacture of amulets and shamanic paraphernalia.

After the Pleistocene, larger land animals were rare. However, small game was hunted and consumed until the Early Colonial period. Aside from reptiles these were also rodents, living close to gardens and villages, such as rice rats (Oryzomyini) and hutias (*Isolobodon* spp.). The ethnohistoric sources indicate that larger mammals and reptiles were often reserved for elites. This is also supported by some archaeological lines of evidence (DeFrance 2013; Newsom and Wing 2004). In Tibes, Puerto Rico, for example, larger reptiles such as iguana (*Iguana iguana*) and several species of snake were on the menu, although due to their scarcity they had likely become an elite-only food by the end of the contact period (Curet and Pestle 2010). Other high status food remains, such as Guinea Pigs (*Cavia porcellus*) have also been found here and in other late pre-contact sites (Oliver and Narganes Storde 2003). Birds were part of the diet since the earliest phase of human occupation of the islands (Grouard 2001; Newsom and Wing 2004). Aside from this dogs – perhaps also used for food – and certain birds were kept as pets (Plomp 2013). Another main reason these animals were kept and exchanged was to serve as sources of raw materials for ornaments (Laffoon, *et al.* in press). Although they have not been preserved, ethnohistoric accounts speak of the use of colourful bird-feathers as ornamentation (Oliver 2000). In addition, perforated and decorated dog teeth have also been used as ornament and are sometimes found together in large caches (Ortega 1978).[4]

What is important to understand is that most terrestrial faunal – and to a lesser extent even floral and maritime faunal – species did not have a uniform distribution over the region. For example, it may be erroneously concluded from the abovementioned presence of guinea pig bones in Tibes that, if the species was present on Puerto Rico, it must have been present on other, nearby, ecologically similar islands as well. However, in this particular case it is more likely that guinea pigs were transported to the island by humans as part of a specific interaction network which may not have extended to (all) other islands in the Northeastern Caribbean (DeFrance, *et al.* 2010: 121). In fact, even with the ecological transformations resulting from the "Columbian Exchange", at present the islands still have their own set of pre-contact animals and plants, some of which can only be found on a single island. The distribution of species is not so much due to the isolation of individual islands and resulting speciation as may be the case in other, more remote island situations. Rather, ecological niches afforded by distinct island environments combined with particular mobility or transportation processes of animals were responsible for the discontinuous floral and faunal distribution map of the pre-colonial period (DeFrance 2013).

Maritime technology and voyaging

The variation in geological zones, terrestrial and maritime ecologies, and functional and symbolical niches of land and maritime species created a discontinuous but interconnected landscape of resources. In order to fully utilize the natural riches of the Caribbean in all their diversity, people either acquired these through partners or needed to travel across the sea to procure them directly. Even if goods would have been directly procured over longer distances, this would have involved interacting with others, either as a result of random encounters while travelling, because of a need to gain permission to access the territories of other groups, or by relying on the hospitality of others, forming a support network that likely stretched across multiple environmental zones. Aside from such social dynamics, pre-colonial naval technology and maritime logistics would have been important parameters influencing the coherence and connectivity of inter-island networks.

---

4   Drawing on ethnographic analogies from the South American mainland, it would be likely that dogs and parrots would have been more than just a source of food and raw material. For instance, research carried out among the Waiwai (Vaughn Howard 2001), indicates that dogs and colourful, speaking birds are part of extended social networks in which they are both social persona and valued gifts. It is possible to surmise a similar role for parrots in the Caribbean, which were kept in houses and often presented as highly prized gifts (Mol 2007; Oliver 2000). Pending isotopic analyses suggest that (decorated) dog teeth were also habitually moved between island regions (Laffoon, *et al.* in press). Whether this means that living dogs were also exchanged is not known, yet that dogs were an inherent part of pre-colonial communal networks is evident from various dog burials found in the Greater and Lesser Antilles (Hoogland and Hofman 2013: 454-455).

The documents from the early period of indigenous-European contact are invaluable for our understanding of pre-colonial maritime technologies. All vessels were man-powered canoes, which differed in size from simple one-person boats to canoes made from giant trees that could transport up to fifty people at a time (McKusick 1970). Thus far none of these large canoes have been discovered in the archaeological record. In fact, due to the exceptional circumstances needed for their preservation, only three (partial) vessels have been encountered in underwater sites. In addition a small number of other associated canoe-faring tools and implements like paddles have been found (Billard, *et al.* 2009; Boomert 2000: 297-298; Callaghan 2001; Conrad, *et al.* 2001). None of the recovered canoes resemble the large vessels of the contact period that were reported by Spanish chroniclers (e.g Bérnaldez 1992: 149).[5]

Little was known until recently about the precise hydrographic properties of Amerindian canoes on larger stretches of open water, until the start of the Martinique-based "*Ioumoúlicou*" project. This project started with the commission of an indigenously handcrafted canoe from the Wayana of French Guyana, named *Akayouman*. After its completion a group of archaeologists and volunteers has endeavored trips between the different islands of the Lesser Antilles – over a dozen at the time of writing (Bérard, *et al.* 2011; Billard, *et al.* 2009). With a trained crew of rowers and a dugout-canoe reinforced with plank boards of a type which were presumably known to the pre-colonial indigenous peoples, they have gathered much practical and hydrographic data. Perhaps the most noteworthy finding thus far is the average hourly speed of an indigenous canoe on open water.[6] A trained crew of twenty physically fit rowers attained speeds averaging *c.* 3to 3.5 knots (5.5 to 6.5 km/hour), depending on local wind, swell and current conditions. As a result the crew of the *Akayouman* can easily complete journeys of 12-20 nautical miles per day (22-30 km). Larger stretches of water such as the passage between Martinique and Dominica could be traversed in a single day, although as Bérard reports: "a journey of over 20 nautical miles is a real trek for us, especially if it

---

5   The Stargate canoe, for example, a rare specimen, found almost intact in an underwater cave in the Bahamas, measured 150x36 cm with a height of only 10 cm. All three canoes recovered thus far have been dug-outs consisting of types described in the historic sources and often found in the region today. With its limited depth the Starlight canoe was probably meant for coastal travel. All of them were sea-worthy vessels, but one type – sometimes referred to as the platform canoe due to its overhanging extensions – was specifically well-adapted to open sea travel. This specific type also has a Circum-Caribbean distribution, probably indicating diffusion of the technology by means of contact (Callaghan and Schwabe 2001).

6   The project has already yielded some highly interesting results, such as the fact that it was easier to row a canoe fully laden rather than empty and that it was difficult to keep the contents of the canoe dry with anything but a mirror flat sea (Bérard, *et al.* 2011; Billard, *et al.* 2009).

includes the dangers associated with the crossing of a channel" (Bérard, *et al.* 2011: 582, my translation).[7]

Although a team of eight or even twenty rowers seems like a small number of people, one should not underestimate the challenges associated with the formation of such a crew. Getting skilled and able-bodied men or women to willingly brave the perils of any extended sea passage – let alone an expedition of several weeks to foreign and possibly hostile lands during which they could not provide for or defend their kin – would have been no mean feat of "interpersonal management". Indeed, it is likely that specific extended kin and other alliance networks would have existed for such expeditions. The existence of precisely such teams of voyagers is recorded for the Early Colonial war expeditions of the Kalinago (Boomert 2000; Bright 2011). Still, as is also well-attested from the historic record, much travel probably took place in smaller boats with smaller groups.

Whatever the size of the vessel and crew, group-owned or personal canoes and their implements must have been focal points of Caribbean social and cultural life. From mainland ethnographies we can establish an impression of what the production and ownership of such canoes entails. The Warao, master canoe builders from the delta of the Orinoco, go through a complex *chaîne operatoire* involving a specifically identified tree, several cycles of adze-carving and burning of the inside of the log, shaping of the hull of the canoe with fire and axe, and an intricate ceremonial process involving many taboos and specific roles filled by various spirits and craftsmen. Even after the canoe has been completed precise ritual and nautical knowledge as well as continued investment by the community are required to operate the canoe (Wilbert 1993). All these ingredients – large, likely cosmologically significant trees, specialized tools, decorations and a degree of ritual and nautical specialization – could have been present in the Caribbean since the first colonization of the islands.

Even with a large supporting community, trained crew, sea-worthy canoes, and good navigational markers, travelling on the open sea would have required a great deal of skill and effort. In the Lesser Antilles the currents in channels and the prevailing winds would have been perpendicular to the direction of travel. Richard Callaghan has therefore suggested that in some cases maritime travel side-skipped a majority of the islands en-route to take a direct, off-shore route to the target destination (Callaghan 2001). His models are based on software that calculates the likelihood of a successful (drift) voyage.[8] With the help of this software

---

7   Whether this speed of travel would have been the same for indigenous canoe crews is difficult to surmise, since speed and distances historically reported from the mouths of indigenous Caribbean sailors are in temporal units like "moons" or "days" and not in geographic distances. Bernaldéz (1992: 167), basing himself on various sources, among which Columbus himself, reports that: "a caravel can sail in a single day as far as the canoes are able to in seven." A standard caravel of that era would have travelled at speeds of up to 8 knots with an average of 4 knots, making *c.*78 to 86 nautical miles a day. In fact, this is around seven times the lower limit of a day trip made by the *Akayouman* crew (12 nautical miles).

8   The model applies modern data on winds, currents, gale and hurricane frequencies, and sea-swell conditions from the U.S. Defense Mapping Agency as input (Callaghan 2001).

Callaghan has undertaken several studies on the likelihood of maritime contacts (e.g. Callaghan 1990, 2001, 2013).

An important part of these models is based on the possibility of a failed open sea voyage, but it is difficult to surmise the exact risks of pre-colonial maritime voyaging (Fitzpatrick 2013a). First of all the level of danger would have been dependent on weather, especially during the hurricane season and crew preparation. The problem is also whether the perceptions of risks and benefits by past communities aligns with that of the model. For example, Callaghan (2001) has calculated that a drift voyage from the South American coast of 4 to 5 weeks with a crew of eight would have involved a crew loss of 10% to 12%. On the other hand a northward directed journey from South America to the Greater Antilles lasting 5 days with rowers taking alternate shifts would only have a little less than 1% chance of a fatality, according to Callaghan. If we transpose this to a more common mortality rate system the latter figure translates to a little under 1000 deaths per 100,000 sailors on an outbound voyage. This number seems acceptably low, but this is deceiving. In fact, it is a relatively high mortality rate compared to that of the more dangerous early modern and modern commercial sailing vessels. For example, the mortality rate of outbound Dutch East India Company sailors was 6700 per 100,000 (Bruijn 2009: 75). Although this is higher than the suggested pre-colonial Caribbean mortality rate, one has to keep in mind that this voyage was at least thirty times longer. In fact, the death rate of a Caribbean crossing proposed by Callaghan dwarfs the deaths associated with the most dangerous modern types of sailing: commercial fishing, which "only" has one hundred and twenty-nine deaths per 100,000 sailors per year (Lincoln and Lucas 2010).

One could argue that the model's suggested death rate per crossing is incorrect. If not, it is unlikely that these cross-Caribbean voyages or similar long voyages were undertaken with a light heart. Naturally the perception of maritime voyages would have depended on the actual frequency of trips made and a community's knowledge and memory of (fatal) accidents on sea. Suppose an individual made generally ten trips with a 1% death rate in a lifetime, which would be on the low side. Based on a crew of ten, this means that he or she likely witnessed one death during his or her "career" as a canoe rower. Being on sea for extended periods of time was probably considered to be one of the more unsafe things to do in a region were the only other natural hazards were destructive but infrequent earthquakes, volcanic eruptions and hurricanes. This would have had an effect on sea-going trade expeditions, resource procurement and (individual) mobility.

On the other hand, suppose that travelling across the sea was generally (assumed to be) safe? What would this actually say about the formation and development of inter-island networks? This is difficult to ascertain a priori. When judging and interpreting models of inter-island connectivity we should not fall for the logical fallacy of probabilistic reasoning.[9] In this case, this means that even if intervisibility or favourable sea currents create the contexts for easy travel and easy travel influences the presence of social relations, then it still does not follow that

---

9   If R then P, P has a large probability of Q, so if R then Q (Oaksford and Chater 2001).

intervisibility or favourable sea currents between two areas equals social interaction. Rather, intervisibility and sea current studies present an environmental spectrum of possibilities (cf. Callaghan 2001: 312). The more probabilistic models are contextualized, the better they will be at approaching historical reality. One should for example take into account that the push and pull of potential or established (social) relations between communities or individuals would have been one of the most important reasons for inter-island travel (cf. Keegan 2004).

The voyages undertaken by the *Akayouman* present a set of meta-data that can serve to contrast such social incentives for Caribbean inter-island travel to current navigational models. It is notable that the canoe always travels between islands rather than bypassing islands in favour of crossings on open stretches of sea. Although the passages often present quite a challenge, as predicted by Callaghan's models, the extra effort is worth it for the crew. This is because, aside from gathering scientific data, the goals of the society are to increase awareness of indigenous heritage and cement the ties between Martinique and the islands that they visit on their trips (Bérard, *et al.* 2011). Indeed, when they arrive at an island this is always accompanied by a public ceremony and media attention. Moreover, this also, interestingly enough, involves the exchange of gifts (see Chapter 4). In the case of the *Akayouman*, bypassing (inhabited) islands defeats the greater purpose of the voyage.[10]

To synthesize my argument, it is clear that navigational models have yielded valuable insights into the spectrum of possibilities for Caribbean maritime voyaging. Yet this probabilities need to be further defined into plausible (local) histories. This needs to be based on agentive simulations for modelling costs, but should also incorporate modelling of voyaging benefits within a wider set of factors. Ideally both sets of parameters would be (partly) data-driven: a model that does not only computes navigational paths but also measures these in terms of cost and benefit and contrasts this with evidence of interaction from the archaeological record. Such a model does not exist yet with reference to the Caribbean.[11] As such, once developed it is sure to benefit from the incorporation of network theoretical models and measures (e.g. Knappett, *et al.* 2008).

Culture history

Traditionally the history of the pre-colonial Caribbean has been divided into three large periods, the beginning and end times of which are subject to debate and vary per region (Petersen, *et al.* 2004): (1) the Archaic Age (6000/4000 BC-500/400

---

10 There is one comparable experiment with canoe travel on open seas in the Caribbean. During the late 1980s a group of Dominican archaeologists and volunteers paddled from the Amazon, up the Orinoco and the Lesser and Greater Antillean island chain, to Cuba. This epic expedition was completed in the indigenously-made canoe called *Hatuey*. This canoe is still on display outside the Museo del Hombre in Santo Domingo. It was named after the famous indigenous leader who took his people from Hispaniola to Cuba in order to escape Spanish oppression. Remarkably, the journey had the same objective as that of the *Ioumoúlicou* project: honouring indigenous maritime heritage and the strengthening of inter-island relations (Harold Olsen, personal communication 2009).

11 Such a new maritime, cost-benefit model will be one of the intended outcomes of an upcoming NWO-funded project by the Leiden Caribbean Research Group.

BC), (2) the Early Ceramic Age (500/400 BC-AD 600/800), and (3) the Late Ceramic Age (AD 600/800-1492). Sometimes these longer periods are further subdivided into an Early and Late phases or transitional periods, such as the Early Archaic Age or the *fase transicional* of the Dominican Republic. Aside from this, every island (archipelago) has its own cultural periodization (Rouse 1992; Figure 1.1). As discussed in the introductory Chapter, these larger and smaller periods are demarcated by means of several criteria, notably material culture type and style, subsistence practices and socio-political system as evidenced by site layout and inter-site patterning. The end of the Archaic and beginning of the Early Ceramic Age has, for example, been set around 500/400 BC in the Northeastern Caribbean when communities using so-called Saladoid ceramics started to appear (see below). However, recent breaks from these standard models are more aligned with the idea of a continuous and connected process of gradual ebb and flow of local, regional and interregional systems of interaction and diffusion, rather than a series of cultural phases. This makes any strict periodization difficult to defend. Nevertheless, for the sake of clarity, I have subdivided the following diachronic discussion into paragraphs reflecting open-ended periods that align with date marks for important developments and processes. Although there are some overlaps with recently proposed period names (e.g. Petersen *et al.* 2004; Rodríguez Ramos 2010b), the paragraph titles are not suggestions for a new periodization, but reflect the most important processes in terms of interaction and mobility during this period.

Foundation: 6000/4000 BC - 2000 BC

The earliest dates of human occupation in the Caribbean originate from the site of Banwari Trace in Trinidad, ranging *c.*6000 BC – although Boomert (2000: 49) discusses a single spearhead from the much earlier Joboid complex. Here, as part of the budding riverine and coastal interaction sphere on the Venezuelan coast and Orinoco, the first settlers exploited the rich resources of the island, while probably remaining in contact with their mother communities across the Gulf of Paria (Boomert 2000). Banwari Trace and the nearby site of St. John both show evidence indicating a way of life that would be typical of much of later Caribbean (pre-)history. Tools for the production of canoes and the faunal remains suggest a rapid shift from a terrestrial subsistence strategy to one that focused on freshwater and marine foods – notably shellfish and crab (Wilson 2007: 39-43). At the western extents of the Caribbean islands another group of settlers, presumably originating from Yucatan, reached Cuba and Hispaniola in *c.*5000 BC (Rodríguez Ramos, *et al.* 2013). In contrast to their counterparts in the southern Caribbean, early Cuban sites, do not display a similar reliance on (shell)fish, still focusing largely on foraging as well as the hunting of larger animals (Kozlowski 1974; Newsom and Wing 2004).

Both these groups originated from a small group of settlers that had colonized Mesoamerica a long time before the Caribbean islands seems to have been. However around the time the Caribbean islands were first inhabited mainland material cultures – for this period defined by various stone knapping techniques and form as well as composition of lithic toolsets – were rather diverse (Kozlowski

1974). As a result, the Caribbean islands were colonized by peoples with two quite different knapping techniques and associated assemblages. The southern lithic material culture group, traditionally called Ortoroid, is characterized by a versatile and opportunistic toolkit and knapping technique, working from small cores to produce flakes applied in a variety of purposes. The western group of lithic materials, known as the (Casimiran) Casimiroid, is distinguished by the presence of larger cores to produce flakes and long thin blades, although over time the percentage of blades in relation to flakes slowly dropped (Rodríguez Ramos, *et al.* 2013; Wilson 2007).

There is another marked difference between the two colonisation waves, as indicated by means of the speed in which they spread and their connections to their original homelands. The Casimiroid-lithic using peoples seem to have steadily extended their range eastwards, with the first evidence for human presence in Puerto Rico by *c.*4000 BC (Rodríguez Ramos 2010: 50). In contrast, the southern migration was concentrated mostly around Trinidad and Tobago, with very little evidence for early sites in the other more northerly Lesser Antilles (Callaghan 2010). It is presumed that the peoples who settled Trinidad were still in contact with their mainland neighbours or could even be alternatively living on the island and mainland. They would have trekked around the Orinoco and Gulf of Paria not in a mainland-island colonisation setting, but in that of a riverine, coastal interaction sphere. In any case, the maritime technology and knowledge required in order to cross the Gulf of Paria would have been limited. Even up to a few decades ago small dugout canoes carrying only one or a few individuals, regularly made the journey from the mainland to Trinidad (Boomert 2000).

In the West, the logistics of navigating the Yucatan channel – the narrowest gap between the Yucatan peninsula and Cuba – or any other waterway between the North American and Mesoamerican mainland and the islands would have been far more taxing, with strong currents prohibiting easy canoe crossings (Callaghan 1993). As a result interactions between the early colonizers of Cuba and their mother community may not have been as intensive as those between communities on Trinidad and the South American mainland. It could be that the proximity of the mainland and strong ties between Trinidad and mainland communities created an "anchor" for the first southern settlement of the islands. The effect hereof was that the southern colonization of the Caribbean advanced very slowly, whereas early communities in Cuba were not "inhibited" by similar social ties.

The preservation of sites for the earliest periods is heavily biased by obscuring or destructive natural factors such as erosion, volcanism, and fluctuating coastlines (Cooper and Boothroyd 2011; Delpuech 2004), making it difficult to say something definitive on human interaction and mobility during this period. To our best knowledge it seems that, if there is evidence for human settlement, total population numbers on islands were very low. Based on site layouts and the evidence for site activities, it is generally accepted that the first settlers of the

Caribbean lived in small social units consisting of not more than ten individuals.[12] Furthermore, the relative low density of early sites suggests that these groups were moving around in large areas. Sites often do concentrate around areas that gave easy access to marine foods, such as fishing grounds located close to shore, salinas and mangroves.

Ethnographic analogies with comparable settings and cultures suggest that most, if not all, individuals in the group were connected to each other through close blood relations. With a small pool of potential marriage partners, even individuals from other groups were closely (genetically) related. For an early inhabitant of the islands, one's social network consisted generally speaking of a small number of related individuals with which one consistently interacted in the course of his or her lifetime. This would have had a corresponding effect on how such small groups were structured, which social strategies were used when interacting with others and how material culture formed a part of these interactions.

Development: 2000-800 BC

Archaeological investigation has thus far only presented a general picture of the Early Caribbean. What does become clear from site excavations and research is that we should not view the period from 6000/4000 BC - 2000 BC as consisting only of two major waves of migration, followed by centuries in which nothing happened. A steadily rising population, the opening up of new territories, and increasing specialization and adaptation to the island environments, ensured that Early Caribbean society and culture was anything but static.

Another major tipping point occurred in c.2000 BC in the North-Eastern Caribbean. This was, according to current consensus, the time and place that peoples from the Southern Caribbean came into contact with peoples from the West. It is not known at what point exactly the networks of these different groups first started to coalesce. Incidental contacts must have been taking place centuries before archaeologists can first see clear proof of their interactions (Ulloa Hung and Valcárcel Rojas 2013). The result is clear, however: a uniquely Antillean combination of two different mainland-to-island traditions (Hofman, Boomert, et al. 2011; Rodríguez Ramos, et al. 2013). This Ortoroid-Casimiroid interface marked the first moment in which the Greater and Lesser Antilles were connected by means of geographically far ranging, but still small social networks.

The number of sites in the Northern Lesser Antilles skyrocketed during the period 2000-800 BC in comparison to the period before. Subsistence economies were focused on acquisition of locally available foods and tools. The one exception to this is the Caribbean lithic tradition, including but not limited to the knapping, use, and distribution of siliceous artefacts. In addition, spheroliths – stone balls

---

12 Sites are often small scatters of materials, sometimes concentrated in a local region and probably the result of temporary camps from which hunting and gathering activities were undertaken. Several larger sites such as rock and cave shelters may well have served as base camps. Furthermore, their larger size and generally deeper stratigraphy suggests that they were the result of many centuries of cyclical occupation (Bonnissent 2008; Crock, et al. 1995; Davis 2000; Hofman and Hoogland 2003; Hofman, et al. 2006).

ranging in size from a pellet to ones measuring more than 1 m. across, the purpose of which is unclear – can be found in Cuba, the Dominican Republic, and Puerto Rico. The typical shapes of celts and the distinct pattern of wear of edge-ground cobbles are also indicative of wide-shared lithic tool practices (Rodríguez Ramos 2010). These examples provide a tantalizing insight into the circulation of knowledge and practices in incipient, regional networks.

Furthermore, many practices that were seen as key traits of culture and society after 200 BC – crafting techniques of lithics and ceramics, foodstuffs, ritual practices such as use of hallucinogenics and carving of petroglyphs, and (semi-)permanent settlements – were also pioneered in the course of this era (Hofman and Hoogland 2003; Keegan 2010; Pagán Jiménez 2013; Rodríguez Ramos 2010a; Rodríguez Ramos, *et al.* 2008; Ulloa Hung and Valcárcel Rojas 2013). During the period 2000-800 BC the movements and interactions of the first settlers in many ways laid the foundations for the diverse yet connected societies and cultures of later periods.

Continuity: 800-200 BC

Caribbean archaeology has always had a special interest in the period between 500 BC and AD 400. It was previously firmly believed that this era saw the arrival of a wave of new migrants that utilised a distinctively new type of ceramics referred to by archaeologists as the (Cedrosan) Saladoid, named after the type site of Saladero in the Lower Orinoco (Boomert 2000; Rouse and Cruxent 1963). Following a theoretical framework based on population movements (Rouse 1986), the idea was that Saladoid colonizers migrated into the Caribbean from the Orinico delta. These "Saladoid peoples" were thought to be the founders of Ceramic Age culture in the Caribbean, which did not only include the use of ceramics, but also traits such as sedentarism, horticulture, a pronounced animistic ideology, tribal organization and long-distance acquisition of exotic raw materials and finished objects. The "Saladoid phenomenon" has also been linked to the spread of the Arawakan language into the Caribbean islands (Granberry and Vescelius 2004; Heckenberger 2013; Rouse 1948a).

It was believed that this influx of Neolithic migrants from the mainland pushed out or otherwise quickly assimilated with the original "Archaic Age" inhabitants. The sudden break-off of the distribution of Early Saladoid ceramics at the western extent of Puerto Rico signalled that indigenous resistance in the western Greater Antilles was more successful, leading to a Saladoid-"Archaic Age" frontier between Puerto Rico and Hispaniola. However, slow acculturation finally dissolved this frontier, which then shifted further westwards. Historical documents of the early contact period still reported pockets of a-ceramic, cave dwelling peoples in the extreme West of Cuba, so the neolithization of the Caribbean was thought never to have been completed (Rouse 1992).

Nevertheless, several facts do not align with some basic aspects of this version of Caribbean history. The newest data suggests that this crucial period was less about the mass migration of culturally dominant colonists than it was about growing and increasingly interconnected island and mainland worlds (Hofman, Boomert, et al. 2011; Rodríguez Ramos 2010a; Rodríguez Ramos and Pagán Jiménez 2006). What is more, this process did not start with the appearance of new ceramic series, but much earlier.

In a recent contribution and following up on earlier studies (Ulloa Hung and Valcárcel Rojas 2002; Veloz Maggiolo 2001), Rodríguez Ramos and his colleagues have shown that the first use of ceramics could potentially be traced to the early 2nd millennium BC. The evidence is clearest for the period between 800-200 BC. These sites that were previously considered to be a-ceramic yielded evidence for a crude but widely distributed ceramic series, called the Caimitoid in Cuba and Hispaniola (Rodríguez Ramos, et al. 2008). The fact that this ceramic series is not connected to the Saladoid phenomenon is especially clear in the case of the Dominican Republic and Cuba where "true Saladoid" has never been found (Hofman, Ulloa Hung, et al. 2007).

There is also solid evidence of certain typical lithic tools and techniques later associated with another series called the Huecoid (see below). Iconic "Neolithic" tools such as edge-ground cobbles, flints, pestles and celts, were part of toolkits that predated the arrival of Saladoid ceramics in the Caribbean (Rodríguez Ramos 2005). Furthermore, proof from starch grains on tools and in the calculus of teeth, has indicated that foodstuffs considered part of a horticultural or even more intensive agricultural diet (such as maize and beans) were also produced and consumed at pre-Saladoid sites (Mickleburgh and Pagán-Jiménez 2012; Pagán Jiménez 2013). Chapter 5 will discuss how the same raw material resources continue to be applied and distributed from the earliest settlement of the islands until the end of the pre-colonial period. All things considered, it is safe to say that there is no clean break between an Archaic and Ceramic Age. Instead we should speak of a 800-200 BC interface period during which two traditions started to mesh together (Hofman, Boomert, et al. 2011).

What does this continuity entail in terms of the deep-time dynamics of Caribbean social networks? Firstly, ceramic and lithic production techniques are not just single dots on the map, but occur at several sites over an extended region and period. Unless independent invention occurred in every single case, diffusion involving social interactions must have been taking place in the Archaic Age. As a result, the foundational groups of settlers would have become evermore tightly knit and interlocked over time. This caused or came together with structural changes in several key areas of human mobility, food economy, and socio-political systems. The exact scale of and interaction mechanisms behind these processes are not yet fully understood, but it is likely that they were partly the result of a structural growth of local movement of goods, people, and ideas and not only the result of outside migration.

So, prior to 500 BC, networks must also have been meshed together with those on the mainland (Hofman, Boomert, et al. 2011; Rodríguez Ramos, et al. 2013). Whether these network paths led through many interlocked archipelagic subgraphs or consisted of a small number of cross-Caribbean long-distance or "weak" ties is impossible to say (see Chapter 3). Unfortunately, the evidence is also unclear as to the extent of which this involved the circulation of information or also of goods and raw materials. It is also important to note that continuity of foundational culture and society does not necessarily contradict earlier opinions on the actual movement of new peoples into the Caribbean (Bérard 2013). It rather suggests that this movement was part of a connected set of developments.

Transition: 200 BC-AD 400

Notwithstanding recent ideas on continuity, the period between 200 BC and AD 400 witnessed many structural revolutions to Caribbean culture and society (Bérard 2013). This came together with an influx of new peoples, attested by the sudden appearance of Saladoid-style ceramics. The most plausible lines of evidence point to East Venezuela as the homelands of these migrants, most likely in the Lower Orinoco (Bérard 2013; Boomert 2000). Their migration into the Caribbean did not follow a stepping-stone fission pattern up the chain of islands as would be the case in a slower, undirected migration. If this had indeed been the case then the most southerly island from the mainland would have the earliest evidence of this migration process. After some time a group would then have fissioned off from the earliest colony to colonize the island further to the north, and so forth. Currently available evidence does not support this. Rather, as was first noted by Keegan (1995) and later substantiated by Fitzpatrick (2006), it seems that the earliest dates of sites with Saladoid ceramics on the islands stem from the northern Lesser Antilles. This would imply that a rather rapid advance to the northern Lesser Antilles and Eastern Greater Antilles had taken place, and not a slow, up the line exploration. This has recently led to a discussion on the ancestral homeland of these migrants (Fitzpatrick 2013b). Still, in terms of historical processes and network dynamics the region of origin is ultimately not that important. What is more interesting is that a direct migration indicates that these movements were *directed* towards a certain objective (cf. Keegan 2004's "pull factors").

If all that the new colonizers were looking for was a new place to live it seems unlikely that they would travel that far north. On their journey they would have passed through mainland and island regions suitable for habitation – which according to the evidence thus far were not or only scarcely populated. Moreover, based on the patterning of Early Saladoid sites, it seems that they were indeed located close to areas with good access to resources that were useful but in no sense critical for survival. Thus, if one rules out a voyage of random drifting, these migrants would have travelled to places of which they already had acquired some prior knowledge passed to them by means of down-the-line information exchange or direct contacts. From this point of view, the rapid advance north is an argument in favour of the existence of an interaction network connecting the first inhabitants of the islands with the immigrants from the mainland prior to 500/400 BC and possible intermingling afterwards.

The fact that they were not cut-off from their previous social contacts is also clear from the increase in evidence for long-distance interactions (Boomert 1987, 2001b; Hofman, Bright, *et al.* 2007). Exotic objects in site assemblages are easily transportable ornaments. In the site of La Hueca and Sorcé, for example, they consist of a range of materials, such as decorated bones from mainland animal and various sorts of worked semi-precious stones. Many feature animal elements and iconography that can only be connected to species found on the mainland, such as jaguar and peccary teeth as well as amulets depicting large birds of prey. Birds of prey amulets made from Puerto Rican serpentinite and found as far south as Trinidad, provide evidence for interactions between the islands and the mainland (Chanlatte Baik and Narganes Storde 1990, 2005; Narganes Storde 1995).[13]

A new ceramic series, the Huecoid, taking its name from the above mentioned site, has been linked to these (geographically) long-distance ties (Chanlatte Baik 2013). Rouse (1992) had originally proposed that Huecoid ceramics simply represented a sub-series of the Saladoid series. Yet, based on their fieldwork on Vieques and in East Puerto Rico, this has been contradicted by Chanlatte-Baik, Narganes Stordes and other Puerto Rican archaeologists (Chanlatte Baik and Narganes Storde 1990). Although advances have been made on the study of its ceramics and associated assemblages (Chanlatte Baik 2013; Hofman and Hoogland 1999; Rodríguez Ramos 2010a), the role of sites with Huecoid-style material culture in the melting pot of the first centuries BC and AD, is still not quite clear.[14]

What dynamics can possibly account for the complex interrelations in the site assemblages of the "Archaic"-Saladoid-Huecoid interface period? Due to its ties to older local and Saladoid assemblages it is unlikely that the appearance of the Huecoid represents a completely unconnected phenomenon – e.g. a separate migration of people making and using only Huecoid ceramics. This also implies that it is not likely that the Huecoid assemblage evolved from either a purely Caimitoid or Saladoid strain. Instead the divergences and similarities in material culture practices and the parallel timing of several structural changes within Caribbean society and culture in a span of a few centuries or even decades is of crucial importance. It seems to me that the only way forward is to understand the developments of this period as the result of what is known in network science as a "phase transition".

---

13   The origins of exotic zoological materials found at Vieques on which isotopic provenance studies have been carried out do not only extend to the Eastern Venezuela, but also to other mainland regions located more to the West (Laffoon, personal communication 2012).

14   It is difficult to ascertain if the Huecoid represents a completely separate set of social and material relations to the Saladoid. Following a system of chrono-metric hygiene, Saladoid is dated earlier than Huecoid with the earliest occurrences at the site of Trants on Montserrat and La Hueca/Sorcé (see Chapter 6). It is furthermore noteworthy that there are very few sites in which only Huecoid ceramics have been found. At present, the only dated and published site that contains only Huecoid ceramics is Punta Candelero in East Puerto Rico. Other Huecoid-style ceramics always co-occur with Saladoid and sometimes earlier components are discovered on the same site. However, few securely excavated and dated sites have an Early Saladoid component only. Indeed, the majority of early sites present mixed Huecoid/Saladoid components. A study on the raw materials and production techniques of both Huecoid and Saladoid ceramics at Trants also shows these were indistinguishable (Reed and Petersen 2001).

Although phase transitions can often not be explained as the result of one place, one process, or one moment in time they can be seen as an event. If a network undergoes a phase transition then a system will "suddenly" evolve that can have completely new dynamics when compared to previous stages (Padgett and Powell 2012). In the case of the Archaic-Saladoid-Huecoid interface, the lead-up to this transition was slow but steady: in the millennia before island and mainland communities had become ever more connected over an ever wider region. Ceramic production, horticulture, and other innovations had already been circulating in the pan-Caribbean region through down-the-line diffusion or intermittent, long-distance ties. Then a "sudden" change occurred. Island and mainland networks across the Caribbean seaboard became and stayed fully connected. There are several parallel revolutions in regional culture and society, consisting of: (a) the sudden presence and spread of both Huecoid and Saladoid ceramics, (b) the increase in (habitation) site size and quantity, (c) new forms of material culture, and (d) changing foodways. This co-temporality is congruent with the idea of a network undergoing a phase transition, suddenly changing shape, becoming more coherent and having greater connectivity.

When a network becomes more connected, the new structure needs to be sufficiently robust or else the system will return into a less connected state. It is thus possible that in the Caribbean greater coherence and connectivity had already occurred at multiple moments in time and at various places (Rodríguez Ramos 2010). Yet, in contrast to earlier occasions, for some reason this time interregional networks were robust enough to not fall back into their previous, less connected state. One way in which this threshold could have been overcome was the movement of migrants into the North-Eastern Caribbean.[15] Migrant groups did not have to be large (cf. Laffoon 2012). Even small numbers could have been responsible for the new forces at work. This idea is not new, but this incarnation of an old hypothesis does need to be strengthened by means of a continued discussion with reference to the timing and causal factors of this transition (Boomert 2000; Keegan 2004). The question remains which specific processes, places, material culture and moments in time caused this transition to occur and succeed? Chapter 5 will present further ideas on and a discussion on these issues.

Waxing and waning of inter-regional interaction: AD 400-600/800

After the first few centuries AD, interaction systems continued to grow both geographically and in terms of the total amount of individuals and social groups taking part in them. Between AD 200 and 500 we see the largest number of sites on the larger as well as the smaller islands in the Northeastern and Southeastern Antilles (Boomert 2000; Bright 2011; Curet 2005; Haviser 1991; Torres 2012).

---

15 Migration does not have to be the (only) factor in creating these robust networks. Any other increase of fitness of more expansive Caribbean networks, such as a breakthrough in (maritime) technology, could have been at its basis (see also Keegan 2004).

This is also the period during which the archaeological record yields the best evidence for regional and interregional interactions (Fitzpatrick, *et al.* 2008; Hofman, Bright, *et al.* 2007; Knippenberg 2007).[16]

It seems that greater network connectivity and coherence does not hold true for all aspects of the archaeological record. At the same time that the record shows an intensification of interaction in the region, we also see that technical and iconographical systems lose their similarities. This resulted in a typical island style of ceramics in the Lesser Antilles, sometimes called the "Late" or "Modified Saladoid" (Boomert 2000; Bérard 2013). A similar process takes place in the Greater Antilles with the emergence of local styles such as Ostiones, Cuevas and Monserrate, which are normally treated as part of a larger (sub)series called the (Ostionan) Ostionoid (Rouse 1992). The same can be said for changes in foodways with archaeobotanical and archaeozoological evidence revealing an increased reliance on marine and horticultural resources, rather than the hunting of small game animals (Newsom and Wing 2004).

It is likely that this was related to a change in the socio-political landscape in the region. Changes in burial practices, an increase of sites denoting an increase in population, and development of more pronounced local and regional cultures indicate a slow change in the political structure of the Caribbean from around AD 200 on (Hofman and Hoogland 2004; Siegel 1992).[17] This argument is strengthened by the increased quantity of personal valuables found in excavations and surveys in the Northeastern and Southern Caribbean islands (Curet 1996). They are mainly small objects designed to be worn or easily carried and were probably crafted in household settings by non-specialists. It has to be noted that these ornaments are fairly standardized with relatively little variation within the same category of objects. Perhaps this is related to the fact that, aside from being personal ornaments, they were also circulated in wide-ranging exchange systems (Hofman. Bright, *et al.* 2007).

The majority of these objects depict animals or fantastic creatures. The identities of others, such as the small three-pointed stone, bone coral and shell artefacts, are less easily interpreted. As will be discussed below to the indigenous people of the Caribbean these were not only objects but inspirited things and other than human beings (Breukel 2013; Petitjean-Roget 1997; Waldron 2010). At any rate, it is clear that by AD 500 a complex system of cosmological relations between humans and non-humans had developed (Hofman and Hoogland 2004; Oliver 1998). The

---

16 For example, new studies indicate that the majority of the jadeitite objects, for instance those from the Royall's site in Antigua reported by Harlowe and Murphy (Harlow, *et al.* 2006; see Chapter 1), date from after AD 400 (Knippenberg, personal communication 2013). However, it now seems likely that at least a part hereof originates from either Hispaniola or Cuba and not from the Sierra de las Minas in Guatemala (Garcia-Caso, *et al.* 2013). It nonetheless represents a movement of materials over a range of several hundreds to over 1000 km Another example of continued long-distance exchange is found at the site of Maisabel in Puerto Rico. Here a few fragments of guanín were recovered, i.e. an alloy of gold, copper and silver for which the knowledge of smelting techniques was only present in the Isthmo-Colombian region (Oliver 2000; Siegel 1992).

17 Although Keegan recently suggested that socio-political hierarchy was present in some form before this period (Keegan 2010), there are few archaeological proxies that may serve to argue for institutionalized social inequality before AD 600 or even intercommunal polities before AD 200.

material counterparts of this system served to create, maintain and contest social relations in new ways (see Chapters 7 and 8).

Regional surveys across the Caribbean suggest that the population still increased rapidly during the period AD 400-700 (Curet 2005; Hofman 2013). Around AD 700 however, we see a relatively abrupt end to the growth of sites both in size and number, particularly in the northern Lesser Antilles. Interaction across the Northeastern Caribbean region also dropped sharply (Bérard 2013; Hofman 2013; Hofman, Bright, et al. 2007). The quality of the ceramics, sometimes referred to as "Terminal Saladoid", was cruder than before and their designs became more rudimentary (Bright 2011; Hofman 2013). In addition, this period is marked by what seems to be the intentional destruction of ceremonial valuables in the northern Lesser Antilles, like the aforementioned three-pointed stones (Petitjean Roget 1993). It has been suggested that these developments were correlated with a change in climate to more arid conditions than before (Blancaneaux 2009; Bonnissent 2013) This does not imply that in the 8th century AD interactions between communities had come to a halt. In the Guadeloupe archipelago, for example, we see a tightly knit system of sites, which are related through specific ceramic decorative and technical practices (de Waal 2006; Hofman, et al. 2004; Petersen, et al. 2004). For example, the site of Anse a la Gourde on Grande-Terre has evidence for the movement of exotic (lithic) materials and individuals in and beyond the archipelago (de Waal 2006; Hofman and Hoogland 2004; Knippenberg 2007; Laffoon and Vos 2011).

Increasing density and complexity: AD 600/800-1492

While the Lesser Antilles seems to have hit a phase of stagnation or even decline, the Greater Antilles, in particular Puerto Rico and Hispaniola, saw the emergence of evermore complex systems of people, things and ideas. With reference to these topics, the development of chiefdoms or *cacicazgos* has been discussed at great length (Curet 2003). Much of our interpretations of the type and dynamics of indigenous political structures during the period AD 600/800-1492 is a projection from late 15th and early 16th century post-contact European documents (Machlachlan and Keegan 1990). These documents describe a system that has come be known as the *cacicazgo*, a regional polity headed by a *cacique*. Traditionally the *cacicazgo* has been seen as a political system that occurred in many of the regions along the shores of the Caribbean Sea and beyond. For example, it has been suggested to be present in some form or other in the Lesser Antilles, the South American coasts and llanos, Amazonia, the Isthmo-Colombian region and parts of Mesoamerica (Blanton, *et al.* 1996; Crock 2000; Heckenberger 2005; Keegan, *et al.* 1998; Redmond 1998; Spencer and Redmond 1992). Yet in how far these systems were similar in their general or specific mechanisms remains very much unclear. The *cacicazgo* should thus be seen more as of a diffuse set of related practices and political roles than as any unified form of cultural or political organization (Curet 2003).

It is safe to say that in the islands the majority of such research was carried out in Puerto Rico and, to a lesser extent, the south and east Dominican Republic. This region, divided by the Mona Passage, has become known as the heartland of *cacical* culture in the Antilles.[18] Here, one of the lines of evidence for regional integration of autonomous communities is the evolution of the earlier village plaza into clearly demarcated, ceremonial plaza complexes that served the wider region.[19] Siegel has argued that the empty space in the centre of habitation sites from the first centuries AD was the starting point for the later evolution of ceremonial plazas and so-called ball courts (Siegel 1999, 2010).

During this period in the Greater Antilles population numbers continued to rise. Sites themselves did not necessarily grow in size, but their density in the late pre-colonial landscape increased. Regional overviews indicate the presence of large sites with many smaller pockets of habitation across the Greater and Lesser Antilles (e.g. Curet 2005; Hofman, *et al.* 2004; Ulloa Hung 2013; Veloz Maggiolo 1972). As was referred to in the previous discussion on Caribbean flora and fauna use, this population growth was sustained by means of evermore sophisticated subsistence techniques.[20] However, it has been suggested that population pressure was partly the reason for the rise of the *cacicazgo* system, although it has been shown that the population in West Puerto Rico was not anywhere near its maximum threshold when the first regional polities appeared (Curet 2005). Nevertheless, larger population numbers also implied a potential larger pool of social partners or competitors now existed (Siegel 2004).

---

18   Ethnohistoric records indicate the presence of similar regional polities in Cuba and Jamaica, but the material culture of these islands indicates that they differed slightly from the Dominican Republic and Puerto Rico. The best evidence for chiefdoms outside of the Mona Passage heartland can be found in the Cuban Banes region. It has a few larger habitation sites surrounded by smaller habitation sites, of which the site assemblages contain many personal decorations and amulets (Valcárcel Rojas 1999; Valcárcel Rojas 2002). For a discussion of possible Lesser Antillean chiefdoms, see Chapter 6.

19   In Puerto Rico the earliest demarcated plazas occur around 650 BC (Curet and Stringer 2010; Oliver 1998; Siegel 1999, 2010; Torres 2012). With the addition of new plazas at the same site, single plazas grew into plaza complexes. From this period, demarcated plaza sites are also known from the Virgin Islands. Here stone alignments do normally not feature petroglyphs. The same applies to Hispaniola, where some of the largest plazas can be found (Alegría 1983). It has been suggested that central plaza sites can also be found in other islands outside of this heartland. Yet, because they are not clearly demarcated, they are not easily recognized (Keegan 2007).

20   Dental anthropological studies suggest that carbohydrate intake increased. A change in food preparation techniques also meant that food from staple crops became more refined after AD 600-800 in both the Greater and Lesser Antilles (Mickleburgh 2013). In addition, islands like Cuba and Hispaniola have evidence for agricultural works, such as terraces and *montones* – small hills functioning as mini raised fields (Ulloa Hung 2013). There was also an increase in the scale and effectiveness of marine food procurement, including new techniques for processing, preservation and distribution (Morsink 2012). Historical sources indicate elite-specific foodways in the Greater Antilles, for which some archaeological evidence also exists in Puerto Rico (Curet and Pestle 2010). Valuable non-food plants such as cotton were more intensively cultivated (Morsink 2012; Newsom and Wing 2004).

For the period AD 1000-1492 Rouse (1992) identified only five larger cultural series (see Figure 1.1), but this is not representative of the actual variability in material cultural repertoires.[21] New research of site and regional ceramic assemblages has indicated that local divergence in decorative and technical styles had continued after AD 1000. This is not to say that there are no similarities at all between local ceramic and other material culture expressions. These larger series should rather be seen as broad "interregional styles". While local technical and decorative choices represented a different way of doing things locally, broadly shared iconographic repertoires meant that ceramics and other forms of material culture were still part of wider socio-cultural systems (e.g. Bright 2011; Hofman, Isendoorn, *et al.* 2008; Hofman, Ulloa Hung, *et al.* 2007; Hoogland and Hofman 1993; Petersen, *et al.* 2004; Ulloa Hung 2013).

Among the artefacts recovered from this period a distinct repertoire of beautifully crafted objects stands out (e.g. Bercht, *et al.* 1997). From a systemic perspective these valuables probably co-evolved with earlier elite networks that culminated into the *cacicazgos* of the proto-historic period (Curet 1996; McGinnis 1997; Oliver 2009; Walker 1993).[22] Although such objects are often identified as chiefly regalia, it would be more accurate to describe them as being part of the system of *cemí* objects (Oliver 2009; Figure 8.1). The material cultural repertoire of the last phase of contact was thus a specific Antillean extension of an Amerindian ontology in which things could be (as central as) people in the context of late pre-colonial social relations (see Chapters 7 and 8).

More than before, production and exchange took place in and with places that were geographically close. This increasingly local focus is particularly clear in the Lesser Antilles, which has been the subject of several studies dealing with stylistic interaction and provenance of raw materials and finished goods (Bright 2011; de Waal 2006; Hofman 1993, 1993b; Isendoorn, *et al.* 2008; Knippenberg 2007). Evidence for interregional ties is still present, but in contrast to the earlier interactions from around the turn of the first millennium AD, coherence of material culture assemblages across the entire region had greatly decreased (Bright 2011; Hofman 2013).

---

21 Meillacoid assemblages are found across sites in the Dominican Republic, Jamaica, the Bahamas and Cuba (Rouse 1992; Ulloa Hung 2013). The Chicoid series is present in the Dominican Republic, Puerto Rico and, after AD 1200, also in the northern Lesser Antilles (Hofman 1995; Rouse 1992). Puerto Rico, the Virgin Islands and the northern Lesser Antilles still had some later forms of the Elenan Ostionoid (Rouse 1992). Suazan Troumassoid can be found in both the Windward and Leeward islands in sites dating to around AD 1000 to just after contact (Bright 2011; Hofman 2013). The Lesser Antillean Cayoid represents a terminal pre-colonial to post-contact indigenous ceramic tradition, which are correlated with the presence of Kalinago peoples (Boomert 1986).

22 A number of these objects have been associated with the evolution of communal displays taking place at plaza sites, for instance stone elbow collars and belts (Walker 1993). Intricately carved three-pointed stones had earlier incarnations as smaller, undecorated three-pointers of various materials that are first found around the beginning of the first millennium. The regional distribution of the largest, most elaborate specimens is correlated with the spread of the central plaza sites and the historic descriptions of classic *cacicazgos*. As a result, these larger three-pointers are also generally associated with elite ceremonies and exchanges (de Hostos 1923; Oliver 2009). The same is often argued for other items like the ceremonial seats called *duhos* and shamanic paraphernalia (Ostapkowicz 1997; Roe 1997).

In short, politics was not the only aspect of indigenous culture and society to display an increasingly complex and locally dense social structure during the last centuries before European contact. The rise of the *cacicazgo* went hand in hand with other dynamics in inter- and intra-communal relations. Growing population numbers meant larger social networks. However, even if there was a total growth of node and tie quantity, the social ties that individuals had did not necessarily expand geographically. The expansion of village centres into plaza complexes serving the wider region must have converged with a new understanding of the collective. This is also supported by evidence for more large-scale communal subsistence strategies such as fishing and agriculture and more refined food preparation techniques. In this period the idea of community was clearly extended to non-kin, perhaps for the first time in the history of the Caribbean (Siegel 2004; Torres 2012).

Between AD 600/800 and 1492 a development took place in which interpersonal sets of relations were transformed within larger social institutions. Most lines of evidence point to a process in which personal relations would have become territorially entrenched, thereby perhaps carving up the Antilles into smaller territorial units. On the other hand it is clear from ethnohistorical studies, artefact provenance studies, overarching similarities in material culture assemblages and other synchronous developments that people, goods and ideas continued to circulate in interregional exchange systems. Thus, after a short period of divergence, from AD *c.*1000 to the end of the pre-colonial period the Caribbean once again became more connected. As I will discuss in Chapters 7 and 8, rather than being the outcome of a type of chiefdom society, this was the result of multiple interacting, dynamic processes.

Cultural, linguistic and ethnic (self-)identification

The result of this long history of pre-colonial encounters meant that at the time of contact the Caribbean had a highly diverse cultural, linguistic and ethnic layout, something which did not go unnoticed by European travelers in the region (Hofman and Carlin 2010). Needless to say it has been always deemed important to utilize their information to be able to know more about how social interactions and material distributions could have been based on cultural, linguistic and ethnic groupings. However, it is becoming more and more clear that the particular mechanics of group membership were not fully grasped by Spanish and other European reporters. Or, if they were, these were not clearly communicated in their chronicles. Nevertheless, attempts to re-construct group affiliations based on historic sources and to apply these labels to material culture assemblages do continue.

"Taíno" is probably the best known of these group labels. It is still a frequently occurring term in Caribbean archaeological literature, nowadays most often serving to denote a widespread Antillean set of cultural practices and norms shared by several or more localized cultures in the Greater Antilles and beyond (Petersen, *et al.* 2004). It is akin to but different from an older use of the term that suggested the existence of a conglomeration of Taíno peoples, sometimes grouped under the header "the Arawak" (Rouse 1948a), who occupied the Greater Antilles from Eastern Cuba to Puerto Rico (Lovén 1935). Linguistically the "Taíno" would all have belonged to the same Arawakan language family that is widely distributed over the South American mainland (Granberry and Vescelius 2004; Heckenberger 2013). Rouse (1992) further divided these Arawakan speaking groups on the basis of (ceramic) material culture traits and socio-political organization: "Sub-Taíno" in Cuba and Jamaica, "Classical Taíno" on the island of Hispaniola, and "Eastern Taíno" on Puerto Rico and some of the northern Lesser Antilles. To many, "Taíno" material cultural represents the aesthetic epitome of the indigenous peoples of the Antilles (Bercht, *et al.* 1997; Kerchache 1994; Regional Museum of Archaeology Altos de Chavon 1991). Several contemporary Caribbean indigenous revival movements both in the region and the diaspora utilze the term "Taíno" as a self-identification and have re-constructed a "neo-Taíno" language and culture.

"Taíno" is just one of several denominations for Greater and Lesser Antillean indigenous peoples that are believed to have inhabited the islands at the moment of contact. The inhabitants of the Bahamas, for example, were and are often referred to as "Lucayo". These, like the "Taíno", are believed to have been Arawakan speaking groups, and would have been identified with an indigenous word for "islander" and are sometimes referred to as Lucayan "Taíno" (Keegan 2007; Petersen, *et al.* 2004). The "Guanahatabey" (sometimes called "Ciboney") of Central and Western Cuba were purportedly an isolated people who lived in caves and used only lithic tools at the moment of contact (Rouse 1948c). The central and northern parts of the neighbouring island of Hispaniola are believed to be the homeland of "Macorix" and "Ciguayo" groups. Several historic sources indicate that people here spoke a different language and these reports were combined with the presence of divergent archaeological assemblages in central and north Haiti and the Dominican Republic (Ulloa Hung 2013).

In the Lesser Antilles historic reports and archaeological material have also been applied in conjunction to reconstruct group formations. The Island-Caribs or Kalinago are the only pre-colonial indigenous group present in the Caribbean that still forms a sovereign indigenous community today (Honychurch 2000). In the past they formed an ethnic group together with the mainland Kalina. The Cayo pottery style, reminiscent of the mainland Koriabo complex, is connected to these people (Boomert 1986). Their language is subdivided in a male and female vocabulary. The female vocabulary consists of an Arawakan grammar and lexicon, while the male vocabulary consists of an Arawakan grammar with a lexicon that has many Caribban loanwords (Breton 1999 [1665]; Granberry and Vescelius 2004). Said to have migrated from the mainland to the southern Lesser Antilles according to their narrated histories, their connection to the late pre-colonial Cayo style also suggest they were late arrivals in the Caribbean. Due to recent excavations and surveys there is now an increasing understanding of the archaeological reflection of this group (Boomert 2011; Hofman and Hoogland 2012).[23] In addition, older literature refers to people inhabiting the Lesser Antillean before the arrival of the Island Caribs as "Igneri" or "Eyrie". Because it was believed that they were pushed out by the arrival of the Island Caribs in the late pre-colonial period, earlier ceramic styles belonging to the Saladoid series have been correlated with their presence (Fewkes 1903/1904; Rouse 1948a: 517 and 545).

It should be noted that the origin and comprehensiveness of the majority of these group labels are vague at best (Boomert 2000; Hofman 1993: Chapter 6; Hulme 1993). However, in academic vernacular these terms have long continued to be used in a similar way as one might speak of an ethnic group: the Dutch, the Romani, the Taíno, the Macorix. This trend still continues in some (popular) historic overviews (e.g. Knight 2011: Chapter 1). However, with the notable exception of the Kalinago, it is not clear how and if any of them correlate to an ethnic or socio-cultural, indigenous (self-)identification.[24] This is especially unclear in the case of the "Taíno" label. It has long been recognized that none of the indigenous peoples of the Caribbean ever referred to themselves or others as being ethnically "Taíno". The term does not appear as a collective name in any of the primary or even secondary sources before the mid-19th century (Rafinesque 1836: 186; Rouse 1948a:note 9). Instead *taíno* probably meant "good", "friendly" or "noble" in at least one Arawakan language spoken on the islands at the time of contact (Hulme 1993).

There is a sizeable contribution from Arawakan, Caribban and maybe some influence from Waraoid and even Tollan languages to the historically reported linguistic register (Granberry 2013). Nevertheless, like is the case with group denominations, a lack of understanding exists with regards to the specific history, identification and distribution of languages. All in all it can be said that, in the case of the pre-colonial Antilles, the marriage of "historical ethnic studies" (i.e. the identification and study of ethnicities through historic sources), linguistics and archaeology is not a happy one. As a result of this mismatch, hypotheses

---

23 Conflicts with the Spanish, English, French and Dutch during the colonial period have led to the historic descriptions of these people's portrayal as cannibalistic, brutal warrior tribes who in prehistoric times were continually raiding the "peaceful" chiefdoms to the north. In the past this has led scholars to draw a cultural fault line between the northern and southern Lesser Antilles at the Virgin Islands (Rouse 1948b, 1948c; Figueredo 1978). Others had even suggested that the northern Lesser Antilles during the late pre-colonial period were something of a perpetual conflict zone wedged between Taíno and Carib peoples in which there were only some marginal settlements. It has since long been understood that especially the latter view was incorrect (Allaire 1987; Boomert 1986; Whitehead 1995), but presuppositions concerning a perceived Taíno/Carib dichotomy continue to plague Caribbean archaeology today (Hofman, Bright, *et al.* 2008).

24 An accurate historic and archaeological characterization of the Guanahatabey is lacking. This has led to the realization that the idea of a Cuban "pre-ceramic" frontier enduring to the contact period is probably false (Rodríguez Ramos 2008; Rodríguez Ramos, *et al.* 2009). The status of the terms Ciguayo and Macorix have also been reconsidered, which has led to a resurgence of fieldwork in the regions that they supposedly inhabited (Ulloa Hung 2013). Perhaps these names represent regional denominations rather than ethnic, culture or language group names. Something similar may have been the case with the Lucayo. Granted, due to socio-cultural-geographic correlations, these labels could have some tenuous links to indigenous perceptions of group identities. In contrast, the existence of the "Taíno" seems to have no firm ground in historical, social or material cultural reality whatsoever.

on the socio-cultural boundaries of groups have traditionally been proposed based on the distribution of types of material culture and the more than likely erroneous identification of historically reported ethnic or linguistic affiliations. Without denying the importance of indigenous perceptions of cultural, linguistic, ethnic and social differences, I feel it is better to let these boundaries potentially emerge from the archaeological material, rather than imposing them top-down. For this reason I will limit the application of these labels in any form to an absolute minimum.

Ontology

An ontological approach focuses on indigenous "theories of being" and is an anthropological adaptation of ontology as it is used in (meta-physical) philosophy. An ontological approach seeks to capture salient, emic understandings and explanations of the features of the world, the place of humans and other beings in it, and how this came to be. In this the term ontology is closely analogous to the concepts of worldview or cosmovision, but it signals a departure from the notion that what (non-Western) people think and feel about their world are variants in expressions of or perspectives on one transcendental reality. Rather, referring to a worldview or cosmovision as an ontology instead starts with the idea that how people think and feel about their world aligns with how this world literally is. This is a radical move away from relativism in favour of the acceptance of the (internal) realism of other ways of thought (Goodman 1978; Overing 1990). This is not without some destructive complications about knowledge and truth-claims in the field of (archaeological) anthropology (Henare, *et al.* 2007). However, the realization that non-Western ontologies are (internally) real and logical already leads to an important shift in our own perception of them. For example, practices that are inconsistent with our reality – in that case referred to in academic vernacular with terms as "magical", "esoteric", or "symbolic" expressions – make sense in the context of the original ontological system and should thus be analysed and interpreted as such (see also Paleček and Risjord 2013).

Due to the quick decline of Amerindian societies and cultures and in particular the repression of beliefs and practices considered to be diabolical by European missionaries, our knowledge on indigenous Caribbean ontologies is limited. In the Greater Antilles all that remains is a smattering of sources on indigenous views on the state of the world and the place of humans in it. Fortunately, there are some sources that can give us a more comprehensive approximation. Manuscripts as for instance the *Account of the Antiquities of the Indies* by Fray Ramon Pané (1999 [1571]) or those of other early ethnographer-style clergymen in the Lesser Antilles such as Breton (1999 [1665]), de la Borde (1684), and Labat (1979 [1722]), are relatively objective descriptions of indigenous ontologies. However, even based on these sources it is not possible to paint a picture of local ontologies with more than a broad stroke.[25] One, time-tested solution to this problem has been to expand the limited sources of information at our disposal by drawing upon analogies to mainland indigenous cosmologies, specifically those of Lowland South America (e.g. Arrom 1975; Boomert 2001c; Roe 1982, 1997; Stevens-Arroyo 2006; Whitehead 2011). Obviously, a one to one correlation between Lowland South American and Antillean indigenous ontologies does not exist. Nonetheless, in comparing Antillean worldviews to those known from narratological and ethnographic research in Lowland South America, the two regions showcase a wide range of similarities in their ontological substrate. When extrapolating this unity into deep-time it is possible to present a base-line for the pre-colonial indigenous ontologies of the Caribbean islands (Boomert 2001c; Roe 1982).

At its basis this deep-historic, base-line model could be called "animistic" (Oliver 1997). Animism is the inclination to believe in spirits or souls that reside in or are identified with (parts of) the natural world (Descola 1996; Roth 1915; Tylor 1871). The problem with this term is it presupposes that what is "natural" and what not is a useful distinction to make. Generally speaking, and specifically in Amerindian ontologies, this is not the case (Viveiros de Castro 1998; Willerslev 2011). Furthermore, animism is too broad a category to serve as an ontological trope in specific cases. Belief in some form of spiritual agency applies to most if not all indigenous ontologies of the Americas. It also applies to (aspects of) the worldview of many who live in societies that have not traditionally been recognized as animistic, like our own (Gell 1998; Knappett 2005; Pels 2010; Skrbina 2005).

As a reaction to the problems with the term animism, in 1998 the ethnographer Eduardo Viveiros de Castro advanced "perspectivism" as a competing model. At the heart of this model lies the concept that Amerindian ontologies are not based on the true natures of beings, but on their perspectival states. An Amerindian theory of being is in a sense multi-"natural", i.e. it recognizes multiple ways of being which can also be expressed or experienced at the same time. In addition, the outward forms of humans, animals, and spirits are not representative of their subjective states. Rather, the inward state of many (but not all) organic and even inorganic beings is of an elementary sameness. Which form and behaviour other types of beings display is not a given, but depends on one's perspective.

For example, in normal circumstances humans are humans. Animals are animals and potential prey *for* humans. Spirits are spirits and as such often prey *on* humans. All are subjects and thus potential social partners – although such roles are often restricted to beings that have been identified as central counterparts of human "symbolic ecologies" (Roe 1982). Roles such as prey and predator are not

---

25   For the pre-colonial Caribbean one finds no evidence of overarching belief systems that were implemented from the top-down such as widely shared political ideologies, organized religions, or even loosely organized "cults" with a larger following. Even if there was a shared ontological substrate, we may consider that different communities and even individuals had quite variable ontologies. This may have been yet another drive towards the variability of material culture expressions we see in the archaeological record. Research thus far has tended to stress overarching patterns in indigenous cosmographies and their material expression in the archaeological record, rather than provide a view on (inter-island) differences. Thus it is presently impossible to discuss the issue of the possible diversity of ontologies more in-depth.

natural, i.e. (biologically) inherent, but based on a being's perspective. So, in their own contexts spirits and animals will act as humans, talk like humans, and have similar material cultural repertoires and practices – e.g. houses, dress, hammocks, foodstuffs (Viveiros de Castro 2004). What is more, because spirits and animals see themselves as humans, spirits will potentially see humans as prey, while animals may perceive of humans as predators akin to spirits.

As such the "manifest form of each species is a mere envelope (a 'clothing') which conceals an internal human form, usually only visible to the eyes of the particular species or to trans-specific beings such as shamans" (Viveiros de Castro 1998: 470-471). Indeed, the outward form of a being is flexible and can undergo rapid transformations from prey to predator or from subject to object and back again (Viveiros de Castro 2004). Sometimes transformations are induced by subjects themselves. More often than not, they are due to the agency of others or transformative contexts – e.g. a shaman that stays too long within the village of Anacondas or eats the food of his animal hosts risks never being able to return again (see Carlin 2004: 511-514). In "before-time", a widespread concept among Amerindian groups, such transformations happened with even greater frequency. These transformations in before-time are also (dialectically) contingent with the outward shape, and essential qualities of human, animal and spirit subjects in the present (e.g. Overing 1990). Many Amerindian oral traditions are based on such present and before-time transformations talking of humans that change into animals, animals that change into humans, spirits that change into elements of the landscape, *etc.*[26] These same perspectivist elements are also found in Antillean indigenous narratives (e.g. de la Borde 1684; Labat 1979 [1722]; Pané 1999 [1571]; Taylor 1938).

This perspectivist model provides us with a deeper understanding of the type of material culture that (for us) represents more esoteric aspects of pre-colonial life, notably the widespread use of shamanic paraphernalia and iconographies of fantastical creatures. Specifically perspectivist animals must have had a central place in indigenous Caribbean ontologies. Starting *c.*500-400 BC we see the incorporation of animal iconography in ceramics, amulets of stone, shell and bone, and other forms of material culture. Often these animal shapes are mixed with anthropomorphic elements or vice versa, creating animal-human hybrid iconography. "Adornos", lugs and handles attached to vessel rims and walls, are found from *c.*400 BC onwards and often have an emphatic hybrid anthropomorphic and zoomorphic character. Ceramic motifs are often more difficult to interpret but it has been suggested that the same set of hybrid animals feature in them, as well (Petitjean-Roget 1997; Roe 2004; Rouse 1992; Waldron 2010).

It is generally believed that this ontological substrate did not change much throughout the pre-colonial period – although this must partly be an artefact of direct historic analogy. There was, however, a slight divergence in the ritual practice and material expression of this ontology on the islands (Arrom 1975;

---

26 For those interested in Amerindian narrative collections and motif analyses, see the excellent series titled *Folk Literature of South American Indians* (1979-1992, edited by Johannes Wilbert) of the Latin American Institute at the University College of Los Angeles.

Boomert 2001c; Oliver, *et al.* 2008; Roe 1997; Stevens-Arroyo 2006; Whitehead 2011). This culminated in an Antillean system of beliefs and practices surrounding a set of superhuman beings often referred to as *cemíism* (Oliver 2009). Even though it was a main feature of Antillean culture and society, beliefs and practices surrounding *cemí* were not in any way part of a centrally organized religion. Any similarities of specific superhuman beings and practices among the islands thus resulted from shared symbolic and ecological contexts, as well as from a diffusion of ritual practices and beliefs (Allaire 1990). It is all the more remarkable that the material expressions of *cemíism* – (idols, amulets, personal accoutrements, ceramic decoration, shamanic paraphernalia and other valuables with pronounced (zoo)anthropomorphic imagery – remained relatively uniform across the islands. A subject that will be returned to in Chapter 8.

One may ask: how would indigenous ontologies have impacted how social networks functioned? In this regard it is important to understand that Amerindian perspectivism is not only a model of "being" or identity, but also of relational subjectivity. With this I mean to say that subjective or "agentive" states are based on outward differences but internalized equalities. Thus having a certain perspective constrains or expands the potential of a spirit, animal or human to interact with the world and others in it. This changes the quality and quantity of possible relations – e.g. a human that has become outwardly animal may inadvertently be hunted and eaten by other humans. In other words, this flexible perspective would have allowed for a wide range of possible (social) ties between humans and other types of beings.

This has repercussions for archaeological interpretations of how past Caribbean communities were "networked". For example, it means that material evidence of connections between humans, animals, spirits and ancestors – e.g. zoo-anthropomorphic designs, carving of petroglyphs, post-mortem manipulation of human bones – should not (only) be interpreted as the result of metaphorical or otherwise symbolic behaviours. Instead, these may have been expressions of literal relations between subjects. Though this ontology pushes beyond the boundaries of what a Western naturalistic framework considers to be "true" and possible social interactions, from an emic perspective such a wider field of inter-subjective relations would have exponentially increased the total amount of potential social partners and competitors. Even if we would only be strictly interested in explanations that align with a modern view of subjectivity, we cannot discount the fact that relations with other than human beings had a great effect on the historical trajectories of societies and cultures in the pre-colonial period.

Substrates and processes of pre-colonial networks

This overview has only highlighted general trends, with many local particularities of Caribbean environments and historical contexts left undiscussed. This bird's eye-view has thus necessarily obscured much of the intricacies of the current scholarly debates (see Keegan, *et al.* 2013). Rather, what this chapter has done is identify and discuss a number of ecological and historical parameters, substrates and processes. These all came together in creating a dynamic geographic and cultural space characterized by a high amount of micro- and macro-level connections.

First of all, as Rouse (1986) had recognized previously, the geographic layout of the Caribbean islands must have had a shaping effect on the patterns of homogeneity and diversity in the region. However, in the case of the Caribbean, the popular perception of the environmental similarity of (tropical) islands is contradicted by the large variety in local ecological and geological systems. This meant differential access to resources, which was conducive for the creation of inter-island networks. On the other hand environments were similar enough to allow analogous local evolutionary developments in subsistence practices, material culture production and distribution and (ecological) base-lines for belief systems. These differential but analogous environments would have reinforced a mixed collective of socio-cultural practices and ways of dwelling within these islandscapes.

Although much remains unknown with regard to maritime logistics and (perceptions of) safety, a high degree of inter-island voyaging, indicated by archaeological and ethnohistoric sources, would have been a logical outcome of this natural, social and material landscape. In this regard it is also notable that the geographic layout of the Northeastern Caribbean correlates with that of a lattice-network. Most islands were intervisible and local archipelagoes were always well-connected through exchange of goods and inter-island residential mobility (Hofman, Bright, et al. 2007; Laffoon 2012; see also Chapter 6). Within island regions, exchange and other interactions would have been quite literally "down-the-line" in the sense that people or goods were geographically moving down (or up) a chain of islands. If voyagers decided to skip certain paths in the island network, this would have been a choice made with reference to other places geographically farther down the line and all the social and material costs and benefits that this entailed.

The history of the Caribbean can be painted in broad strokes as a series of networks that grew and contracted, merging and separating in the process. This view reinforces the deep-time connections between Caribbean societies and cultures and the almost rhythmic cadence of ties between various islands and mainlands (cf. Hofman, Bright, et al. 2007; Hofman and Bright 2010; Hofman and Hoogland 2011; Rodríguez Ramos 2010). This process started with the establishment of the first (mainland-)island networks (6000/4000 BC-2000 BC). Once the connection between westerly and southerly island communities had been made (2000 BC-800 BC), local and regional networks continued to grow and develop, becoming part of intermittently and weakly connected Greater Caribbean interactions (800-200 BC). This growth led to (re-)emerging connections between the islands and the mainlands of the Caribbean as well as to the creation of the first robust interregional networks (200 BC-AD 400). This was initially followed by an increasing density and expansion of local and regional interaction spheres (AD 400-600/800), but was followed eventually by a retraction of interaction networks in the Lesser Antilles around AD 700. In other regions society and culture evolved to become increasingly dense and complex on the local level (AD 600/800-1000).

This was correlated to the solidification of regional polities. From AD 1000 on we see the renaissance of patterns of similarity in material cultural repertoires across the Greater and northern Lesser Antilles (AD 1000-1492). The causal relations underlying these synchronous emergences of local and regional complexities are still very much unclear.

The homogeneity and diversity of pre-colonial Northeastern Caribbean cultures and societies cannot be separated from their geographical, geological, ecological, logistical, ontological, and historical contexts. A good understanding of this is critical to complement, substantiate and interpret the relations in and between archaeological assemblages and other lines of evidence. The resulting base-line expectation should be that these substrates and parameters allowed for a high rate of interaction among islands and regions coupled with strong possibilities for local autonomies and developments of communities and their material cultural repertoires and practices. In order to begin to better understand this pattern of connectivity I will apply a variety of network approaches to the case studies in Chapters 5 to 8. The network science and specifically graph theoretical concepts, measures and models that will be utilized will be discussed in the following chapter.

Chapter 3

Archaeology as a Network Science: Basic Concepts and Measures

Claim 1	*Network science is the study of network models. [...]*
Claim 2	*There are theories about network representation and network theories about phenomena: both constitute network theory. [...]*
Claim 3	*Network science should be empirical – not exclusively so, but consistently – and its value assessed against alternative representations. [...]*
Claim 4	*What sets network data apart is the incidence structure of its domain. [...]*
Claim 5	*At the heart of network science is dependence, both between and within variables. [...]*
Claim 6	*Network science is evolving into a mathematical science in its own right [...]*
Claim 7	*Network science is itself more of an evolving network than a paradigm expanding from a big bang.*

Editorial of the first issue of *Network Science* (Brandes, et al. 2013)

This chapter introduces network approaches in archaeology by explaining some elementary concepts and measures that may be employed in the exploration of archaeological networks. Formal network approaches have a profound mathematical basis, based in graph theory and other topological mathematics. I will specifically discuss the structures of a graph theoretical network data set, concepts and measures of, grouping, cohesion and centrality. While, this chapter focuses on some of the more elementary formal network concepts and measures that have already been or could be applied in archaeological studies, it has to be noted that several general books present richer introductory texts or deeper explorations of graph theory and other mathematical analyses (e.g. Brandes and Erlebach 2005; Newman 2010;

Scott 2012). In addition, the network concepts and measures discussed here are by no means an exhaustive discussion on possible applications of network science in archaeology.

The concepts and measures discussed here will be illustrated by means of a hypothetical network case-study in which nine generic "artefact types" are distributed over twenty-six contemporaneously inhabited sites. These sites are all that remains of a fictional past island world called Chremanesia. The people of this island world had a peculiar tradition. They never moved to, never intermarried with, never befriended or had any other social interactions of any other kind with folk from other islands. The only exception to this norm was when a lone traveller crossed a channel to bring material culture to another island. Another peculiarity was that the inhabitants of Chremanesia only had nine different types of things and did not seem to have the need to alter these in any way or invent new things. This is especially strange since certain items were only produced at certain locations. The result is that only these nine types of things lay at the basis of supra-island culture and any inter-island politics must also have been completely founded on which island supplied which other island with their things. Of course such a system could not have survived for long and some unknown disaster wiped out the people of Chremanesia. A few centuries later archaeologists discover the remains of the Chremanesians. The only key to understanding their shared culture and society seems to be to make sense of how the nine types of things they left behind form an inter-island network.

The embedding of network science in archaeology

In the highly connected world of today, networks are everywhere. From everyday conversation to academia, they are the talk of the town. Networks are also big business. New online only companies like Facebook and Twitter rely on attracting as many members to their respective networks as possible. In these online networks many more people have much more "friends", "followers" or other types of social contacts over a far wider geographical landscape than traditional ideas on human group dynamics ever accounted for (Dunbar 1988; Dunbar, et al. 2010a). Indeed, the manner in which networks intrude into our everyday life seems to be unlike anything ever seen before. Fuelled by connected phenomena such as ICT revolutions and globalization, this gives rise to a number of completely new developments in the history of human society (Castells 2011).

In recent years network theories, models, and analyses have also enjoyed an enormous rise in popularity in academia, including archaeology (Brughmans 2013; Knappett 2013). As such, it seems that archaeology has fallen slightly behind the curve of an upsurge in network studies that occurred in other research fields around the turn of the millennium (Brandes, et al. 2013; Newman 2010). Having observed that this correlates with the growth of networks in our daily lives, it could be argued that the popularity of network-themed approaches in archaeology and beyond results mainly from the tangible reality of networks today. However, though we are now more concretely part of networks than before, this does not imply that the networks of today are categorically different than those from the past. In fact, networks of humans, computers, enzymes, academic papers or food webs are all analogous because as a system they are characterized by means of the relations between their nodal points. In principle these systems, from the most archaic and simple to the most advanced and complex, can be understood by applying a similar set of analyses arising from the incidence structure of relational data sets abstracted from real-world cases.

As a matter of fact, although we see a notable spike in publications on networks at the beginning of the present millennium, the study of networks is nothing new (Brandes, *et al.* 2013; Prell 2011: Chapter 2). Network-like approaches have also always been present in archaeology, even if they were not explicitly recognized as such. For example, one of the core methods and theories in archaeology, chronological or cultural seriation (Petrie 1899; Pitt-Rivers 1906), is an example of network ordering and visualization (Figure 3.1). Seriation is essentially network modelling of data *avant la lettre*: the diagrams are visualizations of systems of relations between site assemblages, objects or periods. Outside of the discipline of archaeology, such seriation models and diagrams have even been of wider interest

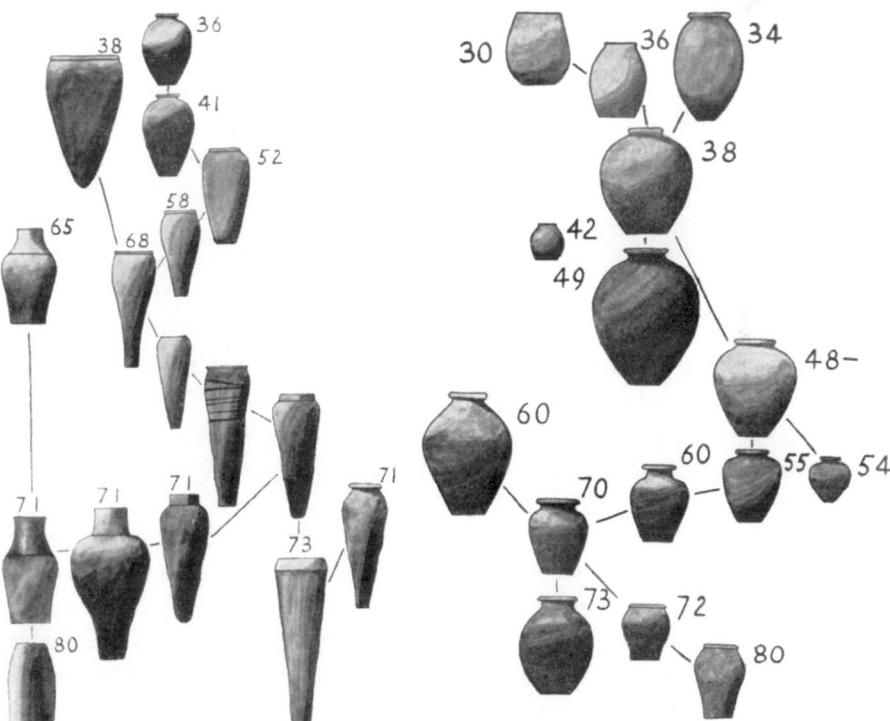

Figure 3.1: A seriation network by Flinders Petrie (1899). The depicted type-vessels are the nodes of the network. The ties are based on the cultural stratigraphy and development of one or multiple morphological traits. For the majority of nodes, there is only one route through the network (i.e. the network is phylogenetic and only partially ordered). In this sense the above network is comparable to what a network based on the modal approach by Rouse (1992; Figure 1.2) could resemble.

with regard to network studies – specifically in discussions concerning matrix re-ordering, a way of organizing that reveals regularity and patterning in a series of data points (Brandes, *et al.* 2012; Brandes, *et al.* 2013; Liiv 2010). Seriation is just one example of how networks are embedded in archaeology. The idea that "hidden" network theories are already an integral part of (Caribbean) archaeology has already been discussed in Chapter 1.

There are various reasons for the rise of network approaches in archaeology. At present their largest attraction seems to be that networks can provide a relational perspective. More specifically, however, a network science approach can provide both a set of models and analyses that intuitively seem to hold some value with regard to an advanced understanding of past (social) relations. Network analyses as "relational statistics" fill a niche that has only recently become available through the increasing size of archaeological data sets and the advent of ever more powerful methods and techniques enabling the study of relations in the archaeological record. Alongside these advances there have also been several developments in the broader network sciences themselves. Of specific significance is the increasing availability of network analytic software and the publication of popular science books on the topic (Terrell, personal communication 2010).

Although the call for a network approach to the study of the past can be heard throughout the discipline, formal network studies in archaeology can be termed as somewhat of a "grassroots movement". Even since their first usage during the 1970s (Kendall 1970; Terrell 1977), their application has arisen directly from questions and developments within regional archaeologies, rather than from an interest in the mechanics of networks themselves (e.g. Broodbank 2000; Cody 1990; Hardy 2008; Graham 2006; Knappett 2013; Knappett, *et al.* 2008; Mills, *et al.* 2013; Mol 2013; Terrell 2008).[1] This is perhaps the reason why, as Tom Brughmans (in press) has shown with a citation analysis of archaeological publications using formal network methods, network studies in archaeology are still paradoxically characterized by a distinct lack of connections between them. Fortunately, this situation is rapidly being remedied by means of new, cross-regionally integrated archaeological network studies (e.g. Knappett 2013), integration between historical and archaeological network analysis, and (upcoming) special journal publications and symposia.

Even if the applications thus far have been largely independent of each other, a number of general trends can be discerned regarding the application of networks within archaeology today. Firstly, the majority of studies make loose references to networks and apply them as a metaphor for trade or other types of exchange systems. Regrettably this is often without providing any form of argumentation or discussion on why it is important that trading, barter, gift or other exchange systems are networks and how they operates (e.g. Schortman and Ashmore 2012). If the term network is applied less loosely this is generally speaking done in order to emphasize the object of study forming a (social) network. This is akin to using the concept of the network as a heuristic device or theoretical perspective. Network

---

1   See Bentley and Maschner (2003)'s work on complex systems for a notable exception.

science is further integrated by theories drawn from the broader field of network studies (e.g. Collar 2007; Mol 2013; Terrell 2008). An example hereof is the recent work presented by Irad Malkin (2011). In his *A Small, Greek World* the idea of Greek cities forming a "small-world network" is used to discuss early Classical colonialism in the Mediterranean (cf. Watts 1999; see Chapter 1). The a-centrally organized Greek colonial system consisted of a group of city states, micro-regions which were only loosely or not at all affiliated in economic and political terms. Nonetheless, based on the connective power of the Mediterranean Sea and a small number of ties, a notion of shared group membership was strongly rooted in all of them. In other words, Malkin presents a perspective of how a "Greek" identity and language was dispersed throughout the Mediterranean and Black Sea area using the rhetoric of small-worlds.

Applied in this more rhetorical manner archaeological network perspectives are part of a meta-theoretical framework that can be referred to as relationism (e.g. Kaipayil 2009), methodological relationism (e.g. Ritzer and Gindoff 1992), or relational theory (e.g. Kineman 2011). Seen in this vein, network thinking is not new, especially not in the European academic tradition (Knappett 2005; LaBianca and Arnold Scham 2006; Malkin 2011: 41). The popularity of relational approaches in academia waxes and wanes, however. Archaeology is currently riding a wave of relational thinking and is (re-)connecting the pieces in the wake of the deconstructive efforts of post-processual Archaeology. It is therefore important to understand that using the concept of a network as a rhetorical device is not the same as applying network theory and analysis. In fact, sometimes the latter is even claimed to be antithetical or detrimental to the former (Ingold 2007a; Latour 2005; Malkin 2011). In Malkin's work an explicit network model or analysis is deliberately left out, since the author feels that network representations of multi-temporal, directional and dimensional connectivity too often lead to oversimplified models that still resemble "spaghetti-monsters" (*ibid.*: 18; e.g. Figure 1.4.2).

Although there is something to be said for this standpoint – there is much work to be done in the efficient visualization of networks, especially in archaeology –, his critique on "messy pictures" misconstrues the actual reason why more formal network approaches may be important new additions to archaeological method and theory. Networks, for example, can be employed as models for possible real-world connections. A good case in point is John Terrells's research on the likely structure of inter-community ties in New Guinea's north coast. For this he created the geographic relational modelling called Proximal Point Analysis already discussed in Chapter 2 (Terrell 1977; see also Broodbank 2000). As was shown there, PPA can serve to give base-line hypotheses for social, cultural and linguistic relations as underlain by geographic distances. Another example of geographic distance-based network modelling in archaeology is the case-study on Bronze Age Aegean inter-site connections presented by Knappett, Evans and Rivers. In order to test ideas on local maritime interaction they developed a software package, aptly named *ariadne* which runs a specific algorithm that was created for spatial modelling of cost-benefit relations in archaeological cases (Evans, *et al.* 2012; Knappett, *et al.* 2008). By means of this cost-benefit measure they looked into possible changes in Aegean

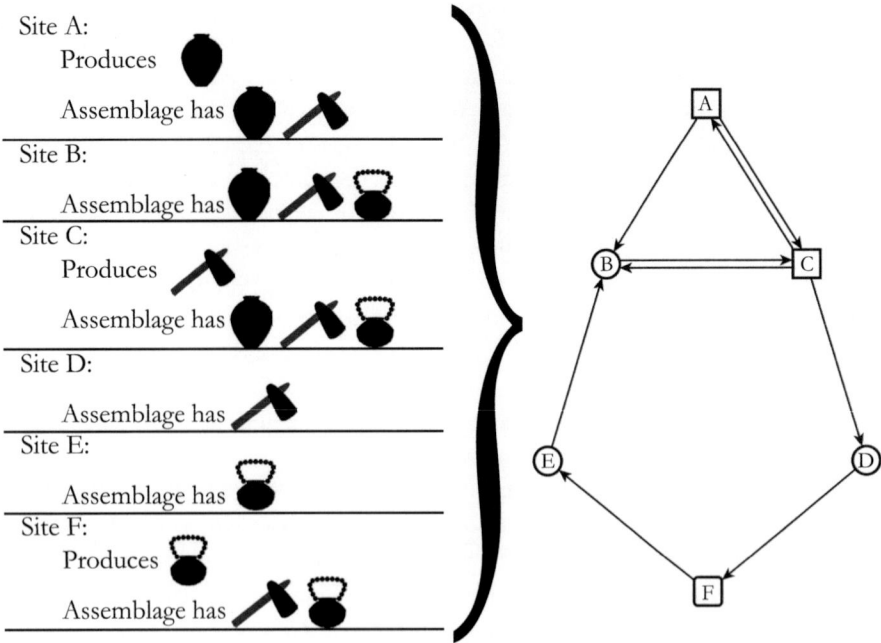

Site A:
 Produces
 Assemblage has

Site B:
 Assemblage has

Site C:
 Produces
 Assemblage has

Site D:
 Assemblage has

Site E:
 Assemblage has

Site F:
 Produces
 Assemblage has

Figure 3.2: From archaeological assemblage to network. Here the archaeological record of the southern Chremanesian islands are combined and "incidences" (i.e. co-occurrences) of artefacts in assemblages and knowledge of production centres is abstracted into a network.

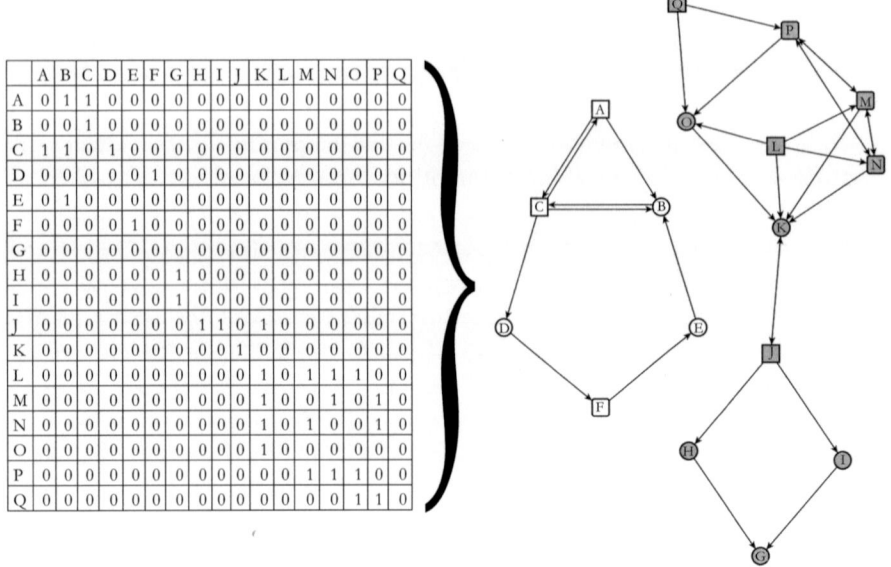

	A	B	C	D	E	F	G	H	I	J	K	L	M	N	O	P	Q
A	0	1	1	0	0	0	0	0	0	0	0	0	0	0	0	0	0
B	0	0	1	0	0	0	0	0	0	0	0	0	0	0	0	0	0
C	1	1	0	1	0	0	0	0	0	0	0	0	0	0	0	0	0
D	0	0	0	0	0	1	0	0	0	0	0	0	0	0	0	0	0
E	0	1	0	0	0	0	0	0	0	0	0	0	0	0	0	0	0
F	0	0	0	0	0	1	0	0	0	0	0	0	0	0	0	0	0
G	0	0	0	0	0	0	0	0	0	0	0	0	0	0	0	0	0
H	0	0	0	0	0	0	0	1	0	0	0	0	0	0	0	0	0
I	0	0	0	0	0	0	1	0	0	0	0	0	0	0	0	0	0
J	0	0	0	0	0	0	0	1	1	0	1	0	0	0	0	0	0
K	0	0	0	0	0	0	0	0	0	1	0	0	0	0	0	0	0
L	0	0	0	0	0	0	0	0	0	0	1	0	1	1	1	0	0
M	0	0	0	0	0	0	0	0	0	0	1	0	0	1	0	1	0
N	0	0	0	0	0	0	0	0	0	0	1	0	1	0	0	1	0
O	0	0	0	0	0	0	0	0	0	0	1	0	0	0	0	0	0
P	0	0	0	0	0	0	0	0	0	0	0	0	1	1	1	0	0
Q	0	0	0	0	0	0	0	0	0	0	0	0	0	0	1	1	0

Figure 3.3: From matrix to network visualization. Here the matrix adapted from Chremanesia's fictional site assemblages is visualized as a network. In the matrix "1" indicates the presence of a tie, while a "0" means absence. A row of zeroes runs diagonally down the centre of the matrix, indicating there are no "loops" in this network (a tie from a node to itself). Moreover, due to the directed nature of this network, the matrix is not symmetrical.

networks based on the model's parameters and the absence or presence of site-nodes in the network. Among other things their model serves to illustrate the long-term network effects of the 17th century BC destruction (due to a large volcanic eruption) of the island of Thera, an important port of trade. According to this model the disappearance of the Thera node from the network caused overextension of maritime interaction routes which possibly heralded the demise of late Minoan culture approximately 50-100 years later (Knappett, *et al.* 2011).

These types of studies are interesting because their results can serve as base-line expectation models for what type of connectivity patterns one can expect in the region of study. This is exemplified by further research carried out by Terrell and his colleagues (Terrell 2010; Welsch, *et al.* 1992). Once again focusing on ties between communities on the New Guinea coast, linguistic affiliations were compared against a relational database based on Sepik material culture assemblages housed in the Field Museum of Natural History, Chicago. Both data-driven graphs were compared to a distance-based model and genetic affiliation, in both cases the model based on material culture similarities provided the better fit. This demonstrated, according to Terrell and his colleagues, that social boundaries in the region cannot be mapped to linguistic barriers, a correlation which is often taken for granted in archaeology. The corpus of data-driven network studies has been steadily growing and a selection of recent studies will be highlighted below

Site	Assemblage	Produces	Distributes	Comp.	Str. Comp.	Core	Clique
A	Type 1, 2	Type 1		#1		2-core	[A,B,C]
B	Type 1, 2, 3		Type 3	#1		2-core	[A,B,C]
C	Type 1, 2, 3	Type 2		#1		2-core	[A,B,C]
D	Type 2		Type 2	#1		2-core	
E	Type 3		Type 3	#1		2-core	
F	Type 2 and 3	Type 3		#1		2-core	
G	Type 4			#2		2-core	
H	Type 4		Type 4	#2		2-core	
I	Type 4		Type 4	#2		2-core	
J	Type 4, Type 5	Type 4		#2		2-core	
K	Type 4, 5, 6, 7, 8, 9		Type 5	#2		3-core	[K,L,M,N] & [K,L,O]
L	Type 5	Type 5		#2		3-core	[K,L,M,N] & [K,L,O]
M	Type 5,6,7,8	Type 6		#2	[M,N,P]	3-core	[K,L,M,N] & [M,N,P]
N	Type 5,6,7,8	Type 7		#2	[M,N,P]	3-core	[K,L,M,N] & [M,N,P]
O	Type 5,8,9		Type 9	#2		3-core	[K, L,M,N] & [O,P,Q]
P	Type 6,7,8,9	Type 8		#2	[M,N,P]	3-core	[M,N,P] & [O,P,Q]
Q	Type 9	Type 9		#2		2-core	[O,P,Q]

Table 3.1 Site nodes in the Chremanesian network. A list of the site assemblages of Chremanesia and production centres, followed by a list detailing to which components, strong components, cores and cliques a node belongs.

id	Degree %	Indegree %	Outdegree %	Closeness %	Betweenness %	Status %
A	4.8	3.2	6.5	5.6	0.0	3.3
B	6.5	9.7	3.2	5.2	8.1	8.6
C	8.1	6.5	9.7	7.7	11.7	6.5
D	3.2	3.2	3.2	4.1	6.3	3.3
E	3.2	3.2	3.2	4.8	6.3	2.6
F	3.2	3.2	3.2	4.4	6.3	2.7
G	3.2	6.5	0.0	0.0	0.0	5.3
H	3.2	3.2	3.2	2.5	3.6	3.1
I	3.2	3.2	3.2	2.5	3.6	3.1
J	6.5	3.2	9.7	7.9	18.9	5.5
K	9.7	16.1	3.2	4.9	21.6	17.0
L	6.5	0.0	12.9	11.1	0.0	0.0
M	9.7	9.7	9.7	9.3	2.0	10.2
N	9.7	9.7	9.7	9.3	2.0	10.2
O	6.5	9.7	3.2	4.8	6.0	8.2
P	9.7	9.7	9.7	7.5	3.6	10.2
Q	3.2	0.0	6.5	8.3	0.0	0.0

Table 3.2 Different measures of network centrality in Chremanesia.

(see also Brughmans 2013; Knappett 2013). Considering their rising popularity, it should be expected there will be more and more varied network studies in the near future.

To synthesize: networks in archaeology have been and can be applied in quite different ways (Isaksen 2013). Still, several general trends are visible in their implementation. At the threat of oversimplifying a dynamic situation, it can be said they are currently used in three different ways: (1) as conceptual metaphors and perspectives, (2) network models as base-lines, and (3) data-driven studies. As should be clear, these approaches are not mutually exclusive. In fact, I would argue that the usefulness of all three types of network is enhanced by combining all of them. If this is done there is much to be won by going beyond the traditional use of networks in archaeology as metaphors for exchange systems.

Key concepts and operation

Nodes and ties are the most basic elements of a network or graph. The term "node" has its roots in computer science and is also known as a "vertex" in mathematics and physics, "site" in physics, or "actor" in sociology. Ties or "edge", "link" or "bonds" are the connections between nodes, creating the incidence structure of the network. Nodes and ties in a single network can literally be anything (e.g. Newman 2010: Chapters 2-5). This also applies to archaeological cases. However, when building a network it is required that nodes are equivalent in terms of their function in the network that is modelled and that they can be connected by relations that belong to an equivalent category. A network model of co-citations within a collection of academic papers, for example, would be drawn utilising references between papers and not based on whether the authors of the papers are personal acquaintances or not.[2] The same would be the case for an archaeological network. For instance, one can designate habitation sites as nodes and connect them if there is co-presence of artefact types in the site assemblage, as has been done in the hypothetical network presented in Figure 3.2 (e.g. Mills, *et al.* 2013; Sindbæk 2007). If one was to treat assemblages of regional surveys, activity sites and habitation sites as nodes in the same network this will presumably present us with a skewed picture. Needless to say, there could be a theory-driven motivation to do so.

The latter is important to keep in mind. A relational database and resulting network model is always contingent upon a theory that explains why a certain set of nodes and ties is deemed to be relevant for the question at hand. This is why formal network approaches always need to be applied in conjunction with a set of supporting ideas and hypotheses. It is entirely possible to create a network of the chronological connections between sites on the basis of stratigraphy, connecting site Y to site Z on the basis of the presence of cultural material in a similar geographic layer, for instance. However, such a network would not be only network theoretical but would also hinge on the geo-archaeological concept that such a geographic layer is indeed a valid type of relation (e.g. Waters 1992: 210-212). In this particular example, the theory is well-supported and it is also clear what such a relation entails: contemporaneous habitation of site Y and Z. However, in the case of shared artefact types across assemblages a shared artefact type will denote a tie. Whatever such a connection may imply in a societal or cultural sense is much more problematical to substantiate (see Chapter 4).

It is furthermore important that the choice of nodes and ties depends on the possibility to collect a database that can be acceptably "completed". It is problematical to measure networks when the structural holes – the empty spaces in the network – arise from missing data rather than actual absence of a tie. This is an especially problematical factor when working with archaeological data, because of the truism that absence of evidence is no evidence for absence. One can carry out a network study of habitation sites that have been excavated thus far, but the distribution of habitation sites will probably not fully correlate with the past distribution of contemporaneously occupied communities. When it is possible to collect a representative data set and abstract this into a collection of nodes and ties one should reflect beforehand upon the added value of a network approach. Analyses of very small data sets or networks with very few relations generally little more insight than can be gained from a cursory inspection of the original data. Nevertheless, network visualization can still effectively serve to communicate the networked nature of the data set.

---

2   One could contrast the citation network of scholars with their professional social networks in two
     separate networks.

In its basis, any archaeological feature can be investigated as part of a relational data set as long as the entities utilized as nodes can be meaningfully related. As a result, the inherent flexibility of that which constitutes a relational data set can be somewhat confusing at first. We find a number of obvious choices for node and tie-types in archaeology. As is clear from the literature, "sites" are most frequently selected as nodes. This echoes a general tendency in archaeology: the (habitation) site and its (ceramic) assemblage is the scalar unit of choice to understand past socio-cultural relations, even if there are many other types of archaeological features that can be used to construct networks (van Rossenberg 2012: 38-39). This is largely justified, since it is undeniable that places of habitation, ranging from the provisional shelter to the metropolis, are critical factors in any human network. Nonetheless, the prevalence of inter-site networks can blindside archaeological network approaches. Sites were indeed prime social, cultural, political and economic nodes precisely because they consisted of a myriad of micro-scale networks (Knappett 2011). In that sense it is remarkable that GIS-based proxemics and the studies of micro-practices, have not yet led to more formal network studies that emphasize networks of household assemblages or other more local scales of analyses (Mol and Mans 2013; Chapter 6). A similar remark can be made on network studies that draw relations between objects or object types based on their attributes (see Chapter 8). These smaller scale analyses could function as a network operationalization of design, materiality and object system theories.

In terms of the ties between site-nodes, distances in geographic or "Euclidean" space have often served as a basis. This development follows a line of earlier archaeological graph theoretical studies partly based on geography (cf. Brughmans 2013), such as publications by Terrell (1979) and later Broodbank (2000). Utilizing the geographic distance between sites provides a basic but profitable ground level for understanding past networks. This also showcases the close ties between archaeological network studies and GIS-based modelling, including space syntax approaches (Hillier and Hanson 1984; e.g. Mol 2012). Furthermore this geographic preference is presumably influenced by the fact that, although archaeologists cannot easily understand the human factors (cultural and social practices) that shaped a past network, physical factors such as distance between sites are more easily recovered. Site assemblage overlaps repeatedly serve as a basis for drawing ties between sites (e.g. Mills, *et al.* 2013; Sindbæk 2007; van Rossenberg 2012). Archaeological techniques that can be utilised in order to find the provenance of specific objects in a site assemblage can also be of great assistance when reconstructing more detailed relations between site assemblages (Golitko, *et al.* 2012; Graham 2006; Phillips 2011). If detailed knowledge can be acquired concerning inter-site steps in the *chaîne opératoire* of individual objects or specific artefact types this can enhance network modelling of archaeological relational data sets even more (Chapter 5).

An elementary form of graph theory, the type of mathematics underlying many network studies, was first put forth by Leonard Euler. In his essay dated 1736 he addressed a standing mathematical question based on the topography of the city of Königsberg (since 1945 Kaliningrad, Russia). This city was laid out across four landmasses connected by seven bridges. The question was whether it was possible to walk a route that covered the whole city without backtracking even once. This problem is similar to a modern diagram-tracing-puzzle in which one has to follow an "Eulerian route" in order to connect the dots and complete the picture. In a series of twenty-two paragraphs Euler first proceeded to abstract the problem, recognizing that its solution was not based on the layout of Königsberg or any other real world example, but on the routes between points – in Königsberg taking the form of bridges between city districts.[3] After surmising that the Königsberg problem had no solution, he then abstracted that for all cases, "if there are more than two areas to which an odd number of bridges lead, then such a journey is impossible." Yet when "the number of bridges is odd for exactly two areas, then the journey is possible if it starts in either of these two areas." Yet if there are no areas to which an odd number of bridges lead, then the required journey can be accomplished starting from any area (Euler in Hopkins and Wilson 2004). These abstractions and theorems later provided the base for what was to become known as "graph theory" – a term popularized in handbooks by the American mathematician Frank Harary (e.g. 1969).

This first example of graph theory delivers an elemental truth about network approaches. In order to find solution to problems regarding relations, one has to (1) abstract a general network theoretical problem, (2) abstract the nodes and the relations of the network, (3) analyse them and (4) abstract a conclusion from this (Scott 2000: Chapter 3). Therefore, in the case of the Chremanesian network an archaeologist may wish to investigate if the collection of sites in the data set forms groups of some kind and if group composition and similarity is centrally regulated or not. He or she could abstract this problem by asking whether there are any nodes in the collection of sites with more ties with each other than with other sets of nodes. If so, are there within these groups nodes with more network power than the average member of the group? The relations between the nodes can be discerned based on the presence or absence of a certain artefact type at a site. This is in turn based on another set of theories implying that such a pattern of presence and absence is meaningful for understanding communal systems in archaeology (e.g. Flannery 1976; Mills 2000). The outcome of the analyses might be based on the type of measure applied to understanding group composition and power within networks (Brandes and Erlebach 2005; Newman 2010: Chapter 6; see below).

Once this first steps has been taken a matrix of relations can be abstracted from a data set. A matrix is essentially a view of the mathematical structure of the graph. In a matrix, nodes make up the columns and rows, while ties are represented by means of the content of the matrix cells. The cells of the matrix of the most regular type of graphs do not have a discrete value, but will often contain binary data, a "1" marking the presence and a "0" marking the absence of a tie. In such a binary matrix, a node will not often be related to itself – a type of self-referential relation

---

3   In contrast to popular belief Euler did not draw a graph of the city of Königsberg but rather labelled the landmasses and routes with letters (Hopkins and Wilson 2004).

sometimes referred to as a "loop". A binary matrix will typically consist of a series of zeroes running diagonally along the matrix, dividing it in half (Figure 3.3).

Not all network data will necessarily reflect two-way or reciprocal relations, but it is also possible to work with tie directions in graphs. If a graph is "undirected" it means that either all ties are considered to be reciprocal or that it does not matter for the model if ties are reciprocated or not. A matrix of an undirected graph can be easily recognized because it will be perfectly symmetrical. A visualization of such a graph will in principle show all ties as single lines. If not all ties in a network are necessarily reciprocal, this makes a graph "directed". This is regularly visualized by means of an arrow-head at the end of a tie indicating its direction. Because certain nodes might be linked by only one directed tie, a directed graph will not (always) yield a symmetrical matrix. Although it is often difficult to understand the direction of relations in archaeological data sets, directed graphs might come into play in certain cases, e.g. a clear grasp on producers, distributors and consumers in a *chaîne opératoire*. In the network of Chremanesia ties have been given directionality based on a hypothetical – and admittedly rather perfect – data set that can identify producers, distributors and consumers. This data set therefore yields an a-symmetrical matrix (Figure 3.3). Finally, ties can also be provided with a value in a matrix. Especially in the case of archaeological networks this can often result in further insights into the specific historic processes shaping the network (Peeples and Roberts Jr. 2013). Once completed a matrix can then be explored and analysed further or be visualized as is.

2-mode networks and ego-networks

The majority of networks plot relations between nodes of the same kind – e.g. a person to other persons or one site to other sites. These types of networks are 1-mode networks. However, networks can also serve to understand the relations between nodes that are not of the same kind. This is based on tracing the incidences of ties between one type of node with another type of node. Such a 2-mode network, sometimes referred to as a bi-partite network, can present a rather different perspective. In a social network it might illustrate how academic scholars visit various congresses and how, through these meetings, they might become acquainted.

A 2-mode model can therefore present a radically different view of a network. There is, indeed, a different type of matrix underneath this graph, because it models information between two sets of nodes. A 1-mode graphs always consists of square matrices. A 2-mode matrix can have varying row and column lengths. It is possible to further explore group formation and other network features from a 2-mode matrix by transforming the matrix from a 2-mode to that of a 1-mode graph. Such a graph is known as an affiliation network. An affiliation network will display the ties between either the nodes in the rows or those in the columns by transposing the original 2-mode matrix into a 1-mode matrix.[4]

Where Figure 3.3 shows a 1-mode network, Figure 3.4 shows a 2-mode network. A 2-mode network can be of assistance with regard to the lack of detail inherent to many archaeological data sets. With many archaeological data sets, such as that of the hypothetical network above, one could also produce a 2-mode rather than a 1-mode graph based on relations between site assemblages and artefact types (Everett and Borgatti 2012). Even if archaeological data sets do not present us with any indication of direct relations between similar nodes, they do testify to the relation between nodes relative to categorically different nodes. Thus, whenever a detailed picture of a site's role in artefact type distributions is not feasible, an affiliation network – e.g. presence in the site assemblage – can be revealing. An archaeological 2-mode network showcases how networks of "people" (sites) and material culture (artefact types) can be part of mutually constitutive networks.

Chapter 6 will make use of ego-networks. The ego-network is not a network mode but rather another type of network altogether. Also known as centred graphs, they were pioneered by the sociologist Linton Freeman. Instead of focusing on the networks as a whole, ego-networks were designed to understand the effects a network has on a particular individual. In Freeman's original paper he observed how a group of academic professionals who had all been invited to a conference communicated with each other independently of the conference organizer. He found that after an initial period of communication, running via the conference organizer, small groups of scholars began to form. These groups dictated how future cooperation took place irrespective of the management of the conference organizer (Freeman 1982). More recently, the ego-network approach has also served to study and find remedies for structural holes – negative spaces in networks in which ties could exist, but for some reason do not (Prell 2011: 123-125).

The ego-network approach is thus all about visualizing and analysing networks that revolve around one node, referred to as the ego-node. The method to create an ego-network is rather straightforward: simply include nodes in the model with which Ego has a direct tie, then draw ties between all nodes that are also in direct contact with each other. This then allows for an analysis of Ego's direct network

---

4   There are two ways in which this can be done in UCInet 6.0: the cross-product method and the minimum method (Hanneman and Riddle 2005). The latter is applied to valued 2-mode data and will not be used here. Cross-product method transposition utilizes binary data (absence/presence).

	Group 1	Group 2	Group 3	Group 4
A	1	0	1	1
B	1	1	0	1

Suppose I wish to determine the affiliation of two row nodes "A" and "B" from the 2-mode network matrix above. This is done by taking entry A and multiplying it with the corresponding column entry of B. Proceed to do this for all other columns. Next the result of all columns is summed: $(1 \times 1) + (0 \times 1) + (1 \times 0) + (1 \times 1) = 2$. The outcome hereof is the strength of affiliation between the row nodes A and B as a tie with value 2. In order to fill a matrix with more than two row nodes the process is repeated for all rows. The same can be done with the Group nodes in the case-study network by multiplying across columns and adding up the rows.

	A	B	C	D	E	F	G	H	I	J	K	L	M	N	O	P	Q
1	1	1	1	0	0	0	0	0	0	0	0	0	0	0	0	0	0
2	1	1	1	1	0	1	0	0	0	0	0	0	0	0	0	0	0
3	0	1	1	0	1	1	0	0	0	0	0	0	0	0	0	0	0
4	0	0	0	0	0	0	1	1	1	1	1	0	0	0	0	0	0
5	0	0	0	0	0	0	0	0	0	1	1	1	1	1	1	0	0
6	0	0	0	0	0	0	0	0	0	0	1	0	1	1	0	1	0
7	0	0	0	0	0	0	0	0	0	0	1	0	1	1	0	1	0
8	0	0	0	0	0	0	0	0	0	0	1	0	1	1	1	1	0
9	0	0	0	0	0	0	0	0	0	0	1	0	0	0	1	1	1

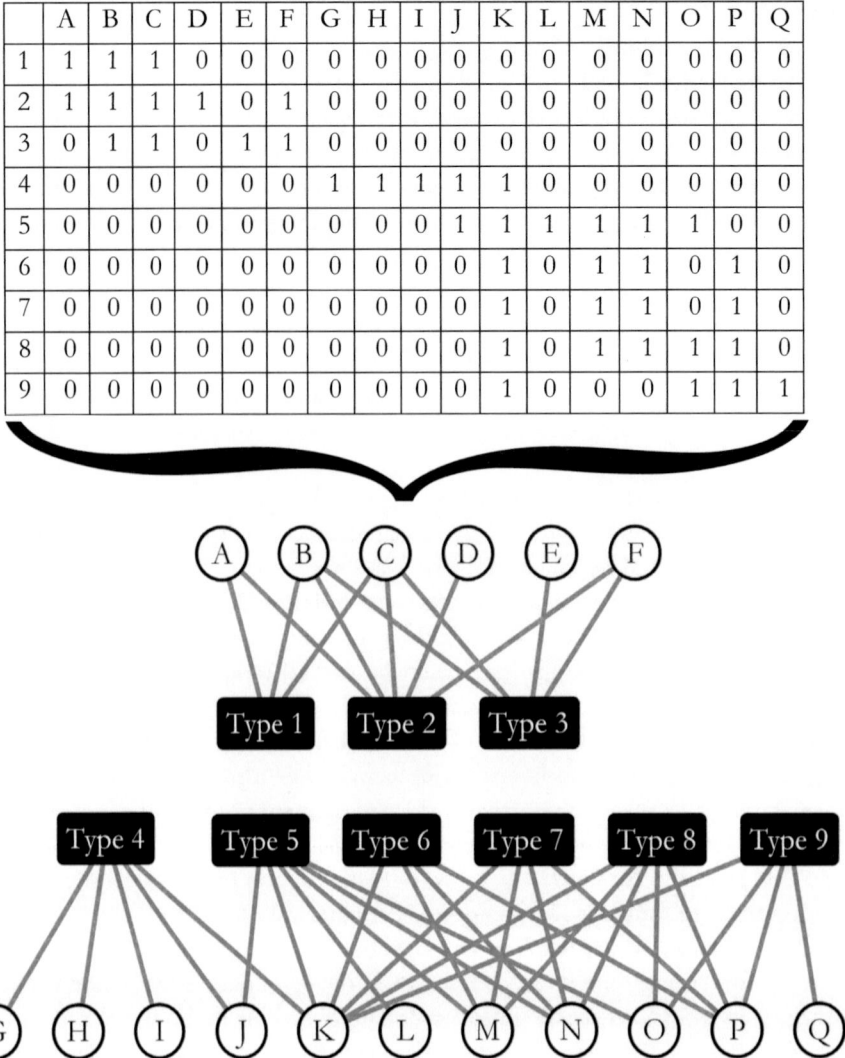

Figure 3.4: From matrix to 2-mode network. This shows a 2-mode network is based on the same archaeological record as the 1-mode network presented in Figure 3.3. Aside from information on site relations this also provides us with an intuitive view of which artefact types have the widest distribution in Chremanesia.

(Figure 3.5). This approach can also serve to compare the networks of different egos, which provides information on how different nodes can have completely different ego-networks and can thus be very different relational entities, even if they are part of the same network.

The fact that nodes and ties can literally be anything also applies to archaeological ego-networks. For example it is possible to designate a specific artefact as Ego and see how it connects to a wider web of things in order to better understand that specific artefact (type). Sites are once again an intuitive choice for an ego-network

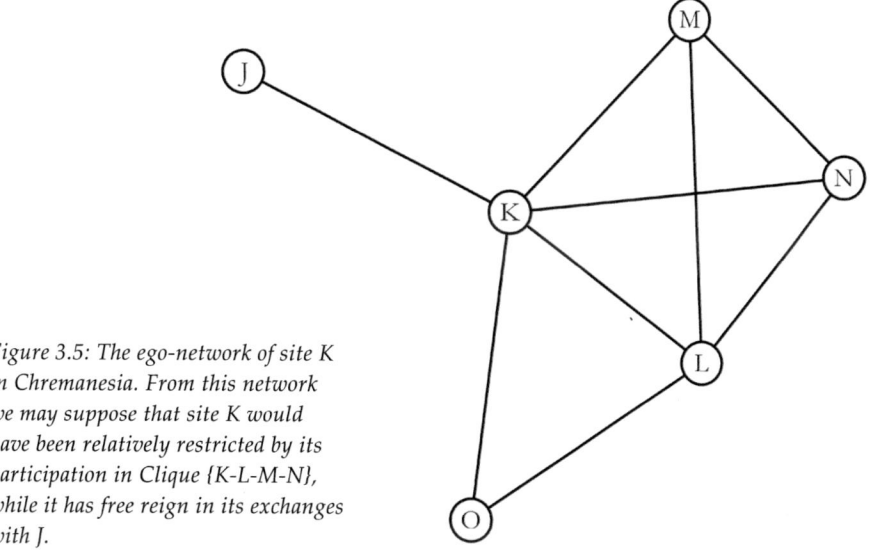

Figure 3.5: The ego-network of site K in Chremanesia. From this network we may suppose that site K would have been relatively restricted by its participation in Clique {K-L-M-N}, while it has free reign in its exchanges with J.

approach. While the majority of archaeological network studies sites connect to sites, a site ego-network model will connect a site to its own relational record. Through an ego-network we can begin to understand a site as a relational entity.

An ego-network is not a completely different type of network, however. Its analysis is also based on graphs and matrices. Thus, problems that affect regular archaeological network models and analyses also affect ego networks. They are for example not any less vulnerable to incomplete archaeological data sets. The reason being that, even if the network is centreed on one site, the same set of information on all other nodes in the network is also needed for the model to fully function. Furthermore, ego-networks need to be handled with care when working with multiple and multi-disciplinary data sets. When modelling an ego-network some relational data sets might turn out to be incompatible with others, even if they are part of the same site assemblage. Whether this is the case or not will be based on the type of data and, once again, a supporting set of theories.

Measuring and visualizing networks

One of the strengths of a graph theoretical approach is that it allows for aspects of networks such as systemic structure, group formation and power to be measured in many different ways. For example, while groups are often treated as (en)closed – you are either in the group or out of the group – network modelling allows for a more flexible perspective on group membership. A varied constellation of nodes can form different network groupings known as "subgraphs". Thus network measures can be used to explore and eventually analyse how, for example, artefacts can belong to multiple types, styles, assemblages or other categories.[5] This flexible view of multi-scalar and nested network cohesion might be applicable when analysing the archaeological record of the Caribbean as a network (see Chapter 8).

The same applies for understanding node power, the structural importance of one node relative to all other nodes, within networks. Looking at power in society it can be perceived to rest in the hands of an important public figure, a leader such as a chief, king or president. On the other hand various types of power can also be seen to lie with persons who have a more covert access to important institutions but who connect two different economies of power: the proverbial *eminence grises*. The same can be said regarding centrality in networks that can be recovered archaeologically. For example, based on settlement patterns it can be said that a site that is close to many other sites was likely an important location. A site may be connected to a few other sites but could still be central for other reasons. For example because it is positioned on a critical juncture of two trade routes. A different view of power will entail a different understanding of central places, processes, persons or things in a system. In other words, the kind of analysis of group formation or network power required depends on the concept of group or power that is relevant for the question at hand. Below I will briefly discuss several basic concepts and measures of network grouping and power before applying these to the case of Chremanesia.

The network measures employed in this work are relatively simple operations. Nevertheless, although it is theoretically possible to carry out graph-theoretical measures by hand, measuring even a small relational data set can be a laborious process. Fortunately, a range of analytic software can be useful for speeding up these calculations. It is necessary to understand the graph-theoretical basis of algorithms in order to comprehend the results of the analysis, yet the relatively easy-to-use interface and reports on many of these programs facilitate a more rapid and increased understanding of the data set. The result is that these relatively easily accessible network analytic programmes have given a boost to network studies across the board.

Although processing algorithms may require a large amount of computing power, the relatively small size of most archaeological networks mitigates this problem. The majority of analyses applied in recent archaeological network studies can be done on low-spec personal computers, with calculations taking only a short time. Of course, as the complexity of graph and other network theoretical models and measures continues to increase in archaeology, more complex calculations will require more computing. For now, most matrices can be created in a simple spreadsheet programme and then exported into a range of programs as a text (.txt) or comma delimited file (.csv) or created and edited in the network program itself. Other often used file types include .gml (Graph Modelling Language), .net (Pajek) and .dl (UCInet).

---

5   Subgraphs are indicated by accolades in the text: e.g. {M-N-P} for the subgraph consisting of nodes M, N and P.

The possibility of visualizing complex networks is a very powerful feature of network studies (Brandes, *et al.* 2006). A single figure depicting a network can illustrate something that a written discussion of a network's structure cannot hope to reveal in several pages. Furthermore, the intuitive mapping of a visualized network can communicate information to non-specialists that a matrix or formula cannot. A visualized network model can present more information than a matrix could hold. A number of network analytic programs offer the possibility to attach more qualities (colour, size, shape, *etc.*) or quantities to ties and even to nodes. These can then serve as visual keys for certain types of information. Larger node sizes are often used to indicate that a node is centrally positioned in the network. This can also be done with non-relational information (e.g. producer, distributor or consumer sites; Figure 3.3).

A growing choice in network analytic software is becoming commercially or freely available.[6] UCInet (Borgatti, *et al.* 2002a) is the most widely used program for network analysis in the social sciences. It is also the one most often found in archaeological network studies thus far. This shareware can handle large amounts of data, offers a relatively easy to use interface, direct saving and editing of matrices, automated matrix handling, and a range of analytic options. Specialized components can also be loaded into the main program in order to enhance its functions. Matrices can be visualized by means of the "Netdraw" software component (Borgatti, *et al.* 2002b). Although some models and measures here have been created or carried out with UCInet 6.0 (indicated per case), most have been done with visone 2.3 and later versions (Brandes and Wagner 2004).[7]

Visone is freeware and offers the possibility to create graphs directly by drawing them. From this network model the program creates the matrix of the graph that can be explored with several basic and advanced measures. These analyses can then also be easily visualized by means of a number of different settings. Nodes and ties can be provided with a different location or appearance and it is possible to attach extra information to them applying a built-in editor. Matrices can be exported and imported to other popular network analytic software, such as UCInet. In addition, the network visualizations can easily be exported into a number of other (graphic) file formats. Visone's visual input offers an efficient way to draw and explore smaller relational data sets. In combination with the option to attach and

6   Currently, a Wikipedia article titled "Social Analysis Network Software" provides the most comprehensive and up-to-date list of available network analytic software (http://en.wikipedia.org/wiki/Social_network_analysis_software, accessed 25-8-2013).

7   When I started my analyses visone was not able to handle 2-mode data, as it automatically wrote a drawn graph as a 1-mode matrix. At that time I used UCInet for 2-mode to 1-mode transformation. The most recent versions of visone do support 2-mode data.

visualize extra attributes to nodes and ties, it is a practical and intuitive alternative to UCInet for (smaller) network archaeological studies.[8]

Measures of the network as a whole

There are many types of network measures. Perhaps the most elementary are those that measure the network as a whole. These can also be used to compare one network to another. Network density or sparseness, for example, is a measure related to the fraction of ties found versus the total possible number of ties. Even without any further analysis the network density can be insightful. One thing that will be clear from a first cursory glance is whether a network is excessively sparse or dense. Although network sparseness or density is not necessarily a defining feature of a network – networks with similar levels of density may have a completely different structural layout –, it does present an initial impression of structure, cohesiveness and connectedness of the overall network. For binary, non-loop matrices the density is easily calculable: $\frac{t}{n(n-1)}$, where t is the sum of all cells in the matrix (i.e. the total number of ties) and n is the total number of nodes. The outcome will be somewhere between 0 and 1, with an outcome of 0 indicating a collection of unconnected nodes and 1 a network that is maximally connected. Thus the density of the Chremanesian graph is, $\frac{31}{17 \times (17-1)} = 0.113$ or, in other words only 11.3% of the network's total capacity is utilized (Scott 2000: 78).[9]

In itself network density is not that informative. It is, however, more useful when contrasted to other networks. Particularly when compared to another, similar network this will establish some first structural similarities or differences between them. For example, Chremanesia's fantastical neighbouring archipelago, the Insulae Rerum, has the same strange practices and limited material assemblage. Closer inspection reveals that the network of the Insulae Rerum has a density of 65%, however. In comparison to Chremanesia this could imply that, regardless of the actual size of either network, greater cultural similarity and more egalitarian relations between sites should be expected in the Insulae Rerum.

Distance is another trait that can be of use for network comparisons. Distance between nodes in a network is always measured by its geodesic or shortest paths. As was already outlined by Euler, a path is a core concept of graph theory, signifying a sequence of ties in which each node and tie is distinct. The length of the path equals the number of ties in it. If a graph is directed, the direction of the arrows is normally taken into account. Thus in the case study the distance between A and

---

8   At the time of writing no software packets were capable of dealing with archaeological relational data. ArcGIS does offer the possibility to apply "Network Analyst" as an extension, but I have no personal experience with this program. The *ariadne* program, created by Tim Evans, was developed in order to model the relations between sites or other geographic entities. It is primarily based on an algorithm of interaction cost and benefit especially created for research that Knappett, Evans and Rivers carried out on Minoan sites (Knappet, *et al.* 2008), but with a different file input can also be used for other (archaeo-)geographic network modelling. Unfortunately, due to a java-based error, it could not run on any of the computers I had access to.

9   It should be noted, however, that the density is here influenced by the fact that the graph is directed. Because non-directed graphs are symmetrical, a two node, non-directed graph will yield a matrix sum of 2, whereas one tie in a directed graph of two nodes will only yield a matrix sum of 1.

E is 4 (A→C→F→E). The diameter of a network or subgraph in the network is the length of the longest path between any pair of vertices for which a path actually exists (Newman 2010: 139-140). In Chremanesia there are several paths leading from node Q to G, but the shortest path between them has a length of 5 (Q → O → K → J → H or I →G). Especially when working with larger data sets measuring the diameter will present a first appreciation of the dynamics of distance in a network.

Subgraphs

Network groups or subgraph will be of especial interest in the case studies presented in later chapters. A dyad is the most basic grouping in a network. As a network entity the dyad is not very insightful, it simply means that a pair of nodes is connected by at least one tie. In fact, one could say that a network consisting only of otherwise unconnected dyads is not a network at all – or not a very interesting one at the very least. In order for a network structure to emerge, it needs to include dyads that intersect, i.e. have one node in common. Such dyads are called incident (Brandes, *et al.* 2013).

Not all (groups of) nodes in a graph are connected by a path. Indeed a network model may consist of discrete "sub-networks" called components, as is the case in the example of Chremanesia. These single nodes or groups of nodes cannot be connected with even a single path. Still, these are considered to be part of the same graph, but will never be part of the same subgraph. Within one graph we may find collections of nodes not related by any ties, other than for the fact they were selected for inclusion in the first place. It is possible to make a selection based on contemporaneity as has happened in the case of the hypothetical Chremanesia network, for instance. Nonetheless, even if there are only nine types of things there is indeed a break in this meagre material cultural repertoire, dividing Chremanesian culture and society into two components: North and South.

Components are the most inclusive form of subgraph. For a node to be part of a component it only has to be connected through minimally one path to all other nodes. When working with directed graphs it is also possible to differentiate between strong and weak components. Strong components are subgraphs with directed ties that still create a continuous path – in other words all relations between nodes are reciprocal – while weak components merely consist of nodes with ties of any type of direction. In the Chremanesian network the nodes {M-N-P} form a strong component while other subgraphs, like component 1 and 2, are simply weak components. The cycle is another type of grouping that dependends on paths between nodes, more specifically: a path that can return to the node from which it started, such as the site cycle C → D → F → E → B → C. Strong components like {M-N-P} are always cycles. Cyclical components are sets of cycles that intersect. Strong components, cycles and cyclical components are examples of further possible subgraph-divisions of a network (component).

Cores present yet another way of looking at groups within networks. A *k*-core is a set of nodes that is related because they are at least adjacent to *k* other nodes in the same component. At low numbers a core is a highly inclusive way of looking at groups in networks. It can, however, be further divided by distinguishing between *k*-core and *k*+1 core members – e.g. the *k*-core members are part of the group but the *k+1* core members have even more connections within that group. In the current example all nodes are members of 2-cores, but only 6, {K-L-M-N-O-P} are member of a 3-core.

A triad is a collection of three nodes that are maximally connected, i.e. every node is connected to all other nodes. There are certain fundamental differences between dyads and triads – as the sociologist George Simmel (1950: 135-137) had already noted. While a dyad is simply a pair of connected individuals, the addition of a third node transforms the network dynamics in crucial ways. With three nodes a so-called group effect is more likely to occur, which undermines the power and autonomy of the individual node (see Chapter 7). A clique is a more expansive, maximally connected subgraph – *ergo* all cliques contain at least one triad (Kosub 2005). Since it requires a subgraph in order to be maximally connected it is the most restricted and tightest form of group inside a network. Within the network of Chremanesia we find five cliques: (1) {A-B-C}; (2) {K-L-M-N}; (3) {K-L-O}; (4) {M-N-P}; and (5) {O-P-Q}. Note that a node can belong to several cliques at the same time, such as site K that belongs to two cliques. There are several variants on the base clique allowing its group membership to be more flexible. The concept of the *K*-cliques waters down the strict requirement of maximal connection in order to allow nodes to be a member of the clique if no more than *k* ties separate them and the other members of the clique. A *k*-clan is a stricter variant on the *k*-clique: specifying that nodes with distance *k* are clique members only if the diameter of the clique is no larger than *k*. Therefore, in the network model nodes A to E belong to a 2-clique but do not form a 2-clan because site D and E are only connected by non-clique member F. Finally, *k*-plexes are collection of cliques that have ties with all but *k* members of a clique.

These various ways of looking at groups inside the hypothetical network model presents us with alternate views of the same relational data set (see Table 3.1). In the hypothetical production and distribution network of Chremanesia the easiest subgraphs to identify are the two different components. Although components are generally easy to spot in any visualization or even in the data set itself, their analytical value should not be underestimated. For instance, it is easy to miss the breadth of the components by looking at a non-relational data set, because it consists of various sites that do not seem to be very connected. Further analysis of the component's connectivity might reveal interesting patterns. Site Q is a good example of this. From one perspective it could be described as a "backwater" of the graph. It functions as a producer of artefact type 9 which it distributes to site O and P. However, even if site Q shares no artefact types with site G, H, I, J, L, M and N, it is nevertheless still part of the same network component. In fact it is indeed part of the 2-clan {K-L-M-N-O-P-Q} and as such directly part of a group that includes the most powerful sets of nodes in the graph (see below).

Realising that this relational database can also be explored as an affiliation matrix of the 2-mode graph it is also possible to look at subgraphs through artefact type connection rather than site connections. The 2-mode graph shows how not only sites but also artefact types are holding the network together. Zooming in on type 6 it shows that this node, like site K, is a central "gathering place" in the network: i.e. it has many different members. In turn these are also members of other artefact types. This perspective can illustrate how an artefact (type) might diffuse through a network and even "interact" with other (types of) artefacts while doing so. Type 1 and 3, for example, are less well connected than type 2, so it could be hypothesized that the latter is more likely to spread through component 1. It also indicates how types themselves might interact at various locations, for example at site K, and thereby possible influence each other.

Centrality

The structural qualities of triads, cliques and other subgraphs demonstrates that aside from network groupings, the degree and paths by which individual nodes are connected are important features of a network. This can be further studied by looking at node "power" or "centrality" in networks (Brandes and Erlebach 2005: Part I; Newman 2010: Chapter 6). There is no common definition of power in networks, yet the concepts builds on the intuitive idea that power is defined by the relations a node is engaged in. Some measures of network power hold that the more connections a node has relative to other nodes the more powerful it is. Others look at relative importance of ties and paths that connect to a node instead of to other nodes. Mizoguchi (2009) provides an archaeological study of network power presenting examples of various centrality analyses in the context of early state formation during Japan's Kofun period.

Degree is the most basic of all the types of network centrality. It simply counts the number of ties that attach to a node and compares these to other the same count for all nodes in the network.[10] The idea behind degree analysis is that the more ties a node has the more influence it has over the rest of the network. Indegree and outdegree are subvariants of normal degree centrality for which respectively only the ties coming in or out count towards a node's centrality. [11, 12] In archaeology, indegree might be of use when researching a tribute-system in which only the incoming relations are of importance. Outdegree on the other hand may come into play when ranking which workshop or production centre has the highest number of consumer sites.

Closeness is a centrality measure based on network paths, rather than on the number of ties attached to a node. A node's closeness is the inverse of its farness, which is the total distance between a node and all other nodes in the graph.[13] Another centrality measure based on paths is betweenness. A node's betweenness

---

10   Degree measure (as calculated in visone, Brandes and Wagner 2004): : $c_v = \Sigma_{e \in instar(v) \cup outstar(v)} \omega(e)$
11   Indegree measure (as calculated in visone, *ibid.*): : $c_v = \Sigma_{e \in instar(v)} \omega(e)$
12   Outdegree measure (as calculated in visone, *ibid.*): : $c_v = \Sigma_{e \in outstar(v)} \omega(e)$
13   Closeness measure (as calculated in visone, *ibid.*): : $c_v = \frac{1}{\Sigma_{t \in V} \delta(v,t)}$

centrality can be gained by determining the shortest paths between a pair of nodes in a graph and calculating which fraction of the path runs through the node in question, repeat this measure for all pairs of node in the graph and summing up all of these fractions.[14] In essence, a node with a high betweenness rating functions as a gatekeeper, controlling access from nodes to other nodes in the graph. Thus, even it does not have the highest number of ties it may have a position that is strategically best. The real power of a node with high betweenness centrality depends for a large deal on the overall connectivity of the graph. If a graph is relatively dense there will be relatively many short paths and therefore a high betweenness will not be valued much: e.g. if all sites in a region have relatively easy access to a certain raw material the one with the easiest access only has marginally more power than if access to a certain resource is highly restricted.

Finally, in some cases status centrality measures, also known as "Katz' status centrality", will be applied.[15] Status centralities fall within a group of centrality measures based on Eigenvector analysis. Like degree, these measures are based on the idea that power in networks can be measured by the amount of ties to and from other nodes. Aside from tie quantity, status measures determine the power of a node based on the power of other nodes that it is tied to. Take the following situation: person A has ten contacts all of whom have fifty contacts and person B has one hundred contacts. Based on degree, B can be said to be the most powerful person. Yet a measure of Katz' status will indicate that A is the more powerful node. Imagine a situation in which a paramount chief C, who does not have a large following but does have ten subordinate chiefs who do, competes with a chief D with a good base of support. Who will be more powerful?

The answer is not immediately clear. Rather, it is dependent on what type of power structure is more applicable for the issue at hand. If it is about exerting influence directly (e.g. intra-communal power) chief D may be regarded as more powerful. If the type of power arises from a larger set of interactions, such as may be the case in larger distribution networks, chief C will be more powerful. This indicates that the selection of centrality analysis should be compatible with the type of network dynamics one is interested in. Beyond those discussed here, many other kinds of centrality analyses have been developed in order to measure specific variations of power in networks. With most network software, exploring power in networks is literally just a matter of selecting a different type of analysis from a menu. Because of this, adopting graph theoretical measures to comprehend power in networks can be deceptively easy. The type of analysis used for understanding centrality can heavily influence the final interpretation of the archaeological network.

In the hypothetical network model of distribution and consumer sites, depending on which type of degree centrality is applied, an individual node's network power will vary (Table 3.2). In terms of the total number of ties, or

---

14 Betweenness measure (as calculated in visone, *ibid.*): : $c_v = \sum_{s \neq v \neq t \in V} \frac{\sigma_{G(s,t|v)}}{\sigma_{G(s,t)}}$, where $\sigma_{G(s,t)}$ and $\sigma_{G(s,t|v)}$ are the number of all shortest *st*-paths and those passing through v.

15 Status measure (as calculated in visone, *ibid.*): $c_v = \alpha \cdot \sum_{(u,v) \in instar}(1 + c_u)$, where $\alpha = \min\{\max_{v \in V} \text{indegree}(v), \max_{v \in V} \text{outdegree}(v)\}^{-1}$

degree, K, M, N and P have the same centrality. With the network of Chremanesia in mind this could be explained as evidence for a sprawling interaction sphere. Yet looking at betweenness and status, K's centrality is far higher than those of the other nodes. This implies that even if sites will have an equal part in the total amount of network interaction, some of them are more strategically located – betweenness – and have a higher total status due to their interactions with other powerful nodes. K would have occupied a very central position within the North component of Chremanesia.

Other types of centrality do not necessarily entail that anode has many connections. Node J, for example, has the second highest betweenness, even if it has only 6.5% of the total degree. Looking at the network model it becomes clear why: J is the bridge between two otherwise unconnected network regions. A similar thing applies for L, who actually has the highest closeness. K on the other hand is relatively far from most nodes, especially nodes P and Q in the outskirts of the network. In this hypothetical case being close to many other nodes can entail a different type of centrality. Suppose that occupants of site L wished to expand their distribution to other communities. A high closeness could indicate that this would require a relatively much smaller investment for L than for other sites in the region.

Network explorations

Chremanesia is an imperfect model for real archaeological networks – it is too perfect. It is a location where only a few ties based on the presence or absence of things form the basis of society and culture. There are furthermore only a few sites that display very little variation in the material cultural repertoire. Historical realities and archaeological records are far "messier" and less one-dimensional than Chremanesia's island world. Fortunately, network modelling and data-driven networks actually do not have to be based on such near "perfect" data sets. In fact, they rarely are (Isaksen 2013). Nevertheless, Chremanesia shows how it is possible to use archaeological assemblages by abstracting, visualizing and applying subgraph and centrality measures to them.

Technically speaking such a data-driven study of incident ties between items of material cultures in archaeological assemblages or other types of relational information should be referred to as "network exploration". This means that, rather than using statistical, analytical or theoretical modelling from the network sciences, concepts, visualizations and some basic measures are employed to lay bare and study in detail the inherent structures of archaeological and ethnohistorical sources of information. This type of bottom-up approach is a necessary first step and provides a good fit for some of the data sets and questions in the discipline itself. In addition, as was discussed in Chapter 1, the goal is not to use network science to find a general theory of pre-colonial network formation and development but rather to use it to check some of the "hidden" network assumptions of existing Caribbean archaeological theories. This will be done in Chapters 5 to 8. However, before that, it is necessary to delve deeper into the nature of the socio-material relations that would have structured the networks in these case studies.

Chapter 4

Ties that Matter, Matter that Ties: A Theoretical Framework for Socio-material Network Studies

I know it may be said that the simple existence of these shells in the ruins from the Gila valley to modern Tusayan can be explained on the theory of barter, and that their distribution does not prove racial kinship of former owners is self-evident. The theory that the same symbolism and treatment of the material originated independently cannot be seriously urged in this case. While I would not say, since I have no proof one way or the other, that these shells were worked by the people who lived in the ancient ruins, I am not sure that their ancestors may not have brought them in their migrations from the south.

Jesse W. Fewkes (1896: 49)

This chapter presents a framework that will make more explicit how the systems of material culture in the Caribbean archaeological record can be said to be interdependent with social networks. As briefly discussed in Chapter 1, the patterns of homogeneity and diversity in the Caribbean archaeological record are underlain by "socio-material networks" (cf. Knappett 2011). Here I will provide a more in-depth and conceptual take on this matter, relating to the ideas of Marcel Mauss, a scholar who has been of institutional importance for thinking about things *and* social relations in anthropology and archaeology. I will follow up on this with a discussion of post-Maussian theories on gift exchange relations and personhood. In addition, a brief ethnographic case-study from outside the Caribbean, based on the famous *kula* exchange, reveals how a dyad of (reciprocal) socio-material relations can quickly expand to form larger systems of objects and persons. Finally, I will also return to the perspectivist model discussed in Chapter 2, which provides a parallel pathway to understanding the impact of socio-material interdependency with a specific reference to Amerindian ontologies.

Jesse W. Fewkes, the same archaeologist who would later carry out important groundwork in the Antilles, discusses in the above quote how to distinguish various types of social (inter)actions. This discussion focuses on the presence of a seashell in Tusayan Pueblo middens in the Midwest of the United States, 400 km away from its possible nearest source. It comes across quite succinctly from this rather tortuous internal deliberation that coming to grips with social factors through the archaeological record is not an easy task. Indeed, the open-ended problem in archaeology is and always has been how to perceive the difference between incidences of material culture in space-time, geographic space and social space. Has there been any progress on this issue since the advent of archaeology as a scientific undertaking? Only the greatest cynic would answer that with a negative. On the other hand, I already discussed the problems archaeologists have with understanding the movements and interactions of people as seen through a diverse but connected pan-Caribbean archaeological record. In other words, the problem at hand is a larger and more convoluted repetition of the fundamental struggle to make sense of the movements of objects in social, geographic and temporal spaces, as showcased above by Fewkes.

Allow me to illustrate what seems like a purely archaeological methodological and conceptual problem with a little thought experiment to make it more relevant for general human experiences. Suppose that we are walking on a beach and you find a shell that has washed up on the shore. You pick it up and bring it home. Because you picked up this shell this does not imply that there is now a social tie between you and the sea. Nor does it imply that there is now a social relation between the creature that produced the shell and you.[1] Now suppose the shell has not been brought by the sea but left there by another human being. Unless this was done with the express intent of leaving it for a certain other person to find, this would not constitute a social bond. Now let us suppose that the shell was transported by the sea but contained some kind of message inscribed on it by another individual designating the shell as a gift to the lucky finder? In this case no personal directionality is given to the action, the donor and recipient have never met, and the recipient will not be likely to reciprocate. In this case the ties between the sea, the creature's shell, the person who left the message, and the finder might tentatively be part of a convoluted network of social "actants" (*sensu* Latour 2005). Hereby the sea and the shell serve as the material parts of a brief, inequitable, and presumably unfulfilling social relation. Now imagine I pick up a shell on a beach and hand it to you. We will immediately recognize the gesture and the shell as a gift – literally a "social fact" (Mauss 1990). What has exactly happened here that sets this apart from the previous (inter)actions? This is the question that will be explored in this chapter.

---

1   Granted, it is possible to have a social ontology in which the sea and shells would be perceived not as material forces but (partly) as social actors. Indeed, the model of Amerindian ontologies presented by Viveiros de Castro (1998) and discussed in Chapter 2 suggests that whether a shell is naturally social or socially natural is simply a matter of perspective. In fact, it seems that Andrezj Antczak and Marlena Antczak (2006) have found evidence for exactly this kind of socio-cosmic entanglements in the Late Ceramic Age shell procurement sites on the Los Roques archipelago (Venezuela). Nonetheless, broadening a traditionally Western view with reference to other social ontologies does not solve the issue of what constitutes a material social tie and what does not. Even if ideas about what constitutes a social interaction differ from ontology to ontology, every society always includes things that cannot be or simply are never socialized (with).

Society and material culture

Theories on how material culture is central to society and vice versa are deeply rooted in the European intellectual tradition. Incipient ideas on this were present in the works of Classical philosophers, in turn inspired by the philosophical and religious traditions of the Middle East and West Asia. In the Early Modern period these earlier views developed into a typically European school of thought (Graeber 2011). Among the numerous works in this tradition, two theories on the origin and evolution of human society, those of Hobbes and Rousseau, are worth explicitly mentioning here (see also Mol, in press). The reason that these two are highlighted here is that they present an argument for living in society and what is needed for it, based on what life was like in an original state of nature or "non-society". Interestingly, both philosophers drew their inspiration for this "original state" from European reports on peoples that lived on the fringes of early colonial empires, among which prominently those of the Caribbean. In addition, both philosophers represent two sides of a debate that has shaped how human sociality is studied in the social sciences and perceived by society at large (Pinker 2011; Sykes 2005). Their social contract theories are still at the basis of modern theories of justice and many other debates on violence, sociality and morality. Of more importance for the present discussion is that both philosophers present an analogous view on the importance of material culture in the formation and development of human social networks.

In *Leviathan* Hobbes (1929 [1651]) devises a theory of society that depends on a social contract enforced by an autocratic ruler. His starting point was a characterization of humans in a "state of nature", as opposed to a state of society, as "solitary, poor, brutish, and short" (*ibid.*: 99). According to Hobbes, humans in the original state of nature have a lack of all things, because they have a "right to every thing" (*ibid.*: 110). This right to appropriate "things" was not inhibited by a code of laws, norms or moral convictions. In modern economic terms, in such a system there would be no moral, social or judicial mechanism to coordinate infinite human wants that clash with equal abilities to gain access to limited means. In Hobbes' view, a lack of reciprocally enforced social contracts will result in an endless war of all versus all.

Discourse on Inequality (Rousseau 2012 [1754]), written a century later, arrives at the same need for a social contract. Here and in other works (e.g. Rousseau 1966 [1762]), Rousseau argues the opposite of Hobbes his position on the natural state. He proposes that the original environment of humans would have given them near infinite ways to foresee in their needs. This was a period in history "in which the state of nature, being that in which the care for our own preservation is the least prejudicial to that of others, was consequently the best calculated to promote peace". Only when humans came together to achieve goals that were out of reach for the solitary individual did conflict and strife and the need for a social contract arise.

The shadow cast by these conflicting theories of a war-like or peaceful human nature has also affected the anthropology and archaeology of non-state societies: the type of social structures that many hold to be closer to a fabled original state of nature than (modern) state societies (e.g. Fry 2006; Keeley 1996; Pinker 2011; Sahlins 1972; Sykes 2005). The debate has surprisingly passed over the ethnohistoric and archaeological record of much of the indigenous Caribbean. Even more surprisingly is the fact that it goes unacknowledged that the central arguments of both Hobbes and Rousseau are partly concerned with the interdependencies between social networks and material culture (Corbey 2000; Corbey 2006; Sahlins 1972). According to Rousseau, due to natural affluence humans do not necessarily have to cooperate with each other in social support networks, while according to Hobbes limited means and infinite wants actively prevents such ties from forming. Innovation or desire for material culture will change both these situations, however. In the case of Rousseau the payoff for acting socially is gained through a cooperative development of things, while in the case of Hobbes cooperation under a social contract means to lay down the ultimately destructive individual's "right to all things" so that certain things can be reciprocally enjoyed.[2]

It is interesting to see how these examples depart from a "state of nature" that is completely opposed but for one thing: a lack of sociality and a lack of things. Both theories of sociality begin in a state of zero inter-personal contact and both the original Rousseauean and Hobbesian human being lack a material culture in the most real sense of the word – their cultures are not material because they do not create anything that endures beyond the grasp of a single individual. By encountering the sociality inherent to material culture, through invention of things by cooperation in the case of Rousseau and by claiming equal rights to things in Hobbes, the need for social cont(r)acts is discovered. Thus, through different routes Rousseau and Hobbes both present theories of the origin of society through the connective properties of material culture. The factors for the creation, durability and evolution of connections between the solitary human "nodes" that gave rise to networks are simultaneously social and material in nature.

Of course, both Hobbes and Rousseau present hypothetical cases of original human nature that likely do not correlate with any human society that ever existed and certainly not with those of what we know of pre-colonial or proto-historic Caribbean societies. Their idea that "natural society" was still present on the banks of the Caribbean Sea and other regions of the world at the advent of contact should rather be seen as a typical result of the perceived superiority of European culture and society inherent to the colonial project. Yet this does not mean that there is no merit in the idea that "having material culture" entails "having society" and *vice versa*. As we shall see this idea is still central to much of anthropology, particularly to (post-)Maussian studies of exchange. In addition, recent studies from cognitive psychology, cultural economy, and the ethnographic and archaeological record also support a deep relation between social interaction and material interests (Coward 2010; Dunbar, *et al.* 2010b; Gintis, *et al.* 2005; Malafouris 2010; Wilk and Cliggett 2007).

---

2   As Hobbes (1922 [1651]: 96) remarks in regards to this: "The Passions that encline men to Peace, are Feare of Death; Desire of such things as are necessary to commodious living; and a Hope by their Industry to obtain them."

Interestingly, in the diverse linguistic, ethnic and cultural landscape of the Caribbean, material culture may also have functioned as a connective factor for "Rousseauean innovations", "Hobbesian pacifications" and other socio-cultural processes. We can see this in practice through the historic documentation of "first contact" situations between Europeans and indigenous peoples:

Sunday, 30 December, 1492

> *The Admiral went ashore to eat and arrived at the same time as did five kings, subjects to Guacanagari. All wore their crowns, showing their high position, so much so that the Admiral says to the Sovereigns that "Your Highness would have been delighted to see their manners." When he went ashore the king came to receive him, taking him by the arm and conducting him to the same house they had been in the day before where they had arranged a layer of woven fronds and some seats where the Admiral sat. Then the king took the crown from his head and put it on the Admiral, who in turn took off a necklace of good carnelians and very handsome stones of most delicate colours which shone in any position and put it on the king's neck. Then he took a richly woven mantle of fine cloth he was wearing that day and gave it to him, and he sent for a pair of colored Moroccan boots and had them put on him. The Admiral put a large silver ring on the king's finger, for it was reported to him that earlier, when the king had seen a silver ring on a sailor, he had insisted that it be given to him. The king was particularly satisfied and content, and two of the kings with him moved up to where he was with the Admiral, and each gave the Admiral his own large gold plate"* de Navarete 1922: 133-134.[3]

The above account from the first voyage of Columbus details one of the many documented encounters of Europeans with Caribbean indigenous peoples during the first years of contact. It tells of the diplomatic manoeuvrings between Columbus and the indigenous "king" or *cacique* Guacanagarí. Some days prior to this get-together, admiral Columbus and his crew, shipwrecked after their ship the Santa María had run aground somewhere on the north coast of present-day Haiti on Christmas Day 1492, had been taken in as distinguished guests by Guacanagarí. Establishing good relations was of paramount and strategic importance for both groups and their leaders. Columbus and Guacanagarí were both in a precarious position – one was shipwrecked, the other faced a group of strangers with superior military technology. Nevertheless, they could both benefit enormously from the

---

3   "Salió el Almirante a comer a tierra, y llego a tiempo que habían venido cinco Reyes subjetos á aqueste que se llamaba Guacanagari, todos con sus coronas, representando muy buen estado, que dice el Almirante a los Reyes que sus Altezas hobieran placer de ver la manera dellos. En llegando en tierra el Rey vino a rescibir al Almirante, y lo llevo de brazos a la misma casa de ayer, a do tenía un estrado y sillas, en que asentó al Almirante, y luego se quitó la corona de la cabeza y se la puso al Almirante, y el Almirante se quitó del pescuezo un collar de buenos alaqueques y cuentas muy hermosas de muy lindos colores, que parecía muy bien en toda parte, y se lo puso a el; y se desnudó un capuz de fina grana, que aquel día se había vestido, y se lo vistió; y envió por unos borceguíes de color, que le hizo calzar, y le puso en el dedo un grande anillo de plata, porque habían dicho que vieron una sortija de plata a un marinero y que había hecho mucho por ella. Quedo muy alegre y muy contento, y dos de aquellos Reyes que estaban con el vinieron adonde el Almirante estaba con el y trujeron al Almirante dos grandes plastas de oro, cada uno la suya" (de Navarete 1922: 133-134).

opportunities offered by these new social ties, as well. This is why, in the days that followed the wrecking of the Santa María, relations between the two groups steadily improved to a point where Columbus decided he would build a small settlement, La Navidad, close to the village of Guacanagarí.

In hindsight, the importance of the interactions between Columbus and Guacanagarí far transcended their own immediate interest and their dealings would have a large impact on the diplomatic history between two previously unconnected peoples. Regrettably, what started out as a series of friendly exchanges soon ended in bloodshed. In November 1493, when Columbus returned to La Navidad on his second journey to the Caribbean, he found the settlement destroyed and its inhabitants killed. Columbus learned from a messenger sent by Guacanagarí that the fort had been attacked by a more powerful *cacique*, Caonabo, who had been angered by expeditions made by a riotous group that left the fort in search of gold and women. When questioned while resting in his hammock nursing his wounds, Guacanagarí vowed he had tried to defend the fort from Caonabo. Nevertheless, many chroniclers and other historians have noted that, since he was likely a vassal of Caonabo, this account is questionable. The exact history of events taking place after Columbus left La Navidad remained unclear, however (Wilson 1990: 68-71, 75-79).

Guacanagarí himself remained Columbus' ally, and continued to send him gifts at the new Spanish Colony of La Isabela (Deagan and Cruxent 2002; Mol 2008; Wilson 1990: 75-79). Yet on a larger scale the destruction of La Navidad was the beginning of a long spiral of violence between Europeans and the indigenous peoples of the Caribbean. In Hispaniola this culminated in the Spanish-indigenous Wars of Higuey of 1502-1504, after which the Spanish colonizers were unobstructed to aggressively assert their dominance over the native population (Churampi Ramírez 2007; de las Casas 1992 [1542]). Unfortunately, put into its wider historic context, this early episode serves as a bloodstained archetype for indigenous and European contact throughout the centuries of colonization that followed.

Aside from Columbus, Guacanagarí, and the dramatic force of colonial history an attentive reader will distinguish another key actor in this passage. There was as yet little or no common language at this point, but during the meeting, crowns, seats, clothing, jewellery and other adornments facilitated and framed the interactions between the two leaders and the peoples they represented. This "material lingua franca" must thus have been of great aid or even necessary for communication. By sharing, exchanging or otherwise incorporating things in their interactions, Europeans and Amerindians alike attempted to create and maintain ties of huge personal and historical interest.

Thus, starting out in a potential state of Hobbesian "Warre" or Rousseauean isolation, over a span of days Columbus and Guacanagarí managed to create a society between them – albeit one that would ultimately prove to be disastrous for the indigenous peoples of the Caribbean. The rapid emergence of this intercultural, social network was only possible because it was being built with mutually intelligible social strategies that were efficiently scaffolded by material culture (Keehnen 2011; Mol 2008; Oliver 2009: Part V; Valcárcel Rojas 2012). The reciprocal gift giving, the creation of hierarchies based on the exchange of prestige items, and other interactions are born out of a desire for (new) things that goes hand in hand with socialization. This example of indigenous-European network creation in practice is a historical example of how social and material factors are inherent to the theories of Hobbes and Rousseau. Such particular person-thing "networks" are tied to a universal human tendency in which material culture "scaffolds" personal and group interactions (Corbey 2006; Graeber 2001; Knappett 2005, 2011; Mol 2007, 2010). Furthermore, viewed from the particular perspective of Guacanagarí and his community, these exchanges were likely mimicking ancient Amerindian ontologies in which things had a central part to play in personal and group interactions (Keehnen 2011; Mol 2008; Oliver 2000, 2009). These can partially be reconstructed through archaeological and ethnohistoric studies, but are also still echoed by the attitude towards material culture in contemporary indigenous communities in Lowland South America (Santos-Granero 2009a).

Mind over matter?

Most of the more traditional archaeological and anthropological theories of material culture and society have in common that they posit a hierarchy between their social and material dynamics. Where there is smoke there is fire, where there are objects there are people. Heuristically, where the former is the *explanandum* (smoke/objects), the latter is the *explanans* (fire/people). This "mind over matter" hierarchy spills over into other fundamental differences between subjects and objects, cause and effect, signifier and sign, agent and dependent, and means to ends (Bourdieu 1977; Keane 2006; Olsen 2010; Preucel 2008; Tilley 1999). As a result, the evaluation of the strategic position of things in networks has often taken a backseat to the strategic position of people. For instance, consider the following famous archaeological parable. In it an archetypal Real Mesoamerican Archaeologist (R.M.A.), reacts to a theory forwarded by his Skeptical Graduate Student. The Skeptical Graduate Student has just presented a paper in which he discussed how Olmec prominence in Early Formative Mexico was largely due to their wealth in highly developed ideas. The R.M.A. has an entirely different view on the matter (Flannery 1976: 285-286):

> *"'Two Indians met on a jungle trail at the Isthmus of Tehuantepec. One was an Olmec from La Venta. The other was a guy from the Motagua Valley, carrying a 200-lb jade boulder with his tumpline.'*
>
> *'Hey soul brother', says the Olmec. 'What'll you take for that jade boulder?'*
>
> *'What have you got?' says the guy from Motagua.*
>
> *'Ideas.' says the Olmec.*
>
> *'Let's hear one.' […]*
>
> *'Our chief is descended from a jaguar who mated with a human female.'*
>
> *'So is ours.'*

'If you'd let me have that jade boulder, I think we could make our chief into a king.'

'What's that mean?'

'That means he'd be semidivine, and have life-and-death power over his subjects; he'd have a monopoly of force, and the power to conscript soldiers, levee taxes, and exact tribute.'

'If our chief tried that, we'd whip his ass.'

The Olmec sighs.

'That's all the ideas you got?' says the guy from Motagua.

'That's all I'm authorized to trade.'

'In that case,' says the Motagua Indian, 'if you don't mind, I'll head on up to the Kaminaljuyú area, where the chief is offering 10, maybe 12 girls from elite lineages for every hundredweight of jade." And that, O Best Beloved, is how the Great Jade Boulder got to Kaminaljuyú.' "

In other words the reason why a large jade boulder came to be deposited in Kaminaljuyú rather than in an Olmec site is that a guy from Motagua rated the "social" benefits of girls from elite lineages above those arising from the favour of an Olmec near-king. The R.M.A.'s theory is meant to be tongue in cheek and he therefore presents a (too) functionalist interpretation of the whole affair. Yet, remarkably, his seemingly straightforward story actually does nothing to explain how a guy from Motagua, elite girls and an Olmec chief came to be part of a set of social relations revolving around a boulder of jade in the first place. Which is strange, when you think about it: the boulder of jade has the highest materiality in this particular set of interactions. Its ties are valued as much as the lives of multiple human beings and more than the support of a nearly semi-divine king, who apparently can use this jade boulder to gain life and death power over other people.

Of course, this parable is just that: a story meant to teach a certain lesson. However, the added lesson is that archaeological theories from high to low are often more focused on the direct networks between and around people.[4] People who were making things, shaping things, using things, moving things, exchanging things, acquiring things, hoarding things, giving meaning to things, generally doing things to, with, and through things in order to establish ties with other people. As a result, what has changed significantly in the course of the history of archaeology is the identification of possible relations behind the distribution of material culture in the archaeological record. On the other hand another vast amount of literature discusses how material culture itself is related in time and space – starting with the typo-chronological frameworks of early scientific archaeology. Therefore, while these domains are often segregated into archaeological theory and method, there is a definite understanding of both humans and things in their own respective

---

4   Another lesson to be learnt here is that R.M.A.'s from the 1970s still thought it humorous to equate women with objects.

systems (Olsen 2010; Schiffer 1999). The problem lies in the interpretive interface in which both domains come together.

This also applies to the Caribbean, where (macro-regional) networks have mostly been dealt with as reflections of ethnicities, identities and cultures drawn from relations between things (Geurds 2011). Whether it is the spread of Saladoid ceramics, distribution of jades, metals, hard woods or ball courts, the interpretative weight lies on the cultural or social and not the material counterparts of these networks (e.g. Helms 1987; Rodríguez Ramos 2010a; Rouse 1992; Wilson 1993). However, it is clear that these things must also have shaped Caribbean social networks. If not, why would they even have been distributed across such distances? Caribbean archaeology cannot be faulted for the particular disregard of objects as a shaping factor in its networks. It is part of a wider context in which "despite the grounding and inescapable materiality of the human condition, things seem to have been subjected to a kind of collective amnesia in social and cultural studies" (Olsen 2010: 2). During the last 10 to 15 years numerous scholars with a broad range of interest in material culture have made a serious effort to remedy this situation. At least in some parts of anthropology and archaeology, thinking about things is enjoying a renaissance.

This "material cultural turn" in anthropology originated from scholars who already had an affinity with the study of material culture (Hicks 2010). Pinpointing the exact beginning of this new wave is impossible, but often the works by Miller on consumerism and materiality are regarded as the starting point (Miller 1987, 2005). *Art and Agency* by Alfred Gell (Gell 1998) is another setting off point that presented a new theory on how things can come to be agents. Both emphasize the influence that material culture exerts on wider societal practices and the lives of individual persons (Dant 2005). More avant-garde thinkers, such as Latour (2005), have completely discarded the idea of difference between social and material factors. Things and people are part of an inclusive "network of actants" that shapes the Social. Actions of things and actions undertaken by humans become part of the same fields. From such a perspective, material culture can (re)act on people as well as the other way around.

Scholars such as for instance Gell, Miller, Dant, and Latour have each in quite variable ways – e.g. the reactions to Ingold (2007b) – shown how human life and society can be shaped by means of "silent" but vital ties between things and persons. This has opened the way for a line of thinking in which life, culture and society is not any longer only created by humans and given meaning to by human minds. Things are part of society and society partly consists of things. As such, this revaluation of the thing has been a timely counter to what Olsen (2010: 2-3) has called the "anti-material sentiment". However, as so many academic counter-movements, its solutions have sometimes been as extreme as the problem it tried to address.

A problem with tracing networks of object agency in society is that things are hardly ever literally perceived as having the same type of agency as human beings. To a Western frame of mind in particular, things lack the necessary qualities that would make them comparable to human agents. Referring to both humans and things as "actants" does not solve this. Things are important in the networks that create and maintain human society, but that does not imply they are commensurate with human subjects. Things are not alive, do not think, do not perceive and are, or should not be, as valuable as persons (Graeber 2011). These inconsistent alignments of humans and objects are based in the rejection of a modern point of view, where the materiality of things comes as somewhat of a "surprise" – a logical process Gell (1998: Chapter 1) calls abduction.

However, such questions of human-thing and subject-object ontologies would likely not have been of (immediate) concern for the indigenous peoples of the Caribbean. This definitely applies to more contemporary Amerindian ontologies, in which things are often simply part and parcel of life. Some things may occupy central positions in the interfaces between social and even socio-cosmic networks (see also Keegan 2007; Oliver 2000, 2009). Nevertheless, as I will explain below, when things become subjects this arises from a certain inter-subjective context, an interaction with a (human) being that brings out their inherent but only partly social nature (Santos-Granero 2009a).

Yet even when taking other, non-Western perspectives on this matter to their extremes, only the most fervent panpsychist would disagree with the fact that, while things and humans potentially share many ontological and metaphysical aspects, they are not the same. People are not things and things are not people, at least not in an ultimate analysis. Consequently networks of people, social networks, are not the same as networks of things, or material networks, and therefore the interdependent system that results from them cannot be quite the same as either. Thus, when there is nothing that directly ties them together, how can one make the conceptual leap from material to social network? In the following I will propose a perspective on the matter that is inspired by (post-)Maussian theories of gift exchange.

The gift: a material total social fact

The burgeoning field of gift exchange theory was created by the virtue of one scholar's singular essay: the French sociologist Marcel Mauss and his "*Essai sur le Don: Forme et raison de l'échange dans les sociétés archaïques*" (Mauss 1923/1924). This publication, translated into English as *The Gift* (Mauss 1990), is a remarkable text when viewed against the backdrop of the history of anthropology (Sykes 2005). It is saturated with concepts, theories and research agendas that are exemplary for the French anthropological project of the early 20th century, yet it is still relevant today (Corbey 2008; Sigaud 2003). It is near unthinkable in anthropology and archaeology to write about forms of exchange without referring to it. It has proven problematic, however, to read and understand this *c.*100 pp. essay in an unequivocal manner (e.g. Corbey and Mol 2012; Godelier 1999; Graeber 2001; Gregory 1982; Lévi-Strauss 1949; Mol 2007; Parry and Bloch 1989; Sykes 2005).

In this sense the *Essai sur le don* is truly a reflection of the type of anthropologist and individual Marcel Mauss was and the personalities engaged in the anthropology of the day with whom he worked, not in the least his famous uncle, the sociologist

Émile Durkheim (Fournier 2006).[5] Mauss followed up on Durkheim's idea of "social facts", promoting the view that society is a real and active force, which prior to Durkheim's studies was not a generally accepted idea (Durkheim 1897, 1982 [1895]). Mauss expanded on the idea of the social fact with the notion that some social facts are "total" in nature, a key concept in the essay (Mauss 1990: 9). A total social fact is a practice that is inherently social and pervades all layers of a society: political, religious, economical, judicial, *etc.* Total social facts are not only present in every aspect of a given society, but they can also be thought of as the "generators and motors of the system" (Gofman 1998: 67).[6]

When the exchange of gifts is considered to be a total social phenomenon, it readily becomes apparent that it does indeed touch on a large number of related subjects. Nonetheless one aspect in particular caught Mauss's attention. He was puzzled by the fact that the reciprocal gift as total social fact is found in so many societies and has proven to be such an effective social mechanism. In his essay he therefore wonders "[w]hat rule of legality and self-interest, in societies of a backward or archaic type, compels the gift that has been received to be obligatorily reciprocated? What power resides in the object given that causes its recipient to pay it back?" (Mauss 1990: 4). For his explanation he turned to the concept of a "spirit" or force contained within the thing given.

An embryonic version of this hypothesis can be found in *Origins of the Notion of Money* (Mauss 1914). In this short lecture Mauss attempted to elucidate the socio-economic phenomenon of money that, as in the case of gift exchange in contemporary society, stems from a pre-monetary stage of history. He claimed that, where no true monetary system exists, the words referring to objects that come closest to our idea of "money" are always directly related the words for magical power in that society. Examples Mauss presented are the concepts of *dzo* among the Ewe, the notion of *mana* in Polynesia, and *manitou* among Algonquin-speaking peoples.[7] Mauss indicated that the items that are perceived as possessing a large amount of "magical force" are often the most prized in exchanges. This is by and large due to the fact that these objects also garner the most prestige for the owner. Joined to this is the idea that the magical force contained within objects is important because it is perceived as durable and transmissible. In this view

---

5   Although an understanding of Durkheimian sociology is instrumental for comprehending the oeuvre of Mauss – and the largest part of anthropology in fact – this does not imply Mauss his works were only influenced by his uncle. Mauss worked closely with and befriended leading French ethnologists and sociologists of the time, for instance Hubert, Espinas, Levy-Bruhl, Leenhardt and Fauconnet. In addition, he was an avid letter writer, corresponding with whom we now consider to be seminal scholars in anthropology such as Boas, Van Gennep, Frazer, Tylor, Radcliffe-Brown, Firth and Evans-Pritchard (Corbey 2008: 9; Fournier 2006: 240-241).

6   In his "*Essai sur le Don*" Mauss actually uses the French terms *des phénomènes sociaux totaux* and *des prestations totales* (translated as "total social phenomena" and "total services" in Mauss 1990) instead of *faites sociales totales* (total social facts).

7   Subsequent research on these concepts and many of their similarly perceived counterparts in other cultures has revealed that their amalgamation with money is an artefact of early anthropological studies of value, rather than proof of the existence of monetary systems before the development of money (Graeber 2001; Parry and Bloch 1989).

exchange valuables are therefore best characterized by the magic force contained in them that serves as a certain kind of transmissible, mystical currency.[8]

In "The Gift" Mauss goes one step further in his attribution of exchange functionality to the magical force contained in the exchanged thing when discussing the Maori *hau*. (*ibid.*: 14). The *hau*, Mauss (1990: 15) explains, is a magical force contained within the thing given that forces it to return to the previous owner:

> "[H]au — *which itself moreover possesses a kind of individuality — is attached to this chain of uses until these give back from their own property, their taonga [valuables], their goods, or from their labour or trading, by way of feasts, festivals and presents, the equivalent or something of even greater value. This in turn will give the donors authority and power over the first donor, who has become the last recipient*"

It is his theory concerning the spirit in the gift that has attracted the bulk of the critique forwarded by scholars who commented on Mauss (e.g. Gell 1998: 106-109; Godelier 1999; Graeber 2001: 178-181; Lévi-Strauss 1997; Parry 1986: 456; Sahlins 1972: Chapter 4; Sigaud 2003; Weiner 1992: 49).[9] Numerous commenters feel that cross-culturally transposing the magical force of the *hau* is essentially flawed. The general sentiment is that a reference to a magical thing within the gift to account for a social practice while leaving the underlying social mechanism itself unexplained resembles the introduction of a *deus ex machina* to tie up loose ends in a story plot.

As one of the first to present his critique on the *Essay on the Gift*, Raymond Firth held that the *hau* Mauss was referring to did not exist, since "[attributing] the scrupulousness in settling one's obligations to a belief in an active, detached fragment of personality [...] is an abstraction which receives no support from native evidence (Firth 1959 [1929]: 421)." Furthermore, Firth held the view that the explanations for reciprocity should rather be understood as the avoidance of social sanctions, such as the desire to continue useful economic relations and the maintenance of prestige and power, that do not have to rely on esoteric credence – in other words, Equality Matching for the sake of Market Pricing and Authority Ranking relations. Lévi-Strauss (1997) likewise laments that Mauss was misled by native "ghosts and goblins" stories. According to Lévi-Strauss any notion of *hau* in the gift was nothing more than a "*truc indigène*" (Godelier 1999).

Remarkably, it seems that the concept of a spirit in the gift has again gained some momentum with the theories of materiality and objects as subjects discussed above. Moreover, the idea that things can be autonomous and somehow can have the same qualitative status as human beings has always been present in works that were influenced by Mauss (1990). Particularly discussions of the status of gifts

---

8   The connection between exchange and magic would be further examined by Thurnwald in his "Economics in Primitive Communities" (Thurnwald 1932).

9   These two distinct lines of critiques both focus on Mauss' application of the Maori concept of *hau*. Aside from the critique on the *hau* as "floating signifier", scholars have pointed to problems when applying secondary data on the *hau* in order to introduce this hypothesis of the spirit in the gift. This line of critique is interesting in its own right, but not of direct concern here (e.g. Graeber 2001: 178-181; Sahlins 1972: Chapter 4; Sigaud 2003).

in contrast to that of commodities refer to the notion that gifts and persons are commensurable (e.g. Gregory 1982).[10] In some recent material culture theories, the spirit in the gift that was independent of individual human actors has expanded in scope under the headings of "thing", "fetishism" and materiality (Dobres and Robb 2005; Gosden 2005; Keane 2006; Pels 2005).

The point of this short critique of the *hau,* spirit and materiality of gift objects is to shift the emphasis away from the idea that persons and things can impact one another because they are categorically similar. Consider the idea that the majority of objects that circulate between humans are not perceived as alive or as "fetishes". In practice, most objects that are exchanged do not need a spirit or force to circulate in human networks.[11] Instead of person-thing commensurability I wish to shift the focus to how humans and objects (systemically) stand in relation to each other and how socio-material dynamics can effectuate a diverse yet inherently linked set of social and material cultural relations. The general idea is that things that are part of social networks have a different dynamic from objects that are not. For example, I can enjoy an artefact I excavated by putting it in my private stash, but the a-sociality of the situation will prevent it from having the same impact on social networks of myself and others as it would have when displayed in a museum – in fact it is likely even my enjoyment of the object would decrease if it was based on a purely solitary relation between myself and the artefact (Graeber 2001: 260).

A physical transfer of objects is also never the same as a "service", i.e. non-materially expressed social relations. In his essay Mauss somewhat conflates the two.[12] However the reality is that, while the former has a physical presence after the exchange has been made, the latter is based only in the cerebra of those that were witness to the exchange – and their perceptions and recollections may vary. Graeber, in an excellent reappraisal of Mauss his discussion (2001: 169-188) also reconnects the *hau* and similar magical forces explicitly to the material condition of human sociality. He contends that because of the functioning of the Maori exchange system (in which a donor can basically request anything from a recipient, leaving the recipient completely in the donor's *tapu,* or "sphere of influence") the *hau* should indeed be considered a type of gift and not as a magical force. The gift of something invested with *hau* is a clever "intentional movement", a material social stratagem, of a thing towards one's creditor in order to avert his or her influence.

---

10 A good example of this concept of "object biography", also popular in archaeology (cf. Kopytoff 1986). Although it is clear that objects can have their own "narratives", a story of its use-life, this is too often directly taken to mean that an artefact may have been considered to be actually alive.

11 Granted, as we shall see below, some objects will have a kind of subjectivity. Nevertheless saying that these objects are therefore commensurable with persons is missing the point. These objects circulate between or are otherwise part of other relations than exist between humans alone: i.e. their defining relational characteristic is that they are part of relations between humans and *other than human* beings (see also Mol 2007, note 1).

12 It has to be noted that this conflation between non-material and material relations is present in the original French term "*prestations*" used by Mauss (1923/1924) to indicate gift relations. However, in the 1990 English version of the essay this term has been translated as "services". This is somewhat unfortunate because Mauss also uses the French "*services*" to denote relations that may only be immaterially expressed.

Furthermore, social relations stick to things and things stick around. Thus, aside from the "externalization through materialization" of human socio-politics, material culture can also function effectively as corporate memory-bases (Dyke and Alcock 2003; Mills and Walker 2008). The relations a human can have with and through things will be there after other people are not present. In such a way things become social by proxy and what are considered as, in theory, predominantly spiritual or social relations will become material.

The interdependency of persons and gifts

It is thus my contention that the value of Mauss's "The Gift" is as a theory of sociality by the mechanism of the materialized social contract (cf. Corbey 2006), rather than as a theory of reciprocity or thing and person commensurability as is often done in retrospect. The former is also how the essay has been used in most ethnographical studies it is referenced in (Sykes 2005). The majority of gift case studies do not focus on the spiritual essence of gifts – although this will generally play a very important in their emic conceptualization – but rather on their social and material dynamics. For those coming after Mauss, exchange does not occur because things *contain* a magical spirit, but because they *stand in relation to* persons.[13] This reading of the gift can also be literally found back in the above-mentioned essay. It is true that Mauss is not outspoken about this particular topic, but he does make the following remark towards the conclusion of his discussion of the *potlatch*. This small sentence already expresses the concept that part of one's own being is material and "external" – that which is visible to others – because it is part of social relations:

> *"The circulation of goods follows that of men, women, and children, of feasts, rituals, ceremonies, and dances, and even that of jokes and insults. All in all, it one and the same. [...B]y giving one is giving oneself, and if one gives oneself, it is because one 'owes' oneself – one's persons and one's goods – to others"* Mauss 1990: 58-59.

Subsequently, anthropologists who have actively framed their research, carried out in various settings and various locations, around the question of the gift consistently engaged the topic of personhood and communal identity in relation to the gift. This has led to numerous culturally specific examples of this phenomenon that have contributed immensely to a cross-cultural understanding of personhood and society. This has shown that, aside from the type of evocative give and take of the type of "Archaic" societies Mauss focused on, gift giving is still a central tenet of many contemporary societies.

In the Soviet Union during the rule of Stalin, for example, it was customary for international and national institutes (ranging from the Supreme Soviet to provincial factories) to present personal gifts to the General Secretary on the

---

13   This is not necessary a novel idea. R. W. Emerson (1844), for example, distinguishes this nuclear element of gift giving. "[I] like to see that we cannot be bought and sold", but that "[t]he only gift is a portion of thyself" (*ibid*: 26).

occasion of his birthday (Ssorin-Chaikov 2006). The thing presented to Stalin was often something that reminded of the gift's origin, regional culinary specialities for example, or of the type of person that Stalin was believed to be. Stalin then often redistributed these gifts, especially the ones that bore his countenance. Interestingly, these things were treated with the highest degree of decorum.[14] One could say that gifts from Stalin that were somehow inherently linked to the person of Stalin are a characteristic example of the distorted nature of Soviet political ideologies. Nevertheless even in capitalist societies relations of persons with things has the power to change the relations between persons, by moving even the most basic "stuff" from Market Pricing models of relations into other social spheres and vice versa (Kopytoff 1986).

For example, in the U.S.A. an event such as a garage sale, in which one sells personal belongings to complete strangers, is not only about making money through the sale of commodities (Herrmann 1997). Prices paid for the objects are small, but values attached to them by either donor or recipient can be great. Often potential buyers receive gifts in the form of discounts or free "stuff" if the person hosting the garage sale feels a personal connection with the buyers. In certain extreme cases donors and recipients imagine that something that was once theirs now has the opportunity for a second life with the new owner, while still remaining tied to their original owner, as well (*ibid.*: 918-920). The gift is in this sense an extension and renewal of the self as a partly Communal Sharing model of relation, but giving or receiving a gift also acts as a constituent of one's status as a person and can therefore create socially and material Authority Ranking hierarchies.

This can even elevate normal persons to a categorically different status such as in the case of the late, saintly monk Thamanya Hsayadaw. His birthday was, as was Stalin's birthday – to make a politically incorrect comparison –, celebrated by means of an extensive presentation and redistribution of gifts (Rozenberg 2004). In generally, such exchanges between Burmese Buddhist monks and the laity are one of material and immaterial asymmetry. A layperson presents a gift to a monk who reciprocates by acknowledging its merit and thus the merit of the person in the gift itself. Additionally, the monk is supposed to renounce the material profit

---

14   For instance, the Russian author Agranovskii recalls the following event that took place during a trip of his orphanage to a confectionary factory involving the person of Stalin and a particularly impressive gift that was on display there: "[I]n a small hall in front of the director's office a huge bust of Stalin, made of chocolate, was exhibited. [...] I don't know who touched the pedestal where the bust was seated. The fact remains that Stalin's bust tottered and fell down, breaking into many large and small pieces. Our teachers were stunned. And the director, when he jumped out of his office and saw what had happened to the chocolate Leader of All the Progressive Humanity, went completely white, then looked at us with suddenly empty eyes [...] and uttered almost without any voice and with only half of his mouth open [...]: 'Eat it!'
    We heard his command, and not just heard it but correctly understood it – and jumped... on the Best Friend and the Teacher of All Soviet Children. The first thing that struck me (and, maybe others as well, but we did not share these thoughts) was that Stalin turned out to be empty inside... I got a huge ear [...]. On another occasion we would have luxuriated on this ear for the whole day... but now we finished Stalin quickly... Nothing was left of Stalin, not a single crumb: the director, we think, even forbade sweeping the floor – which would be an extra blasphemy... – not that there was anything left to sweep; it was Stalin, after all" (Agranovskii in Ssorin-Chaikov 2006).

that the gift provides and would therefore be best off by redistributing his material wealth, although in practice this is more the exception than the norm.

Thamanya Hsayadaw did live up to this expectation of renunciation, even when he received a huge number of presents during this ceremony in honour of his birthday, which could go on for 1 day or more. The large number of gifts and his ability to reciprocate them were a yardstick of his sanctity and in this sense affirmed his living sainthood. At the same time he renounced the gifts by redistributing his material wealth. One portion thereof served to feed those attending the ceremony, while the larger part was redistributed among the other monks in attendance. This redistribution among monks created "a radical rupture" between them. The birthday ceremony materialized the claim that "there is no possible comparison between Thamanya Hsayadaw and the other monks" (*ibid.*: 512). By receiving and giving away material gains Thamanya Hsayadaw doubly reaffirmed his sainthood.

There are many more examples from past and present societies that indicate the way in which persons and things are tangled up in the act of being social: for example, the restitution of gift-souvenirs taken from dead enemies by WW II veterans to their family members (Harrison 2008); the passing on of unopened and unused gifts in Japan (Daniels 2009); literally presenting one's person through the gift of a part of one's own body (Copeman 2005; Simpson 2004); giving to one's spiritual self by extending one's material wealth to one's church and fellow believers (Coleman 2004). This can all be synthesized by the realization that in these situations things and persons, while not necessarily commensurable, are interdependent. In a practical sense, things are of persons and persons are in things. As such, they are tied together in socio-material networks.

While Mauss mostly deals with maintaining relations of people using things, new social ties are also created through this interdependency. This goes back to his original question concerning the origin of the triple obligation to give, receive and give in return. Mauss's answer to this question is twofold. While the essay focuses almost entirely on the reason for reciprocation, a small part concentrates on the reason for giving and receiving. Both are explained rather curtly and culminate in the following statement: "To refuse to give, to fail to invite, just as to refuse to accept, is tantamount to declaring war; it is to reject the bond of alliance and commonality" (Mauss 1990: 17).

It is remarkable that this explanation has not received more direct discussion both from Mauss and his followers (see Corbey 2006; Graeber 2001: 152-155; Sahlins 1972: Chapter 4, 2008), because it states in so many words that a social action – the gift and its reception – is needed in order for there to be a social bond.

It pre-supposes a reality in which it is not the gift that is the total social fact, but the absence of "bonds of alliance and communality", i.e. social networks.[15]

This theme has already been dealt with in the beginning of this chapter, where I discussed how both Hobbes (1651) and Rousseau (1754) found the origin of social morality within communal material interests and how this was reflected in the interactions between European colonizers and indigenous people at the very beginning of contact.

The problem with this concept is that it can result in rather antithetical views on moral and political economies. On one side it can lead to a materialistic, neo-liberal view on human social networks, in which a desire for things – "man's natural propensity to truck, barter and exchange one thing for another" (Smith 2009 [1776]: 19) – is at the heart of their sociality. On the other hand we see the classical Marxist idea of the "material base of society", i.e. the idea that when people "(re-)organize" the production and alienation of things they start to re-organize the ideology that drives their social networks.[16] In essence, both neo-liberal and Marxist theory ground their models of society in a materially-based perspective. However, rather than siding with one of these two overwhelming theoretical traditions, it is more suitable to find out if this reasoning is also present in non-Western social ontologies.

Such a project has already been carried out by David Graeber, whose rational I follow here (2001: specifically Chapter 4, see also 2011). His work is a re-appraisal of Marxist, (neo-)liberal and, more importantly, many non-Western theories of value. It points to the fact that the various forms of "social totalities" – from globalized consumerism to highly ritualized exchange ceremonies in the remotest corners of history and the earth – have in common that they apply "creative energies" arising from the production and exchange of things to "produce people." This need for creating social relations will be discussed more in-depth in Chapter 7 in the context of the "political economy of life" of late pre-contact Hispaniola. Here, communities and their leaders were always looking to draw in new political allies into their sphere of influence in order to compete with others and maintain their own viability (Santos-Granero 2009b).

---

15   This is not to say that war or interpersonal conflict is not intimately linked to social interaction. As Mauss points out here and in other places (Corbey 2006), society is composed of both contracts and conflicts. This is especially true for indigenous Lowland South America where inter-village exchange and raiding networks are often one and the same (Lévi-Strauss 1943). Social interactions can be antagonistic relations (Mol 2007). Direct violent, conflict, whether physical or not, is a form of interaction that precludes all other types of social relations. You cannot solicit gifts while smashing your exchange partners' head. The result hereof is that conflict (inter-personal violence, war, even verbal arguments) and contract (exchange, cooperation, agreements) alternate.

16   The following excerpt from the German Ideology written by Marx and Engels, is a mode-of-production-flavoured echo of Rousseau's idea on the emergence of the social contract: "By producing their means of subsistence men are indirectly producing their actual material life. [...] This production only makes its appearance with the increase of population. In its turn this presupposes the interaction of individuals with one another. The form of this intercourse is again determined by production" (Marx and Engels 1970 [1845-1846]: 42).

The idea of "production of people" starts from the absence of relations. As humans are inherently social, not engaging in social interaction denies their humanity. The opposite is true, as well. Nevertheless, it is precarious to assume that other human beings are inherently sociable. Thus, if you wish to "create a person", it is best to first socialize him or her. Gifts are an excellent way to do this – a concept also found in Lowland South America (Santos-Granero 2007; Vaughn Howard 2001). Obviously, certain things are more suitable than others when creating new social ties, because certain things are more broadly valued (see Chapter 8). What is valued and what is not depends upon local norms (Bourdieu 1984).

This becomes clearer when these relations are being created in encounters between socio-cultural others (Thomas 1991). On the other hand, ethnographic and socio-cognitive case studies suggest that humans have quite a capacity to appreciate – not necessarily agree with – the value of each other's (material) cultures. If value systems roughly align across the cultures involved it is only normal for social networks to evolve from material exchanges, a situation Gosden (2004) calls "middle ground". From this common ground, mutual understanding may follow. As Columbus remarks during his visit to an indigenous village on the north coast of Hispaniola:

> "Some ran here, others ran there to bring us the bread made of yams, which they call ajes, very white and good, and they brought water in gourds and terra-cotta jugs made like those of Castile, and they gave all they had and knew what the Admiral wanted, and they did it all with such an open heart and with such joy that it was a wonder to behold. 'Let no one say,' declares the Admiral, 'that what they gave was worth little and therefore they gave generously, because those who gave pieces of gold did so as generously as those who gave a gourd of water. Besides it is easy, 'continues the Admiral, 'to tell when one gives something with his heart, truly wishing to give" (Navarette 1922: 115, translation from Beckwith 1990.[17]).

This vivid, if perhaps somewhat romantic, account reaffirms that cultural and linguistic barriers are easily negotiated in socio-material networks (see also the above citation from the Diary of Columbus on his interactions with Guacanagarí). However, this type of inter-cultural connectivity was only found in the earliest period of contact in the Greater Antilles. Socio-material ties ultimately proved to be too weak to counter the strong prejudices and lust for gold expressed by the Spaniards (Keehnen 2011; Valcárcel Rojas 2012). In the Caribbean this process resulted in things, which were once freely given or exchanged (Communal Sharing

---

17   "[L]os unos corrían de acá y los otros de alía a nos traer pan, que hacen de ñames, aquellos llaman ajes, que es muy blanco y bueno, y nos traían aguas en calabazas y en cantaros de barro de la hechura de los de Castilla, y nos traían cuanto en el mundo tenían y sabían que el Almirante quería, y todo con un corazón tan largo y tan contento que era maravilla; y no se diga que por lo que daban valía poco por eso lo daban líberamente, dice el Almirante, porque lo mismo hacían, y tan liberalmente, los que daban pedazos de oro como los que daban la calabaza del agua y fácil cosa es de conocer (dice el Almirante) cuando seda una cosa con muy deseoso corazón de dar"
(de Navarete 1922: 115)

or Equality Matching), that had to be paid as tribute (Authority Ranking and Market Pricing). These tribute systems, such as the *encomiendas* established in Hispaniola and other parts of the Spanish American empire, were also socio-material in nature. An *encomendero* would task a *cacique* or other indigenous leader with gathering a certain amount of gold or other goods from his people. If unsuccessful he would face (corporeal) punishment. Yet such an unbalanced Authority Ranking-based relation ultimately only brought death or slavery to indigenous peoples and falling productivity to the *encomenderos* (Valcárcel Rojas 2012). The latter is a negative example in which the balance of "creative energies" was hugely distorted, as so often occurred in colonial or imperial enterprises (Graeber 2011). Nevertheless, in general, colonial socio-material networks were evolutionary stable, since in many cases they were and are still able to bring about mutual profit.

In fact, from a networked cost-benefit analysis, this would be the most logical outcome, since one tie always connects two nodes. In other words, where one person is socialized with a gift, so, from the other's perspective, is the donor. Naturally people also create new connections in material networks when they interact (Kandler and Laland 2009; Levinson 2006; Padgett and Powell 2012; Steele, *et al.* 2010). Various objects and technologies will be connected for the first time, out of which increasingly complex artefact forms, technologies and other material practices may arise – e.g. "terra-cotta jugs made like those of Castile", mantles and shoes as a new addition to the regalia of Antillean *caciques*, indigenous valuables at courts across Europe, and, later, indigenous tobacco creating a wide range of smoker's paraphernalia, potatoes that partly powered the Industrial revolution, *etc.* (Crosby 2003). Socio-material interdependencies were thus also the cause for the production of new ties between things.

Kula: from gift relations to socio-material network

Maussian theories of gift exchange focus on dyadic relations, on a pair of persons and their things. One may wonder if this perspective that emphasizes reciprocal relations between a pair of individuals is compatible with a network perspective, which tries to take account of a whole system of such relations? To answer this I will present a brief case-study based on the Melanesian *kula*, to show that gift relations between persons can quickly grow into a network of persons, especially when material culture is involved.[18] The *kula* is a set of elaborate social practices, centred on the exchange of *vaygu'a*, or "valuables" (e.g. Campbell 2002; Leach and Leach 1983; Malinowski 1922; Munn 1986; Weiner 1992). This exchange phenomenon rose to fame thanks to Bronisław Malinowski (1922), the first anthropologist to develop a clear methodology for anthropological fieldwork as a participant observer (Sykes 2005: 46). During fieldwork in the Trobriand Islands, and attempting to describe Trobriand society as a whole, Malinowski became fascinated by this exchange.

---

18 These exchanges from a graph theoretical perspective will not be discussed here as this issue has already been dealt with extensively by Hage and Harary (1991).

In turn archaeologists examining past exchange systems have often been caught by the exchanges Malinowski describes. In Caribbean archaeology and beyond it is therefore a beloved, but sometimes misconstrued (Spriggs 2008), icon, as well as an evocative analogue for other prehistoric exchange systems (e.g. Knippenberg 2007; Renfrew 1986; Spielmann 2002; Tilley 1996; Watters 1997). This work also adds to this *kula* analogy obsession, but only moderately so. I do not claim that direct analogies between twentieth-century island Melanesia and the pre-colonial Caribbean are in order, but I hold the view that this proto-typical exchange practice does clearly illustrate the interdependencies between social and material networks.

Kula valuables come in two types: necklaces of red shell, called *soulava*, and white shell bracelets, called *mwali*, which are exchanged for one another along *keda* or "paths". This exchange is highly ceremonial, involving magic spells and strict taboos.[19] Sea travel is the only way to reach exchange partners in other regions. Because inter-island travel is too dangerous and costly for a man to do on his own, *kula* expeditions are organized in which a group of men sets out to exchange *kula* valuables with their trade partners on the nearest neighbouring island. During the 1980s the system was still present in approximately thirty communities that stretch out across island Melanesian over an area known as the Massim, sometimes called the Kula ring (Leach and Leach 1983). It is talked about as if it was a game and men exchanging *kula* are referred to as players. Just like excelling in certain sports increases one's social standing, the success of *kula* players influences their and their clan's socio-political status (Liep 1991; Munn 1986).

A *kula* exchange or *wasi* begins when A gives to a desired exchange partner B a *vaga*, an opening gift. This is done with the idea in mind that when B gets his hand on either a desirable *soulava* or *mwali* A will receive this as a *yotile*, a return gift. If too much time passes between the *vaga* of A and the *yotile* of B, B is expected to give a *basi*, a smaller bracelet or necklace, as intermediary gift. This in turn obliges A to return the *basi*, with a *basi* of his own. In the case that B has multiple exchange partners and has a *kula* valuable that is a particularly fine specimen, which is desired by more than one exchange partner, these partners have the option to give *pokala* or *kaributu*, non-*kula* gifts (of which the stone axe *kaributu* is the most valued) These are meant to persuade the exchange partner into exchanging his *kula* valuable. When B finally presents the closing gift to A that will balance the equation. This is called the *kudu* (Malinowski 1922: 98-99). It should be clear that all of these exchanges are social interactions in which the Equality Matching relational model dominates – It does indeed matter what is exchanged, between who, when and how much, but there is no absolute exchange ratio.

---

19   The *kula* valuables are meant to be displayed by women, but their exchange is essentially a male practice (Weiner 1990).

Fiske (1991: 16-17) also references the exchange of *kula* valuables as a proto-typical model of balanced exchange separate of formal economic ratios and rationality.[20] However, aside from *kula* exchange, Malinowski (1922: 96, 176-192), also reported the existence of extensive barter trading or *gimwali*. According to Malinowksi there were huge differences between *gimwali* and *wasi*. While one was Market Pricing barter, the latter was a highly ceremonial activity and signified a precarious moment in the social life of an individual and group in which things could easily fall either way.[21] Interestingly enough *gimwali* would still go on in tandem with *wasi* exchanges, often with the same group of trading partners. However, in the *kula* ring the models of relations belonged to separate "spheres of exchange". This means that, in theory, one exchange networks is completely independent of another, because value conversion between the two spheres of exchange is impossible (Sillitoe 2006).

Although it is a highly important aspect of social life and can be the main model through which relations are framed, it would be highly impractical if Equality Matching was the only model of relation. If a *kula* exchange goes wrong fortunes are lost, but it is always possible to start over again. Yet, if an expedition would run out of supplies, it would be unthinkable to exchange *soulava* or *mwali* directly for *taro* or other foodstuffs. That is why these things can be bartered for outside of the Equality Matching model of relations of highly ceremonial and precarious gift giving between individuals who are competitors that must try to have a balanced, non-ratio relation. In addition, the ingredients necessary for making new *mwali or soulava* often have to be bartered or, nowadays, paid for with non-Kula ring communities (Campbell 2002). Market pricing *gimwali* and Equality Matching *wasi* are linked.

A successful player is due considerable respect in his own community or clan, this does not imply he is a categorically differently ranked person in communal life. Many of these communal relations are built on various types of exchanges that are more Authority Ranking than Equality Matching or Market Pricing. Communal Authority Ranking is built on social contracts with the wider kin network of a person, especially affinal relations. Every year during the yam harvest men are obliged to present part of their harvest to their affinal kin. This harvest is housed and displayed in personally owned yam houses, built and filled by one's affinal kin, especially the son-in-law. At the same time this yam house will be emptied by transferring one's yams to the yam house of one's affinal kin on the side of the

---

20 In fact, the characterization of the *kula* as an Equality Matching model of relations – avant la lettre – had been one of Bronisław Malinowski's main motives (Wilk and Cligget 2007). If 'primitive economics' were at all covered by the economic theory of the early 20th century it followed the neoclassical tradition set out by Adam Smith 150 years earlier (Smith 1776). In this view non-western, non-market economies were considered as a precursor to a capitalist monetary economy and were believed to rely solely on barter in order to see to their wants and needs (e.g. Bücher 1893). Unhappy with the way in which the practice of exchange in non-market societies was approached in *Argonauts of the Western Pacific* Malinowski (1922) set out to disprove neo-economic theories of exchange.

21 *Wasi* and other type of Equality Matching exchanges are often similar. They transcend the everyday practice of give and take between humans and distil it into a focal point – a node – of relations that are 'socio-cosmic' rather than economic (Bourdieu 1997; Dumont 1970).

spouse. This obligation sometimes continues even beyond the death of the spouse. This is not a matter of an exact Market Pricing tribute, one yam for you, three for me. Neither is it framed in Equality Matching terms. Rather it simply is a matter of showcasing who owes allegiance to whom, i.e. it ranks persons and even whole clans on an ordinal scale. Ultimately, stock of yams in Massim villages displays the Authority Ranking of extended kin and, by extension, the Authority Ranking relations in the community itself. Outside of the community or clan, these publicly displayed Authority Ranking networks can then be used in displays of generosity to others – such Communal Sharing models of relation always have a potential for becoming Authority Ranking models of relation, such as in the case of the American Northwest coast *potlatch* (Mauss 1990; Rosman and Rubel 1986), or as a base to acquire *vaygu'a* in order to enter into Equality Matching *wasi* exchanges. These relations then garner social standing or "fame" for the whole of the island community, providing an alternative inter-communal Authority Ranking (Damon 2002; Munn 1986).

The same can be said when referring to the *kula* valuables themselves. Annette Weiner (1992) has highlighted this central role of the most valued *mwali* armband and *soulava* necklaces in the Trobriands. During her fieldwork on women valuables she established that many social relations of Kula playing communities were structured around keeping a certain highly valued *mwali* or *soulava* out of exchange. Instead of focusing on social relations as the shaping mechanism of individual and communal identity, her research concentrated on things excluded from the exchange structure. In a cross-cultural review of similar practices, she postulated that such things are of a nature so inalienable that to exchange or otherwise lose them would cause a change in society that would be extremely detrimental to individual and communal identity. Nevertheless, it is difficult to keep a *vaygu'a* out of the hands of its "suitors."[22]

Kula is a very competitive game played for the highest political stakes. Being a successful player means transcending one's kinship group and connecting oneself with an elite group of men (Munn 1986: 71). Not exchanging *soulava* or *mwali* means not being able to participate fully in the world of inter-communal politics. In addition there is the tug of exchanges that are external to the *kula*. Promising a *kula* valuable to a partner is a way of keeping it safe from being exchanged in a non-*kula* exchange. When one man has many *keda*, or *kula* paths, this offers a way of forestalling the forever ongoing exchange by manipulating them in such a fashion that the choice of who is going to receive what can be postponed and postponed again (Weiner 1992: 140). Some very successful players can put off exchanging the most esteemed *soulava* and *mwali* for the duration of a generation,

---

22 The paradox here lies in the fact that, because these inalienable possessions are the most potent force in the effort to prevent such things from happening, they at the same time represent the threat. Herein lays, according to Weiner, the paradoxical function of the exchange of things: to keep inalienable things out of exchange through the gift of some other object. A good example of this keeping-while-giving are the *basi* gifts consisting of minor *kula* valuables to avoid the alienation of a more precious *mwali* or *soulava* (Malinowski 1922: 98-99).

up to 2 decades. Instead of the threat of the loss of a valuable, the owner risks the danger of *keda* withering and harmful sorcery by covetous or jealous individuals.

In Weiner's original analysis, "keeping-while-giving" practices are underlain by the incest taboo. Be that as it may, to my mind her work shows first and foremost that it is not only persons that are in the middle of social networks. The "fame" of *kula* players and communities is for a great deal dependent on the "fame" of the object itself (Damon 2002; Munn 1986; Weiner 1987). This fame of the *kula* valuable is contained in a narrative of why, when, where and between whom it was exchanged. Therefore, the value of an individual *mwali* or *soulava* is constructed through and during its circulation: if it is held by renowned *kula* players the object's value would have increased accordingly – something Malinowski already remarked upon (Malinowski 1922: 511). Thus, in order to know the value of a *mwali* or *soulava* the players must know the exact itinerary of the *kula* path the object had travelled on and the "fame" of all its individual keepers many of whom a player will never have met, because they had already passed away or lived beyond his range of mobility. For instance, for the documented case of the *mwali* Nonowan the recorded history runs between 1938 and 1976. It comprises a list of twenty-four exchange partners, divided among fourteen communities dispersed over a distance of 300 km (Damon 1980). Advanced *kula* players, who would be partaking in several *kula* paths, needed great skill in tracking multiple networks of things and people in order to be successful and gain personal "fame".

What this aspect of "fame" in the *Kula* ring shows is that the centrepiece of this exchange system, the *mwali* and *soulava*, are socio-material nodes. They are, of course, also things on their own: beautiful ornaments fabricated from local and exotic materials. Yet their most important quality arises from their participation in specific social networks: "tournaments of value" in which individuals and their communities play for the highest stake (Appadurai 1986: 21). Their success was dependent on the keeping and giving of famous *mwali* and *soulava*, which was again based on the fame of its previous keepers, *etc*. The community of players were part of larger communal and inter-island social networks. Nonetheless their "fame" and their community's standing in these networks was for a great deal based on their access to and understanding of the material network-part of the *kula* "tournament of value". In other words, *kula* is not just a type of social network or a collection of (in)alienable valuables (Malinowski 1922; Weiner 1990), it was an interdependent socio-material network.

The *kula* exchange has been studied from a graph theoretical approach (Hage and Harary 1991). However, as can be expected, this analysis has concentrated on how humans have structured the *kula* network. The mini-*kula* exchange model, featuring only 4 players and 2 valuables, in Figure 4.1 is more in line with analyses such as those of Weiner that focus on how the objects themselves have a large impact on the overall structure. The figure depicts a *soulava* A and a *mwali* B that increase in "fame" (size of the node) as they travels along their path, thereby also increasing the fame of its keepers (1-4). These, in turn, increase the "fame" of the valuable. Interactions of past phases are indicated by decreasingly smaller ties. Note that this is a situation in which every keeper remembers all past exchanges of

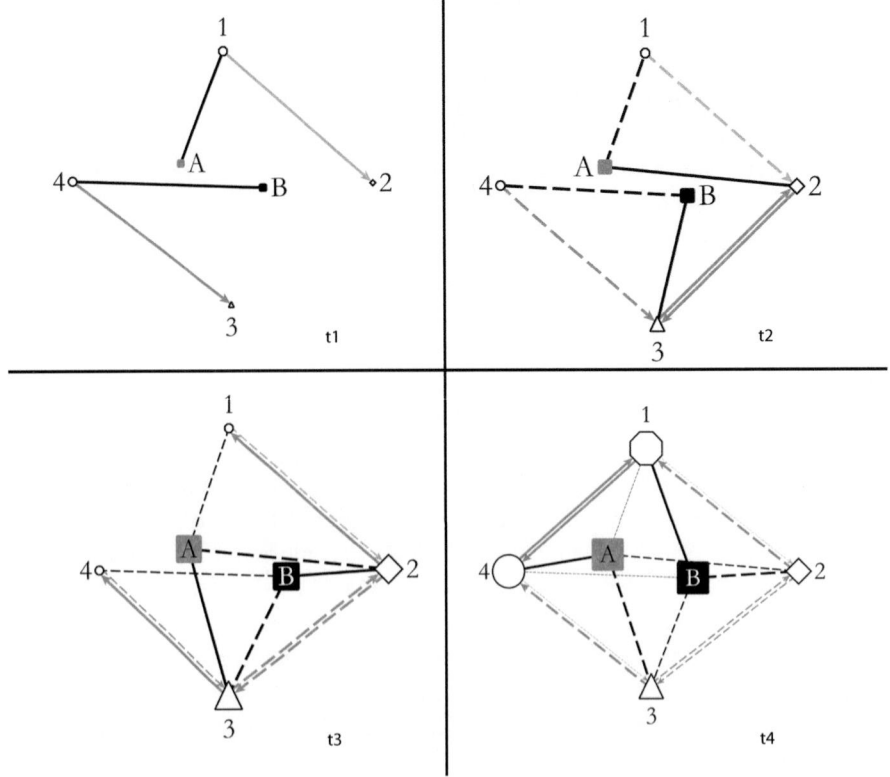

Figure 4.1: One cycle of the kula *as socio-material network The size of the* soulava *A and a mwali B nodes and the "keeper" nodes 1 to 4 indicates the "fame" of the object and person respectively. Because they are interdependent they reciprocally increase each other's fames. In this model past exchanges are remembered (indicated by decreasingly smaller ties). This network memory prompts quite a high rate of inflation (incremental node growth).*

A and B, which prompts quite a high rate of inflation (incremental node growth). Additionally, it should be clear that the "fame" of node A is not only linked to its keepers, but through them also to B and vice versa. Aside from showing the interdependency of *kula* players and valuables, this model also makes clear how easy it is to progress from the Maussian relation of give and take between two persons to a wider socio-material network.

Object perspectivism and socio-material interdependency

What about the confluences between social and material networks in Amerindian theories of culture and society? To answer that question we should re-visit Viveiros de Castro's (1998) model of perspectivism. As Viveiros de Castro pointed out in a further refinement of his model, the subjectivity of any being is not a fundamental given. Rather it is influenced and activated through the perspective of and interactions with others. Here, the state of being a subject, is a quality of an individual that is interdependent with the perspective and agency of other subjects. One way in which this interdependency is manifested is in the widespread Amerindian perspectivist concept of what, for lack of a better term, may be called a "life-force". This life-force rests in human but also bodies of other types of subjects (Århem 1996; Santos-Granero 2009b; Vaughn Howard 2001). It is an integral part of a person but is not contained to a physical body and can "leak" into peoples, places or things with which a subject interacts with. A person's things are conceived of as being infused with a specific person's life-force and thus the personal qualities of its owner. For example, the passing on of a thing from a peaceable person to another is expected to effectuate a pro-social tendency in the recipient (Vaughn Howard 2001). The specific social state of a person is thus directly dependent upon whom he or she interacts with.

This concept of life-force is also closely examined in Oliver's 2009 publication on socio-political alliances and *cemís*. *Cemís* have traditionally been perceived as being a class of objects, specifically three pointed artefacts (de Hostos 1923; Rouse 1992). He shows how persons of great import, both human and other than human beings, were connected through *cemí* exchange and idolatry. In this sense their exchange is a social and material network in which a particular class of things has a central position, such as the *kula* exchange. However, Oliver (2009: 59-60) suggests that *cemí* was (also) a "numinous force", a potency contained in both human and other than human beings that could have been transferred between them.[23] In this sense, there seems to be some local base for Maussian theories of the inspired gift.

In the context of the perspectivism model peoples and things have another type of interdependency, too. While the original model of perspectivism only incorporated humans, animals and spirits as subjects, it has recently been extended to also include the Amerindian theory that objects can also be (multi-) perspectivist subjects. In *The Occult Life of Things*, Santos-Granero (2009a, editor) and other Lowland South American ethnographers present examples of the shifting subjective states of objects in Amerindian ontologies. Their work implies that objects can also change perspectives and subjective states – i.e. see themselves as and often outwardly become more human. Early historic descriptions suggest that the objects humans used to engage with other than human beings were more than ritual imagery or paraphernalia or even carriers of personhood: they were powerful subjects in their own right. This is clearly represented in the discussions on individual *cemís* in the work of Pané, such as below:

> *"This* zemi *Guabancex was in the country of a great cacique, one of the principal caciques, whose name was Aumatex [...] and they say that there are two others in her company; one is a herald, and the other a gatherer and governor of the waters.*

---

23 The Greater Antillean, Arawakan *cemí* can be traced back to a similar term in Lokono (True Arawak). Here *seme* or *semehi* denotes "the good spirits that help the medicine man" and a shaman or curer is known as *sémi-či* . *Seme* also means "sweetness" in Lokono, however (de Goeje 2009 [1929]: 200). Oliver connects these two meanings and re-interprets *cemí* as being a spiritual quality. Following this, what archaeologists call 'cemís' are actually the things that are capable of possessing *cemí*, by that quality becoming a type of "idols" or "fetishes" (Oliver 2009).

And they say when Guabancex grows angry, she moves the wind and water and tears down the houses and uproots the trees. They say this zemi *is a woman and made of stones from that country"* (Pané 1999 [1571]: 30).

In an academic European frame of mind, a spirit who is also a woman made of stones is a contradiction of states and therefore must ultimately denote a metaphoric, allegoric or other type of symbolic relation. Yet in a multi-perspectivist ontology there is not necessarily a contradiction of states and it is possible to literally be a stone-woman-spirit. If we accept this as a reality and not as a *"truc indigène"*, as Lévi-Strauss would call it, this entails that the spirit in the gift or the socio-materiality of relations has an added dimension in the sense that one could not only interact through but also with material culture.

Pané's account has several instances describing such socio-material relations between humans and spirit-things, discussed in great detail in Oliver's 2009 book. These fragmentary examples of human and object relations affirm that where the agency of things is a logical abduction in our society (Gell 1998), from an indigenous Antillean perspective (some) objects literally could be subjects. In this capacity they would have had even more of a formalizing role in the interpersonal and intercommunal networks of humans than the things in the ethnographic examples on gift giving, as discussed above. What is more, these stories indicate that *cemís* even regularly dominated humans. For example, a *cemí*, called Baibramá, "brought diseases to those who had made that *zemi*, because they had not taken him *yuca* to eat" (p. 27).

On the other hand, even if objects sometimes lorded over humans, further exploration of their status as subjects shows they were actually quite dependent on humans. In Lowland South America the subjectivity of material objects will be activated by coming into contact with humans. In fact, in many of the Lowland South American cases that are discussed in *The Occult Life of Things* objects cannot reach full agentive potential without their intervention. Only when activated by a human subject, do material objects become semi-autonomous agents taking their own decisions and exerting influence over humans. This story from the Warao provides an example of how this happens and the sometimes undesirable effects it can cause to human beings:

"Once a young man went along the river all alone, carrying a bow and arrow in his hands. Without realizing it the young man was heading toward Skull. On and on he went until he came to a basket lying there on the ground. The young man touched the basket with his arrow and the basket ran up to him and hugged him around his neck. As it hugged him, it said it would be easy to cut his throat. The young man said, 'Don't cut my throat. Let's be partners. We can talk and I will go with you.' So with Partner went Skull, hanging onto his neck" (Wilbert 1970: 170).

Subsequently, the young man reluctantly hunts animals for the basket for some time, until he deliberately misses his target and has to search for the arrow. He then takes this opportunity to run away and hide from the basket. The basket tries to follow and kill him, but ends up falling in the river and transforms into a *caribe*, a carnivorous fish. The interchange of the subjective state of the Skull, the basket, and Partner, the man, is straightforward in this example: the young man touched the basket by which it changed from an object into a spirit-thing. This then literally created a socio-material tie between the young man and the basket. The basket even becomes the dominant subject by enforcing its will by means of physical threats. Yet when the contact between the human and the thing came to an end, the basket was literally lost, falling into the river and loosing (some of) its potential to inflict harm.

This idea that objects become powerful subjects through mediation of a human being can also be found in the invaluable account delivered by Fray Ramon Pané (1999 [1571]: 25-26). It includes a small excerpt on how the subjective state of a "natural" feature can be activated through encounters with humans and how its life-force can be further enhanced by trans-specific beings such as the shaman-like *behiques*:

> "*The ones of wood are made in this way: when someone is walking along and he says he sees a tree that is moving its roots, the man very fearfully stops and asks who it is. And it answers him: 'Summon me a* behique, *and he will tell you who I am!' And when that man goes to the aforesaid physician, he tells him what he has seen. And the sorcerer or wizard runs at once to see the tree of which the other man has told him; he sits next to it and prepares* cohoba [*a hallucinogenic mixture of the* Anadenanthera peregrina *plant and chalk] for it [...].*
>
> *Once the* cohoba *is made, then he stands up and tells it all his titles, as if they were those of a great lord, and he asks it: 'Tell me who you are, and what you are doing here, and what you wish from me, and why you have had me summoned. Tell me if you want to be cut down or if you want to come with me, and how you want to be carried, for I will build you a house with land.' Then the tree or* zemi, *turned into an idol or devil, answers [the behique], telling him the manner in which he wants it to be done. And he cuts it and fashions it in the manner he has been ordered; he constructs its house with land, and many times during the year he prepares* cohoba *for it*" (Pané 1999 [1571]: 25-26).

Ties between persons and things can lie at the root of personal transformations, but on a societal level Amerindian life can also be shaped by (before-time) acquisition of material culture. Aside from socio-material ties based on gift exchange and the other social relations that were already discussed extensively above, there is also a higher level of interdependency between what it entails to be (culturally) human and the possession of things. Coming into possession of (material) culture is at the root of many South American Lowland narratives on the origins of society. Distinctively human things, such as tools, fire, ornaments, and dances, have often been introduced by "culture heroes" who acquired the objects themselves or the knowledge to make them from other than human beings. This can occur either through theft or as part of gifts from non-human beings in before-time (e.g. Lévi-Strauss 1969: 66-78). Thus, primordial humans have only become the "true" humans of the present day because they have acquired certain material cultural traits.

Among the Warao, the so-called *Haburi cycle* is chief among such origin narratives (Wilbert 1970: 279-310; 1993: Chapter 1). In it the protagonist Haburi, or sometimes the Haburi brothers, travel across a before-time version of the Orinoco Delta and its neighbouring regions. Along the way he interacts with a variety of animals and spirit beings. Through them he gains key knowledge on societal and material culture practices, some of which shape the daily life of the Warao to this day – e.g. bow and arrow hunting, canoe travel and the acquisition of stone tools and ornaments. For Hispaniola, Pané's document describes a comparable journey in which the culture hero Guahayona travels around a before-time version of the Antillean archipelago in search of women (Pané 1999 [1571]: 5-12). During his travels he encounters several other than human beings, among which the aquatic spirit-woman Guabonito, who presents him with *guanines* and *cibas*, precious metal and valued stones that adorned the *cacique* and other important personages (Oliver 2000). The latter narrative elements also have a noteworthy analogue in a Lokono origin story that describes a human who became the first shaman when he received sacred rattle stones from a water-spirit (Boomert 2000). Through such narratives from Lowland South America and the Caribbean, it is possible to see how universal socio-material dependencies are framed within local ontologies.[24]

A Maussian and Amerindian ontological framework

By now it has become clear that matter that ties and ties that matter are inextricably, but not necessarily inexplicably related. Often things and persons come together to such an extent that they seem to be more than two sides of the same coin; they are part of interdependent socio-material relations and networks. This is not a new insight. In the introduction to this chapter it was discussed how in some Enlightenment views, such as those by Thomas Hobbes (1929 [1651]) and Jean-Jacques Rousseau (e.g 2012 [1754]), the origins of society and material culture are inherently linked. This kind of thinking culminated in a specifically European intellectual tradition that focused on how owning and alienating material goods was one of the constituents of society, as can be read in influential works on economy, ideology and society by thinkers such as Karl Marx and Adam Smith (Graeber 2001, 2011a; e.g. Marx 1893; Marx and Engels 1970 [1845-1846]; Smith 2009 [1776]; Weiner 1992).

Obviously, thinking about the material roots of human social networks has progressed far beyond these earlier theories, not the least in archaeology and other material culture studies. One example hereof were concepts and theories resulting from the "material cultural turn" (Hicks 2010). Aside from this there are also interesting new developments in cognitive archaeology and (palaeo)anthropology – in particular how the "social brain" has developed as a "distributed mind" that can extend from the human body into the realm of things – providing a deep historical perspective on the way humans utilize material culture to build their

---

24 For further information on this subject I recommend the index and the relevant volumes on Guyanese and Orinoquoid peoples in the series "Folk Literature of South American Indians", published by the Latin American Centre of UCLA and edited by Johannes Wilbert, as a starting point.

social networks (Coward 2010; Dunbar, *et al.* 2010b; Malafouris 2010). Recent "fragmentation theories" that stress the links between "dividual" personhood and "fragmentation" of things propose a similar line of thinking (Chapman and Gaydarska 2007; Oliver 2009). Furthermore, in his book *the Archaeology of Interaction*, Carl Knappett (2011) has also put forward an intuitively appealing, archaeological network approach that seeks to integrate material culture theories with (social) network perspectives. These contributions seek to bridge in their own way the interfaces between social and material fields and offer good starting points for archaeology as a more emphatically social and material (network) discipline.

In the present chapter I have presented an alternative, but possibly complimentary view of this issue, based on (post-)Maussian theory and Amerindian perspectivism. Hereby I did not mean to imply that transposing the total social material facts of gift-giving is an all-purpose solution. Rather, theories of the gift provide one pathway in order to understand the dialectic or even cyclical relations between things and persons, as was exemplified by the discussion of fame in the *Kula* ring. This may result in a position that is less materially focused than several other current theories, but it stresses the importance of things as nodal points of human social life.

While things and people have an existence outside each other's sphere of influence, when they come together a different sort of relation emerges from their combined dynamics. By themselves such relations have a high impact on the identities of persons and things and, by extension, on the history of societies and (material) cultures. What is more, because they consist of objects that were part of social relations between humans in the past, the networks we encounter in archaeology will always be socio-material interdepends. As a result, based on archaeological data, the only social networks we can meaningfully abstract, analyse, interpret and discuss are those that have co-evolved as socio-material networks.

With regards to Caribbean pre-colonial networks the key is, in my opinion, to view such co-referential socio-material ties in the light of both Maussian person-thing relations and a broadly shared Amerindian ontology that Viveiros de Castro (1998) tried to capture by means of the "perspectivism" model. As such it is noteworthy that, as far as it is possible to understand this based on ethnographic studies, humans and things *are* interdependent subjects from an Amerindian perspective. Humans and specific items of material culture can literally change, enhance or otherwise affect each other's status as subjects. Furthermore, (human) culture is seen as partly resulting from the primordial and present-day appropriation of material objects. In other words, it seems that Amerindian perspectives align well with the basic premises of socio-material interdependency.

In the Antilles pre-colonial personhood and society may literally have been perceived as socio-materially interdependent. In sum, we can identify at least three types of interdependencies: (1) a "Maussian" type based on the exchange of "life-forces" and the shaping influence of gifts on personhoods, (2) connected to (1) is a "perspectivist" type based on the idea that the perspectival states of others can be influenced through interaction, something which many objects need to become subjects, and (3) a local variation on the "Hobbesian-Rousseauean" type of interdependency discussed at the beginning of this chapter, based on the idea that "having society" entails possession of (material) culture.

Interestingly, numerous romantics have contrasted a more detached and often spiritual indigenous valuation of material culture with the rampant materialism of European societies, painting a picture of an Amerindian pastoral society wholly unperturbed by the "materiality of things" (e.g. Bond 2006; de las Casas 1992 [1542]; de Montaigne 1958 [1580]; Michener 1989; Rousseau 2012 [1754]; Torres Santiago 2009). Although it has a specific Amerindian character, the importance of socio-material interdependency in the constitution of personhood, subjectivity and society goes against this widespread supposition that Amerindians are anti-materialists.

Obviously, it is by and large impossible to re-discover and understand specific individual biographies or past subjective statuses of objects from the archaeological record. Nevertheless, the following chapters will show that, rather than being of ephemeral importance, socio-material interdependencies were highly important for creating the patterns of homogeneity and diversity that characterize the pre-colonial Caribbean.

Chapter 5

A Heart of Stone: Lithic Networks from 3200 BC to AD 400

No one could ever find a stone
that from splendour of sun or inner light
had such power or stood out so bright.

Excerpt from Dante Alighieri's *the Stone Beloved* (Kline 2008)

Following through with the main themes of this work, patterns of homogeneity and diversity and the socio-material networks of the Caribbean, this chapter will examine how lithic production and distribution is informative of the early socio-cultural history of the region, in particular that of the "Archaic"-Saladoid-Huecoid Interface period.[1] This will be done by discussing continuity and changes in the production and distribution of stone material sources endogenous to the Northeastern Caribbean from the period 3200 BC-AD 400 (Figure 5.1). With regard to a number of these materials a precise *chaîne operatoire* can be reconstructed presenting us with an insight into their production and (down-the-line) exchange (Cody 1990; Crock 2000; Knippenberg 2007; Murphy, *et al.* 2000; Watters and Scaglion 1994).

These lithic networks will be traced over a time-span of 3600 years, divided into five segments: Period A (3200-2000 BC), Period B (2000-800 BC), Period C (800-200 BC), Period D (AD 200 BC-100), and Period E (AD 100-400). The initial occupation of the islands in this study is dated to *c*.3200 BC at sites such as,

---

1   Corinne Hofman, Sebastiaan Knippenberg, Reniel Rodríguez Ramos and I collaborated on the case-study presented here and of which the network explorative and interpretational part is further dealt with. Working from an incipient idea developed by Hofman several years earlier, we focused on the role of lithic exchange – specifically in intercommunity gatherings such as feasts – with reference to the evolving social networks of this period. Knippenberg and Rodríguez Ramos undertook the lithic analyses and identifications that lie at the basis of the distribution networks. All credit for this should go to them, and any mistakes or generalizations made here are entirely my own. Hofman and I collected other relevant (site) data, such as the C-14 database (assisted by Anne van Duijvenbode), site classification and ceramic stylistic affiliation. The network data was explored by the present author and presented by Corinne Hofman as a paper at the 24th Congress of the International Association for Caribbean Archaeology in Martinique (Summer 2011). It is currently in preparation for a publication called *Islanders on the Move* (University of Alabama Press, edited by Corinne L. Hofman).

for instance, Jolly Beach I (Antigua) and Angostura (Puerto Rico), indeed – several hundred years later than the islands located beyond the western and southern extremes of the study region for example Hispaniola and Trinidad – which evolved into a local set of material culture practices during Period B. Period C witnessed an important shift: communities that had long been present in the Caribbean were presented either with (groups of) new settlers or with technical, cultural and social changes that must have taken place in a relatively small window of time. At the conclusion of period D permanent habitation sites, ceramics and subsistence practices partially based on garden farming had become the norm. These developments continued throughout and beyond period E. By that time the typical pre-period C a-ceramic, smaller temporary places of habitation or activity had been largely phased out and became a less ubiquitous feature of indigenous culture and society – although such sites never ceased to exist throughout the pre-colonial period and even up till today.

Figure 5.1: Local stone of the Northeastern Caribbean. A: Long Island Flint Blade and Flake (Photograph courtesy of Menno L.P. Hoogland). B: Puerto Rican serpentinite in the shape of a bird of prey amulet (Photograph courtesy of Reniel Rodríguez Ramos); St. Martin Greenstone axe, note that the original hue would have been a far more muddier green, but the material has weathered over time (Photograph courtesy of Sebastiaan Knippenberg); Carnelian beads, half-fabricates and raw material (Photograph courtesy of Arie Boomert).

This marks these periods out as being of formative importance for later Caribbean cultures and societies, as discussed at greater length in Chapter 2. Within this time frame, as I will outline below, the period between 800 BC and AD 400 sees the largest quantity of change in the networks under study. Although opinions differ on when, how and whence these changes were initiated, it is clear that around the start of the first millennium the previous ways of life led by small, mobile groups had been replaced by a full-fledged form of village society and a uniquely Caribbean material cultural repertoire. However, these revolutions did not occur as discrete events but are linked processes. Here, a series of network models will serve to explore how these overarching histories of societal and culture change are dialectically related to developments within interaction networks based on the production and distribution of stone raw materials and finished objects.

The network explorations will be contrasted to a hypothetical network model based on a more traditional view of this period focusing on migrations of peoples who only had limited interactions with each other, as forwarded in works by Rouse (e.g. 1986, 1992). Based on the rapid diffusion of Saladoid ceramics and (absence of) mixing of material culture styles, he suggested that during Period C and D culturally superior migrants moved in to the Northeastern Caribbean, supplanting the original inhabitants. It is their societal and material cultural practices that were believed to be at the base of the Early and Late Ceramic Ages. If this is explicated in terms of lithic distribution network structures and dynamics, this "migration network" is one in which new, culturally unified subgraphs (i.e. sites with "pure" ceramic assemblages) will be introduced in period C or D within which we would see a focus on shared lithic material cultural practices and repertoires, but between which little to no lithic materials would be exchanged (Figure 1.5.A).

Nodes and ties

The networks will be discussed at the scale of the region (running from St. Vincent in the south to Puerto Rico in the northwest; Figure 5.2) and, like other archaeological network studies of its kind (Golitko, *et al.* 2012; Phillips 2011), the majority of nodes represent sites and their assemblages. On the basis of more than three hundred C-14 dates a division into five network periods was developed, dating from between 3200 BC and AD 400, which have been labelled A to E. This division is based on mean data intervals coinciding with major socio-cultural processes in the region over time. It starts at the earliest securely dated site in the region and cuts-off at the time that the full arc of the Lesser Antilles has been occupied by ceramic using horticulturalists (Hofman, Mol *et al.* 2011).

During the earliest period several sites included in the sample are find scatters, temporary camps or sites with a presumed semi-sedentary occupation. For the latter periods all sites are considered to have been places of (semi-)permanent habitation – as geographically fixed and temporally contiguous parts of the network. With regard to the network models an extra layer of information has been added to node sites in order to establish their main cultural affiliation at that moment in time. This identification, based on the characteristics of the site's assemblage is indicated

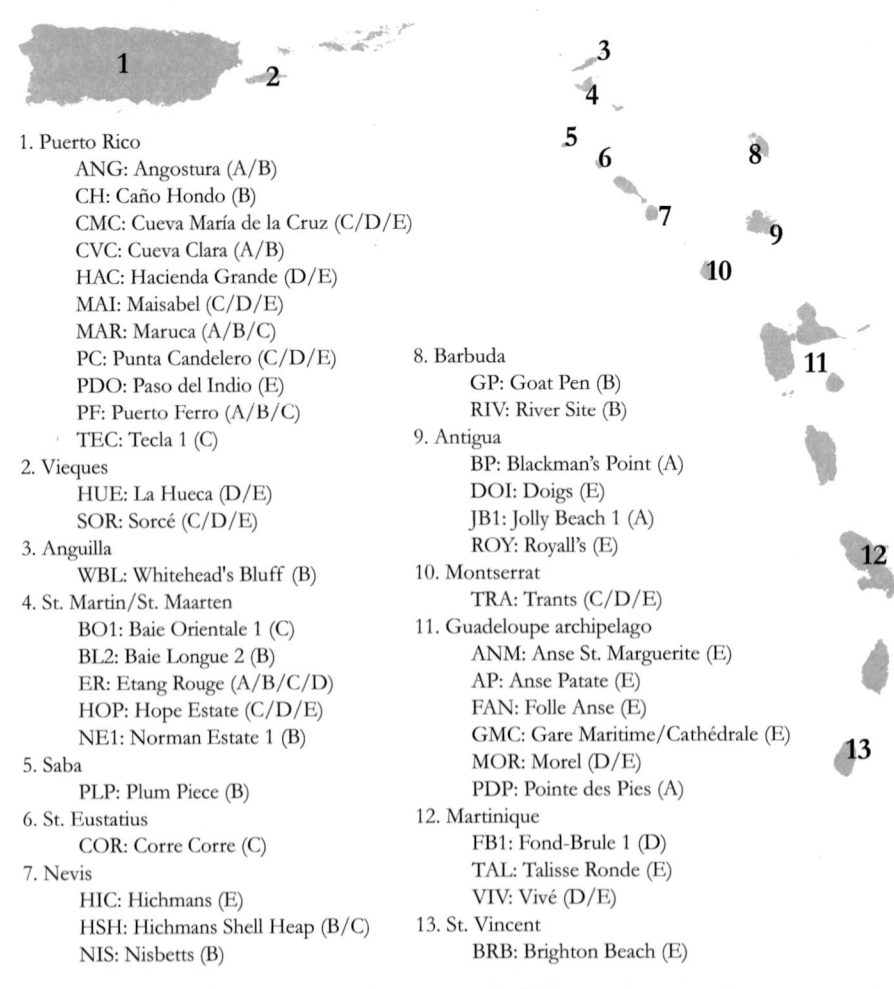

1. Puerto Rico
    ANG: Angostura (A/B)
    CH: Caño Hondo (B)
    CMC: Cueva María de la Cruz (C/D/E)
    CVC: Cueva Clara (A/B)
    HAC: Hacienda Grande (D/E)
    MAI: Maisabel (C/D/E)
    MAR: Maruca (A/B/C)
    PC: Punta Candelero (C/D/E)
    PDO: Paso del Indio (E)
    PF: Puerto Ferro (A/B/C)
    TEC: Tecla 1 (C)
2. Vieques
    HUE: La Hueca (D/E)
    SOR: Sorcé (C/D/E)
3. Anguilla
    WBL: Whitehead's Bluff (B)
4. St. Martin/St. Maarten
    BO1: Baie Orientale 1 (C)
    BL2: Baie Longue 2 (B)
    ER: Etang Rouge (A/B/C/D)
    HOP: Hope Estate (C/D/E)
    NE1: Norman Estate 1 (B)
5. Saba
    PLP: Plum Piece (B)
6. St. Eustatius
    COR: Corre Corre (C)
7. Nevis
    HIC: Hichmans (E)
    HSH: Hichmans Shell Heap (B/C)
    NIS: Nisbetts (B)

8. Barbuda
    GP: Goat Pen (B)
    RIV: River Site (B)
9. Antigua
    BP: Blackman's Point (A)
    DOI: Doigs (E)
    JB1: Jolly Beach 1 (A)
    ROY: Royall's (E)
10. Montserrat
    TRA: Trants (C/D/E)
11. Guadeloupe archipelago
    ANM: Anse St. Marguerite (E)
    AP: Anse Patate (E)
    FAN: Folle Anse (E)
    GMC: Gare Maritime/Cathédrale (E)
    MOR: Morel (D/E)
    PDP: Pointe des Pies (A)
12. Martinique
    FB1: Fond-Brule 1 (D)
    TAL: Talisse Ronde (E)
    VIV: Vivé (D/E)
13. St. Vincent
    BRB: Brighton Beach (E)

Figure 5.2: Map of sites with codes corresponding to the node names mentioned in the network visualizations. The name of the sites is followed by the period to which it can be dated (indicated in parentheses).

by means of node shape in the network models. The relational database compiled for this case-study also consists of various types of nodes, notably the sources of the lithic raw materials distributed between these sites, which are known to be local to the region (indicated by a rounded, horizontal rectangle in the network).

The nodes in the database are of two types: raw material source and habitation sites. The former are indicated by rectangles and the latter by triangles, squares and circles and a two or three letter code (see Figure 5.2 for a key). As dealt with in Chapter 3, one way to handle such variances in node character is by modelling them in 2-node networks, in which a site can be a "member" of a certain type of lithic material. As such the earliest periods (3200 - 200 BC) can be discussed in terms of their 2-mode network dynamics, which include sites, raw materials but also various technical lithic styles that can be found in the assemblages. These present us with insights into how early Caribbean sites were connected through time and space by means of lithic sources and technologies.

Thanks to the relatively high resolution of the data set it is also possible to draw a somewhat more interpretive 1-mode network for later periods that treats lithic sources and habitation sites as part of the same network. When drawing such a 1-mode model, site contemporaneity is of paramount importance. That is the reason why nearly all sites in these networks have absolute dates taken from two larger C-14 databases: one for Puerto Rico (see Rodríguez Ramos *et al*, 2010) and a second one covering the entire pre- and proto-colonial period of all the Lesser Antilles as assembled by the Leiden Caribbean Research Group.[2] The dates in this database originating from the sites that were part of the sample period and region have been selected based on the parameters for chrono-metric hygiene (Fitzpatrick 2006). As a result, the dates for the earliest sites in the case-study refer to a period lasting for several of thousand to several hundred years. Faced with the disparity of dates we cannot be certain of or even guesstimate whether sites dating from the earliest periods were contemporaneous or not.[3]

In the 1-mode, more interpretive models to be constructed for the later periods, ties between nodes are drawn on the basis of a number of characteristics. When constructing this network the production and distribution chain of the Antiguan Long Island Flint was of paramount importance. This, together with the production and exchange of other lithic materials, has been the feature of a highly valuable line of research carried out by Sebastiaan Knippenberg (2007). Based on an extensive study of lithic assemblages in the Northeastern Caribbean, he was able to map the distribution of Long Island Flint and St. Maarten greenstone and calci-rudite. The latter is not found in assemblages of these periods, but the other two are found over a large region from early to late pre-colonial times. What is more important is that, based on a fall-off analysis of production debris and flake size (cf. Renfrew 1977), it has been possible to distinguish sites with direct access from those that procured these materials through various degrees of down-the-line exchange.

Similar, if somewhat courser, distribution models could be established by means of other lithic raw material sources in the Caribbean as well, notably Puerto Rican serpentinite and carnelian (a yellow or orange variety of chalcedony) from Antigua. The latter two have obvious production centres respectively located in Puerto Rico and on the islands of Antigua and Montserrat from which other islands would have been supplied with raw materials and (semi-)finished objects (Narganes Storde

---

2   This database will be included in the forthcoming *Islanders on the Move*, edited by Corinne Hofman (University of Alabama Press).

3   Later periods comprise only a few hundred years. The one-sigma range of C-14 dates from most sites overlap during this period. These are still arguably long lapses of time allowing for all sorts of movements and interactions to take place. However, these habitation sites seem to have been permanent places in the social landscape, continuously occupying the same location for several hundred years in some cases (Bright 2011). Although such longevity of a village is almost unheard of in modern ethnographic examples from Lowland South America (that often serve as an analogy for pre-colonial Caribbean communities) it has been argued to be a feature of island habitation sites (Samson 2010). Thus, although one can never be sure of anything in archaeology, it is assumed that these nodes represent discrete social collectives that engaged in exchange or other types of relations, which is reflected in the connections between lithic material culture assemblages.

1995; Watters and Scaglion 1994). In other words, in the 1-mode model, ties between site-nodes are based on the production and distribution of local lithic materials which is in turn based on the absence and presence and quantity of material. This presents an in-depth perspective on site relations during the later period of this case-study that can go far in creating a lithic distribution network.

Nevertheless, these models still lack certitude of tie direction required for a true, directed network model. Thus, as a final step to create a 1-mode network model of Period D and E in the fullest detail possible, the geographic distance between distribution and consumer sites has also been taken into account. By doing so the network based on the ties between a consumer site and the closest distributor could be further differentiated. This might resemble an unwarranted guidance of the original data set, yet two reasons justify this geographic constraint. Firstly, the simple fact of the geographic layout of the – almost literal – island chain must be considered. As discussed in Chapter 2, even if this does not necessarily mean that possible interregional voyagers must have travelled through this island bridge, this stepping-stone character will have had a large impact on interactions within the region. Secondly, the distribution model of Knippenberg (2007) supports this geographic constraint, where the fall-off model is proven to be correlated with geographic distance, suggesting that sites preferentially attach themselves to geographically close neighbours.

The downside of these 1-mode models is: they treat habitation sites and lithic raw material sources as equal nodes. Hence, because raw material nodes are donors in this directed network rather than groups of which sites can be a member of, this does not yield a comparable insight into the power of materials as a 2-mode network would. That is why 2-mode and 1-mode modelling has been jointly applied when referring to certain periods. To be sure, these models are not meant as absolute reflections of exchange or other type of socio-material networks. However, combined with an absolute chronology and insight into presence and absence of materials and in some cases even their production and distribution chains, the result is a model that provides a longitudinal view of the presence, production and distribution of endogenous lithic materials between 3200 BC and AD 400. Together with more substantive lines of evidence, these can then be used to draft further hypotheses on the history of society and culture in the early Northeastern Caribbean.

Period A: foundation

At first glance, the lithic network model of Period A, representing the first occupation of the Northeastern Caribbean, is clearly rather small. It nonetheless contains all sites that have been securely dated between 3200 BC and 2000 BC in the region of study. Other sites and finds have been identified as belonging to the earliest phase of human occupation on Antigua and other islands (Davis 2000; Nicholson 1994), but their site chronology is unfortunately only supported by one or no absolute dates. In addition it has to be mentioned that just to the south and the west of the region we find similar systems, for example those in Hispaniola which were already part of a small but burgeoning lithic network in the vicinity of the Barrera Mordan flint source (Pantel 1988; Veloz Maggiolo 1972).

Structure and subgraphs

Even though it represents the earliest phase of the human occupation of the islands the region seems to be relatively well connected. (Figure 5.3). If the flint sources and knapping techniques are taken as qualitatively similar nodes, an affiliation network from a 2-mode to a 1-mode site network can be made (using UCInet). This shows a maximally connected component, in other words a clique of all nodes. It has to be noted, however, that this is primarily based on the inclusion of flint knapping techniques as part of a multi-mode model. All sites with siliceous materials have evidence for both blade and flake knapping techniques in their assemblages. These visualize that, regardless of raw material acquirement strategies, ties to can be drawn between early users of chert material in the Northeastern Caribbean. Rather than being a region with isolated material repertoires and practices, we find a certain measure of connectedness in this incipient network.

In terms of lithic sources the small network is divided into a number of subgraphs, which revolve around the two main types of flint encountered in sites attributed to this Period. The {ANG-CCL-PF-MOC} 2-clique consists of site

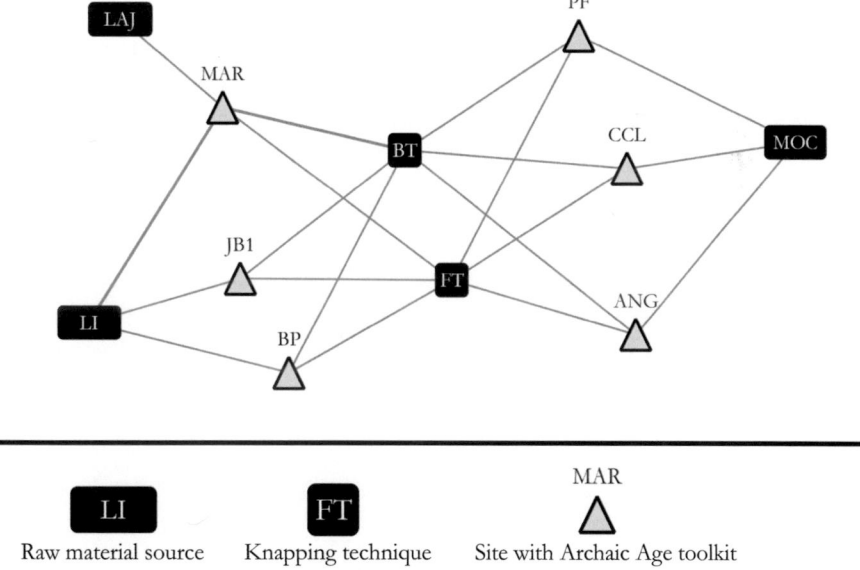

Figure 5.3: 2-mode network of Period A illustrating sites tied to raw material sources of which material is present in their assemblages. Nodes are also connected to a knapping technique node in order to indicate the presence of tools produced with that technique that were found at the site.

nodes that exploited the Mocca flint source in Puerto Rico.[4] Another 2-clique, {BP-JB1-MAR-LI}, centred on the Long Island flint source. Finally, the dyad {MAR-LAJ} is based on Maruca's exploitation of the Lajas material.[5] The network's cohesion is somewhat enhanced by the adoption of Long Island Flint at the site of Maruca (MAR). Such a transfer of Long Island Flint from Antigua to Puerto Rico at such an early stage in the development of regional networks would represent a significant achievement in terms of logistics.[6] On the other hand, unlike the other Puerto Rican sites, Maruca is not affiliated with the Mocca (MOC) but with the Lajas (LAJ) flint source. The tie only serves to connect the MAR node to the subgraph that makes up the "Long Island Flint" 2-clique. It is thus not truly a network bridge.

Interpretation

What can this network model say about overarching cultural and social interaction patterns of the early past of this region? Not much, to be fair: the low temporal resolution and small size of the data set warrants a very careful consideration of any inferences drawn from this model alone. It has to be stressed that the networks represented here are not models of social interaction. Rather they provide a view of how material cultural repertoires and practices are connected through time and space. This is particularly true for Period A, which has so few reliable data-points that it is impossible to say anything meaningful about social processes that could underlie this distribution.

Blade knapping techniques have traditionally been considered to be representative of the peoples that settled the Greater Antilles, while flake knapping is found in both the southern and western lithic traditions (Knippenberg 1999; Walker 1990). The cohesion in terms of flint knapping techniques of this small lithic network supports the idea that this region was the location of the first interactions between previously unconnected western and southern lithic traditions. This is also supported by the site contexts of two sites from the network, namely Jolly Beach I (JB1) and Maruca (MAR). Both present evidence for an interaction between two alternate knapping traditions in their lithic assemblages – blades with a much smaller quantity of typical Greater Antillean ground tools in the case of Jolly Beach I and Casimiroid and Ortoroid flint knapping styles in Maruca – and other evidence for interactions, such as converging subsistence practices (Wilson 2007).

---

4   All 2-cliques mentioned in this Chapter are also 2-clans (see Chapter 3).

5   Alternatively this can also be achieved by removing the knapping technique affiliations. If left out of the equation, a picture of a much less connected network emerges, breaking down in four separate components.

6   There are some qualifications to be made here. Firstly, although it has been documented in the assemblage by Jeffrey Walker (Rodríguez and Winter 1999) and later by Reniel Rodríguez Ramos (personal communication, 2011), it is not entirely clear that Long Island Flint can indeed be found in the earliest period at Maruca. Secondly, Long Island Flint constitutes only a minority of the lithic material found at the site, the majority of the siliceous materials originates from local sources.

However, there is a breakup in multiple small 2-cliques based around the various lithic sources. These mostly correlate with geographic proximity. If Long Island Flint is indeed found in the lower strata of Maruca this provides a bridge between the northern Lesser Antilles and Puerto. Nonetheless this far-reaching geographic distribution fails to truly connect the material networks of this period. The likelihood that social networks would have spanned the entire region – at least as can be deducted from the potential cotemporaneous direct procurement of the same lithic source – is minimal. This would be in line with an early human occupation of the island chain that consisted of local, small and mobile groups that would have only been loosely connected at the regional level.

Period B: growth

The multi-mode network of Period B (2000-800 BC) consists of "Archaic" sites, flint stone materials and knapping techniques (Figure 5.4). An added element is the presence of numerous unconnected sites dating to Period B. Their assemblages (many of which have been examined by Knippenberg and Rodríguez Ramos) have no known (i.e. published) flint or other non-local siliceous material connecting them to the larger network. The status of these unconnected components goes beyond the current analysis, but it has to be kept in mind that this network is based on the presence of stone materials not on discrete social or cultural ties. It is unlikely that unconnected sites were not frequented by similar (or even the same) peoples who left their lithic materials in sites connected by means of this network. These sites too were an integral part of the socio-economic system of the peoples living in the region, just not one that can be modelled applying the available data. The same goes for many small sites that would presumably fall in this Period, which are not part of the model here because they are not and often cannot be securely dated. Examples hereof are the isolated finds of Long Island Flint blades on sites such as Dog Island and Flower Avenue (Anguilla) or the Level in Saba (Cherry, *et al.* 2012). There is also a new raw material node: an unnamed flint excavated at the site of Caño Hondo that is probably local to Puerto Rico (Rodríguez Ramos, personal communication 2011). Maruca once again is connected to both Lajas and Long Island Flint.

Structure and subgraphs

In comparison to the model from the 1200 years before, the network has hugely expanded. Site node quantity shows a growth of 375% and the total amount of affiliation ties has increased with 182.2%. Naturally, this picture is partly biased by archaeological preservation. However, it is unlikely that the superior archaeological detection of later period sites is the only reason of this growth. Although the site nodes and ties have increased in quantity, relatively speaking the affiliation network has become more sparse and disconnected. During Period A 47.5% of all possible

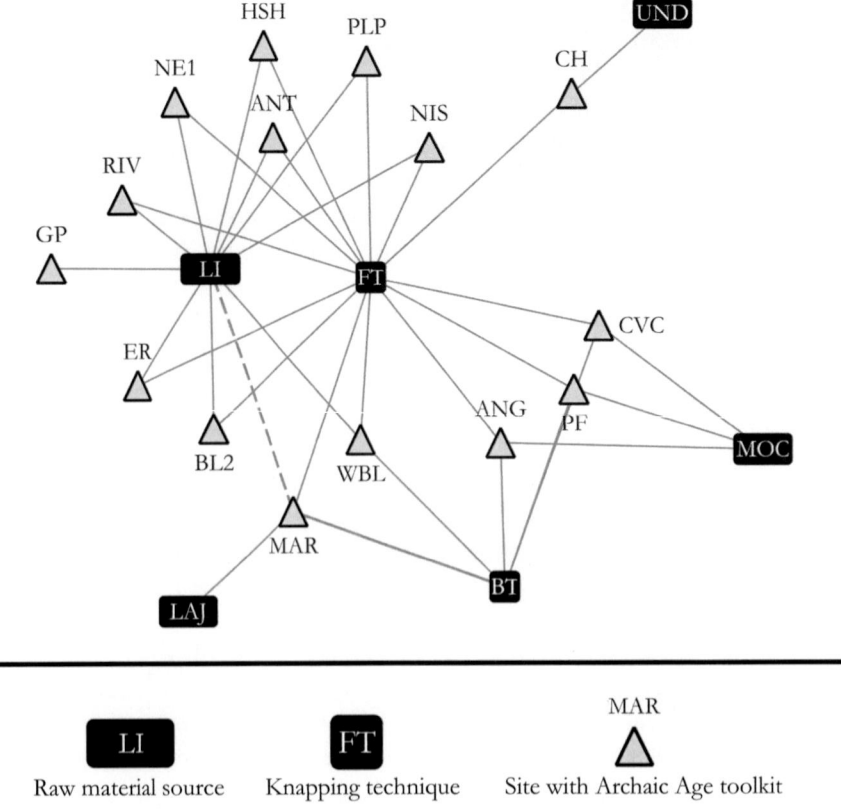

LI — Raw material source   FT — Knapping technique   MAR — Site with Archaic Age toolkit

Figure 5.4: 2-mode network of Period B with sites tied to raw material sources of which material is present in their assemblages. Nodes are also connected to a knapping technique node in order to indicate the presence of tools produced with that technique that were found at the site.

affiliations were present versus 19.4% in this model.[7] In general, this is related to the fact that many sites that are securely related to this Period are without (published) evidence linked to the use of flint or other cherty material: fifteen out of thirty (50%) of the site nodes are not affiliated with any lithic material or technique in contrast to two out of eight (25%) attributed to Period A. If these unconnected components are left out of the picture the connectivity of the network increases to 31.5% of all possible affiliations. This is partly related to the fact that node sites are affiliated with only one type of lithic raw material, with the exception of MAR that is once again affiliated with both the LAJ and LI flint types.

This trend is also visible in the difference in total affiliations between lithic blade and flake technologies. Five sites belong to both the blade and flake knapping clique, four of which are located in Puerto Rico and one in the Lesser Antilles; the

---

7   As nodes are not directly related in this 2-mode network, the network density is not calculated here as indicated in Chapter 3, but by means of this calculation: , where *n* is the total amount of site nodes (columns in the matrix) and *m* is the total amount of lithic group nodes (rows in the matrix) and *t* the total amount of ties (sum of all cells in the matrix).

majority of the sites (ten) where siliceous materials have been reported employ only flake knapping techniques.

If we compare the degree centrality, in this case the total number of site node affiliations to raw materials nodes, it becomes clear that the clique surrounding Long Island Flint source has become much larger with eleven out of fifteen nodes affiliated to a lithic raw material linked to Long Island Flint, while the degree of the others has remained the same. On the other hand it is interesting to note that the network of Period B is structurally quite similar to that of Period A. The only real change is the addition of one extra but small clique: the CAN node and the unknown, presumably local source of its flint. In general, the large component consists of cliques merely connected through their lithic technology not their raw materials. Thus, the materials are at the centre of cliques of which the members have no ties with sites that make use of other lithic materials.

Interpretation

In the light of the development of the networks of the first colonists it is interesting to compare the model of Period B to the period before. It shows a mixture of sites already present during Period A and sites that are new. All the new sites, with the exception of Caño Hondo, can be found in the northern Lesser Antilles and not in Puerto Rico. Although influenced by the variances in archaeological coverage of the Period, the model suggests that Long Island Flint was an important attractor during this era. Moreover, the large number of shell-only sites in the northern Lesser Antilles, for example on St. Martin (Bonnissent 2008), suggests that the marine resources of the reasons also served to draw new settlers or enable the growth and fissioning of groups already established in the region.

The patterns in the model visualize what we already know from previous non-network analyses, for example the increase of the total number of sites. In addition, the differences in blade and flake affiliation are congruent with previous findings that suggest a gradual demise of the blade knapping technique on all of the islands (Hofman, Mol, *et al.* 2011). The model also reaffirms that it is not the access to good knapping material that causes the shift, but rather a change in flint knapping practices. While Whitehead's Bluff on Anguilla and Angostura, Maruca and Cueva Clara still have flint blades in their assemblages, in the majority of sites chert materials are only reduced using the flake knapping technique (Crock *et al.* 1995; Rodríguez Ramos 2010). Whether this is due to preference or loss of knowledge is difficult to surmise, yet it is interesting to observe that sites in Puerto Rico retain the blade knapping tradition for a longer period than those sites in the northern Lesser Antilles. However, even though we see an increase and the continuation of traditions, the relatively low overall connectedness of the network model indicates that as the region becomes more densely occupied (total number of sites) the lithic affiliation landscape does not show any greater cohesion. This suggests that the growth of social networks of this period is primarily at the local level.

The fact that this build-up seems to take place in localities where Long Island Flint was procured is telling. This pattern is best interpreted through sites that are known to have been semi-permanent settlements. Plum Piece in Saba, for example, shows a habitation pattern, faunal assemblage and toolkit that is typical of a seasonally occupied campsite (Hofman, *et al.* 2006; Hofman and Hoogland 2003). Plum Piece presents evidence for small, temporary shelters and the specialized procurement of black crabs (*Gecarcinus ruricola*) and Audubon's shearwaters (*Puffinus lherminieri lherminierii*), both species with a seasonal presence on the island. Several other of such seasonal resources can be identified in the local archipelago. Furthermore, Knippenberg has found that Long Island flint nodules were probably directly acquired from Long Island itself as part of the mobility cycles of these groups (Knippenberg 2007). However, in contrast to seasonal resources or many other faunal and floral resources of which the ideal procurement area must have shifted around over time, Long Island flint, applied in many day to day activities, was always in high demand and permanently available at the same spot.

Aside from being easily accessible and the best of the few chert resources in the region, the Long Island flint source would thus have represented an often frequented and fixed spot in the landscape (Davis 2000; Knippenberg 2007; Nicholson 1994). It is presumed that this popularity and fixedness of the Long Island flint source implied that human habitation gravitated towards the islands in its general proximity. It is also telling that, in spite of the numerous small sites in the area of Long Island, no single large site during this or any later period seems to control access to the material.

Period C: transition

The model of Period C, which runs from 800 to 200 BC, is presented in two variants here. Figure 5.5.a presents all the sites datable to this period and their connections to Long Island flint, Mocca flint, Lajas flint and local chert sources. Blade and flake technology nodes are no longer part of the model, since blades have all but disappeared during this phase. The shape of the site nodes denotes the original interpretation of their ceramic assemblages: (1) a triangle for a site with a toolkit that is representative of the "Archaic Age", (2) a circle for a pure Saladoid assemblage, and (c) a rounded rectangle for a Huecoid site with Saladoid components. Figure 5.5.b is an expanded version of this model. It includes two new elements of the lithic networks in this region: down-the-line exchange (visualized by the northern Long-Island Flint distributor node) and the presence of semi-precious stones.

In this period down-the-line exchange, in contrast to the direct acquisition of material, can for the first time be attested on the basis of lithic studies. According to Knippenberg (2007) it can be confirmed for the site of Hope Estate on St. Martin and La Hueca and Sorcé on the island of Vieques. It has also been suggested to have been the means for the dispersal of Long Island flint to the site of Maruca and Paso del Indio in Puerto Rico (Rouse and Alegría 1990; Rodríguez Ramos, personal communication 2011). In order to investigate the structural position of a distributor node down-the-line exchange is simulated by adding a hypothetical distributor node.

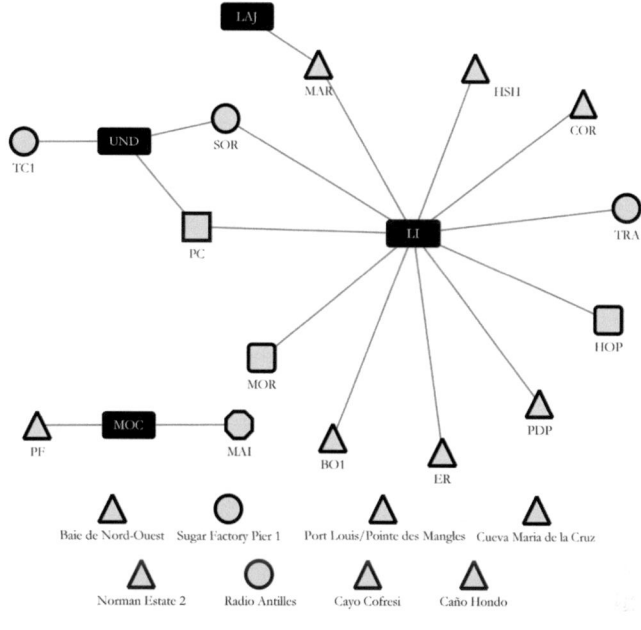

a.

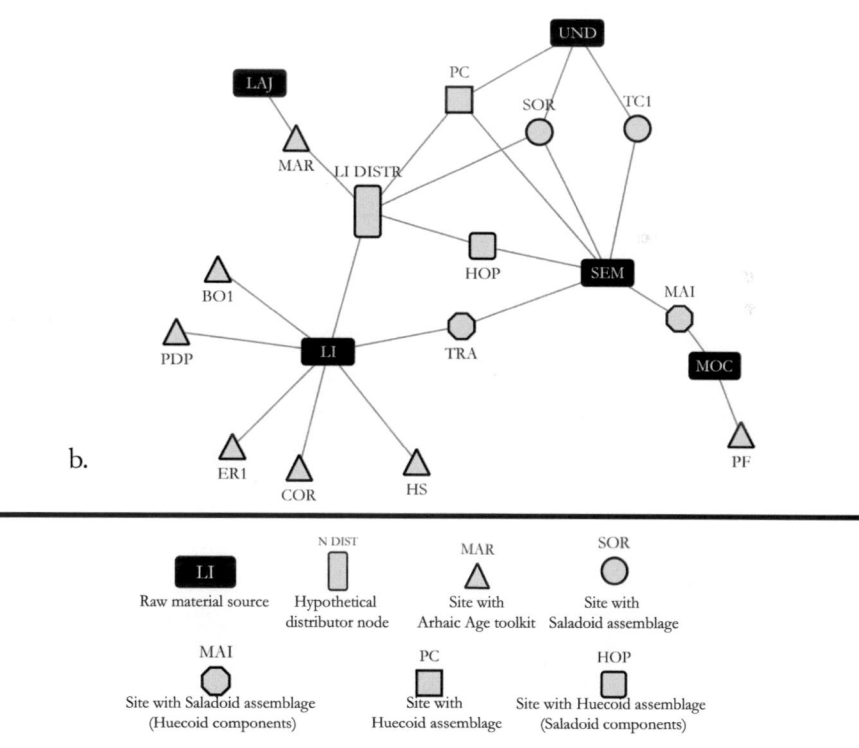

b.

Figure 5.5: 2-mode network of Period C, illustrating sites tied to raw material sources of which material is present in their assemblages. Model A shows only the presence of chert sources, while Model B shows the presence of semi-precious materials and a hypothetical distributor node.

In the indigenous Caribbean we find a wide range of semi-precious materials: agate, amethyst, aventurine, diorite, quartz, jadeite, nephrite, malachite, topaz and turquoise (Narganes Storde 1995; Knippenberg 2007; Murphy 2000; Watters and Scaglion 1994). The exact sources of the majority hereof remains unknown. However, based on the geological layout and current known lithic sources of the region it is presumed that in general these materials originated outside the Caribbean. The semi-precious lithic node represents a type of stone materials that were and are primarily chosen for their aesthetic qualities in small decorative objects, mainly personal adornments. The adjective "semi-precious" is slightly misleading, since any ranking of lithic materials into precious, semi-precious and non-precious materials is not indigenous but a construct of modern gemology. However, certain material qualities, for instance translucency and brilliance, are shared among all specimens of rock that were regularly utilized during this period (Rodríguez Ramos 2011).

Down-the-line exchange of semi-precious stones is difficult to model because it is represented by a structural void in this period: it is suspected that one or more nodes and ties were responsible for the distribution, but we have no clear view of how communities acquired the material. Lithics in this Period could have travelled through various ways from various locales to their final place of deposition. In addition, the exact stratigraphic location of semi-precious lithics in sites, for example, is often not mentioned in reports. When they are indicated it is clear that the lower levels contain only very few semi-precious lithics. Later periods do have better evidence for a fully developed network with down-the-line exchange of endogenous lithic materials, among which semi-precious stones.

Structure, subgraphs and centrality

The number of sites in the network has diminished somewhat (now twenty-three), but the Period is also shorter by half than the ones before. When this is taken into account the model shows the same trend: other siliceous materials are being used but Long Island Flint continues to grow in affiliate ties (eleven members). Due to the absence of a distinct blade and flake technology group, the network in Figure 5.5.a falls apart in one large and one smaller component and many unconnected nodes. Once again sites from which no lithic materials have been reported. It is noteworthy, however, that the majority of the nodes are now connected.

A slightly different picture evolves when taking into account the down-the-line exchange and semi-precious stone presence in the site assemblages. Aside from the a-lithic sites, the network is now a single component. This is brought about by the distribution of semi-precious stone materials found in several sites not connected through their flint or jasper assemblages. Interestingly, this component can furthermore be divided into several subgraphs. This is most evident when taking a closer look at clique formation in an affiliation network (2-mode to 1-mode; here and below carried out with UCInet 6.0) of the graph in Figure 5.6. As explained in Chapter 3, such a network models the affiliations based one set of nodes of a 2-mode graph, in this case ties based on the co-affiliation of site nodes to a lithic group node.

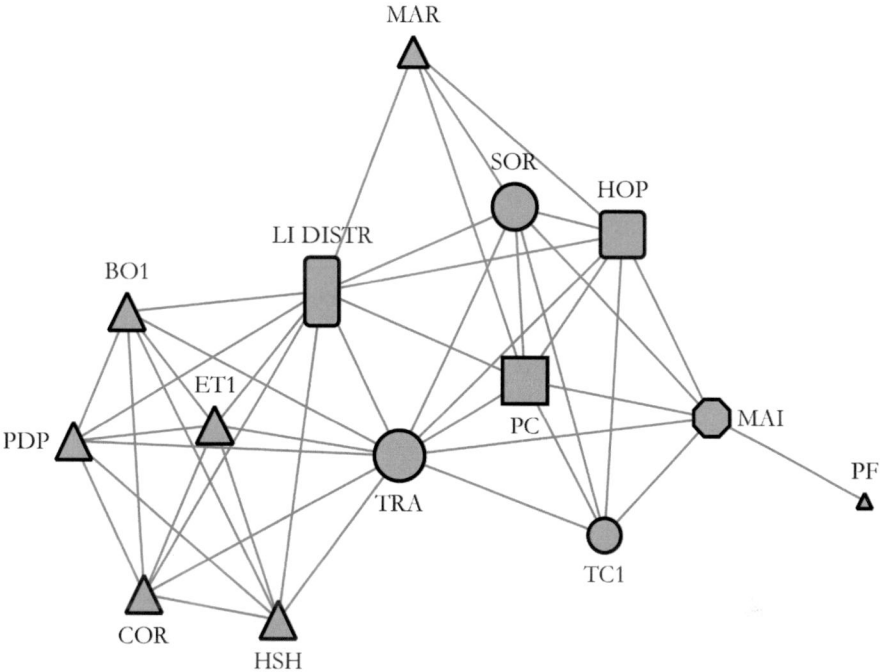

Figure 5.6: Affiliation (site to site) network of Period C. The node size is based on degree centrality.

All nodes are reachable from any other node and all nodes, except for PF (Puerto Ferro), are in fact part of a 2-clique. Therefore, because all nodes except Puerto Ferro can reach all other nodes in no more than two steps, this means that the network is rather "small in size" (i.e. with a small diameter). Nonetheless, the affiliation network is not exceptionally dense (44 ties = 48.35% of all possible ties). When looked at closer the network can be roughly divided in two regions: the 6-core {BO1-COR-ET-HSH-TRA-Distr} and the 5-core {HOP-MAI-PC-TC1-SOR}, where the Distributor and TRA node share the role of gatekeeper. These core areas are more or less contingent with a geographic focus on the southerly region of the network for the 6-core and the Puerto Rican and northerly Lesser Antilles for the 5-core. These cores can furthermore be divided into four cliques: A {BO1-COR-ER-HSH-PDP-TRA-Distr}; B {HOP-MAR-PC-SOR-Distr}; C {HOP-MAI-PC-SOR-TEC-TRA]}; D {HOP-PC-SOR-TRA-Distr}. These groups of nodes correspond with: Long Island Flint direct acquisition (Clique A), down-the-line acquisition of Long Island Flint (Clique B), presence of semi-precious stone in the site assemblage (Clique C), and, a focal point in the network of gateway nodes, Long Island Flint down-the-line acquisition and semi-precious stone presence.

Definite conclusions cannot be drawn based on this data set alone, but in terms of control of lithic resource distribution in the region it seems that both Trants (TRA) and the hypothetical distribution node would have occupied a central position. Trants even has a slightly more central position with a degree of 11 instead of 10 and a better structural position in the network. This is caused by the fact that it participates in the "semi-precious stone clique" to which a hypothetical node does *de facto* not have access. Based on the structural equivalence of the distributor node and Trants it could even be suggested that Trants is in fact the distributor node. In regards to network power, a note should be made about the triads in a valued affiliation matrix of this Period. Although there are sixty-seven triads in total,[8] one triad {HOP-PC-SOR} is exceptional since it is the only subgraph for which the link strength between all nodes is 2 rather than 1. This has to do with the fact that all three nodes are members of both the Long Island distribution and the semi-precious stone group. If this was to be calculated with merely the Long Island flint presence instead of down-the-line acquisition, Trants would also be added to this clique of ties with strength 2.

Interpretation

From a culture historical perspective, Period C is highly interesting because it covers the centuries in which many so-called "Archaic Age" resident and newly arrived, "Early Ceramic Age" communities contemporaneously occupy the islands. What does this network model and its analysis tell us about this Archaic-Saladoid-Huecoid interface period?

Firstly, the model is clear with regard to the presence of connections between resident commuities and sites that were in all likelihood communities of newly arrived settlers. Both types of sites take part in the same lithic network groups. During the entire Period several sites with an assemblage representative of "Archaic Age" communities were present on the islands and had direct access to Long Island, Mocca and Lajas flint. In the case of Long Island flint at Maruca this access was acquired through down-the-line exchange, suggesting that this site was either relying on pre-Period C distribution networks or able to tap into new ones. In addition we come across a host of evidence for a strong presence of "Archaic Age" communities on Antigua and other Lesser Antillean islands during this time. These sites are not part of the network because no secure dating is available. The same is true with reference to several possible Early Saladoid sites and finds in this region and on the Windward islands to the south.

Nonetheless, as to the second half of the Period, these latter materials can be clearly located and dated on Montserrat, St. Martin, Vieques and Puerto Rico. From that moment on, at least the Saladoid site of Trants had direct access to Long Island flint. Down-the-line, other Saladoid sites such as Sorcé also managed to acquire this now farspread material. The same goes for the Huecoid site of Hope Estate on St. Martin. A similar yet smaller version of this Archaic Age-Saladoid-Huecoid sharing of raw material sources is suggested by the ties of affiliation between Maisabel and Puerto Ferro – based on the presence of Mocca flint in their assemblages.[9] However, the overall model indicates it can hardly be argued that

---

8   As calculated by means of UCInet 6.0's "triad census" technique.
9   It has to be noted that absolute dating does not fully support site contemporaneity (Siegel 1992).

original residents of the islands were quickly displaced or assimilated upon the arrival of new settlers from other regions.

Analysis of lithics alone would suggest that (down-the-line) exchange is introduced with the arrival of new settlers. It seems unlikely, though, that exchange was not part of prior network strategies. It is unparsimonious to argue that for, example, the spread of cultivated crops into the archipelago was initiated by direct acquisition from donor areas rather than a phased region-by-region introduction. The same would be true for ceramic technology. The reason for the late introduction of down-the-line lithic distribution is impossible to surmise. It could be related to increased interaction due to new settlers or further population growth. Another possibility is a boom in the popularity of Long Island Flint. Perhaps these processes were even dialectically related, implying that a first increase in exchange of lithic materials like Long Island flint led to growing and better connected networks.

It should be remembered that there was already a long indigenous tradition of Long Island flint procurement. With this in mind it could be argued that newcomers arrived in an island region that had been connected by indigenous networks dating back for millenia. One version of this view would see migrants that were already tapped into these age-old networks because of previously established ties between their mother communities and mobile groups that were (partly) resident in the northern Lesser Antilles (Hofman, Mol, *et al.* 2011). In that case information on Northeastern Caribbean resources, such as Long Island flint, gained through prior trade contacts could have functioned as a motive for migration to the islands in the first place.

Precisely these kinds of processes could be behind the slight structural differences between nodes such as the centrality of Trants or the stronger triadic ties between the sites of Hope Estate and Sorcé. This increasing hierarchy and diversification indicate the evolution of new forms of network dynamics. In addition, Period C sees the existence of "networks within networks" for the first time in Caribbean history: based on the presence and absence of semi-precious stone. In this regard it is significant that the only nodes taking part in this clique are sites with either Saladoid or Huecoid ceramics (Hofman and Hoogland 1999; Oliver 1999). Semi-precious stone production, distribution or even presence is simply not reported from any of the sites with an assemblage typical of the earlier "Archaic Age". This suggests a certain limitation to at least some aspects of the Saladoid and Huecoid phenomena other than their specific ceramic styles. Any detailed conclusions on the Archaic-Saladoid-Huecoid interface to be drawn from the model are naturally hampered by the large timespan of the period. However, because absolute dates of many sites overlap, at the minimum we can state that contemporaneous acquirement of the same lithic resources was taking place over increasingly larger geographic distances and between culturally more differentiated groups.

Period D: robust networks

The growing availability of absolute dates from the following two periods allows for a smaller temporal resolution and thus an increasingly refined picture of their possible network dynamics. The network model of Period D depicts the relations between sites and notable stone resources from 200 BC to AD 100 (Figure 5.7). Aside from the by now familiar Long Island and Mocca flint sources, four new lithic raw material complexes are now part of the network: carnelian, St. Martin greenstone, serpentinite and jasper. As can be expected, numerous other types of (semi-precious) stones can be found at sites dating from this period; yet all four nodes represent raw material groups that can be sourced to a location in the region. Carnelian is found on the island of Antigua. There is furthermore evidence for a large carnelian (bead) workshop at the site of Trants on nearby Montserrat. In later times production also takes place at sites on Antigua (Murphy, *et al.* 2000). The

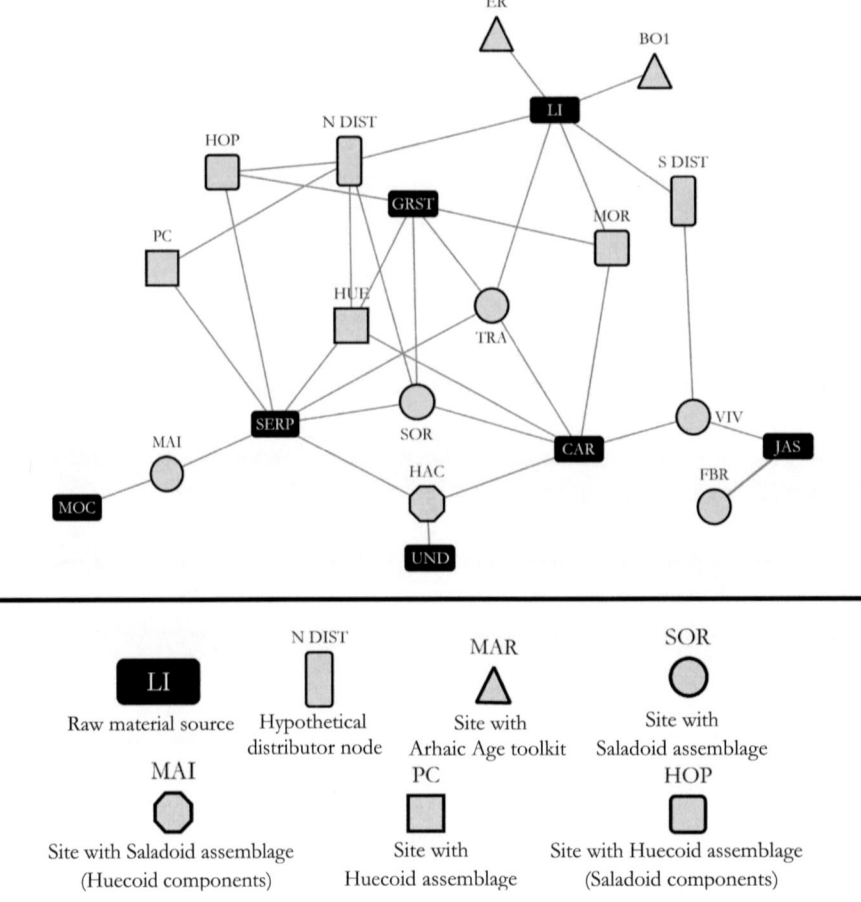

Figure 5.7: 2-mode network of Period D, showing sites tied to raw material sources of which material is present in their assemblages. The model also has a hypothetical distributor node (N DIST) to which some nodes are tied in order to indicate they did not have any direct access to Long Island flint.

name of the muddy green St. Martin greenstone is self-explanatory in terms of the provenance of this raw material source. Interestingly, the only site with direct access to St. Martin Greenstone is also found on St. Martin, namely Hope Estate. We do not know the exact location of the Puerto Rican serpentinite source, a greenstone material used for the production of beads, amulets and other personal adornments. Several serpentinite workshops were discovered on the island of Puerto Rico, one of which is the Saladoid-Huecoid site(s) of Sorcé and La Hueca, of which only the Saladoid component can be securely dated to this period. Finally, the source for red jasper, another chert material, is likely to be found on Martinique, which had an active lithic economy based on the material (Bérard 2004).

For Period D it is also possible to draw inferences beyond simply lithic presence in site assemblages, utilizing the information from the lithic production and distribution studies by Knippenberg and Rodríguez Ramos who have personally examined almost all sites in the network. Therefore this network does indeed not entail the same level of speculation as that of Period C. Based on this and other guidelines put forth in the beginning of this Chapter, I also suggest another hypothetical model below. This model equates flint sources with site nodes and plots them in a directed, 1-mode model of site interaction based on lithic exchange patterns. The validity of this interpretation is much strengthened by the evidence for direct acquisition of different semi-precious stone material and workshops in La Hueca (serpentinite), Trants (Long Island flint and carnelian) and Hope Estate, which held a monopoly on the distribution of St. Martin Greenstone (Knippenberg 2007; Rodríguez Ramos 2010).

Structure, subgraphs and centrality

The most striking difference between Period D and the periods before that is that lithic group node quantity has increased to seven different local groups. Once again the number of site nodes has decreased (n = 18), which is again explained by the shorter duration of the sample period. Long Island flint reigns supreme in the flint category with a degree of 9. Other flints and the jasper from Martinique only have a membership between one and three. Nonetheless, the presence of semi-precious stone types, such as carnelian (degree = 7), serpentinite (degree = 6), and St. Martin greenstone (degree = 5), now come close to being as central as Long Island flint. The network now has a southern down-the-line subgraph, a distribution network that caters to the Vivé site on the island of Martinique.

The network of site co-affiliation based on this 2-mode distribution network shows a possible slight increase in density (54.9% vs. 48.3%) compared to Period C (Figure 5.8). A direct comparison is somewhat skewed: the density of the Period D network in comparison to Period C is downplayed by the subdivision of semi-precious lithic materials and the addition of another hypothetical distributor site. A k-core analysis shows that the network has become more cohesive, the {HAC-HOP-HUE-MOR-SOR-TRA-VIV} six-core now dominates the graph, with a five-core including all nodes but FBR.

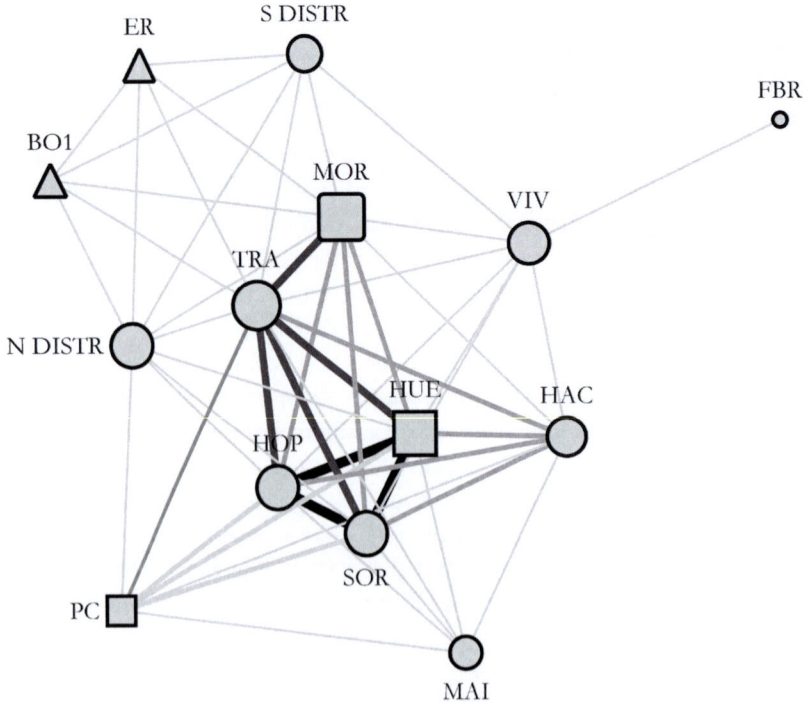

Figure 5.8: Affiliation (site to site) network of Period D. The tie colour and size is related to tie strength (from low to high = light to dark, thin to thick). Node size is based on degree centrality.

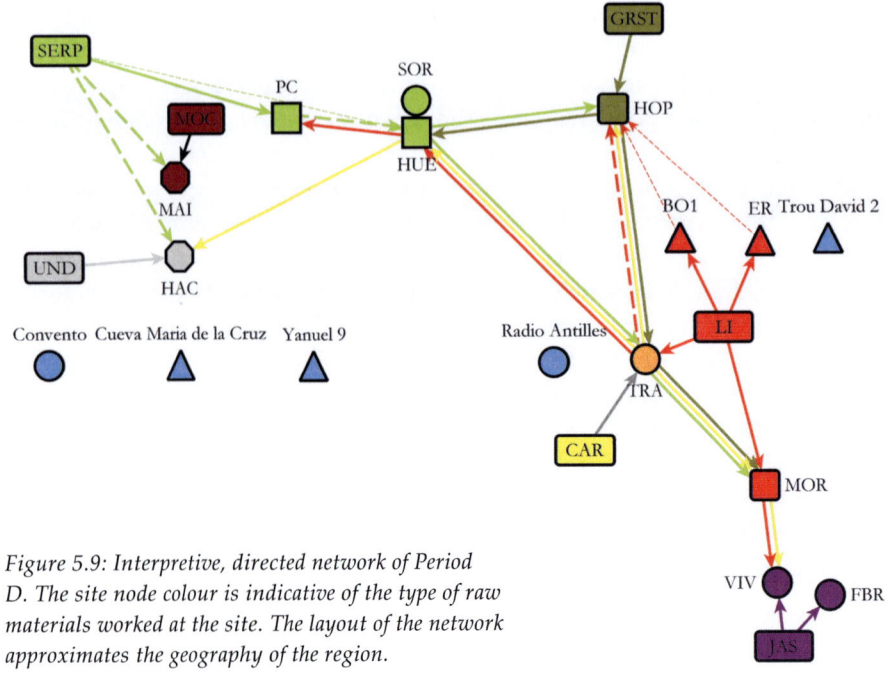

Figure 5.9: Interpretive, directed network of Period D. The site node colour is indicative of the type of raw materials worked at the site. The layout of the network approximates the geography of the region.

The site affiliation network contains eighty-two triads. These are part of six large cliques: A {BO1-ER-MOR-TRA-SDistr-NDist}; B {HOP-HUE-PC-SOR-NDistr}; C {HAC-HOP-HUE-MOR-SOR-TRA-VIV}; D {MOR-TRA-VIV-SDistr}; E {HAC-HOP-HUE-MAI-SOR-TRA}; and F {HOP-HUE-MOR-SOR-TRA-NDistr}. Clique A and B correspond to the direct and Northern distribution acquisition networks of Long Island flint. Clique C corresponds to the sites with access to carnelian, after Long Island flint the widest distributed local lithic material. Clique D represents a merger of sites that are affiliated through semi-precious stones and long island flint in the central-southern part of the region. Clique F fulfils a similar structural position for sites in the central-northern part of the network. All nodes, except for FBR, are part of a 2-clique. All of this suggests a strongly cohesive network with several possible paths through which sites may be connected.

However, not all paths are supported by equally strong ties. Most ties have strength one, implying they are connecting nodes that only share one affiliation. Yet at the centre of the network we see an increase in tie strength. There the "strong clique" {HAC-HOP-HUE-MOR-SOR-TRA} can be found. This clique consists of nodes connected by ties that have strength 2 or more. This subgraph can be further compartmentalized into a 2-clique with tie strength three {HOP-HUE-MOR-SOR-TRA}, which represents those sites that had access to all local semi-precious lithic types and Long Island flint. The subgraph is only a 2-clique because the site of Morel (MOR) does not connect with a 3-strength tie to any other site, except for Trants (TRA). This is because this 2-clique represents the full geographic distribution of Long Island flint, divided into a southern and northern group and connected by a central area. Finally, in the northern area we see a clique of tie strength 3 formed by the sites of Hope Estate, Sorcé and La Hueca and an even stronger triad of 4-strength ties between Hope Estate, Sorcé and La Hueca.

The 3-strength tie clique at the centre of the graph provides a possible indication of candidates for the role of distribution nodes, here substituted by hypothetical nodes. The network illustrated in Figure 5.9 presents an interpretation hereof, based on the evidence for direct acquisition of raw materials and workshops. It suggests that the three sites in the centre of the graph, Trants, Hope Estate and La Hueca, are not only a triad but as such were also a strong cyclical component (Chapter 3).[10] From this it should follow that they hold the majority of the power in the network. This is true: Trants, Hope Estate and La Hueca hold 44% of all the ties (i.e. relative degree). However, between the members of this powerful triad there is a further differentiation to be made. This can be analysed with alternative measures of centrality such as closeness, measuring the distances to all other nodes in the network, and betweenness, which measures the total amount of shortest paths on which a node lies and thus is a good indicator of a node's strategic position. These measures prove that Trants and La Hueca share the same closeness centrality, which is higher than Hope Estate (12.85% over 10.5%). These nodes have the absolute

10 The reason why Sorcé is not considered to be part of this component has to do with evidence for a workshop at the neighbouring site of La Hueca, yet no such workshops have been found at Sorcé itself (Rodríguez Ramos, personal communication 2011).

closest paths between them and all the other nodes within this network. In addition Trants and La Hueca have a much higher betweenness than Hope Estate (13.05%), but Trants (39.15%) has an even higher betweenness than La Hueca (32.60%). This indicates that Trants is located on most of the shortest paths between nodes in the network. Based on a sequential analysis of subgraph identification, tie strength, 1-mode remodelling, and centrality measures, Trants appears to be the node with the most central position of the Period D lithic network.

Interpretation

Period D has received relatively much attention from Caribbean archaeologists (Boomert 2000; Bérard 2013; Fitzpatrick 2013b). This is partly because it is often seen as an extension of the 500/400 BC hypothesized migration(s) from the mainland in which settlers slowly spread over the Northeastern Caribbean. Indeed, where Period C marked the first dated appearance of two new ceramic styles, Saladoid and Huecoid, this represented only a hesitant start. Sites with new ceramic series were still outnumbered by sites with more traditional assemblages. In Period D these new types of sites are now in the majority. Period C included five Saladoid and one Huecoid site, while Period D counts nine Saladoid sites and three Huecoid sites.

Continuing on where the discussion was left in Period C, this suggests that the so-called Archaic-Ceramic interface has started to fade and communities of descendants from migrants and the original inhabitants of the Northeastern Caribbean had started to coalesce. At the same time this saw the rise of two new "archaeological cultures", typified by differences in Saladoid and Huecoid assemblages and often thought to represent dissimilar communities with separate ancestries (see Chapter 2). What can the network of Period D teach us about the the relations between the Huecoid and the Saladoid?

The preliminary conclusion of this is that any notion of a complete social boundary between communities that were using either Huecoid or Saladoid ceramics can be rejected. Firstly, based on presence, there is no difference between lithic preferences of sites belonging to either series. Beyond the fact that Huecoid and Saladoid sites are equally strongly connected to all local lithic groups they also helped distribute them to each other. The most efficacious interpretation hereof is that lithic materials would have had an unrestricted flow between Huecoid and Saladoid sites. The best evidence for this actually comes from the heart of the network: the "strong clique" {HAC-HOP-HUE-MOR-SOR-TRA}. From Northeast to South it consists of almost alternate iterations of Saladoid and Huecoid sites.

This fact is already given away by the hybrid quality of the securely dated sites in this period. Of the nine Saladoid sites in the model three have some sort of Huecoid element and of the three Huecoid sites only Punta Candelero is supposedly a pure Huecoid site. Here, too, the mixed nature of the central triad is most telling. This triumvirate of nodes consists of a Saladoid site with some Huecoid influences (Trants), a Huecoid site with Saladoid components (Hope Estate) and a Huecoid site located within 100 m. of a Saladoid site (La Hueca and Sorcé). All three were lithic workshops, crafting materials found in the other two sites. The strong, mutually directed flows between these sites are exemplified by the cyclical nature of their clique. Furthermore the 1-mode, directed model suggests that between the three of them they were able to completely dominate the flow of lithic materials in the region. Such strong triadic connection would have included a downside. Being part of a clique comes with a price. With an increase in overall network power, cliques also increase the internal depencies between its members. Furthermore, a rise to power of one node can be countered by the other two members of the triad. Thus, it could very well be that the networks of the communities of La Hueca, Hope Estate and Trants were deeply interwined. Such a community of material cultural practices goes beyond any notion of cultural division between Saladoid and Huecoid as it might arise from previous culture historical pathways or different stylistic and technical differences in material cultural repertoires.

On the other hand, this was not an Arcadian paradise and competition, perhaps because of differential access to resources, seems to have been part of these exchange systems, as hinted at by the differences in the centrality of nodes in Period D. These suggest that there were major differences in access to raw materials between some sites and also minor variances between the three members of the central triad. This is also indicated by the boom in the quality and quantity of exotic stones and other materials, particularly ornaments and smaller amulets, found in sites dating from this period. The manner in which such a potential struggle for power affected the inter-communal relations within the region will be further evaluated by means of the model of Period E.

Period E: emulation

Period E does not witness any changes in lithic group nodes (Figure 5.10). There are, however, a number of new site nodes. Especially the southern region witnesses quite an increase in number of sites with the first securely dated ceramic site south of the Martinique passage in St. Vincent. St. Lucia and Dominica remain empty. Whether this represents a structural hole in archaeological practice or in the social networks of the period is difficult to surmise. Dominica has not seen much pre-colonial archaeological work and even then early sites in both islands are likely to be covered under several meters of volcanic deposits or to have been destroyed due to coastal erosion (Delpuech 2004). Antigua, although probably occupied continuously since Period A (Davis 2000; Nicholson 1994), also sees its first securely dated ceramic sites, like Royall's (ROY) and Doigs (DOI).[11] They have ceramic assemblages that are pre-dominantly Saladoid, although a fair number also have a Huecoid component. Puerto Rico still has a number of sites with assemblages that are characteristic of the period before the Huecoid and Saladoid appeared in the archipelago. It is unclear how they are related, yet some of these

---

11 Several sites with Saladoid components on Antigua of this period, such as Elliots (Murhpy, *et al.* 2000), are not dated.

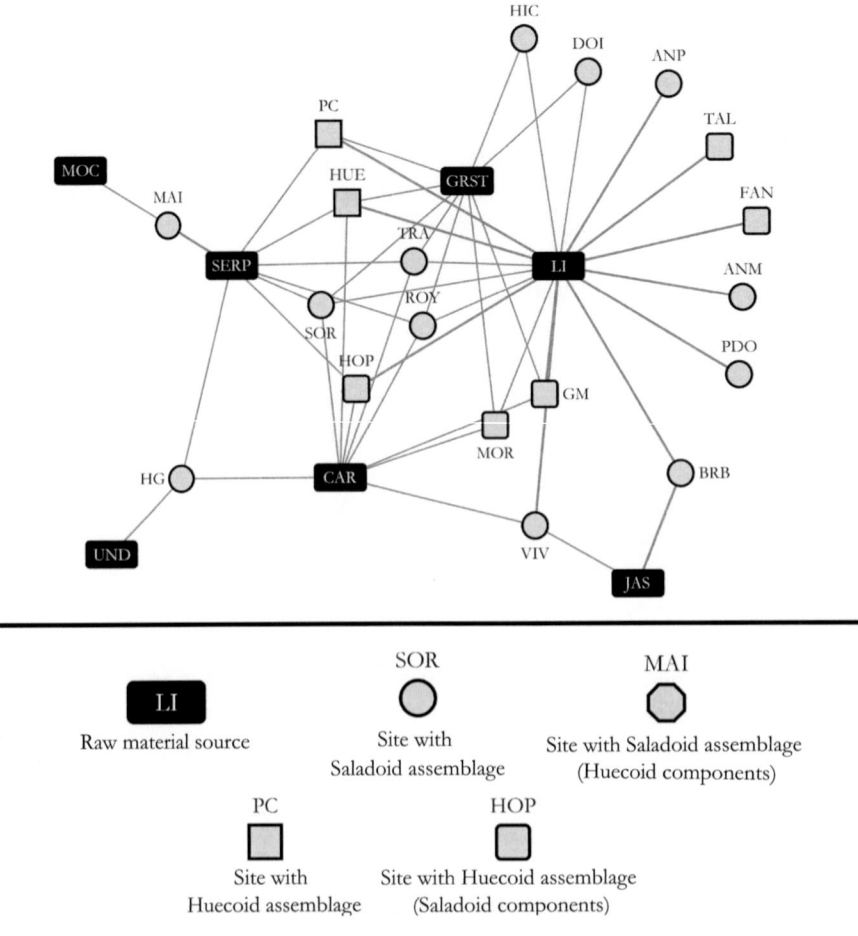

Figure 5.10: 2-mode network of Period E with sites tied to raw material sources of which material is present in their assemblages.

sites, such as Cueva Maria de la Cruz, are located in the vicinity of the Saladoid and Huecoid sites (Rodríguez Ramos 2010). This suggests movement and bilateral interaction, although this is not visible in the lithic network of this period.

Structure, subgraphs and clique strength

Interestingly, this Period once again witnesses growth in node quantity. Since it covers the same span of time as Period D (300 years) and lithic groups this increase is not dependent on any difference in temporal scales or node selection. It is therefore fully attributable to a rise in site nodes of which the network contains twenty-four in total. Of these, nineteen are connectable to any of the seven lithic group nodes in the network. Of the lithic group nodes, Long Island flint, which has already been the most popular lithic material through Periods B to D, sees its node affiliation almost doubled to seventeen. The presence of other lithic sources in sites also grows: carnelian (degree of 9), serpentinite (degree of 9), and St. Martin greenstone (degree of 8).

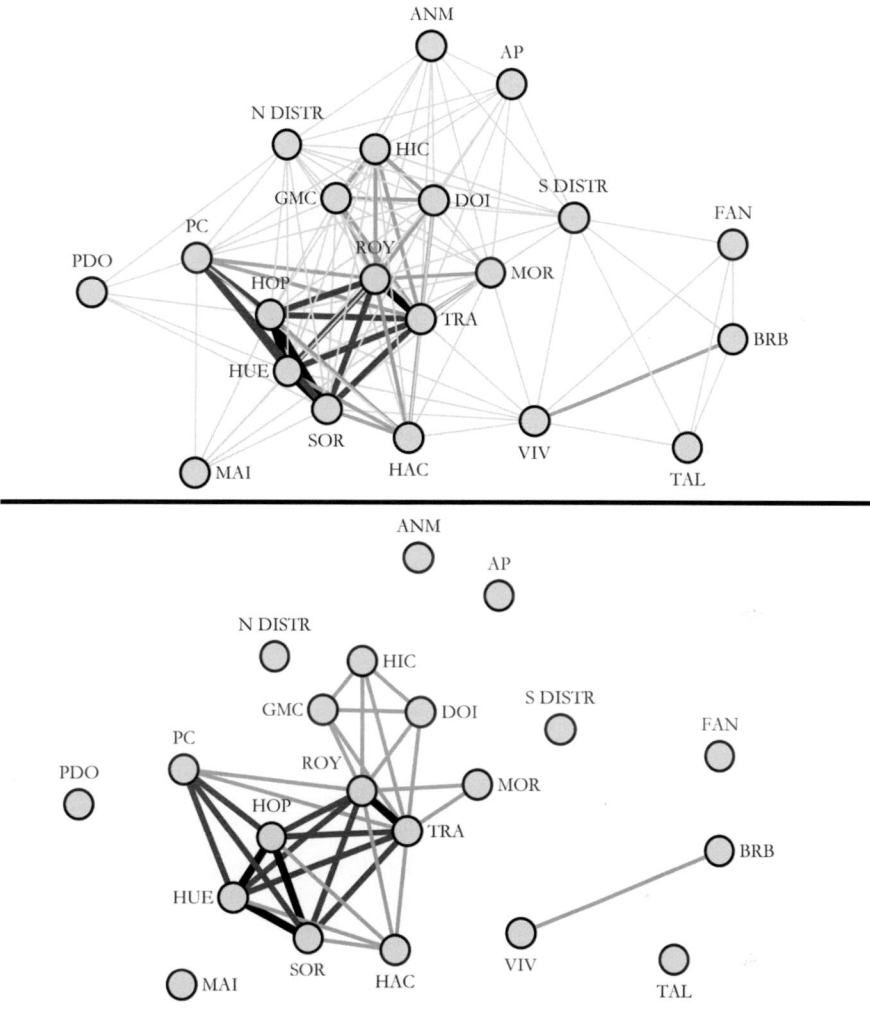

Figure 5.11: Affiliation (site to site) network of Period E. Tie colour and size is related to tie strength (from low to high = light to dark, thin to thick). The network above displays all ties, while the network below illustrates exclusively the ties with strength 2 and higher.

These increases in nodes and node membership are reflected in the down-the-line affiliation network of sites too (Figure 5.11). The graph consists of one component that looks rather cluttered with many ties crisscrossing the network at the centre. Nonetheless, appearances may deceive: the affiliation network of Period E is much sparser than that of Period D (27.6%). This is a result of the fact that the growth of nodes with Long Island flint affiliation occurs at the centre as well as southwards and northwards. This implies that, because of the down-the-line exchange once again modelled through a hypothetical node, some nodes will not be directly affiliated through the network's otherwise best path. In addition, several new nodes connect to only lithic material, often Long Island flint.

Predictably, a *k*-core analysis shows large subgraphs with high coreness values. The twelve members of the 10-core {DOI-GMC-HAC-HIC-HOP-HUE-MOR-PC-ROY-SOR-TRA-NDist} are all found in the North-central and central part of the network. In the Northeastern and Southern extremes of the network we find nodes related to fewer other nodes in the component, such as BRB, FAN and TAL (4-core) and PDO and MAI that have a coreness value of 5 and 6 respectively. Moreover, we see sites in the geographic extremes of the network like Vivé that connect better to the centre core (VIV; coreness value of 8). Overall, the network consists of only two 2-cliques with many shared members. The farthest nodes in this affiliation network are only separated by 3 degrees.

There are ten cliques in this network (see Table 5.1). Some of these maximally connected subgraphs correlate to central, Southern and Northern distribution regions (Clique A for the centre, Clique I for the South and J for the North). The majority of the cliques present network groups separated by geographically long-distances, such as Clique F {HAC-HOP-HUE-MOR-ROY-SOR-TRA-VIV} that affiliates for example the site of Hacienda Grande in Puerto Rico to the site of Vivé in Martinique. This is based on the presence of semi-precious material in their assemblages, which is not differentiated by a Northern and Southern distribution system for this graph.

ID	*k*-core	member of 2-clique	Member of clique
ANM	9	A, B	A
AP	9	A, B	A
BRB	4	B	I
DOI	10	A, B	A, B, C, D, E
FAN	4	B	I
GMC	10	A, B	A, B, C, D, E
HAC	10	A,B	C, D, F
HIC	10	A, B	A, B, C, D, E
HOP	10	A,B	B, C, D, E, F, H, J
HUE	10	A,B	B, C, D, E, F, H, J
MAI	5	A	H
MOR	10	A, B	A, B, C, F, G
NDist	10	A, B	A, B, E, J
PC	10	A	D, E, H, J
PDO	6	A	J
ROY	10	A, B	A, B, C, D, E, F, G, H
SDist	9	A, B	A, G, I
SOR	10	A,B	B, C, D, E, F, G, H, J
TAL	4	B	I
TRA	10	A, B	A, B, C, D, E, F, G, H
VIV	8	A,B	F, G, I

Table 5.1 The subgraphs of the affiliation network of Period E showing k-core numbers, and (2-)clique membership of nodes in the site-to-site affiliation model of the 2-mode network of Period E (Figure 5.11).

Here too we can find a differentiation in the tie strength of cliques. A progressive removal of ties with strengths 1 to 3, results in network decay. This starts at the fringes with cliques without access to Long Island flint or semi-precious stone and progresses to take apart all cliques but for the most strongly affiliated site nodes. Again we find the nodes of Trants (TRA), Hope Estate (HOP), La Hueca (HUE) and Sorcé (SOR) as part of the subgraph that withstands lower strength tie disintegration (Figure 5.11). This select group is now joined by two new members: the sites of Royall's (ROY) in Antigua and Punta Candelero (PC) in Puerto Rico. Together these five sites form a 2-clique that can be further subdivided in the four tie-strength triad {HOP-HUEC-SOR} and the strong dyad {ROY-TRA}. These shifts in the higher echelons of the affiliation network also have their impact on the 1-mode, directed network of lithic distribution during Period E.

Centrality

For this final directed model two possible networks were created to discuss centrality in the exchange networks of Period E (Figures 5.12 and 5.13). The outcome of the centrality measures are collected in Table 5.2. This has been done in order to mimic two possible scenarios, both of which have some plausibility. One (Figure 5.12) presents a situation of preferential interaction. Ties are wired based on the idea that sites with a longer history in the network would hold on to the exclusive nature of their contacts and access to raw material sources in the subsequent period. This introduces a form of hierarchy within the model and old nodes such as TRA, HOP, HUE and MOR have more ties then new nodes like ROY and PC. Being around for a longer time, older site nodes often have had the opportunity to acquire more ties over time, therefore attracting even more ties and thus gain more access to and control over the entire network – conform the preferential attachment model discussed in Chapter 3. The other model is based on the idea of "unrestricted trade" in the region. Whenever a material occurs at a site this is modelled as if it was drawing these materials from all possible partners at the same time. The result hereof is that the latter model has many more ties than the preferential interaction model. For both networks tie wiring is restricted in the case where a down-the-line chokepoint must have been positioned, based on the study of Knippenberg (2007).

In the preferential model Morel has the highest absolute degree, which is based on the high number of outgoing (outdegree) ties through its distribution network to the South of the region (Figure 5.12). Trants, however, has the highest closeness and betweenness rating, providing it with the best strategic position within the network. La Hueca and Morel follow at some distance in terms of betweenness and closeness. Even though it still holds the monopoly over St. Martin Greenstone distribution, Hope Estate has overall lower centrality measures. Growing hinterlands in Puerto Rico and the Martinique and Guadeloupe archipelago provide the power distribution in Period E with a more diffuse character. Indeed, the triad {HOP-HUE-TRA} has lost some of its absolute power within the network. Nevertheless, these sites as yet form the only strong and cyclical component in both models.

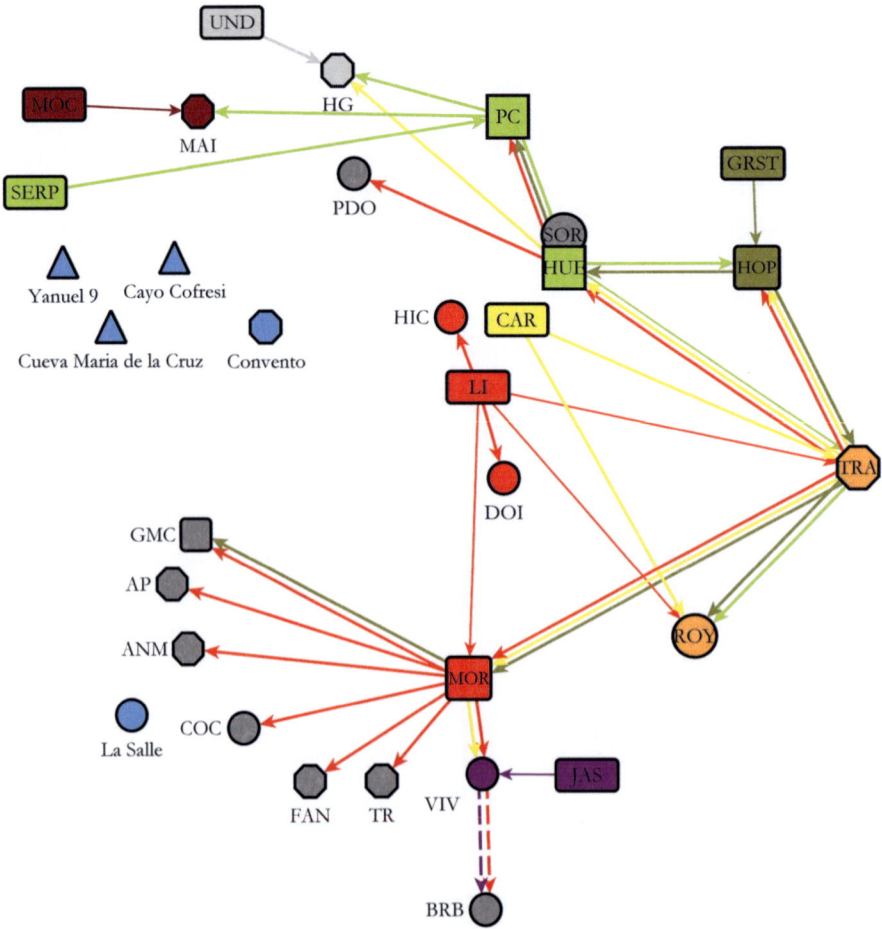

Figure 5.12: Directed network of Period E with preferential attachment to sites which were also present in previous periods (interpretation). The node colour is indicative of the type of raw materials worked at the site. The layout of the network approximates the geography of the region.

In the unrestricted model Royall's (ROY) is added to that central subgraph (Figure 5.13). Royall's is in many respects structurally similar to Trants in a 2-mode or affiliation network: presence of all local semi-precious material and direct acquirement of Long Island flint and Carnelian. However, when referring to both directed models the centrality of most sites, for example La Hueca and Sorcé (HUE/SOR), Vivé (VIV) and Hope Estate (HOP) remains roughly the same, the sites of Royall's and Trants are prime examples showcasing the differences between the preferential and unrestricted model. When serving as a supplier of Trants in the preferential model, in the unrestricted model it is on an equal footing. The other large difference is the site of Morel, which has also lost a fair amount of its network power. The reason being it is not modelled as the de facto down-the-line distributor of lithic materials making their way from North to South.

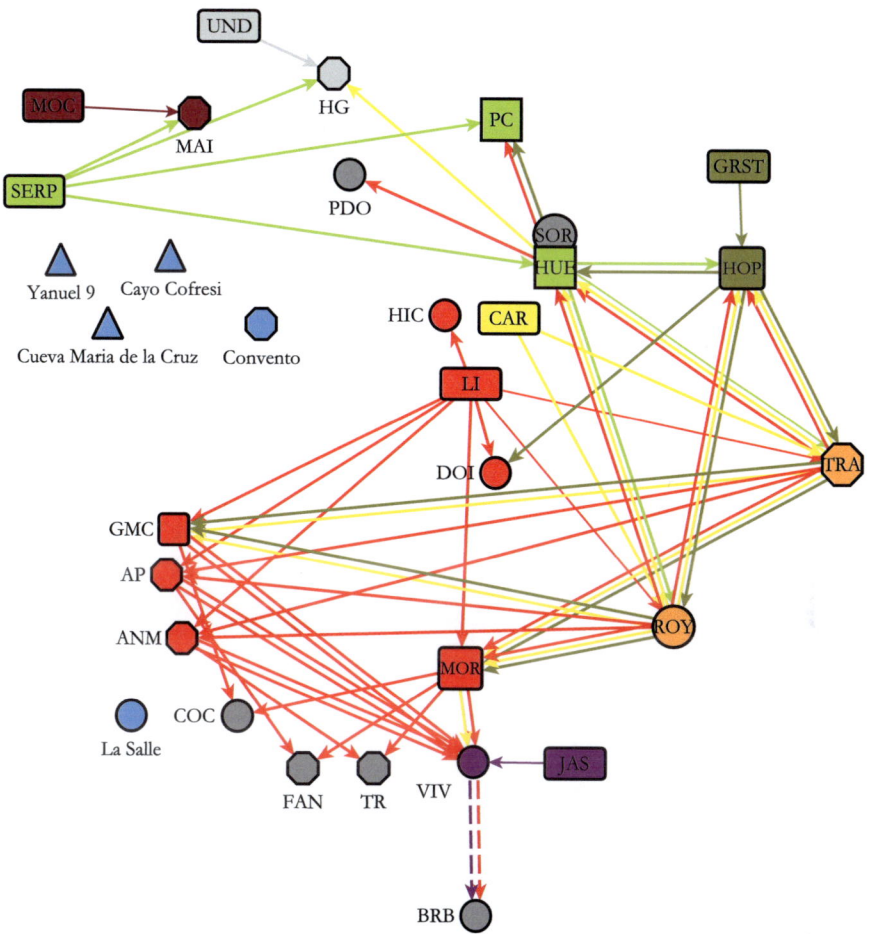

Figure 5.13: Directed network of Period E without preferential attachment to sites which were also present during previous periods (interpretation). The node colour is indicative of the type of raw materials worked at the site. The layout of the network approximates the geography of the region.

Nonetheless, the importance of these models lies not in their differences but in their similarities. Both models point to the same five highest ranking nodes: Morel (MOR) in Guadeloupe, Trants (TRA) and Royall's (ROY) on Montserrat and Antigua respectively, Hope Estate (HOP) on St. Martin and La Hueca (with Sorcé; HUE/SOR) on Vieques. Together these "big five" represent an aggregated 55.4% (preferential) and 60.4% (unrestricted) of the total value of centrality measures for both models. These are all, with the exception of Royall's, sites present in the models of Period D and some are even found in Period E, such as in the case of Trants. It seems that, at least in terms of lithic interaction patterns within the region, social networks had evolved towards a lasting differentiation of power between communities. However, in contrast to Period D, any power is somewhat more equally distributed through the network. We see differentiations between

ID	degree (%)		indegree (%)		outdegree (%)		closeness (%)		betweenness (%)		Rank	
	6.12	6.13	6.12	6.13	6.12	6.13	6.12	6.13	6.12	6.13	6.12	6.13
ANP	2.9	4.6	5.9	4.6	0	4.6	0	2.8	0	3.1	13	7
ANM	2.9	4.6	5.9	4.6	0	4.6	0	2.8	0	3.1	13	7
GMC	2.9	4.6	5.9	4.6	0	4.6	0	2.8	0	3.1	13	7
BRB	2.0	1.5	3.9	3.1	0	0	0	0	0	0	15	13
CAR	1.0	1.5	0	0	2.0	3.1	6.8	8.6	0	0	11	9
COC	1.0	1.5	2.0	3.1	0	0	0	0	0	0	17	13
DOI	2.0	1.5	3.9	3.1	0	0	0	0	0	0	15	13
FAN	1.0	1.5	2.0	3.1	0	0	0	0	0	0	16	13
HAC	2.9	2.3	5.9	4.6	0	0	0	0	0	0	15	13
HIC	1.0	0.8	2.0	1.5	0	0	0	0	0	0	16	15
HOP	6.9	7.7	7.8	9.2	5.9	6.2	9.6	9.4	6.1	13.5	5	5
JAS	2.0	1.5	0	0	3.9	3.1	2.7	2.5	0	0	14	11
HUE/SOR	9.8	10	7.8	9.2	11.8	10.8	10.3	10	18.0	20.2	3	2
LI	3.9	6.2	0	0	7.8	12.3	10.7	12.7	0	0	6	6
MAI	2.0	1.5	3.9	3.1	0	0	0	0	0	0	15	13
MOC	1.0	0.8	0	0	2.0	1.5	1.4	1.3	0	0	16	14
MOR	17.6	9.2	7.8	10.8	27.5	7.7	9.7	5.2	24.4	15.2	1	4
PDO	1.0	0.8	2.0	1.5	0	0	0	0	0	0	17	15
PC	4.9	2.3	5.9	4.6	3.9	0	2.7	0	3.4	0	7	12
ROY	6.9	10.8	9.8	6.2	3.9	15.4	8.4	11.9	8.1	17.2	4	1
SERP	1.0	3.1	0	0	2.0	6.2	6.7	8.5	0	0	12	8
SRPDis	2.9	/	2.0	/	3.9	/	8.2	/	6.1	/	6	/
GRST	1.0	0.8	0	0	2.0	1.5	7.5	7.1	0	0	10	10
TAL	1.0	1.5	2.0	3.1	0	0	0	0	0	0	17	13
TRA	13.7	10.8	7.8	6.2	19.6	15.4	12.7	11.9	30.5	17.2	2	1
UND	1.0	0.8	0	0	2.0	1.5	1.4	1.3	0	0	16	14
VIV	3.9	7.7	5.9	13.8	2.0	1.5	1.4	1.3	3.4	7.4	8	4

Table 5.2 The centralities of nodes in the directed networks of period E, showing the centralities of the nodes for the two models in Figures 5.12 (preferentially attached) and Figure 5.13 (non-preferentially attached) in percentages. Note that there are quite a number of shifts in the individual centralities and aggregated centrality ranks ("Rank" in the table) of the nodes. This rank is not based on one graph theoretical measure, but on the aggregate of all centrality measures presented in this table.

various types of centralities – e.g. Morel has a larger hinterland, yet Trants and Royall's occupy a better structural position, while La Hueca and Sorcé are all-round and consistent high scorers and Hope Estate has its monopoly of St. Martin Greenstone.

Finally, these models also present an interesting alternative view of clique formation, with much more regionally restricted subgraphs. It is to be expected that such a directed, 1-mode network is far less dense (4.8% and for the preferential and 6.5% for the unrestricted model of all possible ties present) than their 2-mode counterpart. However, even taken on the whole, both models do not show much cohesion. Path analysis of the diameter of the network indicates that the farthest sites are separated by 6 degrees, a relatively small social distance for an area with a Euclidean diameter of *c*.850 km It is important to note that the only paths that cover the whole of the network run from the Northeast to the South and not vice versa. This is the reason why the only strong component is the one mentioned above. The same applies to any cyclical subgraphs, even on the level of the dyad. On the other hand the network contains quite a few two-cliques and even cliques: twelve two-cliques and four cliques in the preferential model and fourteen two-cliques and thirteen cliques in the unrestricted model. Most of these can be found in the central and Southern part of the network.

Interpretation

One might wonder which forwards a truer version of social networks during this era: the preferential or the unrestricted model? In fact, the question whether, for example, Trants or Royall's or Morel was more powerful is difficult to answer without looking more in-depth at the contexts of these sites, incorporating more lines of evidence and adjusting for imbalances in the collection of data. Even then it might be impossible to establish a complete picture of network relations between these specific sites. In my view, with regard to the matter at hand and at this level of analysis, such specific questions are ultimately not that important – or even interesting. What does fascinate is that all the models – 2-mode, affiliation, 1-mode preferential directed and 1-mode unrestricted – indicate the same trend: enduringly and increasingly powerful nodes, manoeuvring for power by new network players and down-the-line distribution of materials across the entire archipelago. It is obvious that these patterns are not the result of a disjointed socio-cultural landscape, divided into Saladoid and Huecoid spheres of influence. These models indicate that between AD 100 and 400 the network comprised of an integrated whole embracing several smaller interaction spheres (Boomert 2000; Hofman, Bright, *et al.* 2007). This integration suggests a stabilization of the potentially volatile situation as it had arisen when new cultural practices and, presumably, settlers had reached the islands during the previous centuries. In a matter of 1 or 2 centuries the old and new networks of people and objects had become enmeshed. A new Caribbean socio-cultural reality had been born.

This integration is clearly shown by the size and strength of subgraphs in the region. Based on the suggested scenario from Period D that presents us with incipient inequalities in network power, a falling apart of the social network in various competing, non-interacting factions might have been the case. Surprisingly, as the affiliation model of this period displays many connected sets of nodes. On the other hand there is also new evidence for strong dyadic formation, such as in the case of the new dyad {ROY-TRA}. Such strongly paired sites would have potentially been cooperating more closely than other dyads in the network.

The site of Royall's supports this. It is in many respects the "younger brother" or perhaps the "offspring" of the site of Trants. Being a larger habitation site, its assemblage contains a range of (semi-precious) lithic materials and there is evidence for carnelian bead production (Knippenberg 2007; Murphy, et al. 2000). We find a similar symbiotic, or at least, co-evolutionary bond between the La Hueca and Sorcé sites on the one and Hope Estate on the other hand. The dates for habitation are almost contemporaneous. What is more, all three sites include exotic materials originating from beyond the local region that were produced in one of the two other sites (Hofman and Hoogland 1999; Knippenberg 2007; Narganes Storde 1995; Rodríguez Ramos, et al. 2010). It remains unclear whether similar dyadic relations existed in the southern region of the archipelago. It is notable, however, that the relations between Vivé and Morel had a time-depth of several centuries. Furthermore a number of new habitation sites within the archipelago of Guadeloupe and Martinique were at the least integrated in the exchange network of Long Island flint, but possibly partook in other types of interactions, as well (Bérard 2004, 2013).

Although the core of the network provides us with an insight into the dynamics of networks around the turn of the first millennium, the fringes of the network show an equally interesting picture. The site of Brighton Beach in the southern extents of the network, recently investigated by Leiden University's Caribbean Research group, delivers a good case in point (Mol and Boomert 2011). The village at this site was, for all intents and purposes, able to see to its own needs. The direct location provided plenty of opportunities for food procurement. In addition, siliceous materials on the neighbouring islands of St. Lucia and Carriacou could serve to produce tools and personal adornments. Most of the ceramic assemblage at the site is typical of the late Saladoid, yet at the lower cultural strata we see several layers of early Saladoid material (Figure 1.3.f). C-14 dates of Cal. AD 150 that were acquired from just above these deposits suggest that this material dates from before the previously suggested starting point of Saladoid presence of AD 400 (Fitzpatrick 2009). Interestingly, a majority of the siliceous material found in these layers originates from the Long Island flint source – including a few, almost completely exhausted cores (Knippenberg, personal communication 2011). Although the Brighton Beach site is located at what is now regarded as the fringe area of the advancement of Saladoid communities in the area, the presence of Long Island flint at such an early phase shows it was already connected at the core.

The recent findings at Brighton Beach thus argue for a full integration of the southern Lesser Antilles into the island networks of the 1st century AD. If more archaeological fieldwork is carried out in the region and more absolute dates of early ceramic sites become available this might push this date back to well before AD. It also shows that, even though exotic materials were coming in from various other regions in the mainland, within the islands itself Long Island flint held great attraction for sites located far away from its source – in the case of Brighton Beach,

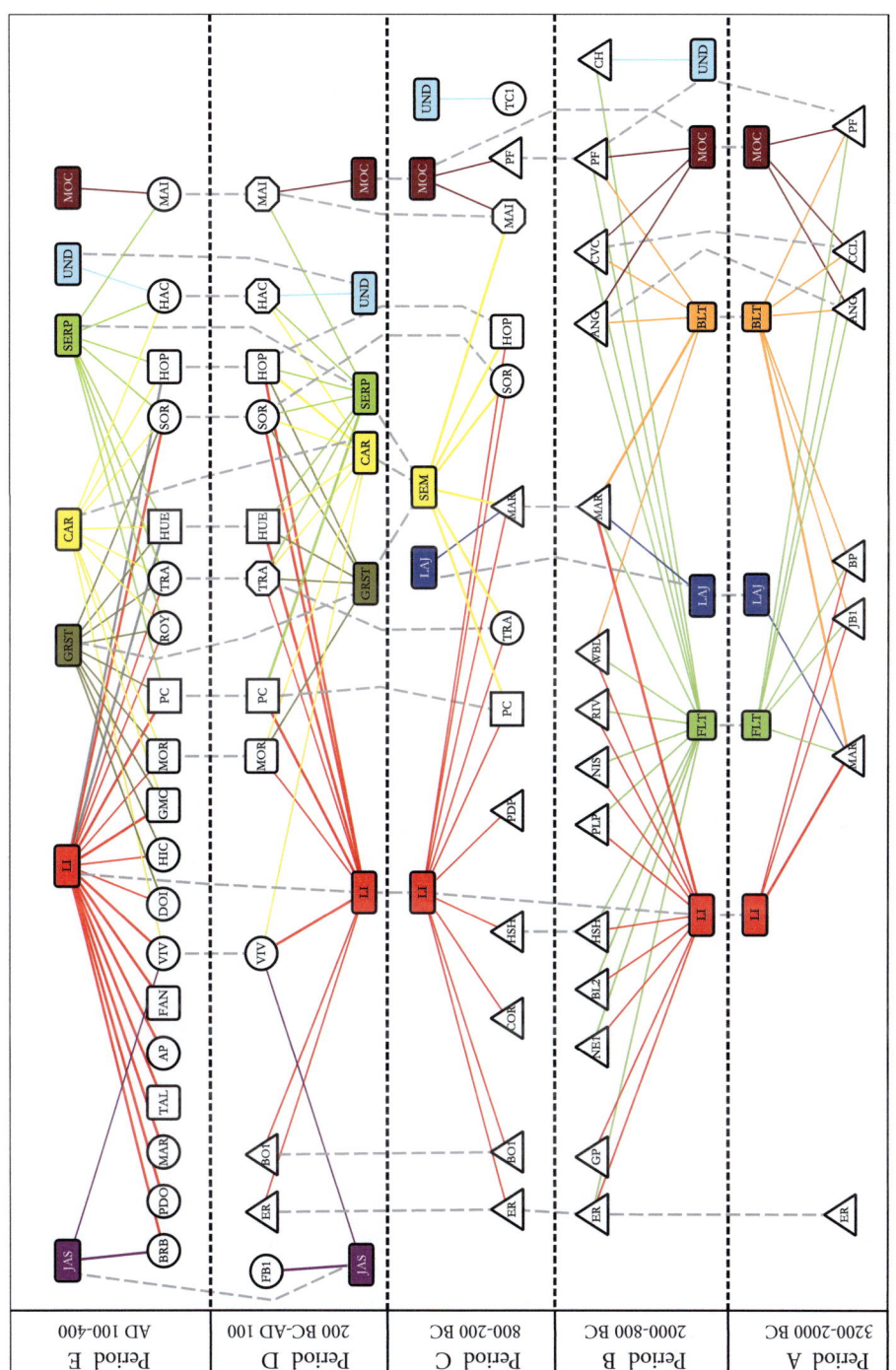

Figure 5.14: A longitudinal view of the 2-mode networks from period A to E (3200 BC–AD 400). It illustrates sites tied to raw material sources of which material is present in their assemblages. In period A and B the nodes are also connected to a knapping technique node in order to indicate the presence of tools produced with that technique found at the site. Sites are also connected to other sites with a dotted line, indicating their continued habitation and use during later periods. The same applies to raw material and knapping technique nodes.

c.450 km away. Even though the distances and the logistic difficulties of navigating the islands could be huge, through its widespread circulation Long Island flint created a socially small(er)-world in the North-eastern Caribbean and beyond.

Longitudinal trajectories of lithic production and distribution networks

The network in Figure 5.14 is a collection of all 2-mode networks dating from the Periods A to E. It shows the connections between sites and lithic groups within the region for each stage and between the stages for those sites and materials with a continued presence. As stated above, this network is not a social network. Its ties do not directly reflect social interaction and, even if they were, it would be difficult to almost impossible to substantiate this with any currently available archaeological methods and techniques. The network may also be considered as a simplification of a large amount of variability in material repertoires and practices throughout time. Because this network is based on currently available and dateable archaeological evidence, it is necessarily a simplified model of a situation that was in reality much more dynamic. Furthermore, because of its huge time-span it is also unlikely that it directly reflects a conscious reality in terms of the historical sense of the peoples themselves. The question is then: what does this network refer to?

This model of affiliations between sites and lithic raw material sources reveals an image of networks across time and space. It shows that from the earliest colonization of the islands humans and things were continously related to each other through networks that were both social and material. The connections and contrast between the lithic nodes in the network was dependent upon the social practices, landscape knowledge and passing on of time-honoured crafting traditions. On the other hand the social networks of these peoples were also founded upon the materiality of these stone materials, such as intrinsic material qualities and the geographic position and availability of the raw material sources. The temporal durability and structure of the network most certainly arose from mutually reinforced relations between people and things. Certain site nodes became increasingly central due to their participation in certain lithic networks and certain materials become increasingly popular the more they were distributed among (central) communities in the region. Cliques and other subgraphs arranged themselves around the distribution of local lithic materials and the distribution of these materials was possible due to the social networks between communities.

The first social networks (3200 - 2000 BC) of the region are shrouded by their light archaeological footprints. At this point the Caribbean presumably had only few inhabitants, which is indicated by the small number of nodes in the network. From analagous situations across the world we know that in such a sparse social landscape all or the majority of the social interactions between people were founded on close kin relations. In other words sharing of food, shelter and other resources was based on the sharing of blood.

This Communal Sharing models of relations seems to have been followed through in later centuries (2000-800 BC). Even though the (social) landscape was rapidly becoming more densely settled in Puerto Rico and the northern Lesser Antilles, this did not lead to an appropriation of important resources, such as sources for critically important flint tools. Rather, groups seem to have been incorporating these resources within their cyclical patterns of migration and probably made return-trips to these sources during the year. Analogous situations in Melanesia teach us that such stone material gathering expeditions can be highly important occasions, infused with communal and ceremonial aspects (Godelier 1973). Similar examples exist closer to home, such as the Warao expeditions in search of chert and other lithic materials from beyond their stone-less Orinoco delta homeland (Wilbert 1993). Building on the inherent social nature of these expeditions and the neutral and immobile quality of lithic sources it is not unthinkable that these developed overtime to become significant social events and the sources themselves important spaces – e.g. communal, perhaps intergroup, meeting places.

It seems that social networks grew beyond the local scale starting somewhere in c.1800 BC, but that they are best attested by archaeological evidence dating from 800-200 BC. The "cultural when, where and how" of the introduction of new materials and ways of life must be left in the middle for now. These local lithic networks do not present a clear view of this process beyond anything already known for certain, which is preciously little. At present, even more remains unknown concerning the social mechanics of an Archaic-Ceramic interface. This model suggests that the communities hiding behind the nodes in Period C were certainly contemporary to each other and their shared utilization of the Long Island and Mocca flint sources suggests they were also in contact. However, those already inhabiting the islands and any newcomers were simultaneously divided and united by their access to and treatment of (lithic) material culture. The accumulated force of interregional interactions and confrontations with new settlers, attested by the inclusive quality of Long Island flint and the exclusive nature of semi-precious lithics and ceramic assemblages, created a new dynamic in social networks. The differential presence of semi-precious lithic materials in Saladoid, Huecoid and "Archaic" sites, suggests a number of variations in the social value that was afforded to these materials. In turn this proposes a slight but critical difference in status based on personal objects. Perhaps this indicates a divergence between communities relying upon Communal Sharing models of relations to those increasingly concerned with fair exchanges (Equality Matching) and inter-personal hierarchies (Authority Ranking). In the network models this most clearly manifests itself in Period D (AD 200-BC 100) by cliques and nodes that come to hold more power in the network than others.

Outside of the lithic network this new dynamic is best visible in the way the Saladoid and Huecoid phenomena are connected. It is undeniable that (parts of) the Huecoid and Saladoid assemblages are distinct and this dissimilarity must have had some effect on the interactions between peoples practicing different material cultural repertoires. Nevertheless, more often as not, sites were internal hybrids, evidencing the incorporation of one another's social and cultural practices, the copying of stylistic motifs and the exchange of raw materials, tools and valuables.

More importantly, however, is the fact that the lithic network model of Period D shows that Saladoid and Huecoid groups were at least partially connected. Communities such as La Hueca, Sorcé, Hope Estate and Trants, together with older sites on Antigua and the surrounding islands, jointly participated in the lithic networks. The emergence of strong cliques in the network suggests they were even joined in their preferences for and distributon of local (semi-precious) stone materials. Therefore, at the very least it can be said that Huecoid and Saladoid communities did not view each other as contraposed groups of social others that were categorically inaccesible.

Thus, one may wonder whether there is even a "La Hueca problem"? Denying such a thing would amount to brushing over the intricacies of Saladoid and Huecoid assemblages. On the other hand it seems that the problem is not one of social incompatibility but perhaps the exact opposite of it. The root of the controversy can be found in an awkward dyad within the network: the sites of La Hueca and Sorcé. From the models it becomes clear that in every respect – but for the slightly earlier dating of Sorcé due to chronometric hygenic procedures – the sites are the same. The sites are located directly next to each other, as well. What, according to the Puerto Rican archaeologists who have excavated and studied the assemblages for nearly 30 years, is vastly different is the material culture styles, forms and techniques that are segmented across horizontal boundaries.[12] Yet even if it was culturally and horizontally divided, the social and material history of La Hueca and Sorcé is clearly connected. In fact, like a knot (*nodus*) consisting of various materials, it could be that a diversity in cultural practices of La Hueca and Sorcé actually benefited these two joined communities, augmenting their possibility to engage in sociable interactions with groups with a diverse range of cultural backgrounds. On the other hand a knot or node is only as strong as its ties. Perhaps this is the reason why peoples with different cultural backgrounds living at La Hueca and Sorcé sought to establish lasting relations with other communities, such as at Hope Estate and Trants, in the process excerting a homogeneizing cultural influence on the rest of the region.

Indeed, the differences in material cultural repertoires become less sharp during the last phase of this case-study (AD 100-400). Perhaps as a reaction to the emergent competition of Period D, cliques and site pairings increase. In this regard the clique of sites in the central and North-central part of the network, with increasingly stronger relations since Period C, is interesting. While all these sites are closely linked, some are more closely linked than others. For over several centuries La Hueca and Sorcé has continued close relations with the site of Hope Estate on St. Martin, for example. Early Trants perhaps had a similar relation with

---

12   As of yet, we can only guess which social mechanics were responsible for such a strong segmentation. However, it seems unlikely no social ties existed between the two sites while social ties were present across the region. These fixed identities were perhaps caused by internal competition and factioning – different clans, moieties, etc. It is still possible that a classical Greek-style of "colonialism" (Malkin 2011), in which Saladoid colonists would settle close to an autochthonous community, working and living together but upholding separate cultural practices, could be the cause of this dichotomy.

the other early site on Montserrat, Radio Antilles.[13] Later Royall's was to take up this role. Such a methodical formation of coalitions has already been discussed by Keegan (2007: 155). The main difference between Keegan's model and this one is the type of distance thought to be important: Keegan identifies geographically close sites as possibly paired settlements, while this pairing is based on the exchange of (lithic) materials.

What can be said about possible changes in the dominant models of relations during the Archaic-Saladoid-Huecoid Interface period? It seems reasonable to suggest that most of the social relations underlying the lithic acquisition and distribution of the earliest periods were predominantly about Communal Sharing models of relation. In most cases it seems to be the case that Archaic Age communities had direct access to raw material sources. Starting in Period C an emulation process starts with the advent of new endogenous and exotic semi-precious materials. If we accept the idea that the dyadic and clique ties resulting from this would have consisted of other models of relations becoming more dominant – it is unlikely that they were absent altogether in the earliest periods. This implies the development of a more "complex" socio-political structure.

The down-the-line distribution of raw materials, especially of semi-precious stones, and the influx of other exotic materials suggests first and foremost a web of reciprocal exchanges and thus the pre-dominance of Equality Matching relations (cf. Knippenberg 2007). It could be that the movements of exotic stone and other materials was based in the idea that leaders were those most successful in creating and maintaining ties with extra-communal others, which would have given them the possibility to come out on top in communal exchanges. This would have involved an early version of Authority Ranking relations, but it seems unlikely that such hierarchies had long-term sustainability. New opportunities for "networking" abounded in this dynamic period and political roles of individuals were more likely achieved than inherited (Boomert 2001a). The exchange of raw materials could also have been aimed at incorporating social others into one's own social sphere as a social life-line, which would be more of a Communal Sharing motive (Mol 2010). If so, this could still have also heralded greater socio-political complexity, based on an incipient variant of an Amerindian political economy of life (Santos-Granero 2007, 2009b).

All in all, it is very difficult to say something concrete about prevalent models of relations based on the developments and directions in lithic networks. Even when considering other available lines of evidence the picture is altogether unclear. Nevertheless what is clear from the lithic networks is that there were major shifts in the social structures of the Archaic-Saladoid-Huecoid Inteface period (Boomert 2001a; Hofman, Mol *et al.* 2011; Rodríguez Ramos 2010). Although, the research focus on changes and growing "complexity" in socio-political systems has traditionally focused on the period from AD 600/700 to AD 1000, the longitudinal developments dicussed here seem to indicate this was a process that started several centuries earlier.

---

13   Radio Antilles has a few dates but little has been excavated. Unfortunately, due to the volcanic eruptions on Montserrat, little more can be said about this subject.

The dynamics of lithic networks

Looking at the collected network of Figure 5.14 two patterns can clearly be discerned: (1) the increasingly small diameter of the network: even though there are more nodes in later phases the network does not lose full integration and geographically widespread nodes remain at roughly the same non-Euclidean distance to each other and (2) the growth of the Long Island flint group through time. Long Island flint starts out as a group with only two affiliates, both located in its direct vicinity. Next, it evolves into the material with the most members and furthest geographic distribution of them all. It is a fact that this increase is followed by some other lithic raw materials, such as carnelian and serpentinite and even some sites with increasingly more ties in the affiliation or 1-mode networks. When referring to the lithic raw material sources of the Northeastern Caribbean it seems to ring true that the longer they are around the "richer" in affiliations they become and that the rich only get richer.

This implies that the network, for an important part, structurally depended on Long Island flint distribution. It was not only the most important resource during the earliest periods but as the network grew, so did the distribution of Long Island flint. This pattern of sequential growth and preferential attachment tentatively suggests that Long Island flint functioned as a hub (cf. Barabasí 2003). We see nonetheless two issues with this tentative identification of a scale-free lithic network. Firstly, too few data-points substantiate such a claim. [14] Secondly, even with sufficient data, the scale-free model would have no real interpretive value.

Although the increase of the network between Period A and E seems to coincide with the concept of sequential network growth, this view is skewed. One set of nodes in this 2-mode network, the raw material sources, are not part of the growth of the network. Even if merely exploited (on a larger scale) from Period C onwards, semi-precious raw materials were already present in the "ecology" of the network during earlier phases. In other words, they could have been included as raw material nodes in the network of Period A and B, but they simply would have no ties to site-nodes (that we know of).

What about the notion that preferential attachment is the cause for the popularity of Long Island flint? As discussed in Chapter 3, in the scale-free model the concept is that if a node is present and connected in the first phases, this will pan out favourably for that node in the long run. Being the most central node in a growing network in this case simply means being the first well-connected node. This could be the case with Long Island flint which occurs in some of the

---

14   The overall data set per period is too small to find the fat-tailed equation that is so characteristic of scale-free networks. A collection of all the affiliations of all the lithic group nodes results a slightly better fit. Although providing only a few data points, a linear Log-Log plot of each of them comes close to being a good fit to a power-law (R2 fitness test = 0.82). On the other hand a similar plot of site node affiliations provides no such fit, suggesting that relations between sites alone were not based on a scale-free network. A combination of lithic group and site nodes does produce a Log-Log scatter with a good fitness (R2 = 0.96). In addition, even if the blade and flake tech nodes are "knocked out" – deleted from the model so that their connections do not count towards node degree –, the large network component remains connected and a similar, if a less pronounced power law trend is present (R^2 = 0.92).

earliest sites in the region. Yet this does not explain why it grew in popularity while the distribution of chert sources that are equally connected in period A and B, such as Mocca flint, were mostly contained to their respective islands during later periods. This indicates that selection processes are, even in the beginning phase of a network, based on more than preferential attachment to resources that have been around the longest.

This was also the case for many of the other real world scale-free networks that were studied. In order to remedy this problem, Barabasí (2003) introduced the concept that nodes have an added "fitness"-parameter that determines if they will be selected for connection with another node or not. Whenever the fitness ecology alters – the fitness of the nodes changes or new nodes appear–, this will sequentially impact the degrees of nodes. Although this seems like an intuitive solution, from the perspective of an archaeological network study, this is an unsatisfactory solution. With modern networks it may be possible to substantiate a claim of increasing or decreasing fitness of nodes – e.g. in his book Barabasí provides the example of early web search engines that were simply outcompeted when the much more "fit" Google came on the scene. Adding a fitness-parameter to an archaeological network however pre-supposes something that most studies would set out to investigate: the evolutionary dynamics behind the continuity and change in the network.

Thus, even if the dynamic behind the popularity of Long Island flint was based on preferential attachment, the question remains: how did Long Island flint and other "beloved stones" connect culturally diverse communities? Why did Long Island flint in particular become the most widely exchanged local stone material in the Archaic-Saladoid-Huecoid interface period? A stone does not move on its own accord and it certainly does not float, so ultimately human beings are the driving force behind its distribution. However, it is obvious that continuity and change in both supply and demand in these interaction networks was also driven by the material qualities of the stones themselves. For example, the reason that Long Island Flint shows such an expansive longitudinal and geographic pattern of distribution, while another chert such as the Puerto Rican Mocca flint did not, is that Long Island flint simply was by far the best chert available in the wider region (Knippenberg 2007). I would hypothesize that the Long Island flint source served as a fixed temporal and spatial point in the mobile lives of the earliest inhabitants of the region. In other words, while other resources were shifting across the landscape due to seasonal or ecological fluctuations, Long Island Flint was simply always there. I suggest that this "fixity" would have rendered it an early nexus of economic activity within the wider archipelago. What is more, following the idea of Amerindian perspectivism laid out in Chapter 4, it could be that such fixed raw material sources and the materials taken from them were also perceived as (the home of) non-human subjects. Combining an indigenous ontology of wider socio-cosmic conflicts and contracts with other than human beings to the quality and fixity of Long Island flint and other stones, we could perhaps understand how these materials made reliable social "partners".

With regards to the later period it is noteworthy that endogenous North-Eastern Caribbean Antiguan Long Island Flint and later on also carnelian, St. Martin greenstone and Puerto Rican serpentinite possessed the material cultural qualities to fit within a range of social strategies and structures as they evolved. The incipient importance of Long Island flint was thus transferred into the Archaic-Ceramic Age interface period, either by virtue of the material qualities of Long Island flint itself or, more likely, as part of exchange and information networks. These flints as well as other endogenous materials were not phased out when the range of (semi-precious) stone material originating from outside the region and even from outside the islands expanded during later periods. In fact it seems that production and distribution only increased (Knippenberg 2007). Endogenous lithic materials are also regularly found in correlation with more exotic stones. It can be hypothesized that the early and widespread distribution of these local materials functioned as the major affordances of other types of (lithic) exchange networks.

Cultural practices and affiliations obviously changed hugely in the course of 3500 years. Moreover, Caribbean cultures and societies were at all times diversifying in ways these "slow shutter speed" models cannot hope to capture. However, the models do serve to bring across the point that these changes cannot be the result of any single type of interaction or movement of peoples. As such they contradict the previous "hidden" network models about this formative period that was mentioned at the beginning of this chapter. Even at such an early state the Caribbean shows simply too much interconnected diversity for Rouse his standard model to hold. The explanations of underlying cultural and societal relatedness of Archaic-Saladoid-Huecoid interfaces cannot be explained by recourse to a culture history that stresses event-like migrations or attempts to identify one donor-region (cf. Rodríguez Ramos 2010; Hofman, Boomert, et al. 2011).

Throughout the period of this case-study and beyond, the societies and cultures of the Northeastern Caribbean were ever-changing. However, in some ways it remained an integrated whole. Endogenous stone sources continued to have a clear value and place in social and cultural systems. They remained part of the changing material repertoires and practices and even had increasingly greater areas of distribution. In Chapter 2, I suggested that the rapid societal and cultural changes taking place in period C could be considered as a "phase transition". In some ways, the societal and cultural "phase transition" of Period C may indeed have been a break with those of Period A and B. The network exploration in this chapter has confirmed that even if some aspects of societies and cultures of this period underwent dramatic changes, some material practices and repertoires were more durable (Rodríguez Ramos 2010). As we will see in Chapter 6, some of these materials, like Long Island flint and St. Martin Greenstone, would retain this connective property up to the late pre-colonial period. This implies that, from the perspective of lithic networks, the cultural history of the island can be connected from the first entry of humans into the region to the start of European expansion into the region – and perhaps beyond. Even when cultural practices had passed beyond tradition into obscurity or when the first migrants had become the locals that encountered new migrants, the "heart of stone" around which social networks partly revolved remained in place. Although it is on a different scale than the interpersonal networks discussed in Chapter 4, this is another example of how the interplay of social interactions and material practices and repertoires can give temporal and cultural transitivity to networks of persons and things.

Chapter 6

Remotely Local: Ego-networks of Late Pre-colonial (AD 1000-1450) Saba

Saba, Oh Jewel most precious,
In the Caribbean sea.
Mem'ries will stay of thy beauty,
Though we may roam far from thee.

Excerpt of Saba's anthem *Saba you rise from the ocean*

In this chapter the multi-levelled networks attested in the archaeological record of the 14th century Saban site of Kelbey's Ridge 2 will be traced from an ego-network perspective (Freeman 1982; see Chapter 3). This is done in order to explore through its ego-network how one can best characterize what type of site Kelbey's Ridge 2 was. This is interesting because it provides a window on the socio-cultural dynamics of a community in what some have considered a fringe area (Rouse 1992). What is more in order to show how these networks developed I will also contrast the ego-network of Kelbey's Ridge 2 to that of the earlier Spring Bay 1 site (cal. AD 1000-1200). This follows up on the regional networks discussed in the previous chapter and provides a view of how these regional networks developed in the late pre-colonial period.

Saba, the island on which these sites are located, is one of the smallest, inhabited Lesser Antillean islands. It has an area of only 13 km², and, since it is a mountainous, volcanic place, has many steep slopes and very few level surfaces. Therefore at present it does not boast large settlements or extensive agricultural fields, a feature which also characterizes its pre-colonial habitation. However, aside from its stunning natural beauty and the friendly local population, Saba has another great treasure: the Saba Bank. This bank is the largest submarine atoll of the Atlantic Ocean, located *c*.4 km southwest of the island and provides a very rich fishing ground. As a result the sea is one the mainstays of the modern local economy, as is still the case in the present.

Saba is also one of the best archaeologically understood islands of the Caribbean. During the 1920s archaeological research here was initiated by the Leiden University-based cultural anthropologist J.P.B. de Josselin de Jong (1947). The island did not see any further research until the early 1980s, when Jay Haviser (1985) carried out a 10-day survey. During the late 1980s, Corinne L. Hofman and Menno L.P. Hoogland, also researchers from Leiden University, started a fieldwork programme that continues until today. In the course hereof several pre-colonial sites have been excavated including the earliest sites with evidence for human habitation (Plum Piece: Hofman, Bright *et al.* 2006) up to the late pre-colonial period (Kelbey's Ridge 2 and Spring Bay 1c: Hofman 1993; Hoogland 1996; Hoogland and Hofman 1999, 2013) and the majority of the cultural phases in between. One of the, due to the small size of Saba perhaps counterintuitive, results of this ongoing research project is that the island has played a central role in the interaction networks of the Northeastern Caribbean. This is attested by a variety of multi-disciplinary lines of evidence, including household archaeology, ceramic decorative and technical stylistic analysis, petrographic and geochemical ceramic analysis, lithic provenance studies, zoo-archaeology, osteo-archaeology, thanatology, isotope and dental anthropological studies (e.g. Hofman 1993; Hofman, Isendoorn, *et al.* 2008; Hoogland 1996; Hoogland and Hofman 2013; Laffoon 2012; Mickleburgh and Pagán-Jiménez 2012).[1]

The site assemblage showcases that even a small community in a relatively marginal local environment was impacted by and exercised at least some influence on networks stretching across the Northeastern Caribbean. Another benefit for a network study of the site is that the settlement was probably discontinuous with previous habitation phases of the island and relatively short-lived with a period of occupation of only 50 years (Hofman 1993; Hoogland 1996; Hoogland and Hofman 1999). This leaves a relatively small window of time spanning a few generations in which the site was occupied. As we shall see, this relatively small window of occupation did not prevent the inhabitants of Kelbey's Ridge 2 to have been a well-integrated part of regional and interregional networks.

Thus far only a single other site, Spring Bay 1c, has been found on Saba that may have been contemporaneous with Kelbey's Ridge 2. Spring Bay 1 is a multi-component Ceramic Age habitation site, which was abandoned and reoccupied a number of times after its initial settlement in *c.*AD 350. Spring Bay 1c is located close to the site of Kelbey's Ridge 2, and consists of an extensive midden area, comprised predominantly of faunal food refuse, particularly crab. A single burial was recovered from the upper levels of one of the trenches. Radiocarbon dating of the infant interred here indicated a date of 535 ±85 B.P., (Cal. AD 1450), making one component of the site, Spring Bay 1C, roughly contemporaneous with the occupation of Kelbey's Ridge 2. This assumption is also supported by close similarities between the ceramic assemblages of Kelbey's Ridge 2 and Spring Bay 1c (Hofman 1993; Hofman and Hoogland 1991; Hoogland and Hofman 1991, 1993, 1999).

---

1   This chapter is based on close cooperation with various members of the Caribbean Research Group at Leiden University, most notably Corinne Hofman and Menno Hoogland. Aside from the fact that the network discussed here is based on their previous studies, they commented extensively on drafts of the text, invited me to their January 2013 field trip to Saba, and provided additional information. With Corinne Hofman and Menno Hoogland as co-authors, a more theoretical and methodological discussion of this ego-network case-study will be featured as a paper that is currently under review for publication in a special issue on archaeological network analysis for the Journal of Archaeological Method and Theory (to be published in 2014).

The potential of a network model centred on one site has not often been explored in archaeology – discounting the socio-spatial networks of space syntax approaches (Hillier and Hanson 1984). However, no network theoretical reason would prevent such a construction (see Mol and Mans 2013). As with inter-site or other regional networks, the limitations for network modelling and analysis within sites are generally speaking practical. They rely upon the depth of understanding of relations within site assemblages. The record of Kelbey's Ridge 2 and its island neighbours provides enough detail to present at least some cautious inferences concerning networks in the Northeastern Caribbean. In contrast to the regional study of the previous chapter, this second network case-study of one site assemblage therefore provides a more localized insight in pre-colonial Caribbean networks.

This insight is of particular interest to evaluate existing hypotheses on what sort of community Kelbey's Ridge 2 was. Based on the identification of a set of "Taíno" elements, Hoogland and Hofman had originally proposed that Kelbey's Ridge 2 was a colony or outpost that had links with a Greater Antillean *cacicazgo* (Hoogland and Hofman 1999). After reviewing the evidence they have recently suggested four reasons why this type of community may have developed on Saba (Hofman and Hoogland 2011: 28-30). Firstly, Kelbey's Ridge 2 could have been a group of "refugees", settling there after fissioning from a Greater Antillean community. Conversely it may have been the case that Saba was settled as an outpost of a *cacicazgo* and served as a gateway to the more southerly located Antilles and the South American mainland. Another incentive to reside in Saba may have been the wish of a politically independent group to control and exploit the rich resources of the Saba Bank. Finally, Hofman and Hoogland consider that a combination of these factors may have been involved "in which the first option represents an incentive for colonization, whereas the second and third options legitimize the existence of this small outpost largely socio-politically and economically dependent on the Taíno heartland" (*ibid.*: 30).

In the latter part of this chapter I will explore these hypotheses and those of other researchers dealing with the position of the site in the region. This will be done by looking at the centralities of nodes in the ego-network and by trying to identify dominant relational models in the archaeological record of Kelbey's Ridge 2. I suggest that in the first hypothesis, the "refugee"-model, one may expect that intra-communal relations are strong and the most central. The dominant model of relation in such a secluded community may be one of Communal Sharing or, if there were strong authority figures present, Authority Ranking. One would expect little or no importance for regional ties and Equality Matching or Market Pricing models. The "outpost model", with its political strategic importance and gateway to trade in the region, would see a dominance of Authority Ranking mixed with Equality Matching or Market Pricing relations and an emphasis on interregional ties. Thirdly, the "entrepreneur model", viewing the community as a group that seeks to control raw material sources and rich fishing grounds, would see Market Pricing as the dominant relation and a central role for nodes and ties in the region and perhaps between regions. Finally, the "mixed model" would have an ego-network that has a mixed set of most important ties and no clearly dominant model of relations.

Northeastern Caribbean geographic networks continued

Kelbey's Ridge 2 lies on a flat terrain located at *c*.140 m. above mean sea level in the Northeastern part of the island. This vantage point commands a clear view of the surrounding bays and coastal valleys, which provide some of the few spots on the island that would have been suitable for canoe landings. The strategic location Kelbey's Ridge 2, a vantage point with access to the sea that was still relatively difficult to access from the coast, clearly suggests that maritime routes and interisland interactions held some larger importance for the people living there. A further characterization of the geographic location of the island of Saba itself should thus be helpful to understand the position of the community in the networks it participated in. Chapter 2 already featured a rough network characterization of the geographic layout of the Northeastern Caribbean islands and island regions by means of Proximal Point Analysis. However, "Maximum Distance Networks" or MDNs (Evans, *et al.* 2012), based on a series of fixed geographic radial distances rather than a fixed number of geographically close communal ties, present another view of the geographic integration of the region.

As with the PPA-model, the distances in this fixed radius model are based on straight travels across open sea, rather than overland distances. Straight lines across open bodies of water were drawn between the headlands of islands, which were once again islands larger than 10 km² and island regions of islands that were larger than 1000 km². Needless to say, the connectivity in the network is greatly influenced by the distance chosen for the cut-off point of the ties. Based on the data of the *Ioumoúlicou* project (Bérard, *et al.* 2011; Billard, *et al.* 2009), a stretch of 30 km of open sea travel was taken as the base-line for a cut-off point. Rather than with regular fixed radius models this distance was applied in iteration to create multiple spheres of distance: model 1 0-45 km (Figure 6.1.a), model 2 0-105 km (Figure 6.1.b), model 3 0-195 km (Figure 6.1.c), model 4 0-285 km (Figure 6.1.d). These ranges were kept broad in order to take into account variability in sea currents, winds and approximate distances between islands. As such, rather than treating them as absolute distances, another way to consider these ties is in relation to Bérard's statement that an open sea voyage of 30 km is a strenuous day trek for him and his crew. Thus, roughly speaking, model 1 refers to a 1-2 day trip, model 2 to a voyage of up to a few days, model 3 to one that would have taken up to several days, while model 4 concerns all ties between islands that could have been reached by a return journey that would probably have lasted at least several weeks.

Model 1 shows only connections between islands located in the proximity of other islands. As a result the overarching area is broken up into multiple island networks consisting of five larger components and three individual nodes. This view can be equated to inter-island travel within archipelagos or in the case of Puerto Rico and Guadeloupe journeys that connect regions within larger landmasses. Model 2 is a network that links both close islands and networks at more extended distances. This model resembles the PPA-network in that it separates the area into two larger network components separated by the Anegada passage (see Figure 2.1). There are also some differences, such as the relative geographic remoteness of East Hispaniola. From the perspective of the more easterly located islands, it is

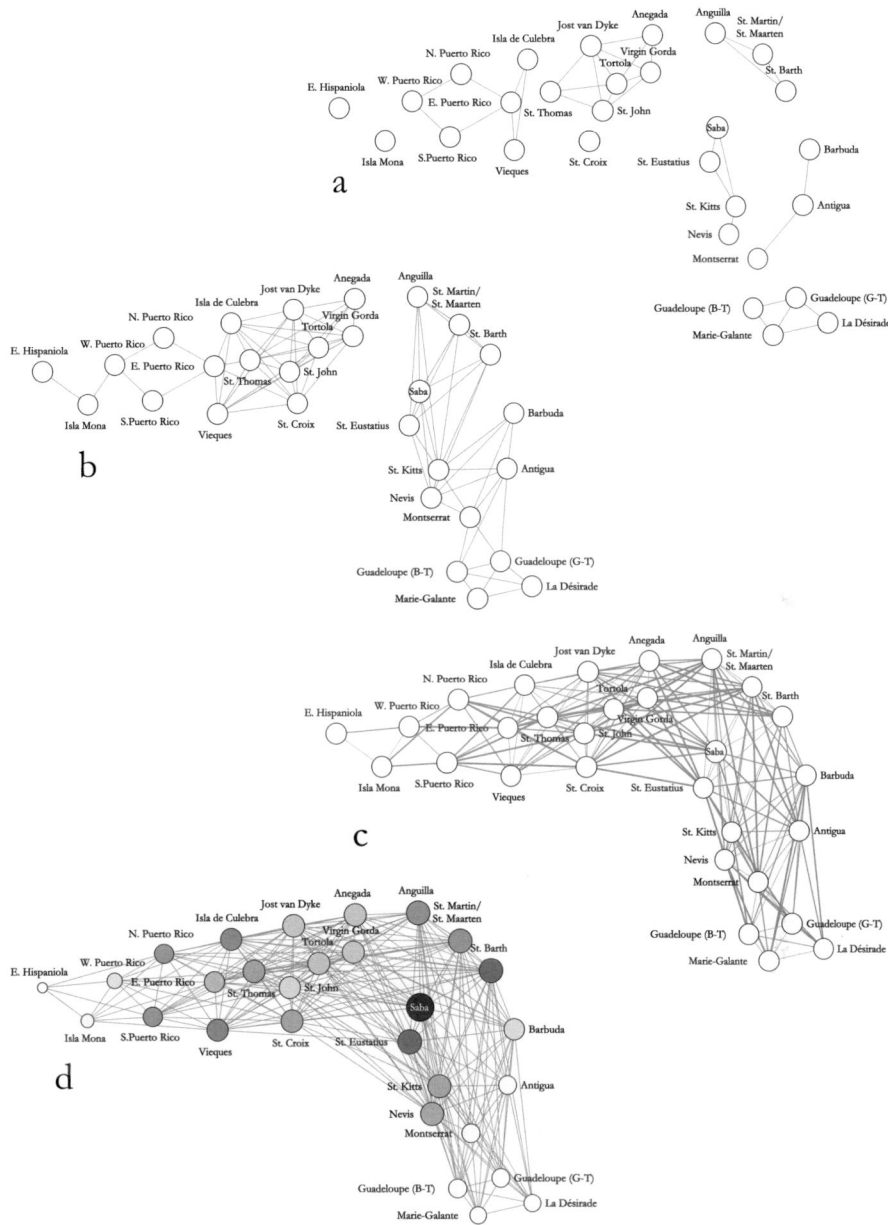

Figure 6.1: MDN of the Northeastern Caribbean. a: 0-45 km; b: 0-105 km; c: 0-195 km; d: 0-285 km. degree centrality is indicated by means of node size. Betweenness centrality is indicated by means of node colour from light (low) to dark (high).

only reachable through Isla Mona, which in turn only connects to Western Puerto Rico. Furthermore, while the northern Lesser Antilles displays a "string of pearls" layout, it is clear that there are multiple paths through the islands and that a strict island by island stepping-stone journey would not be required when setting off on extended open sea-voyages.

The extended distance models 3 and 4 show a fully bridged Northeastern Caribbean. In Figure 6.1c the network model variant of the Anegada passage is now closed by means of seven ties with distances ranging between 105-135 km between certain locations on the Virgin Islands and the islands of Anguilla and St. Maarten. At the 105-165 km, range Saba and St. Barth's also connect to several islands in the Virgin Island archipelago for a total of sixteen ties in total. At the 195 km-plus range (Figure 6.1d), the Anegada passage is crossable at least sixty-six times. In this last model the average degree of nodes is 16.25 (median = 18), implying that a generic island within this region linked to sixteen or seventeen other islands within 300 km. In network terms, therefore, for those prepared to set off on extended, often open sea voyages, the Northeastern Caribbean was quite well traversable with points of departure linked to a high number of destinations that could be reached within a couple of weeks travel.

On the other hand, the shear geographic size of the area should not be underestimated, even in networks of extended travel distances East Hispaniola and Guadeloupe are still separated by three steps. Indeed, with two hundred twenty-six ties connecting twenty-nine nodes even at these scales the network is far from being perfectly connected.[2] Even with a relatively large fixed distance radius, the geographic network of islands in the Northeastern Caribbean holds the middle between a small-world network and a dense lattice model. Looking at the relative centralities of nodes in the network is also insightful, especially in the case of Saba. Considering the progressively larger fixed radius models it becomes clear that the structural position of the island of Saba is advantageous at every level. Together with St. Eustatius, St. Kitts and Nevis it is part of a two-clique component, forming an extended archipelagic system at the lower distance ranges. In model 2 this two-clique has expanded to include the majority of the Leeward Islands, except for the Guadeloupe archipelago. Within this larger region Saba does not seem to hold a specifically central position (see below), yet looking at the extended distance models (Figure 6.1b and 6.1c) it is obvious that Saba holds a pivotal geographic position in connecting the Greater Antilles and Leeward islands. In this regard it is even more centrally located in terms of degree than other strategically located islands such as Anguilla, St. Martin and several Virgin Islands. In fact, Saba ranks much higher than these other islands in terms of its betweenness centrality (9% of the relative betweenness measures versus 4.5-7% for the other islands). This implies that aside from being a highly connected point of departure it is also located on the majority of the shortest, fixed radius paths across the archipelago. This geographic model allows for a preliminary and tentative approximation of Saba as a small but strategically located place in the Northeastern Caribbean (cf. Hoogland and Hofman 1999).

---

2   The density is 29%.

Local, region and interregional ties at Kelbey's Ridge 2

The post-hole patterns of the house structures recovered at Kelbey's Ridge 2 are quite important for the understanding of the patterns in the site ego-network, because several key features of its archaeological record can be linked to them. Seven structures were originally identified at Kelbey's Ridge 2, of which five or possibly six were round houses, measuring between 5 and 8 m. (Hoogland 1996). The site's house structures seem to have been rebuilt and moved a number of times, with at least four phases in the house's trajectory (Hoogland 1996; see also Samson 2010 for an Eastern Hispaniolan example hereof). Other features at the site point to an area that integrated residential, food preparation, and ceremonial spaces. Because the site has been partially destroyed it is not completely clear whether there was more than one residential structure present at any one time during its 50 years of occupation, but it is presumed that community members spent most of their time in a shared and mostly open living space.

The ceramic assemblage of Kelbey's Ridge 2 was quite large (sherd n = 33.000) but due to depositional processes most sherds consisted of small, often badly weathered fragments. Only 0.7% of the sherds was decorated. Based on these and other features, Hofman (1993) characterised the ceramics as belonging to the Chican Ostionoid subseries, which is only loosely related to the preceding Mamoran Troumassoid series or the Suazan Troumassoid of the more southerly located islands (Allaire 1977; Bright 2011). Other lines of evidence, for instance the absence of scratching, various pot shapes and burnishing, also clearly indicate a break in tradition with earlier ceramic assemblages found on the island.

Provenance analysis of the clays of a collection of ceramic sherds from Saba has shown that c.66% of the clays used for making ceramics by both the inhabitants of previous occupation phases and the later Kelbey's Ridge 2 settlement were locally obtained (Hofman, Isendoorn, *et al.* 2008). Two locations on the island, Rendezvous Point and Booby Hill, provided clay of sufficient quality to produce pots. Due to high non-plastic grain content, low-firing and high shrinkage, the local types of clay often resulted in pots that were easily cracked or broken. One source on the nearby island of St. Eustatius yielded more workable clay and, in addition, a clay suited for the production of the red slip found on 3.2% of the pottery assemblage (Hofman 1993). The islands of St. Martin/St. Maarten and Anguilla had several workable clay sources, which would have perhaps been procured by peoples living on Saba. An analysis of the clay microscopic fabric hints at this. Although most types of clay show microscopic inclusions (as is normal for clay from volcanic islands), certain sherds have inclusions only found in clay sources from limestone islands. Even if this does not prove that clay was procured at a specific location, it shows that several types of clay or perhaps even finished pots were procured from Saba's immediate island neighbours (Hofman, Isendoorn, *et al.* 2008; Hofman, *et al.* 2005).

The zoo-archaeological assemblage, dental anthropological studies, and carbon and nitrogen isotopic studies of the diet illustrate that subsistence practices at 14th century Kelbey's Ridge 2 were mostly oriented towards the procurement of marine foods. This is in line with expectations acquired from other, similar sites in the Northern Lesser Antilles. The community resided in close proximity to the rich fishing grounds of the Saba Bank, of which it probably took keen advantage. However, osteological analysis of the skeletal material encountered at the site also suggests it was not a necessarily highly affluent community. Pathologies and wear patterns reveal that the inhabitants of Kelbey's Ridge 2 led arduous lives, with heavy physical activity. In addition, the composition of the burial assemblage suggests a large mortality rate among infants (Hoogland 1996; Weston 2010).

The site layout and size, structural, locally marine oriented subsistence patterns, and local procurement of most raw materials together, present a first rough characterization of 13th and 14th century Saba as a small social network. In such a network members would all have been in frequent and close social contact, perhaps the majority of them being related. Even if this was a settlement consisting of colonists without previous blood or affinal relations, living and providing together would have forced them to literally become close, with all the social bonding and friction implied.[3]

This is prominently reflected in the manner in which the individuals were interred at Kelbey's Ridge 2 (Hoogland and Hofman 2013). Seven pits containing the remains of eleven individuals were found during excavation.[4] Their bodies were placed in small round or oval burial pits in a seated, strongly flexed position. Mortuary practices at the site are quite distinct from the local and wider region (Hoogland 1996; Hoogland 1999). For example, it features the only documented case of cremation in the Lesser Antilles – a burial practice more popular in the Greater Antilles (Hoogland 1999; Mickleburgh 2013). It is also out of the ordinary that many of the individuals found at Kelbey's Ridge 2 are secondary interments of infants with older adults (Hoogland 1996; Weston 2010). The deceased were kept in open burial pits and bones were removed from interments. The open pits or removed bones served to materially anchor (part of) the deceased community member within the social networks of the living.[5] Body and body parts of dead individuals were regarded as more than just mementos, however. From an Amerindian point of view dead bodies were not soulless and at least part of his or her "life-force" remained inside the body after passing away. (Chacon and Dye 2007; Hofman and Hoogland 2004; Petersen and Crock 2007).

---

3   Analogous types of kin networks and the social contracts and conflicts that accompany them have been extensively documented by Lowland South American ethnographers, among other works serving as the main subject of works such as the classics *Les structures élémentaires de la parenté* by Claude Lévi-Strauss (1949) and *Individual and Society in Guiana* by Peter Rivière (1984). See Ensor (2013) or Keegan (2007) for Caribbean archaeological perspectives on kin networks. See Mol and Mans (2013) for a network case-study that contrasts contemporary Guyanese and proto-contact Hispaniolan indigenous kin networks and the distribution of material culture in them.

4   Note that the part of the population that is normally most active – male and female adults – are not represented in the burial assemblage (Weston 2010; Hoogland and Hofman 2011). Hoogland and Hofman (personal communication, 2013) suggest that this may have to do with the fact that the adults that were part of this community would most of the time be away from the settlement on extended fishing or exchange voyages and that after death their remains would not have been brought back to the site.

5   See Hoogland and Hofman (2013) for a more extensive description and interpretation of the burial practices encountered at Kelbey's Ridge 2.

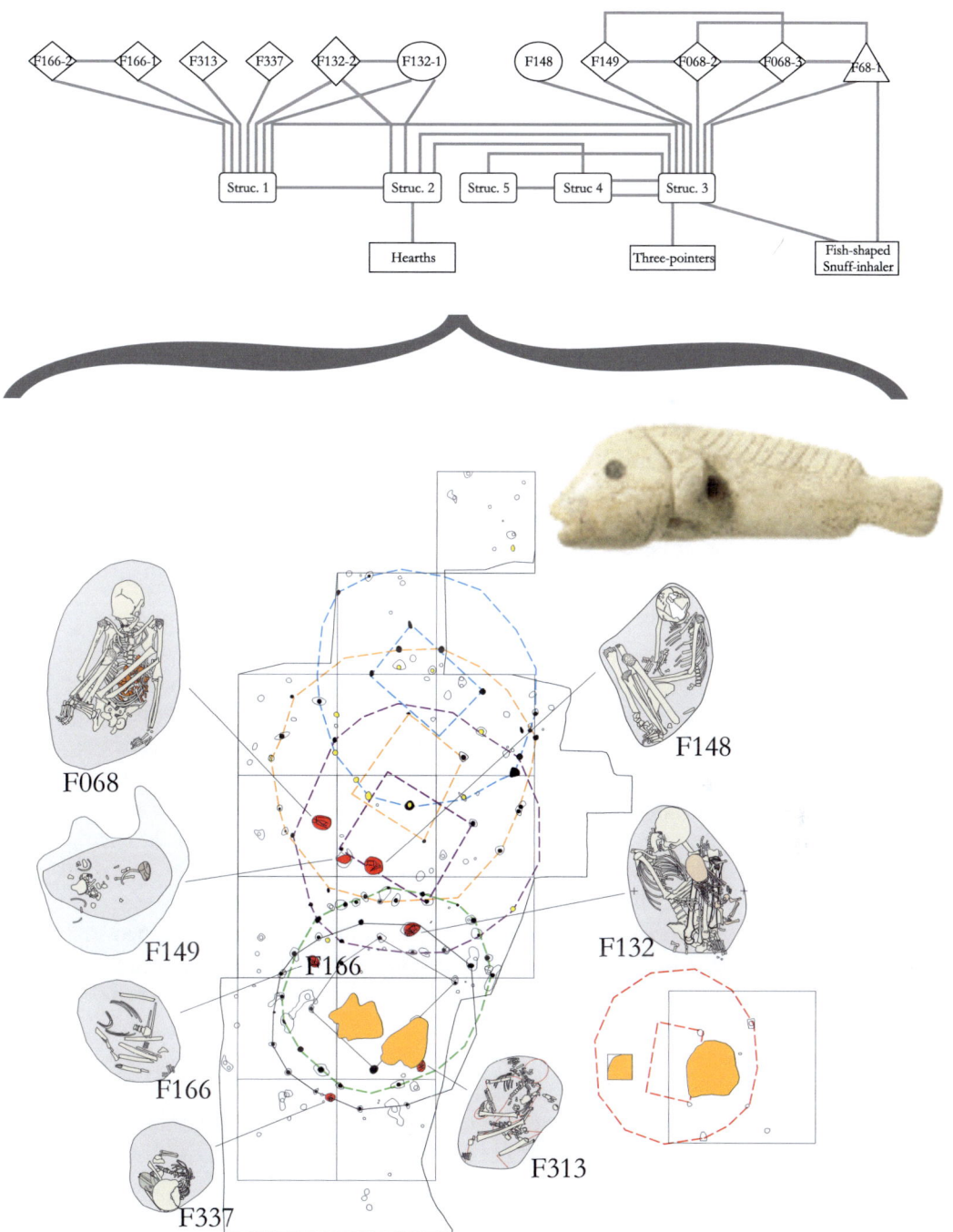

Figure 6.2: Features and finds at Kelbey's Ridge 2, viewed as a network. As can be seen from the bottom half of the picture the ties between burials, structures, hearth and the object nodes are based on spatial correlation (Hoogland 1996). Illustrations and photograph courtesy of Menno Hoogland.

In this regard the associated finds also point to the fact that the bodies of the deceased were still seen as individuals that remained part of communal life. Firstly, objects have been found that were widely valued as important shamanic tools: a finely crafted, fish-shaped snuff inhaler and hollow avian bones that could have been inserted into the inhaler. This potent item can be associated with burial F168, a triple burial of an older man with two young children.[6] Two three-pointed *cemís* were also found near the graves. These spiritually charged objects may have been deposited near the burial pits on purpose, but this is difficult to ascertain because they were collected on the surface of the site. Nevertheless, these objects and all burials can be linked to the house structures that could be re-constructed from the patterns of post-holes at the site (Hoogland 1996). The associations between structures, burial features and finds can serve to reconstruct an intra-site network of socially important "architecture" that probably spanned the 50 years during which the site was occupied (Figure 6.2; after Hoogland and Hofman 2013)

This shows that ancestors at Kelbey's Ridge 2 were literally integrated into the social life of the community. What is more, the physical presence of the (open) burials, the displayed bones of ancestors, and the houses with their interlocked post-hole patterns served to connect the social networks of the living and ancestors through time, as well. The overlap between the post-holes of the structures connects the network of ancestors buried beneath the floor of the houses. Similarly, genealogical histories, perhaps exemplified by the practice of secondary interments, would have connected the material networks of the houses, as well (Hoogland 1996). Even though the precise ebb and flow of everyday personal interactions and life histories remains archaeologically largely invisible, their material counterparts are remindful of smaller Amerindian communities from Lowland South America (Mans 2011). It is clear from the precise reconstructions of burial practices that day-to-day social interactions between the living members of the community were greatly entwined with their deceased. The death of a community member did not mean a breaking of ties between community members.

Saba and especially Kelbey's Ridge was not an optimum location in many ways. Indeed people living here faced all sorts of hardships, leading to for instance general health problems and a high infant mortality rate (Weston 2010). Nevertheless, in spite or perhaps because of this interpersonal ties were strong and were carried across several generations, providing a sturdy basis for 14th century Saba's interactions with its wider island world. All in all, the image arising from the micro-networks of Kelbey's Ridge is that of a tight-knit community.

This strong local base was beneficial when engaging with other communities in the wider region. Regarding this, it has often been noted that the last 3 to 2 centuries before contact witness a sharp decline in site quantities with regard to the Northern Lesser Antilles (Crock and Petersen 2004; Hofman, Bright, *et al.* 2007; Knippenberg 2007; Rouse 1992). It is not known exactly what the reason

---

6   Although the snuff inhaler was not found in the grave, but next to it, a small, tubular bird bone was part of the burial assemblage. Hoogland has convincingly argued that this bird bone must have been a part of the snuff inhaler, by being inserted into it to allow for inhalation of narcotics (Hoogland 1996).

behind this was. Various ethnohistoric sources report that the region was mostly depopulated due to raids carried out by the inhabitants of the Southern islands (Figueredo 1978; Petersen, *et al.* 2004; Rouse 1948a; Siegel 2004; Whitehead 1995). The evidence for inter-communal strife at Saba and other sites in the area is not exactly overwhelming; the evidence for such regional conflicts is mostly circumstantial in Kelbey's Ridge 2 (Weston 2010). This might be proof of inter-communal violence, but it could also be a result of violence from within the community. On the other hand, the choice for the site's location may have been prompted by increased intercommunity conflict and competition, especially when compared to prevalent site locations in the centuries before (e.g. Morne Cybèle 1, Hofman 1995). Its position high-up on the slope would have afforded good defensibility and a clear visibility of the nearby beach, neighbouring islands and sea-traffic approaching from a North-easterly and Easterly direction. All in all, the region was probably not a peaceful Rousseauean paradise, but evidence for large-scale inter-communal warfare or raiding throughout the archipelago is lacking.

It has been suggested that from AD 1000 onwards a growing inter-island polity, possibly based in Anguilla, tried or even succeeded in politically dominating the wider archipelago (Crock 2000; Haviser 1991). This is partly based on the idea that communities from Anguilla had begun to adapt the Greater Antillean chiefdom political system to the inter-island networks of the Northern Lesser Antilles. This was carried out by controlling exchange networks within the wider region, exemplified by the distribution and production of St. Martin greenstone axes and calci-rudite three-pointed stones at Anguillan sites (Crock 2000). In addition, objects with Greater Antillean stylistic characteristics such as shell *guaízas* and elaborately crafted (calci-rudite) three-pointed stones were also encountered in Anguillan assemblages (Petersen and Crock 2004).

The Saba Bank represented another strategic network node that was directly connected to archaeological features at the site. These marine resources formed, as discussed above, the mainstay of the local diet at Kelbey's Ridge 2, but these rich fishing grounds would have provided such a quantity they were probably also exploited for intercommunity trade (Hoogland and Hofman 1999). Recently, Keegan and colleagues (2008) and Morsink (2012) have re-emphasized the importance of smaller islands in marine subsistence webs. Fish and other kinds of sea food could have easily been salted or dried, stored and be circulated as exchange objects. Hoogland and Hofman (1999) have suggested that this activity was one of the main reasons for the existence of the late pre-colonial settlement at Kelbey's Ridge. Remains of sea food are plentiful here, as well as in the closely related Spring Bay 1c site. In addition, Kelbey's Ridge 2 features four large hearths, located within the area of Structure 1, 2 and 3, which yielded evidence for shell and fish preparation (Hoogland 1996). The size of the hearths is relatively large, indicating that substantial catches were prepared in or dried above large fires, perhaps for later storage and circulation. Such a circulation of food stuffs could have taken place as Market Pricing models of relations in which fish was bartered for other goods. Evidence acquired from elsewhere suggests that such food circulation could have been the result of delayed reciprocal strategies between groups – which is most akin to an Equality Matching model.[7]

When Hoogland and Hofman first shared the results of their fieldwork with a wider archaeological audience (e.g. Hoogland and Hofman 1991), the prevalence of Chican Ostionoid ceramics at the site came as something of a surprise. At the time, this assemblage and the assemblage of Spring Bay 1c represented the farthest Eastward spread of this Greater Antillean style. Elements of the Chican subseries were later also encountered on the ceramics of sites on other Leeward Islands (Crock 2000; Petersen, et al. 2004), but Kelbey's Ridge 2 remains the only site in this region to have a completely Chicoid assemblage (Hofman 1995). Its identification at 14th century Saba was partly responsible for a re-framing of the typo-chronological and culture history of the Northern Leewards, which was subsequently labelled "Eastern Taíno" by Rouse in his 1992 publication. According to the latter's ideas on the matter, parts of the Northern Lesser Antilles would have been occupied by a cultural group related with, but also clearly different from the Classic Taíno of Hispaniola and Puerto Rico.

In this regard it is noteworthy that several other lines of evidence point to a higher-level network connection to the Greater Antilles. Firstly, a microscopic fabric analysis, carried out as part of the ceramic provenance analysis mentioned above, indicates that at least one sherd with Chican characteristics consists of a sedimentary clay that most certainly had its provenance in one of the larger islands to the West (Hofman, Isendoorn, et al. 2008: 28). A similar composition has not been reported for any of the other clay sources tested on the islands of the Lesser Antilles (Crock, et al. 2008; Hofman, Isendoorn, et al. 2008; Isendoorn, et al. 2008). Other material remains at the site reflect "Taíno" influences, too. Stylistically, the fish-shaped snuff inhaler of manatee bone displays distinct Greater Antillean influences, which would logically connect it to the cohoba-ritual complex (Hofman and Hoogland 1991, Hofman 1995; Hoogland and Hofman 1999). Kelbey's Ridge 2 is not unique in this. A variety of objects with Greater Antillean stylistic connotations has been found in Chican, Suazan and Cayo contexts as far South as the Grenadines (Hofman, Bright, et al. 2008). As such objects often display small stylistic deviations from a Greater Antillean norm or consisted of local raw materials, it has been suggested they did not necessarily represent direct contacts with Greater Antillean communities but rather a sphere of esoteric interaction (Allaire 1990).

The combined evidence for Greater Antillean relations with the small island and the late and short-lived nature of the settlement, led Hoogland and Hofman to characterize Kelbey's Ridge 2 as a "Taíno" outpost, (Hoogland and Hofman 1999: 107). In light of the strong local embedding of the site it is perhaps odd it is identified by a relatively minor component of its assemblage. Through these few

---

7   For example, the role of the Surinamese Trio village of Amötopo is to supply game and fish for the wider Trio community, not as part of barter trading but in the form of communal aid networks functioning as social lifelines (Mans 2012; see Chapter 4).

ties Saba was nonetheless plugged into more geographically distant networks. As a result, from a view that integrates the networks encountered at Kelbey's Ridge 2, the materiality of these exotic ties would have been higher than the local ties. This is related to the power of inter-cluster ties in sparse networks, as discussed in the context of the small-world phenomenon. Even one tie that goes beyond the local cluster may completely re-arrange paths in the network – in the case of the small-world example from a "cave system" to an incipient small-world. In other words, a tie referring to an exotic node has greater power than a collection of ties referring to the same set of nodes (compare Helms 1988). Seen from this perspective, even if local and regional ties were strong, a characterization of the site of Kelbey's Ridge 2 based on its integration within interregional cultural, material and perhaps even social networks is also justified (cf. Hoogland and Hofman 1999).

The ego-network of Kelbey's Ridge 2

Figure 6.3 combines the evidence of the ties discussed above into an ego-network. It is clear that the ties giving rise to this model are to a certain degree dissimilar. Ceramic or lithic provenance analysis does not lead to the same type of relational data as an analysis of burial practice at the site, for example. Furthermore certain data sets that present substantive information about the role of Kelbey's Ridge 2 in the wider archipelago are unbalanced and incomplete. In order to truly balance these data sets it would require repeating the equivalent of the fieldwork and analysis carried out on Saba on all the islands in the Northeastern Caribbean. However, as a basis this model serves to explore the interrelations of the local, regional, and interregional interactions evidenced at the site.

It seems counterintuitive to join intra-site features to exotics from places hundreds of kilometres away. Remember however that this ego-network tries to move away from geographic distances and scales to present a model of the interactions as seen from the perspective of the community. In other words, an ego-network can and should include ties on what would traditionally be seen as separate scales of analysis. In an ego-network the impact of nodes from various scales can be weighed against each other. In Chapter 3, I discussed how the original goal of an ego-network analysis was to indicate which nodes outside the ego-node have the largest number of incidences and thus are likely to exert the highest influence on the network of Ego.

The result of this is something that may normally be perceived as different scales of analyses – intra-site, regional, and interregional – are here part of interdependent tie sets. This collapse of multi-scalarity into a single model is of specific interest for archaeological network applications. One of the critiques on archaeological network approaches that has been forwarded by scholars such as Carl Knappett (2011) is that they have until now mainly served as site-to-site models. These are regional networks, or macro networks as Knappett calls them, leaving a large part of the local materialities of networks out of the equation. Site ego-networks might be one of the ways around this: Kelbey's Ridge 2 network site assemblage can only

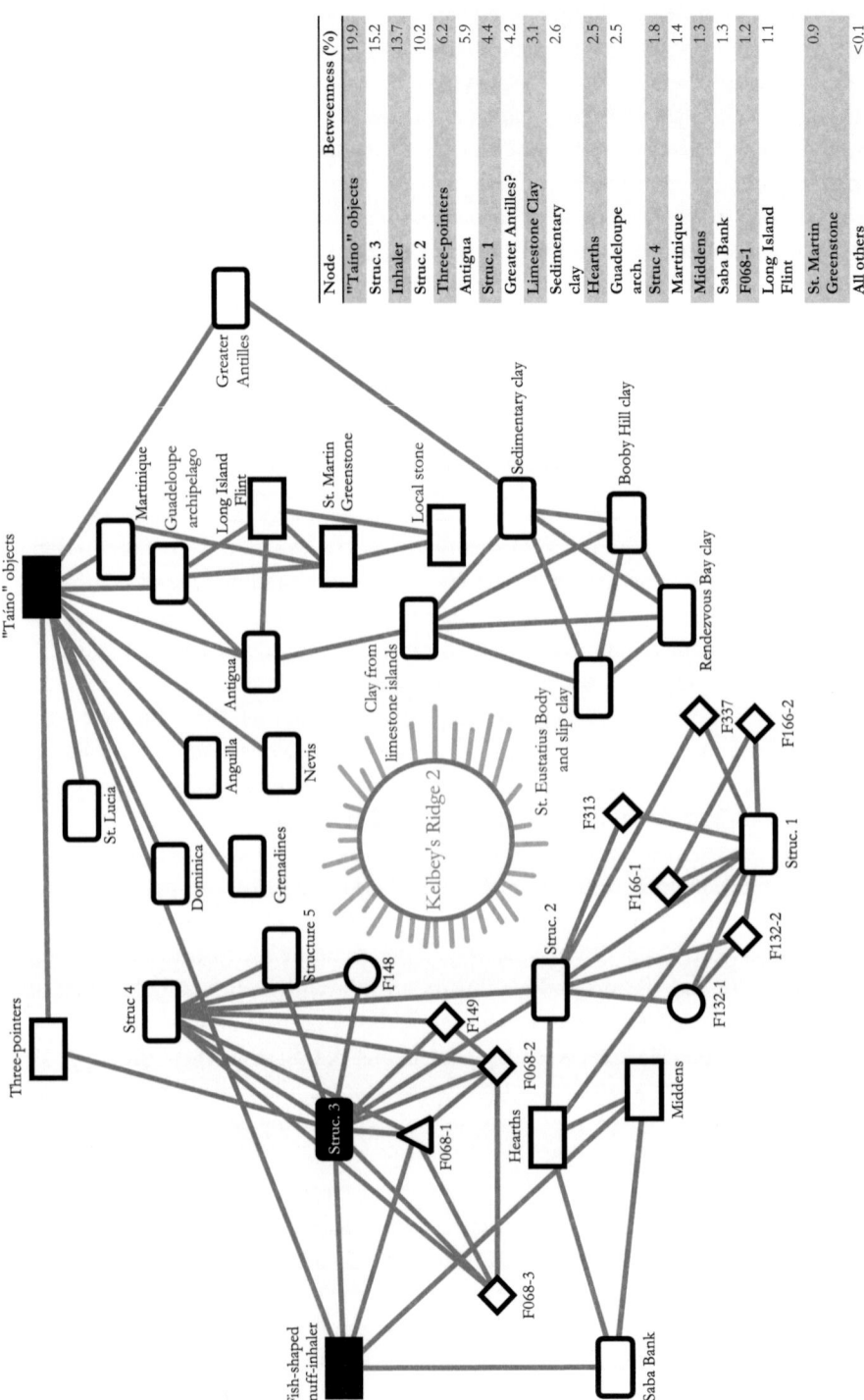

Node	Betweenness (%)
"Taíno" objects	19.9
Struc. 3	15.2
Inhaler	13.7
Struc. 2	10.2
Three-pointers	6.2
Antigua	5.9
Struc. 1	4.4
Greater Antilles?	4.2
Limestone Clay	3.1
Sedimentary clay	2.6
Hearths	2.5
Guadeloupe arch.	2.5
Struc 4	1.8
Martinique	1.4
Middens	1.3
Saba Bank	1.3
F068-1	1.2
Long Island Flint	1.1
St. Martin Greenstone	0.9
All others	<0.1

Figure 6.3: Ego-network of Kelbey's Ridge 2. The node size correlates with node betweenness centrality. The black nodes indicate the presence of "Taíno"-style valuables. The light grey nodes denote stone material distributions. Dark grey nodes combine the two, showing that the ties between islands are by and large based on the presence of "Taíno"-style valuables. This network also clearly proves this at the local level, with an important set of socio-material dependencies that focus on the fish-shaped snuff-inhaler.

be understood as a multi-scalar model, incorporating evidence for both micro, meso and macro networks.

The network is moreover not only interdependent across network levels, but is also an interdependent network of people and their material culture. Interestingly, this specific network consists of more than just objects as things and biological individuals as persons, but it also links diverse set of nodes that interconnects houses with ancestors, fishing grounds, shamanic paraphernalia and hearths with regional trade. Additionally, the objects found at the site of Kelbey's Ridge 2 references a diverse set of material practices and beliefs of the island communities in the wider region. This showcases the possible breadth of material-based network models for understanding the impacts of local, regional and interregional connections between people and their things.

Aside from degree centrality, Freeman (1982) employed betweenness centrality analysis in order to establish which nodes have the highest impact on the network of the ego node. The more central certain subgraphs or nodes are for paths in an ego-network, the more relative power they will exercise over the way in which the ego node is able to independently interact with others in its network. It is important to understand that here, network "power" cannot be (directly) equated to political power nor does it show exchange networks – although some exchange networks are part of the relational database. The reason is that this type of ego-network is not a political or exchange but a site assemblage-based network. In order to make sense of this site assemblage network we need to apply a support theory that can explain what relations in sites portray.

Although archaeology is a site-centric discipline, it is difficult to find a general theory concerning relations of features of site assemblages that is both social and material (Pauketat 2001). This may have to do with the fact that the majority of sites are social and material palimpsests and as a result the archaeological record of even a relatively small site like Kelbey's Ridge 2 is dense with relational information. An ego-network analysis can help us to understand these diverse sets of relations. Indeed, although the terms are not fully synonymous one could say that seeing a site as an ego-network can be equated to perceiving the site as being entangled (Hodder 2012). Therefore, taking a small conceptual leap, a site ego-network actually presents a model of how a community was "entangled" in its relations with the things archaeologists encounter in its records. Interestingly, if the record at Kelbey's Ridge 2 is viewed in this manner, an analysis of betweenness centrality can point out where these entanglements were the thickest. In a sense, a site ego-network analysis can point out the types of material repertoires and practices that were most relevant for the people living here vis-à-vis other aspects of the site record. Hence we can start to hypothesize how certain material foci correlated to social ties at the local, regional and interregional network level. Figure 6.3 shows a visualization of betweenness centrality in the ego-network of Kelbey's Ridge 2.

Let us now look into certain characteristics that appear from an exploration of this particular ego-network. In terms of access to raw material sources, Kelbey's Ridge 2 seems to have been able to position itself as a relatively well-integrated community, partaking in a variety of distribution networks. Saba had its own types of clay as well as a good clay and red slip source on the nearby island of St. Eustatius. Clay from limestone islands also connects Kelbey's Ridge 2 ceramic assemblage to clays found on Anguilla and Antigua. In contrast, sedimentary clay and clay from Saba have not yet been reported on other islands and uniquely connect Saba to a larger landmass where such kinds of clay could have been found. In general the large majority of ceramics is produced from local clay sources, so it may be that the exotic clays represent finished ceramic vessels that were moved to the island, perhaps as part of an exchange or intercommunal visit. This implies that 14th century Sabans had access to wider island clay distribution networks but were far from dependent upon them. The exotic lithics, Long Island Flint and St. Martin Greenstone have a similar position in the network: they serve to connect Kelbey's Ridge 2 with communities on other islands throughout the Lesser Antilles, but they are only found in limited quantities. The difference is that here we see evidence for production and down-the-line distribution, which does not seem to have been the case with the production of ceramics (Knippenberg 2007). In short, regarding the supply of basic raw material sources Kelbey's Ridge 2 seems to have been able to be more or less self-sufficient.

In terms of individuals nodes the snuff inhaler has the highest centrality in the network. This is underlain by the fact it connects a set of cliques that would otherwise remain unconnected. Its fish-shape alludes to the importance of Saba's rich fishing grounds.[8] Its association with Structure 3 and the triple burial also connects it to the living and ancestral community members. In addition, its style and function clearly mark it as part of a Lesser Antillean group of objects that connected local socio-cultural practices to a Greater Antillean social, cultural and material system that has been referred to as "Taíno". Furthermore, its function as a deliverer of hallucinogenics would have connected the community not only to a pan-Antillean form of ritual practice, but it would have given some individuals trans-specific properties, i.e. the ability to make shamanic journeys and thereby shift perspectives. Through the snuff inhaler the community was linked to a multi-perspectivist network of other-than-human beings (Allaire 1990). The specifics of this communal and intercommunal network will remain invisible to archaeological inquiry, but central material nodes such as the snuff inhaler are nonetheless indicative of its importance by proxy.

House Structure 3 is an important node for connecting various parts of the network. For example, through a set of overlapping post-holes it connects other house structures through time, incorporating the relations of the present house into that of past houses. It also features a highly idiosyncratic triple burial (Hoogland and Hofman 2013). One of the individuals, the older man (F068_1) has the

---

8   Menno Hoogland (personal communication, 2013) suggests it is a grouper (*Epinephelus* spp.) a large
    fish that is present in large quantities at the Saba Bank.

highest betweenness rating of all the buried individuals. It is telling that the highest betweenness ratings in the network can be found at Structure 3 and the fish-shaped snuff inhaler, making them important connectors for the wider network.. The snuff inhaler and Structure 3 connect to each other by means of the network paths of an ancestor, the man buried in F068_1. They are also connected, through the hearths associated with Structure 3, to the important marine component of the subsistence economy. Furthermore, through its overlapping post-holes Structure 3 is also tied to a network of houses dating from before and after it. its associated material culture, specifically the three-pointers and the fish-shaped snuff inhaler, connects it to an interregional network of so-called "Taíno" valuables, all objects that share a similar connotation and style. As it can be reconstructed archaeologically, this indicates that Structure 3 was the central spatio-temporal nodal point of socio-material practices at Kelbey's Ridge 2.

Relational models at Kelbey's Ridge 2

Which relational models can explain the patterning in the ego-network? It has to be said that not one distinct set of relations seems to dominate. All in all, it is likely that Communal Sharing, with its focus on egalitarianism, strong reciprocity and sharing of tasks, food and most other items, would have informed daily social practice and community morals. Communal Sharing models of relations would be continued when the living became ancestors, although the relations now took place within more "materially" – house structures, shamanic burial gifts, bones as inspirited matter – oriented networks than before.

There is not much evidence for intra-site Authority Ranking models of relations. These models of relations can perhaps be indicated by means of the differential interment of grave goods. However, except for the notable example of the fish-shaped snuff inhaler, there are no easily identifiable grave goods. The burial assemblage, particularly the post-mortem manipulation of remains, does seem to hint at an Authority Ranking model of relations between the differently aged members of the community. The secondary interment of younger children next to or in the skeletonized bodies of the older members of the community – and not the other way around –mimics Authority Ranking models of relations that would have been a main feature of village life: adults providing and caring for or watching over the younger members of the community.

Nevertheless, it is also clear that these Communal Sharing and Authority Ranking models of relations would have been counterbalanced by intermittent interactions with outsiders challenging communal models of relations. Interpersonal violence, interactions with spirits and ancestors, and trading missions to other islands would all have necessitated a response other than the relatively mutualistic Communal Sharing model of relations. Realising that the community at Kelbey's Ridge 2 had quite a varied regional resource acquirement strategy makes it unlikely that inter-site relations were dominated by Authority Ranking models, preventing the community to have access to particular resources. This is in contrast to what has been suggested previously by Crock regarding the period from AD 1000 on.

In Crock (2000)'s original identification of Anguilla as the head of an inter-island *cacicazgo* two lines of evidence have served to strengthen the argument: control of lithic resources and ownership of Chicoid-styled valuables, suggesting links with Greater Antillean material repertoires. A first look at the ego-network shows that from the perspective of the 14th century site of Kelbey's Ridge 2, relations between island communities in this period were much more nuanced. In contrast to the previous centuries there are much fewer sites and thus fewer communities and a lower population. This is not only the case for Saba, but also for the island of Anguilla and others in the region. This would have made the needs for and benefits of any centralized authority much lower. Indeed, the ego-network shows that Authority Ranking relations would not have been strong enough to actually bring the local network under full control of Anguilla: the betweenness centrality of Anguilla is only slightly higher than those of other islands. Especially when seen in the light of the possible connections of this and other communities to the Greater Antilles, Anguilla would have just been one of several island regions with which the inhabitants of Saba were in contact. In other words, by the 14th century AD we see no indications that Anguillan communities had any type of control whatsoever over the inhabitants of Kelbey's Ridge 2.

In fact, (resource) network control can also be found at Kelbey's Ridge 2: its assemblage has objects with links to a wider material cultural repertoire and evidence for direct acquisition and exchange of Long Island flint. Saba was procuring and producing both St. Martin Greenstone and Long Island flint. These two stone material networks with their deep history (Chapter 5) had begun to contract at the beginning of the Late Ceramic Age and continued to do so. However, these materials and their raw material sources must still have been important to the communities that remained in the region. As such it is noteworthy that Saba was the most Southerly potential distributor of St. Martin Greenstone and the most

Northerly potential distributor of Long Island Flint. In other words, Saba was located at the interface of two lithic distribution networks and three regional interaction spheres (Knippenberg 2007). The Minimal Distance network also illustrates that it held a strategic geographic position that would have established it as the gateway between the more Southerly located islands, the Northern Lesser Antilles and the Greater Antilles.

Based on the evidence for Greater Antillean connections, geographic position and strategic marine and lithic resources, Kelbey's Ridge 2 has the potential to have been somewhat of a hub in the sparsely populated region rendering Saba an attractive site for an outpost (cf. Hoogland and Hofman 1999). Based on this

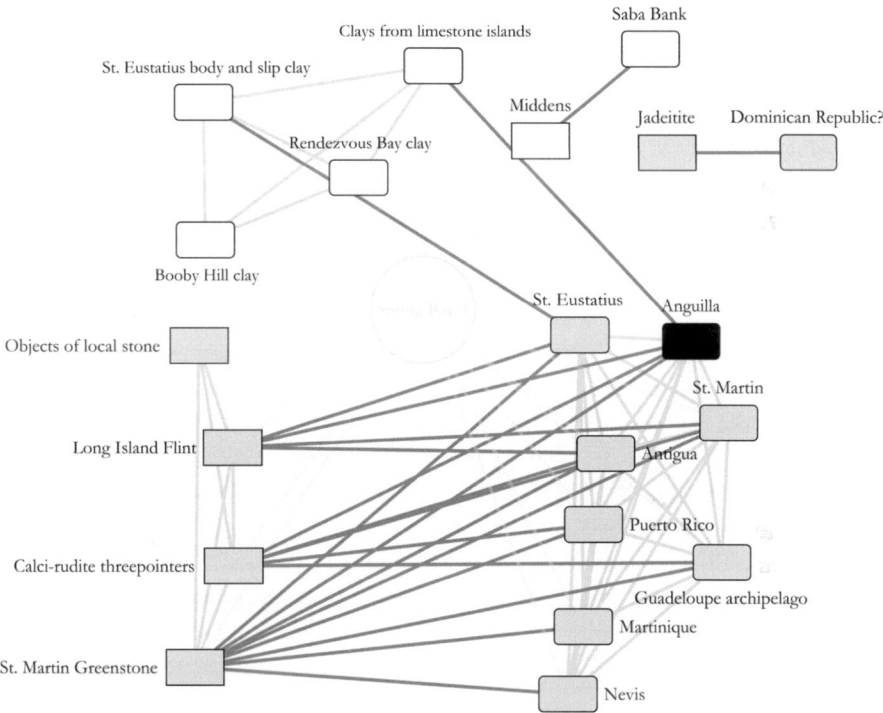

Figure 6.4: Ego-network of Spring Bay 3. The light grey indicates nodes correlated with types of stone distributions. The dark grey of the Anguilla nodes indicate the presence of "Taíno"-style valuables and stone material distribution centres. This indicates that the ties between islands are by and large based on the stone raw material distributions, in contrast to the ego-network of Kelbey's Ridge 2.

relatively tentative evidence, it would go too far to place this community at the head of an inter-island network based on Authority Ranking models of relations. All in all, it seems that the 14th century Northern Lesser Antilles were somewhat of a frontier zone. This is more suggestive of a situation in which Equality Matching and perhaps Market Pricing – perhaps based on sea food export – network strategies would have pre-dominated (Hoogland and Hofman 2011).

This idea is strengthened by a comparison between the ego-networks of 14th century Kelbey's Ridge 2 and those of the earlier (cal. AD 1000-1200) Spring Bay 3 site (Figure 6.4). [9] Spring Bay 3, positioned in the bay valley at the foot of the hill on which Kelbey's Ridge is located, represents a phase of habitation unrelated to the later settlement (Hoogland and Hofman 1999). As such the ego-networks of the two sites should not be longitudinally connected. From those aspects of the network that can be compared (not all types of relational data are the same for Spring Bay 3 and Kelbey's Ridge 2), a clear drop in number of sites and (calci-rudite) lithic distribution to islands in the wider region after AD 1200, and an increase in the distribution of Greater Antillean-styled objects differentiates the two. [10] It is furthermore notable that Spring Bay 3 provided a jadeitite axe of which the provenance study is currently pending (Knippenberg personal communication, 2013). Whatever its source, it is indicative of a lithic distribution network of a scope for which there is no evidence at Kelbey's Ridge 2. [11]

Interestingly we see a shift in the prevalent stylistic ascription of ceramic assemblages after AD 1200 (Hofman 1995). On Saba the Spring Bay 3 ceramics belonging to diverse Northern Lesser Antillean ceramic styles, were replaced by a mostly Chicoid assemblage. Ceramic decorative traditions and vessel forms of Spring Bay 3, among other sites from Saba, have links with the assemblage of Sandy Hill on Anguilla. They also show some similarities to ceramic assemblages from the Virgin Islands and Puerto Rico, in addition to overlaps with Troumassoid ceramic styles from the Windward Islands. However, in contrast to the ego-network of Kelbey's Ridge 2, the Spring Bay 3 network shows neither evidence for the use of sedentary clays nor for the full-fledged incorporation of Greater Antillean stylistic traits (Hofman 1993, 1995).

It is still difficult to understand which changes between AD 1200 and 1300 caused the shifts in stylistic traditions, generally lower number of sites, and the collapse of the lithic distribution system. Was this due to a collapse of an inter-island polity after AD 1200? This could be the case, if it were not that the evidence

---

9   A note has to be placed here with reference to the comparability of Spring Bay 3 and Kelbey's Ridge 2. First of all, the former was not as extensively excavated as the latter site. As a result it was impossible to re-construct entire structures at Spring Bay 3. This means it may be the case that Spring Bay 3 was simply a series of temporary camps. However, even if the cultural and social dynamics would have been different for both sites this does not imply that the ego-network of the assemblages cannot be compared. It does mean that it is impossible to extrapolate from this comparison that Spring Bay 3 was a permanent settlement and part of an inter-island chiefdom.

10   Actually, the only place where calci-rudite artefacts have been found in this phase of the "Late Ceramic Age" is in Anguilla itself (Crock 2000; Knippenberg 2007). In other words, in the 14th century the calci-rudite three-pointer exchange network of previous centuries consisted of only one node.

11   It has to be noted that in the case of such incidental finds such as a single jadeite axe, absence of evidence is no evidence for absence. In other words it may be the case that the community at Kelbey's Ridge 2 was also tapped into a jadeitite distribution network extending to the Dominican Republic or further, but that evidence for this may simply not have been preserved or recovered. Of course, the ego-network models of Kelbey's Ridge 2 and Spring Bay 3 are not the alone in suffering from this problem. The robustness of inferences that are drawn from ties based on the presence or absence of singular finds like jadeitite axes needs to be evaluated in future applications of (ego-)networks in archaeology.

for these changes extends well beyond the possible extents of an Anguillan based chiefdom (Hofman 2013). Another theory is that ethnohistorical descriptions of raids on Puerto Rico suggests that Island Carib aggression in the region had become so fierce it drove the majority of the inhabitants out of the region (Rouse 1948b). Although this remains an option, little actual archaeological evidence for such large scale inter-communal violence exists. It could also be the case that a slow but steady change unfolded in the social and cultural layout of the region due to the encroachment of Greater Antillean polities into the region (Hoogland and Hofman 1999). At present this theory is best supported by a comparison of the ego-network of Kelbey's Ridge 2 and Spring Bay 3. In Spring Bay 3 the regional distribution of stone materials was the greatest connector, as indicated by means of dark grey and light grey nodes in both models. In contrast, elaborate three-pointers, amulets, statuettes, shamanic paraphernalia and seats with Pan-Antillean stylistic and ritual links hold together the regional network of Kelbey's Ridge 2 (cf. Allaire 1990; Hofman, Bright, *et al.* 2008).[12]

Beyond the Ego

Even if your island is small, your Ego(-network) does not have to be. This definitely holds true for the island of Saba. In some senses Saba may have been a small place, far away from the Greater Antillean islands and their blossoming societies and cultures, but it was ultimately only remotely local. As discussed in this chapter, during late pre-colonial times Saba's local networks were expanded with connections to other material practices and places that were often geographically or even cosmologically alien. Nowadays the situation is much the same, with Sabans and visiting itinerants who, as the local anthem says, "may roam far from", but will always have strong ties to the island.

Returning to the hypotheses drafted by Hofman and Hoogland (2011) on the reasons for the existence of the community at Kelbey's Ridge 2, it is interesting to note that the ego-network model supports an importance of a varied set of relations and that there is no clear indication of a dominant model of relation. From the MDN it is clear that it had a highly strategic location, making it more likely that a Greater Antillean focused network of values and valuables extended to the small island. On the other hand, Kelbey's Ridge 2 was also well-integrated in regional networks of exchange. The communal ties, indicated by the house structure and burial patterns at Kelbey's Ridge 2, were also strong. Whether this implies that it was a settler community, leveraging its Greater Antillean roots in favour of trade opportunities

---

12 It is important to note that this pattern is somewhat tentative. A majority of the artefacts showing Greater Antillean influences have not been dated. Instead, based on relative chronology, stratigraphic placement and their stylistic ("Taíno" or Chicoid) affiliations these objects are regularly placed in the final phase of the indigenous cultural chronology of the Antilles (cf. Rouse 1992). It is interesting to note that Anguilla boasts some of the earliest sites, dated to around AD 1200, which have objects that evoke the notion of Greater Antillean connections, such as shell faces, large and carved three-pointed stones and even a similar snuff inhaler as was found in Kelbey's Ridge 2 (Crock and Petersen 2004; Mol 2007). It could be the case that, if an Anguilla-based, regional polity had existed around AD 1000 to 1200, it was responsible for tightening the bonds with similar polities in the Greater Antilles.

in this region, or whether it was a local group that somehow became involved with Greater Antillean communities is currently impossible to say. A strontium isotope-based study of residential mobility at the site is, so far, inconclusive (Laffoon 2012). The mixed network ties and strategies of Kelbey's Ridge 2's ego-network are perfectly illustrated by House Structure 3, which as a socio-material node encapsulates communal, spiritual and inter-communal ties. All in all, this ego-network seems to most coincide with Hofman and Hoogland's fourth hypothesis: a variety of factors contributed to the occupation Kelbey's Ridge 2, all of which are expressed by the archaeological evidence for social interactions at and beyond the site.

Needless to say, the micro to macro-scale ego-network model cannot provide a fully comprehensive view of the larger structure of the networks that the inhabitants of Kelbey's Ridge 2 participated in. It remains unclear whether the overarching network was hub-like with a political or cultural authority, such as could have been the case when it was colonized by a far-off chiefdom from the Greater Antilles? Or perhaps this system was structured like a small-world, with strong local clusters with some ties leading from Saban to Greater Antillean communities? This could have been the case if Kelbey's Ridge 2 was a community of "entrepreneurs" that utilised their already strong regional position and the proximity of the Saba bank to extend their social and material networks. Was Saba perhaps "randomly" connected to other places? Its local population could have been complemented by drifters from the Greater Antilles, bringing its strong local networks in intermittent contact with wider regional networks – a situation that cannot be dismissed when looking at individual mobility at the site (Laffoon 2012). Perhaps Saba's network arose out of a combination of all three or even other dynamics. What is certain is that the model presented in Figure 6.3 contains possible ingredients for each of the above larger network structures. Unfortunately deciding between them is difficult when viewed from the ego-network of one site alone.

Nevertheless, the results of this network exploration show that, thanks to the long-running fieldwork programme on Saba and the extensive multi-disciplinary analyses of its archaeological record, it is possible to gain some more insight into the local effects of the multi-levelled networks in the region. Future archaeometric analyses on the assemblage of Kelbey's Ridge 2 and other sites in the region will allow for a more in-depth study of wider network processes. For now an enhanced understanding of the type of networks dynamics that shaped the site assemblage is only possible by other, more regionally focused studies. The model and analysis of the ego-network of Kelbey's Ridge 2 and its comparison with that of Spring Bay 3 identified two material culture practices that may shed further lights on patterns of homogeneity and diversity in this region of the Caribbean: inter-island distribution of raw materials and finished goods and a loosely affiliated inter-regional system of values and valuables. The incorporation of lithic distribution networks in the ego-network of this chapter can be seen as an extension of the case-study on lithic exchange in the Archaic-Saladoid-Huecoid interface period. In Chapters 7 and 8 I will discuss two themes encountered in the present chapter: the political system known as the *cacicazgo* and the importance of the dissimilar and widely distributed set of "Taíno" valuables.

Chapter 7

Caciques and their Collectives: An Ethnohistoric View of Political Networks

[T]he Admiral found out that they called the king cacique in their tongue.[1]

Excerpt from the diary of Columbus, as told by Bartolomé de las Casas (de Navarete 1922: 110)

In the final part of this work I will focus on two larger and interconnected forces behind the patterns of homogeneity and diversity in the late pre-colonial Caribbean: the political economy and the material cultural repertoires and practices referred to as "Taíno". The latter was also discussed in the previous chapter as the one group that held the network of 14th century Kelbey's Ridge 2 together, perhaps as the result of the growing influence of Greater Antillean peoples over the region. This chapter will take a more top-down view and discuss the structure of the late pre-colonial socio-political system known as the *cacicazgo*. I will contrast a network exploration based on ethnohistorical information on socio-political relations to a standard model that suggests *cacicazgos* were strong, institutional hierarches based around the figure of the *cacique*. The corresponding model is one in which we see a strong hierarchy in political networks that are controlled by one political actor (see Figure 7.1).

Although the *cacicazgo* is a term often applied to refer to the political systems in the Caribbean and beyond, the Greater Antilles and specifically Hispaniola and Puerto Rico are the only islands for which the multi-tiered, regional polities headed by an actual *cacique*, can directly be substantiated from the available historic sources (Curet 1992, 2003; Rouse 1992; Siegel 1992). All other "*cacicazgos*" are extrapolations of either early colonial Spanish colonial administrations or present-day scholars seeking to find one model for the socio-political systems of the indigenous peoples of the Americas. Consequently it has often been equalled to the chiefdom model from socio-political evolutionary theory (Curet 2003). As I will discuss here, on some level the structure of the *cacicazgo* can be compared to

---

1   "[...] y allí supo el Almirante que al Rey llamaban en su lengua *Cacique*" (de Navarete 1922: 110).

other types of political systems, but it also has some features that make it uniquely Antillean.[2]

In the Greater Antilles, the estimates on the number and size of the existing *cacicazgos* at the end of the 15th century vary: some scholars claim there were only five regional *cacicazgos* on the island of Hispaniola, others identify up to twelve smaller polities (Wilson 1990). The number and extent of Puerto Rican *cacicazgos* at the time of contact is less clear, but there were at least a few powerful *caciques* (Oliver 2009). As discussed in Chapter 2, the initial development of these polities and their leaders, taking place around AD 700, also coincided with population growth and the contraction of long-distance exchange networks. As a result of the political solidification, increasing population pressure and decreasing long-distance contacts it could be expected that communities would have become much more territorially entrenched. This could have resulted in more competition and conflict between groups and a cultural and social landscape that had more and more, strongly demarcated boundaries, like it did in many other parts of the world.

Generally speaking, historic sources seem to indicate that *cacicazgos* were more likely to ally than compete with each other. We know that their leaders were mutually connected through several types of elite relations, e.g. exchanges of gifts, marital partners and even the exchange of personal names known as *guaítiao* (Mol 2007; Oliver 2009). It is for instance well-documented that the eastern Hispaniolan *caciques* had strong alliances with several Puerto Rican *caciques* (Oliver 2009; Samson 2010). These bonds may have even been the reason that the *cacicazgos* in the east of Hispaniola were among the longest enduring after the initial contact with Europeans in 1492. Only after the *Wars of Higuey* of 1504, in which a force of Puerto Rican and Hispaniolan peoples openly confronted the Spanish, did the Spanish manage to break the indigenous power in this region (Churampi Ramírez 2007; Oliver 2009). So, although competition was a natural part of inter-*cacical* interactions – even including mock battles –, this rivalry does not seem to have easily spilled over into inter-group violence or cultural segregation.

This solidarity could have been the result of political unification against the greater threat of the Spanish *conquistadores*. Nevertheless, the post-contact archaeological record shows a similar picture of interaction instead of conflict in the region of the Mona Passage – the sea strait dividing Puerto Rico and Hispaniola. Albeit extreme long-distance networks between regions had declined, the last centuries before contact showed a range of frequent and stable connections across the region (e.g. Hofman, Isendoorn, *et al.* 2008; Keegan 2007; Morsink 2012; Oliver 2009; Ulloa Hung 2013). In addition, as was discussed in the previous chapter, material cultural practices and repertoires from the Mona Passage region seem to have diffused to the surrounding island regions (Atkinson 2006; Crock 2000; Hofman, Bright, *et al.* 2008; Hoogland and Hofman 1999; McGinnis 1997; Mol 2007; Oliver 2009; Valcárcel Rojas 2002).

---

2   This chapter is an extension of part of a book chapter I co-authored with Jimmy Mans (Mol and Mans 2013). Here we contrasted the politics of exchange networks of the Trio community of Amötopo (Surinam; see also Mans 2011) to those of proto-contact Hispaniola.

This diffusion includes such examples of "Classic Taíno" culture as (variants of) the Ostionoid ceramic series (Rouse 1992; Veloz Maggiolo 1972), stone belts, elbow stones, (zoo-)anthropomorphic three-pointed stones (Walker 1993), *guaíza* shell faces (Mol 2007), (zoo-)anthropomorphic pestles, and high-backed *duho* seats (Ostapkowicz 1997). Aside from having a large area of distribution these items seemed to also have formed a specific subset of highly valued material culture (McGinnis 1997; Hofman, Bright, *et al.* 2008). It has also been suggested that the diffusion of these objects was the result of their circulation within elite exchange networks (Oliver 2009). It is also noteworthy that archaeological evidence for any larger scale inter-polity conflict is lacking. In the Northeastern Caribbean there is only scant evidence for interpersonal violence to begin with (e.g. Calderon 1975; Siegel 2004; Weston 2010), but the available evidence is certainly not reflective of endemic (group) conflicts. In other words, the observed patterns of connectivity between regions and its relative peacefulness seem to defy the projected evolution of a culturally and politically "balkanized" Northeastern Caribbean.

There does not seem to be any easily identifiable cause for this unity. Although it has been suggested that this was the result of a shared pan-Antillean cultural identity (cf. Rodríguez Ramos 2010: 10, see also pp. 210-212; Oliver 2009: 27-30), there are, for instance, no archaeological indications of widely shared political or religious ideologies (e.g. Anderson 1991). In fact, any form of top-down identity formation seems to be completely lacking. Rather, this and the following Chapter investigates the idea that this was not the result of top-down ideological or identity processes, but due to the pressures of indigenous political economies. I will specifically discuss why, even in the context of potentially increasing political hierarchies and territoriality, those in power could never afford to look too much inward or outward, always needing to connect to various types of political economies. Subsequently, Chapter 8 will follow up on this with the idea that this pressure partly found an outlet and was mediated by inspirited objects (see also Curet 1996; Mol 2007; Oliver 2009; Siegel 2010).

Cacical networks: a fragmentary archaeological view

Archaeological indicators of economic relations between sites can potentially serve to connect nodes and reconstruct flows of past political networks. This can be applied alongside other archaeological indicators of power differentiation between and within sites. The value of such a network is highly dependent on the size and variability of the data sets. Unfortunately, such data are hard to come by in the case of the heartland of the *cacicazgo* or as Oliver (2009: 45) has recently explained in his publication on *cacical* networks or "webs" in the late pre-contact and early contact Mona Passage region: "[T]he patterns of pathways connecting different sites between and within islands cannot be specified, and thus the configuration of the web (nodes and pathways or vectors) remains vague. At best what can be observed is the sphere or area of interaction."

On the other hand investigations in this region provide more and more information on pathways flowing from and to sites, either based in GIS or archaeometrical analysis. Torres, for example, has shown that a GIS-database of site locations and periodization can greatly augment our current understanding of the influence of Euclidean distance on indigenous networks of power (Torres 2012). This study was, however, based on a large database of regional surveys and excavations carried out in southwest Puerto Rico, one of the regions with the best archaeological coverage of the Caribbean.

In Hispaniola most regions simply have not received that kind of substantive attention. One of the zones with the best archaeological coverage to date is the province of Higuey, in the east of the Dominican Republic. It has been extensively surveyed by Dominican and foreign archaeologists since the 1960s. Numerous sites discovered through these surveys have been subject to additional research in the form of both small and large scale excavations, especially in the east and south (Samson 2010: 26-36, 97-105). The resulting image is one of a relatively dense population living in small hamlets and larger villages with some of the larger sites probably fulfilling the role of regional socio-political centres. However, research on the exact direction and nature of interactions between these archaeological sites and their possible political integration is still in its early stages.

Higuey is one of the few regions and sites for which this may be possible. In this region the settlement of Punta Macao, a 1 km^2 large site facing the Mona Passage in the East of the province, holds a special position (Samson 2010: 87; Veloz Maggiolo and Ortega 1972). Ethnohistoric sources concerning the region mention that a large village named Macao was located in a *cacicazgo* with the same name, suggesting it was the centre of this *cacicazgo* (de las Casas 1909: Vol. 1, Chapter 9). Due to its size, which had no parallel in the direct vicinity, archaeologists have suggested that Punta Macao was the location of the historic Macao. Unfortunately, the site itself was destroyed in 2006/2007 due to a golf-course development. Although rescue archaeology was carried out and in spite of the fact that several excavations have taken place in the past, few accessible publications on the site exist.

Punta Macao had a long history of habitation, the chronology of the ceramics found at the site point to a continuous use since AD 200/400 (Samson 2010: 33).[3] Additionally, the ceramic assemblage shows a transition from a local variant of the Ostionoid-series into the Chicoid-series, which suggests that it might have been one of the key sites for the development of the Chicoid international style (Veloz Maggiolo and Ortega 1972; Rouse 1992). The Macao collection of the Fundación Garcia-Arévalo includes Early Colonial ceramics reputedly found at the site (Samson, personal communication 2010). This suggests a continued usage during Early Colonial times.

---

3   Over the years eight C-14 samples were taken at the site. They were dated between AD 825 and 1200 (Olsen Bogaert 2008: 26).

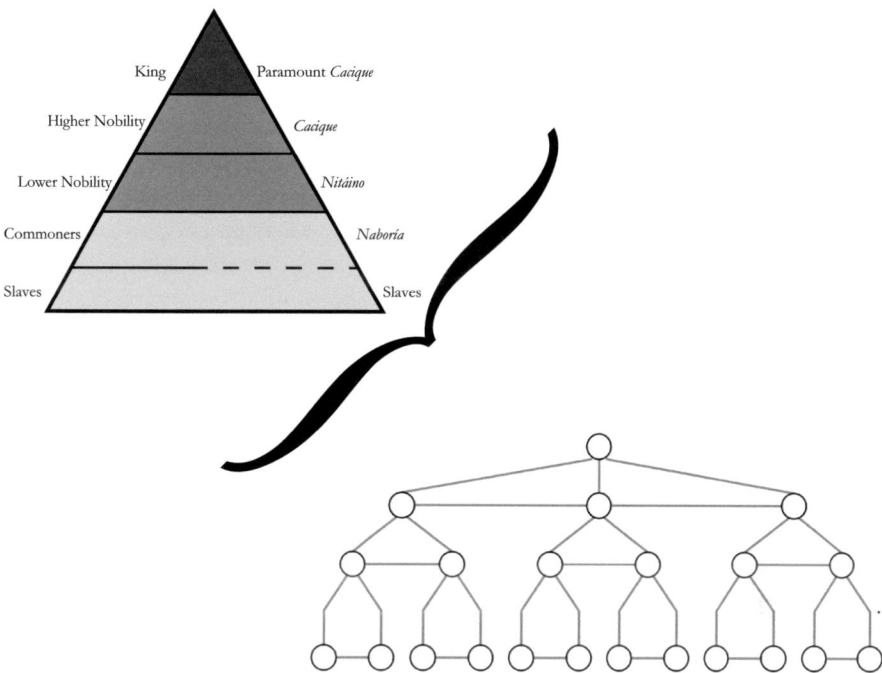

Figure 7.1: A political pyramid as a network.

Pollen analysis, a formal study of part of the ceramic assemblage, and a geological survey of the site imply that, although inhabitants of Macao were exploiting coastal and marine resources, crops such as manioc, sweet potatoes, zamia and chilli peppers as well as non-edible crops (tobacco, cotton) were cultivated on a moderately large-scale (Nadal 2004; Ulloa Hung 2008). A total of twenty-six burials have been recovered in 2006 and are currently being examined at the Museo del Hombre Dominicano in Santo Domingo (Tavárez María and Calderón 2005). A dental study of the remains reveals wear and pathology consistent with a mixed agricultural and marine diet (Mickleburgh and Pagán-Jiménez 2012). Although enlightening, these findings do not point to an extra-ordinary role in terms of subsistence or other economic networks for a site of this period. Punta Macao was just one of many more or less economically autarkic site systems in Higuey (Samson 2010; Veloz Maggiolo and Ortega 1972).

Quite a few personal adornments made of shell, fishbone and stone were reportedly found during the rescue excavations. Objects found at this site and now kept at the Museo del Hombre Dominicano (Santo Domingo) include a large stone axe, fragments of stone belts, ceramic body stamps, a ceramic three pointer, shell and bone beads (including one perforated dog tooth and a shell frog pendant), a badly weathered shell face, and a small sceptre-like object with a big-beaked bird at its head (Ulloa Hung, personal communication 2010). Before its destruction, parts of this site were subject to heavy looting. Therefore it has to be expected that numerous objects from Macao are currently included in unknown local and international private collections. Compared to contemporaneous sites within this region, such as El Cabo (Samson 2010), items recovered from the archaeological record of Macao do not necessarily suggest a central position in local political networks.

Recent studies of clay composition from other contemporaneous, habitation sites in Higuey have pinpointed Macao as the possible source of ceramic clay or completed ceramic vessels (Conrad, *et al.* 2008; van As, *et al.* 2008). Results of a neutron activation analysis of ceramics collected ($n= 175$) at the Mananantíal de Aleta, nearby Aleta Plaza sites, La Cangrejera in the Parque Nacional del Este and Punta Macao show that one hundred and forty-six sherds could be assigned to five compositional groups (Conrad, *et al.* 2008). Although a majority of the clays of the ceramics ($n= 122$) were collected within the regional of the site, several non-local ceramics show a strong correlation with the composition of the ceramic sherds from Punta Macao ($n= 24$). Additionally (van As, *et al.* 2008), specimens were collected in the eastern and south-eastern coastal region in order to gain insight into the provenance of the clay of the ceramics at the site of El Cabo. Further archaeometrical analysis of this material is pending, but a preliminary clay-suitability study indicates that a majority of the clays or ceramics presumably originated from the immediate vicinity of the Punta Macao site.[4]

Using this information it is in theory possible to build a network based on probable clay provenance of the ceramics from several sites in the region. For this purpose the results from the La Aleta and El Cabo study were combined (Conrad, *et al.* 2008; van As, *et al.* 2008). The resulting 2-mode graph is shown in Figure 7.2 (affiliation of absolute quantity of sherds to the various compositional groups). The analysis of the fragmentary ceramic network data based on absence and presence of network connections shows that the group of ceramics related to the Macao region seems to take a somewhat central position within the network. Nevertheless, it is clear that Macao was in no way the most important source for clay with regard to the more southerly located community inhabiting the La Aleta region. Even if it was, the network has too few data points and is too fragmentary to allow for a wider interpretation of political networks in the region. Even based on this relatively large data set it is impossible to conclude anything in detail on whether the political networks of the region were interdependent with Punta Macao's ceramic distribution network. In this sense, Oliver (2009: 45) is correct: even the best available archaeological database from the Hispaniolan heartland of the *cacicazgo* does not present a ready handle that can help us to understand the socio-political structures and strategies that were at play in the region, let alone *cacical* networks in general.

---

4   Another alternative for clays with similar suitability are the areas surrounding the modern city of Higuey in the centre of the province and Boca de Yuma in the Southeast, but Van As and colleagues deem Macao to be the most likely provenance (Van As 2008: 72).

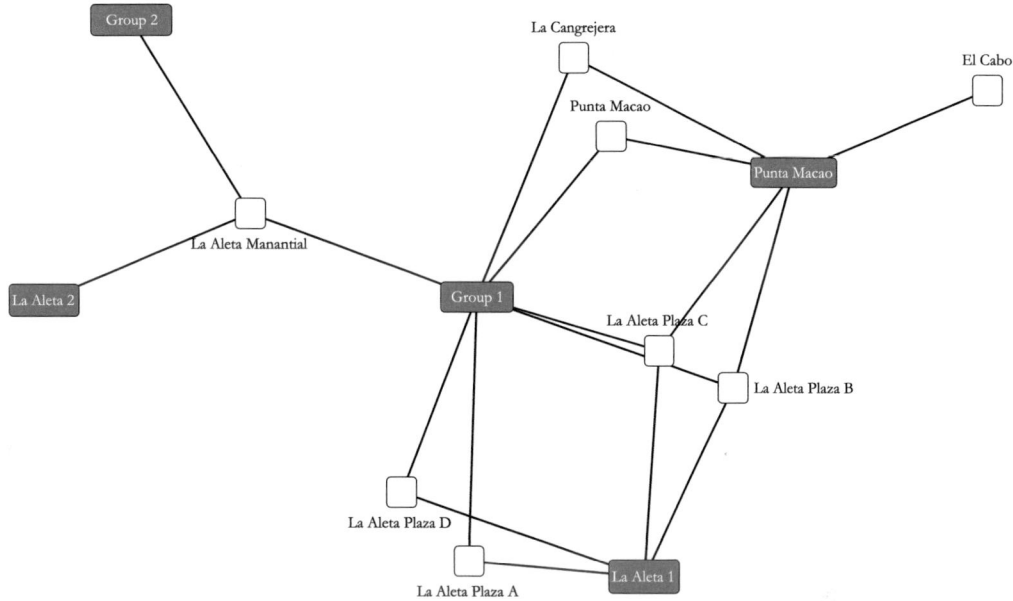

Figure 7.2: Fragmented 2-mode network of an incomplete view of Higuey's ceramic distribution, based on the provenance studies by Conrad and colleagues (2008) and van As and colleagues (2008). White nodes represent the ceramic assemblages of sites or site loci, while dark grey nodes correspond to clay compositional groups.

Cacical networks: a view from ethnohistory

In Caribbean archaeology, ethnohistorical documents have played an important role in the reconstruction of pre-colonial political structures and social practices ever since the beginning of the discipline (e.g. Lovén 1935). The majority of these sources have stressed the *cacique* as being the political office where most if not all political power was held. It is revealing that by and large chroniclers referred to *caciques* as "*reyes*" or "kings" and that even their personal adornments were synonymized with regalia: e.g. feather headdresses became crowns in the citation from Columbus's diary describing his interaction with Guacanagarí (Chapter 4). This seems to place the type of relations *caciques* had with non-*caciques* firmly within the realm of the Authority Ranking models of relations. As I will argue here, this view misconstrues the complex and heterarchical nature of *cacical* political economies. To Spanish chroniclers the role of *caciques* may have seemed comparable to that of late medieval European royalty, but in fact the political networks of which the *cacique* was a part were very dissimilar to those of an absolute, divinely ordained monarch.

Indeed, in more recent scholarly literature the *cacique* is often referred to as a type of chief, rather than king. However, partly because the *cacicazgo* is considered a Caribbean synonymic-type of chiefdom from the viewpoint of socio-political evolutionary theory (Curet 2003; Redmond 1998; Steward 1948), the political system in the Antilles has been characterized through the authority of the *cacique* as an (increasingly) absolute leader (Keegan 2007; Moscoso 1977, 1999; Roe 1997). This has resulted in a "pyramidal" view of the late pre- and early colonial Greater Antillean society, with the *cacique* at the pinnacle (Figure 7.1). This top-down view of indigenous socio-politics can also be found in Caribbean society today: versions of indigenous resistance stories often focus on the personal exploits of *caciques* in their struggle against the Spanish conqueror and in the Dominican Republic the term *cacique* is even today utilized when referring to petty bosses who behave as despots.

This pyramidal model of power was dominated by a set of nested Authority Ranking relations. Regional *cacicazgos*, such as in Higuey, were headed by a paramount *cacique*, who had influence over a number of less powerful *caciques*. According to some sources this class of elites is called the *nitaínos*, "the good ones". The class of the *naborías* (literally meaning, "the rest") is considered to have been the commoner's class (Keegan 1997; Keegan, *et al.* 1998; Moscoso 1977, 1999). It has even been suggested that this pyramidal power structure was already firmly in place by the beginning of the contact period to a degree that the *caciques* were perceived as divine kings, akin to those in Polynesia (Sahlins 1963, 1975), who were venerated with great decorum (Keegan, *et al.* 1998; Oliver 1997, 2000). In this view the only politically relevant network interactions supposedly take place in hierarchical "old boy networks" between a few paramount *caciques* and, from the top down, between paramount *caciques* and their subordinate *caciques*, who in turn ruled their communities (Mol and Mans 2013).

This view of *cacical* authority has received considerable critique. Part of this criticism focuses on the disparate levels of detail between archaeology and ethnohistory. However, the problem is not that this view is largely based on ethnohistorical rather than on archaeological studies (cf. Machlachlan and Keegan 1990; Keegan and Rodríguez 2004). Where the view of the pre-colonial Antillean political structure is most fraught with difficulties is that it is largely based on socio-political evolutionary models. In this model there is one chief, reigning supreme over a certain territory, who is hard at work in turning his chiefdom into an incipient state (Chapman 2003; Pauketat 2008). Aside from the fact that such quasi-evolutionary thinking is based on a teleological fallacy, there is as yet no undisputed ethnohistorical and archaeological evidence indicating that the male *cacique* was in fact an absolute leader. On the contrary, a socio-political network investigation of the ethnohistoric sources will show that the *cacique* is only one of several powerful figures in indigenous political economies.

Cacical nodes and ties

A close reading of the prominent historic sources referring to the early contact period of Hispaniola presents us with a variety of important network actors in pre- and early Colonial Greater Antillean political networks.[5] Based on this information the interrelations between political actors can be modelled. These various nodes in the network fulfilled different but important roles in diplomacy, brokering, and

---

5   Drawn from the standard historic sources, discussed at length in Wilson (1990: 7-13).

competition in the political arena. As such several types of actors can be identified that would have been relevant for the political process from an *emic* perspective: spirits, ancestors, and other superhuman beings, *behiques* or magico-religious specialists, *caciques*, *cacical* communities, and *cacical* kin such as the preferred heir and his wife or *cacica*. [6]

It is clear that the *cacique* was the one individual who was first and foremost responsible for the everyday management of his or her community and extended network of kin. Indeed, it may be presumed that the term *cacique* originally referred to the head of an extended family, a Greater Antillean form of the "*pater familias*" so to speak (Oliver, personal communication 2007). However, at the time of contact there were evidently definite hierarchies dividing *caciques* and *cacical* communities. Larger *cacicazgos* were headed by a paramount *cacique* who supervised a number of less powerful *caciques*. Nevertheless, even if we would accept that they were semi-divine beings, an individual *cacique* was not the only demi-god on earth.

Various readings of the early documents suggest anywhere between five and twelve paramount *caciques* on the island of Hispaniola around the time of contact (Wilson 1990). These regional *cacicazgos* all consisted of numerous smaller political entities. Ethnohistoric sources suggest that at least three *cacical* ranks were distinguished: (1) *matunherí* for the highest ranking *cacique*, (2) *baharí* for a *cacique* of the second rank and (3) *waherí* for the lowest *cacical* rank (Oliver 2009: 25). This essentially added several other layers to the *cacical* network in which the most powerful *caciques* were exchanging and competing in a higher, yet permeable political sphere, while attempting to retain the support of their followers consisting of subordinate *cacical* collectives. Following up on the idea of *caciques* as heads of family-based collectives, there were probably as many minor *caciques* as there were kin collectives (Oliver 2009). These minor *caciques* jockeyed amongst themselves for wider popular support and favourable political alliances, the more powerful among them sometimes even challenging paramount *caciques*. This could have been the intention of Guacanagarí when he attempted to forge an alliance with Columbus (Wilson 1990: 79; Mol 2007).

Other members of the *cacique*'s community were responsible for the creation and maintenance of network relations as well. For instance, it is a recurrent theme in interactions between groups of Spaniards and indigenous peoples that before the leader of the Spanish group meets the *cacique* they first interact with another, less authoritative member of the *cacique*'s community, who perhaps determines the dispositions of the strangers (e.g. de Navarete 1922: 105-108, 154). These trustees, likely family members or other close allies, would also assist the *cacique* during the large communal exchanges in which he was the main acting party. In such exchanges other high-ranking individuals had subsidiary roles to fulfil (such as presenting smaller gifts, partaking in the feast, socializing with the guests, forwarding advice to the *cacique etc.*). This seems to be the power relations

---

6   It is undeniably true that male political leaders seem to be the most prominent in the historic descriptions. However, we should not discount the fact that the historic sources are *de facto* male focused and that the colonizers applied the structure of the *cacical* office as the basis for the later *encomienda*-system, which closely mimicked similar Iberian, male dominated, feudal institutions.

that inform the actions and behaviours of the five unnamed "kings" that were subject to Guacanagarí (Chapter 4). Moreover, gifts were seemingly sent through intermediaries, the proxy was probably a member of the *caciques'* lineage (Keegan 2007; Mol 2007).

The late Puerto Rican scholar Ricardo Alegría found a shipping list from the second voyage to the Caribbean, the so-called "Columbus Shipping List", in the *Colección de Documentos Inéditos* of the Seville *Archivo General de Indias*. It catalogues a string of exchanges between Columbus and Guacanagarí, at the newly founded colony of Isabela between the first quarter of 1495 and the second quarter of 1496 (Alegría 1980; Mol 2007, 2008). The author of the list mentions on several occasions that Guacanagarí sent Columbus various items. It is notable that at least two of them are brought by one of the nephews of Guacanagarí; a similar gift had also been sent with one of his family members, presumably a nephew (de Navarete 1922: 133 and 229).

This particular strategy of involving the *cacique*'s extended kin in exchanges with outsiders is especially relevant with regards to *cacical* succession. It seems that, after his death, the vast majority of the *cacique*'s wealth was returned into circulation during a funerary feast in which his extended kin gave away his possessions to 'foreign' *caciques* (de Oviedo y Valdés 1851: Vol. 5, Chapter 4, p. 134).[7] It is not known which member of the *cacique*'s extended kin supervised this feast. The debate on the rules of descent and inheritance for the *cacical* title has not yet been settled. It has been suggested that this title passed to the sister's son of the *cacique* (Keegan 2006), which would comply with the reference to the nephews of Guacanagarí acting as an emissary.

However, I agree with Curet (Curet 2002, 2006) that, although there probably was an established practice of succession of the *cacique* by his sister's first son, the rules of succession were flexible. This allowed some room for political manoeuvring of the various actors and factions vying for the *cacical* office. Having the right type of network skills and relations offered a decisive advantage in such a competitive environment. Once the old *cacique* had passed away the new *cacique* would inherit the former's title and a set of reciprocal obligations resulting from the funerary exchanges after his death. However, the new *cacique* would not directly inherit material wealth that could serve as capital for existing and new political alliances. For prospective *caciques* it would therefore have been even more important to accumulate social and material capital by means of a strong network of one's own. This would have been strengthened by his duties as a semi-official *cacical* emissary.

Some confusion exists concerning the political status of the wife of the *cacique* or *cacica*.[8] We know that in at least one case (concerning the *cacica* Anacaona, wife to the prominent *cacique* Caonabo) the wife of a *cacique* fulfilled his political duties after his death. It has been claimed that this was the result of stress in the indigenous political system due to some particularly disruptive Spanish actions, including the

---

7   See Curet (2002, 2006), Keegan (2006) Oliver (2009: 104) for an extended discussion hereof.
8   In fact, *caciques* were probably polygamous and their wives perhaps even ranked (Oviedo y Valdes 1851: Book 5, Chapter 3, p. 134).

abduction and later death of Caonabo, held to be responsible for the destruction of La Navidad (Wilson 1990: 119; see Chapter 1). Nevertheless, there seems to have been an important role for the *cacica* and other women in indigenous networks of the proto-contact period. In pre-contact times this position was probably rooted in the matrilineal systems of descent, which made it impossible to hold on to and build a material base of wealth through the male line (Ensor 2013; Keegan 2007). Rather, material wealth and, for that matter, titles and obligations were owned and passed on through the maternal line.[9] In the case of the *cacica* Anacaona it is presumed that, even after the death of Caonabo, she had several houses at her disposal. They stored valuable items that were released into circulation at strategic moments (Martyr D'Anghera 1912: 124-125; Mol 2007: 86-88).

Additionally, the sources are unequivocal about the fact that she was a master at dancing and conducting *areítos* (e.g. de las Casas 1875: Vol. 1, Chapter 114, p. 138-139; de Oviedo y Valdes 1851: Book 5, Chapter 1, p. 127). These *areítos* were ritual, communal dances, which were performed on special occasions serving as mnemonic devices with which history could be recorded and re-enacted. They functioned as highly prestigious intellectual capital (de las Casas 1875: Vol. 1, Chapter 121, p. 171). The records also indicate that the *cacica* and other women of her community were responsible for the redistribution of food when receiving visitors (Wilson 1990: 57). Thus, although *cacicas* such as Anacaona did not have a network role that led directly to the establishment of many new network connections, she and other women of the community were in charge of maintaining existing networks.[10] This network role and strategy is in line with general discussions on the "conservative" role of women in social networks and particularly gift exchange.[11] It is assumed that she and other females of the *cacique*'s community remembered details of past network interactions, exerted control over network relations through the distribution of their lineage's material wealth and were of vital importance to the local infrastructure behind political networks. As is clear in the case of case of Caonabo and Anacaona, a *cacica* was more than capable of taking control of *cacical* collectives and their network relations to other collectives in the absence of a (strong) *cacique*.

It is important to understand the larger social universe in which political contracts and conflicts were created and mediated. Chapter 2 and 4 discussed how, within the broader perspectivist model of Lowland South American and the Caribbean, political economies were driven by acquisition and control of the "life-forces" of social others. This life-force shapes a being's subjective state and therefore the larger ebb and flow structures communal and inter-communal networks. It

---

9   See Strathern (1996) for a cross-cultural perspective hereon.
10 Deagan (2004) argues that the high measure of cultural continuity in Early Colonial Hispaniola (as attested at the contact period site of En Bas Saline) is based on the enduring social influence of indigenous women.
11 See also Mol and Mans (2013) for a perspective on this issue from the viewpoint of the Guianas; see Godelier (1999), Strathern (1986, 1996) and Weiner (1992) for a discussion on this matter with reference to Melanesia and beyond. In addition, psychologists like Komter (2005) and Cheal (1996) have found similar strategic positions for women in Western gift bonanzas such as Christmas and *Sinterklaas*.

cannot, however, be indefinitely or efficiently produced internally – within the person or group –, but needs to be externally acquired through interaction with social others In Lowland South America and the Caribbean the direct objective is to literally acquire life-forces of other subjects and "make them work" for oneself and one's social group (Santos-Granero 2009b).[12]

In a perspectivist worldview where a range of subjects could potentially possess *cemí* or life force, the political economy of life would also have been extended to incorporate non-humans (Oliver 2009). Pané (1999 [1571]: 25-26)'s account on the creation of a *cemí* statue for example, shows that trees, rocks and material culture objects could make their wishes known and thereby enter into contracts with human beings. If these contracts were not honoured by their human counterparts these materialized spirit beings could retaliate by inflicting diseases on them or by simply leaving the community, as in the case of Opiyelguobirán. It was reported to Pané that this partly canine, partly humanoid spirit-statue regularly left its house at night after which it had to be recollected from the forest in the morning (see Figure 8.1.i). At a certain point it was tied down in order to prevent it from leaving but it managed to escape nonetheless and disappeared into a lagoon forever (*pp.* 28-29). It should be noted that this type of politicized residential mobility was probably also open to human members of the community (Laffoon 2012; compare Rivière 1984).

Behiques, trans-specific, shaman-like specialists, were capable of communicating with beings that were outside of the range of normal human interaction. They did this by entering a state of trance during rituals in which they purged themselves and sniffed the pulverized seeds of the *Anadenanthera peregrina* mixed with chalk up the nose. Through this mediation with the spirits the *behique* was also able to cure diseases (Roe 1997). The *behique* seems to have been important as a spiritual advisor to the *cacique* and local communities, too, for example as a medium through which other members of the community could interact with deceased relatives (Pané 1999 [1571]: 23-24). *Behiques* were thus necessary intermediaries for the interaction with other than human subjects.

In addition, the *behiques* themselves were interacting and competing in networks of their own. An example hereof would have been the sharing and exchanging of magical, ceremonial and ritual knowledge (Allaire 1990). Aside from such sociable interactions, *behiques* would also have been locked in perpetual cosmic combat with malevolent superhuman forces that sought to harm the *behique* and the community of which he was a part. Especially in Lowland South America the influence of such malefactors is that significant they are thought to be the major or

---

12   This can be contrasted with other political economies, such as those of capitalist societies in which more metaphorical "life-forces" (i.e. a person's time and energy) are circulated (Graeber 2011).

sole cause behind any misfortune that could befall a person or village. Often these beings are believed to be under the control of hostile shaman-like specialists.[13]

Despite their considerable power, *behiques* would not have dominated everyday politics. First of all, the sources indicate that they were probably very much subordinate to *caciques*. The latter also encroached upon the specialism of the *behique* by being a centrepiece of various socio-religious rituals and ceremonies (Roe 1997). Indeed, *behiques* were not always treated with the same respect that other (elite) people were. Pané (1999 [1571]: 24-25) recounts the incidence of an unfortunate *behique* who is clubbed to death by a mob (only to return back to life later) having caused the death of a family member. As befits his status as a liminal figure, it seems that the *behique* was to some extent a social other within his own community.

Cacical network structure and strategy

The roles and strategies mentioned in the historic sources for the Greater Antilles can serve to construct an idealized political network model (Figure 7.3).[14] Rather than being a direct Authority Ranking, pyramidal model with a clear nested, hub-like structure, this network shows a set of diverse relations, which could be characterized as Equality Matching (sets of interdependent dyads) or even Communal Sharing (cyclical sets of node ties). This is in contrast to previous "hidden" suppositions about political network structure and strategy (Figure 7.1). It also directly contradicts the notion that the *cacique* was the dominant force in political networks. Indeed, based on a Katz status centrality analysis (see Chapter 2), it becomes clear that, even if he was the most powerful actor, the *cacique* was far from the only player of importance in Late Ceramic Age power structures. Instead power was distributed throughout his *cacical* collective – a 2-clique subgraph in the network. In this model various network economies are entwined and jointly provide the political status of the collective as a whole: intercommunal, ritual and communal economies. Within this collective we see certain other key figures. The relative centralities of these actors are listed in Table 7.1.

The positions of the various actors result from the network strategies they represent. *Cacicas* are important network brokers, having access to mnemonic devices in the form of corporate valuables such as *areítos*. Lower-ranked elites such as potential heirs would have acted as go-betweens during interactions with

---

13 This was definitely the case with the historic Kalinago of the Lesser Antilles, who greatly feared the Maboya, a cannibalistic deity who devoured the moon, *opouyem*, and other malicious spirits that were sometimes sent directly by ritual specialists within the own community or shamans from enemy villages. Albeit that the evidence for the Greater Antilles is coloured by the Spanish belief that all Amerindians were devil-worshippers, it is assumed that the group of "devils", where feared above all others, such as certain *zemis* and the *opía* spirit. The latter is probably a cognate form of the Kalinago *opouyem*. *Behiques* would have been able to exert a measure of control over them and direct them to bring harm to individuals and even entire villages (Mol 2009).

14 The fact that this is an "idealized" model has two reasons: (1) it is a reflection of the socio-political system through the eyes of Spanish chroniclers; and (2) the socio-political system is likely to have been much more fluid in practice. For example, some collectives may perhaps have had access to two *behiques* or a number of categorically different spirits (e.g. ancestors and spirits that were not kin).

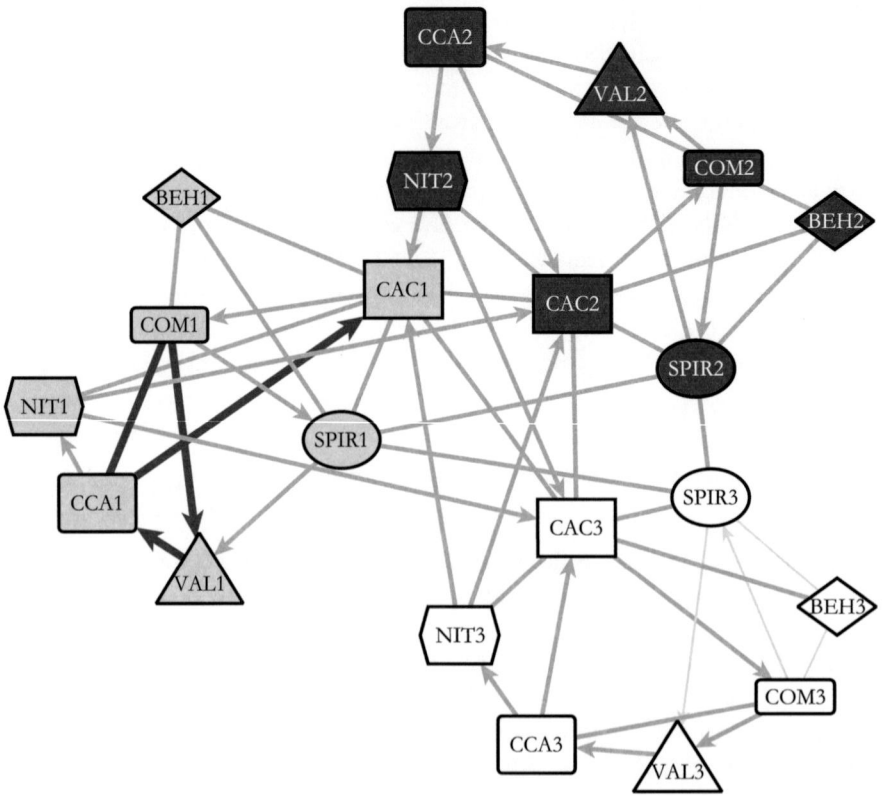

Figure 7.3: Model of political organization of three cacical *collectives. Tie colour and size are indicative of tie strength (darker and wider = stronger ties) in the network.*

outsiders. *Behiques* were other types of go-betweens and of huge importance for sustaining network relations with the spirit world. Thus, although they have specialized roles, depending on which subgraph and type of power one looks at, the network power of *cacicas*, *behiques* and *cacical* heirs rivals that of the *cacique*. Most notably, interaction with superhuman spirits carried out by *behiques* and *caciques* takes a central role in the network. This confirms that mediation with, and manipulation of, these beings was a highly significant political strategy (Oliver 1997).

It may now appear that there was no need in the network for the *cacique* himself. However, it has to be understood that although important network roles and strategies were also executed by other types of actors the *cacique* was a "jack of all trades and master of none" in network terms. Although operating with go-betweens, he was ultimately the face of the community in elite interactions, supervised ceremonial communal redistributions, served as a wartime leader, and was able to enter into network relations with superhuman beings as well. It is exactly this versatile character that would have made *caciques* central players in pre- and early historic political networks. Nonetheless, the concept of the *cacique* as standing alone at the top of a rigid, political pyramid should be adjusted.

Indeed, due to the variety of roles in the network, a political actor required strong relations in order to reach her or his full power potential in the network. Furthermore, the success of one type of network actor was not only based on his or her own tie quantity and strength, but directly related to the degree of success of the other actors in the network. This can be illustrated by changing the strength of the ties between nodes in the various subgraphs to mimic fluctuations in power relations between actors and subgraphs in the network, which will result in a strikingly different status centrality (compare the "status" and "valued status" rows in Table 7.1).

Subgraph 1 illustrates a situation in which the communal economy is extra strong (the ties are valued at two, rather than one). One can call this the "Anacaona-effect": a capable cacica (CCA1) is able to strengthen communal ties (with COM1), the benefits of which are invested in communal valuables (VAL1). Because the *cacique* (CAC1)'s status among other *caciques* is partly dependent on the valuables he brings to the table in political exchanges, this has an impact on his own centrality. In fact, this boost in the communal political economy can be felt among all nodes in subgraph 1: the *behique* (BEH1) and the group of *nitaíno* (NIT1) also have an increased status centrality.

Subgraph 2 depicts a situation that is unchanged relative to the non-valued network, but subgraph 3 presents a situation analogous to the "Opiyelguobirán-crisis" (cf. Pané 1999 [1571]: 25-26). In it the ritual economy is somehow distorted (tie-strength is halved). This leads to limited tie-strength between the *cacical* community at large (COM3), superhuman beings (SPIR3) and *behique* (BEH3). Like the increased tie-strength had a beneficial effect for all of the subgraph members in subgraph 1, this ritual crisis spreads throughout the network affecting the network power of other members such as the *cacique*. Even though he himself has equally strong relations with the spirit world as his *cacical* competitors in subgraph 1 and 2, he suffers a 0.3% point

Node ID	Status %	Valued status %
BEH1	4.6	4.9
BEH2	4.6	4.4
BEH3	4.6	2.9
CAC1	10.2	11.4
CAC2	10.2	9.9
CAC3	10.2	9.6
CCA1	2.0	4.7
CCA2	2.0	1.8
CCA3	2.0	1.6
COM1	3.9	5.6
COM2	3.9	3.7
COM3	3.9	3.0
NIT1	2.8	3.3
NIT2	2.8	2.6
NIT3	2.8	2.6
SPIR1	7.3	7.3
SPIR2	7.3	6.8
SPIR3	7.3	5.7
VAL1	2.6	4.1
VAL2	2.6	2.5
VAL3	2.6	1.6

Table 7.1 Shifts in status centrality in cacical *collectives showing the status centralities of the* cacical *collectives without ("Status") and with ("Valued status") valued ties. The valuation of ties refers to a strong communal economic ties (collective 1) or weak ritual economic ties (collective 3). Note how weakness in a particular part of the network can affect the centralities of nodes that do not directly participate in these economies.*

drop relative to the "normal *cacique*" (CAC2) and a gap of 1.8% with the *cacique* from subgraph 1 (CAC1). This is due to the fact that his status suffers from the combined effect of his own interactions with the less communally-sustained spirit realm, the less-powerful *behíque*, and communal valuables that do not benefit as much from the incorporation of the *cemí* of the angered superhuman beings.

The subgraph aggregate of status centralities illustrates these power fluctuations with even more clarity. In a non-valued link centrality measure the collectives would all hold a third of the total status in the network. However, in the valued measure the normal *cacical* collective (subgraph 2) holds 31.8% of the total network's status, while subgraph 1, boosted by the "Anacaona-effect" has a combined status centrality of 41.2%. With this they easily out-compete the *cacical* collective that is suffering from the "Opiyelguobirán-crisis", which has an aggregate status centrality of only 27%. In other words, the strength and weaknesses of actors in this network are not contained to their direct network position and the political position of one actor is based on his or her subgraph neighbours. Therefore even if the differences between categorically similar network actors (e.g. all the *caciques*) seem relatively minimal, these small differences would have signified great collective power differences. A *cacique* did not rule by setting himself apart from others (Authority Ranking), but by interacting and being involved with them (Communal Sharing and Equality Matching).

Triadic roots of the *cacical* collective

From a network point of view, this interdependence between actors entails that at some point the *cacicazgo* became stable as a political system – knocking out one node or even more does not automatically lead to disintegration of the network. The *cacical* network did not extend this stability to the individual actor or collective, however. Political fortunes would be affected by ripples in both the lower and higher strata of the network. On top of this, node power would have been curbed by the interdependent structure of the network: every node is at least connected to two other nodes, which means that there are always at least two pathways to consider when wanting to control a network. As such it is possible to characterize the *cacicazgo* as a triadic political system. This is in contrast to a dyadic political system: i.e. any system with vertical hierarchies with a chain of command in which any misbalance in power can only be adjusted by destroying the system as a whole. The reason for this is that all nodes are critical for the coherence of the network – e.g. absolute political systems; a *cacical* pyramid of power. It seems that this triadic political system of the late pre-colonial and early colonial period was rooted in the first regional social networks of the Antilles.

Based on archaeological evidence, correspondences with more recent mainland indigenous political systems and analogous contexts in other parts of the world, especially Melanesia, the political systems of this period have been characterized in various related ways: complex tribes, big men systems, great men systems, cycling chiefdoms. The main underlying idea connecting these characterizations is that leadership positions were achieved and that, even when in power, the grip of a leader on his or her community was tenuous and political fortunes could easily sway. The reason being that the power of a leader in these political systems is based on the strengths of their networks which are, in contrast to leaders with ascribed statuses, dependent on how good "network leaders" are at fulfilling their social obligations.

Boomert (2001), for example, based on an overview of several archaeological correlates of big men collectives, likens the political system of the early first millennium AD to those of the so-called Melanesian big men societies. In this political system one must be a charismatic networker if one is to gain and hold power (Godelier and Strathern 1991; Sahlins 1963). In other words, early leaders in the Antilles needed to be capable networkers, mastering various types of social strategies in order to come to and remain in power (Curet 1996; Siegel 1996b). In such an achieved status political network, in general, strategy leaders employ when interacting with their community or collective are delayed redistribution as part of a wider pattern of reciprocal altruism.[15]

Within such a redistributive system all exchanges take the form of indirect or direct, delayed reciprocal exchanges. This implies that, rather than a Communal Sharing-model in which we see a free flow of unaccounted exchanges, all goods and services that such a network leader demands from his collective need to be reciprocated with a commensurable gift at some time in the future. In other words, the politically important exchanges in a "big men system" are based on Equality Matching models of relations. In order to meet his reciprocal obligations the network leader can attempt to entice more persons into joining his collective to draw on their support as well, but in order to do that he needs to give them more gifts, putting him into even larger debt. Delaying a return-gift provides a network leader with some leeway in his debt repayments. However, because persons in his local cluster also exchange goods and share information with each other, it is quickly discovered if the network leader tries to "freeride" on one of his exchange partners, i.e. cheats by refusing to reciprocate (Roscoe 2009).

From a network perspective this implies that a leader is caught in a mesh of triadic, Simmelian ties. These ties, named after the sociologist Georg Simmel, occur when network ties directly and reciprocally connect three or more nodes with each other in triads, or n-cliques for larger groups (Kosub 2005; Krackhardt 1999). The characteristics of such Simmelian ties differ greatly from dyadic network relations. The fundamental distinction between a dyad and a triad (or larger clique) is that in triads nodes are less individual, have less power, but command a better chance at resolving conflicts (Simmel 1950: 139-141). The latter increases the stability of the collective and suits the goals of a network leader in theory. However considering it is his or her aim to stand out from the collective as a powerful individual, the first and second aspect of the triad work directly against prospective network leaders.

---

15   Sahlins (1963: 293) states on the workings of the big men system of Melanesia: "For his help they give their help, and for goods going out through his hands other goods flow back to his followers by the same path."

One way to break out of the constricting mesh of Simmelian ties is to gain access to nodes outside the local network cluster. This strategy of drawing on exotic, out-group relations in order to increase one's in-group power is one of the most documented features of big men collectives (e.g Godelier and Strathern 1991; Sahlins 1963; Sillitoe 1979; Strathern 1971). In Melanesia when men are successful at entering into relations with others and thereby generate a flow of exotic valuables, alliances or esoteric knowledge that they can siphon into their local collectives, they become regionally famous as "men of renown" (Munn 1986; Sahlins 1963; Strathern 1971).

This is a classic example of the way in which power resulting from the in-group distribution of exotic valuables, alliances or knowledge is directly related to the control over such out-group sources of power (Helms 1988). Out-group power is difficult to achieve. Increased distance means an increase in time and energy investment in acquiring exotics valuables for in-group redistribution. In addition, network leaders have to extend their relations beyond the local scale to people with which they are not linked by means of longstanding social contracts. These out-clique exchange partners are thus largely outside the direct sphere of generalized and redistributive reciprocity of a network leader. "Do it yourself. I'm not your fool!" is the typical response from an outsider to a direct request of a big man (Sahlins 1963: 290). This implies that potential leaders will have to establish ties with others outside their collective that are based on a more direct type of reciprocity, giving even less leeway for reciprocal delay or manipulations. Therefore, in order to enter into outside relations, network leaders need to draw on the material wealth of their collective presenting outsiders with gifts, honours and other things of value.

This is the true problem for the big man and other types of triadic, network-based leaders: in order to become a central node within the cluster of nodes and Simmelian ties they are pressed to reciprocate. To be able to do so they need to draw upon the local cluster to demand wealth that can serve to create ties with outsider nodes. This is a network theoretical phrasing of the fundamental instability of big men and other similar networked collectives: a network leader can remain in control of his cluster only so long as he is successfully able to balance both the demands of his collective and his exchange partners. In an attempt to counter this, a successful network leader will stimulate collective production of exchange goods and actively seek to acquire and distribute exotic valuables in the name of his lineage, moiety or community (Boomert 2001a; see also Spielmann 2002).

Nonetheless, network leaders and their collectives play a high-stake game that in the end they cannot hope to win by themselves (Sahlins 1963; Weiner 1992: 143). Because it is based on personal reputation and social wealth rather than an inheritable office or material wealth, the leader's account is settled after his demise. Since everything the network leader is, he owes to others, his wealth will be distributed amongst his social partners, often in large and prolonged give and take between his lineage and those of his exchange partners. Subsequently, any offspring of the "self-made big man" needs to acquire a position without the aid of a "trust fund" of social or material credit.

Despite these challenges, at a certain point Antillean indigenous communities managed to overcome the inherent instability of the self-made network leader. Through time the indigenous political system now took on the more fixed and temporally durable structure of the *cacicazgo*. In some locations this system was so successful that multi-tiered and regionally integrated *cacicazgos* arose. Why this two-stepped transition occurred is one of the most debated issues in Caribbean archaeology. Needless to say, a simple answer cannot be given. Across the globe and in the Caribbean, emergences of such political structures would have followed a myriad of locally variable pathways. As such it is too large an issue to tackle here in its entirety. A comparison with the more purely triadic structure does, however, provide us with a new view on the way in which *cacical* networks differ from the presumably short-lived and more purely triadic form(s) of leadership in earlier times.

Some have suggested that the evolution of open places in villages into the communal plaza systems of the late pre-colonial period was an important aspect in this development (Siegel 1992; Torres 2012). Indeed, it could be the case that this development is correlated with potentially more political competition that was mediated by a communal drive towards larger and more durable collectives (Siegel 2004). Others have pinpointed to a similar shift in material culture repertoires from objects that gave individual prestige to corporately owned valuables (Curet 1996; Walker 1993). The idea that the communal leaders of the first centuries AD, who needed to achieve their status by balancing group and inter-group politics, had transformed into a collective of political network specialists by early contact times fits well with these developments.

Diversification of network roles allowed some power but also some obligations of leaders to be shifted to other specialists. Evolutionarily speaking, a reliance on kin-based mutualism presents a relatively failsafe and profitable way of giving away some power and obligations that came with a leadership position. Thus, any direct kin of a leader would have been likely candidates to be the first to profit from this diversification (the NIT nodes in the network). Tightening relations with affinal kin would have also been important in this regard, as they would have provided a socially and evolutionary more convoluted but still relatively straightforward way of increasing one's material and social capital. This is presumably also the reason that, as has been suggested (Keegan 2007; Oliver 2009), elites in late pre- and early contact Hispaniola would have been polygamous.

Such in-group benefits would have been useful in out-group politics. Looking at the valued status centralities (table 7.1) of the network in Figure 6.2, it is clear that the *cacical* collective represented by subgraph 1 would make the most powerful ally for a *cacique* from another political region, i.e. a *cacique* that is not otherwise connected to the local network. These exclusive relations with an outside collective would only increase the local network power of sub-graph 1: a rise in aggregate status of *c.*24%.[16] Obviously, such a connection beyond the local cluster would have

---

16 This is relative towards the average collective network power in an undifferentiated situation (from three to four collectives implies a 33% to 25% aggregate status) and based on the assumption that the new collective entering the network is a "normal" one, like subgraph 2.

similar effects with regard to the political status of the newly allied *cacique* in his segment of the network. As a reaction other locally strong collectives would either join this alliance or start forming their own in order to compete. Gradually, this would cause a shift in power that would create a new tier of the political network: a multi-tiered *cacicazgo* has come into being. In short, the success of Caribbean indigenous leaders and their collectives was probably based on the attraction of extra-local social others into the own sphere of influence (see also Santos-Granero 2009b). Once a *cacical* collective had become part of the interregional core of the political network, it members cannot afford to sit back and enjoy the fruits of their labour. This level of the network provides even more competition than before. Not only did one continue to be subject to events at home – there was always the threat of upstarts such as Guacanagarí who challenged the authority of vested *caciques* such as Caonabo – , but also to the waxing and waning of the political fortunes of one's political allies in other collectives.[17]

Even if power was interdependent with and vested in the attraction of social others, the chances to influence them were contingent with the possibility to showcase one's social strength effectively. Realizing that by and large a *cacical* collective's status was based on the strength of their internal and external relations, *caciques* and other political actors needed a way to signal the collective's strength. This was often found in the materialization of communal systems of value. As was discussed in chapter 2, such a communal, material identity became more and more important towards the final 500 years of the pre-colonial period. Where there once had been focus on ancestor cults during the earlier periods, in this phase other, more communally accessible superhuman beings became important (Hofman and Hoogland 2004; Siegel 1997; Stevens-Arroyo 2006). In other words communal identity became less about the essence of one's lineage and more about communally shared values and practices that could and needed to be materially expressed.

Other examples of such a formation of communal identities through connected practices are the *areítos* dances and the plazas on which they took place. Such corporate valuables would have served to underline communal identity while making that identity more conspicuous to non-group members at the same time. The techniques for incorporating extra-social others became increasingly sophisticated (Hofman, Bright, *et al.* 2007; Mol 2007; Oliver 2009), leading to evermore complex network ties and strategies. This process is also prominently reflected in the incorporation of other than human beings in the sphere of politics. Here, an increasingly larger emphasis was laid on interactions with non-humans such as spirits and ancestors.[18]

---

17 As illustrated by an early event in the Spanish struggle for dominion of Hispaniola that took place after Caonabo was captured. During the so-called "Night of the fourteen *caciques*" a pact was made to rescue Caonabo and start a joint war against the Spaniards. Rather than utilise his absence to improve their own positions, these fourteen *caciques* risked life and limb to restore their political ally to power: a clear sign that political authorities were entwined beyond the local level. Unfortunately for them, their ploy was discovered and all were killed or incarcerated. (Wilson 1990: 97-102).

18 Archaeologists and ethnographers have witnessed a similar form of socio-cosmic network intensification in other regions around the Caribbean (Heckenberger 2005; Helms 1995; Oyuela-Caycedo 2001).

The complexity of the *cacicazgo*

Complexity is an awkward term within socio-political theory, because it is often conflated with hierarchy (Chapman 2003). From an alternative point of view true hierarchies are actually less complex than other social constellations. In the Caribbean, too, it has often been assumed that as local, regional and interregional networks of people and things became more complex they became more strictly hierarchical. As I have tried to show by means of the *cacical* network model, this is not necessarily the case. The complexity of the *cacicazgo* arises from an increased diffusion of power, rather than a concentration hereof.

This opinion goes against more traditional ideas on socio-political evolution in the Caribbean. Rather than a transition from tribe to chiefdom, I hypothesize that socio-political networks developed from a prototypical network leader in which network economies were condensed into one political actor. The *cacique* is the continuation of this form of leadership, but he has transferred the management of certain network economies to specialists. This does not imply that there were no Authority Ranking relations, such as would have been the case in multi-tiered political networks. Here too, the creation of inter-collective hierarchies may be considered as just another example of political network diversification. It is important to understand that where and when network hierarchies arose they did not spring from the increased power of the *cacique* himself, but from the political strength of his collective that connected various network(ed) economies: ritual, communal and intercommunal.

Ethnohistory provides less firm ground than the "absolute" layouts of webs of relations elucidated by archaeometrical provenance studies. However, even if such data are present as in the case of the Punta Macao site, the collected evidence rarely affords an in-depth view on intercommunal networks of power. Unfortunately, it will often not be possible to carry out a network analysis of power based on archaeological relational data. Nevertheless, as I hope to have shown here, there are alternative lines of information on people and things with power that can be explored with a network approach. Although this model does not have a one-to-one correlation with historically real socio-political networks it does express the complexity of the systems and the underlying social strategies that would have been in place.

As the opening quote of this chapter makes clear, Columbus and other Europeans identified the *cacique* and other political notaries based on the political system they knew from home. It should be obvious from the analysis in this chapter that the *cacique* was not a king. The *cacicazgo* can in fact not easily be equated to any other type of political structure, not even to other supposed analogues like Polynesian, Sub-Saharan African, Migration Period, or even other Amerindian "chiefdoms". One could say that it would even be a stretch to call the *cacique* a type of chief. The reason for this is that, even if it was built on "classical" triadic conundrums of group power, by late pre-colonial times the *cacicazgo* had evolved into its own specifically Greater Antillean system, typified by the engagement of a larger collective of specialists with different economies of power.

All in all, the dependencies the *cacique* had with other political actors does not seem to justify his characterization as a politically or even metaphysically different type of being. Even if Caribbean *caciques* were set apart from others, as seems to be indicated in some ethnohistoric descriptions, their authority ultimately rested in an expansive political network economy in which the smallest power fluctuations could make or break individual *cacical* collectives. The success of the Antillean *cacique* was thus for a large part interdependent with the success and failure of others to efficiently harness and direct relations in communal, intercommunal and spiritual economies. Unlike the class-based society of the divine kings of Polynesia or, indeed, the divinely ordained monarchs of late medieval Europe with which the Spaniards were familiar, the power of the *cacique* ultimately rested in the careful management of a complex set of typically Antillean relations.

It is also notable that, in contrast to the courts of Europe, hierarchies were not based on amassment of material wealth as a form of economic power (Graeber 2011). Instead ethnohistoric sources indicate that political power stemmed from the responsibility brought about by engaging with social others. This is still the case in many of Lowland South America's indigenous societies (Carlin 2012, personal communication; see also Mol and Mans 2013; Rivière 1984; Santos-Granero 2009b). For the *cacique* material wealth rather seemed to be something that needed to be distributed to others. Indeed, corporate possessions were probablly held through the maternal (i.e. the *cacica's*) line to begin with (Keegan 2007). This is also why the knowledge and personal qualities of *cacicas* and other members of the *caciques'* direct community had a high impact on the intercommunal political process.

Authority Ranking models did not dominate in the ritual economy either, such as may have been the case if the will of divine or superhuman spirits was communicated to sacred kings or priests. Even if the *behique* and, to a lesser extent, the *cacique* were ritual specialists, they did not have a monopoly on interactions with ancestors, *cemís* and other superhuman beings. This was partly due to the fact that these superhuman beings seemed to possess quite some subjectivity themselves in their materialization as statuettes, amulets, and other forms of valuables. Indeed, these spirits were embedded within communal and inter-communal life-force networks that were tangible aspects of the larger societal cosmos. Often these ties were explicitly acknowledged and engaged with in a public setting (Oliver 1997, 2009).

In these flexible and complex political economies, Equality Matching relations with other than human subjects were highly important. Other than human beings like spirits and ancestors represented valuable life-forces that were perceived of as being more potent than those of normal beings. In contrast to the ultimately limited supply of humans, these superhuman reservoirs were essentially infinite: all deceased individuals, animals, trees, rocks, caves, *etc.*, potentially represented another social partner whose life-force could be connected or incorporated with one's own. Although there were still hierarchical differences between these beings these could be influenced through various, relatively efficacious means. First of all, one could try to "trade up" by exchanging one's spirit partner for another. If no options for transactions were available, theft was always an option: it is in general much easier to steal an object than a human being. Esteemed spirit members of the community could even be pitted in ritual battle against each other. This would have resulted in a win-win situation for both victor and loser: transfer of life-force without the actual loss of human life-forces (Oliver 2009: Part III and IV).

It seems counterintuitive, but materialized spirit beings were in reality more controllable and reliable than human exchange partners. This seems to be at odds with our as well as with Amerindian concepts that consider spirit beings to be powerful and sometimes whimsical entities. However, the writings of Pané and other chroniclers show how materialized spirit beings were more or less controlled through the actions of *caciques*, *behiques* and other members of the community. *Cemís* were placated by means of houses of their own and gifts of fruits, drinks and tobacco. It may be that they were even forcefully restrained at some times, although this was ultimately unsuccessful in the case of the dog-headed Opiyelguobirán. So, although this did not happen without a struggle, the material counterparts of other than human partners of the *cacical* collective were controlled and in turn were used as tools to control the larger community or impress other polities.[19] In the next chapter I will discuss how powerful *guaíza* spirits that could not be physically matched were nonetheless materialized and exchanged in the form of shell ornaments.

To sum up the main conclusions of this chapter, the *cacicazgo* can be distinguished from a more purely triadic political institution by: (1) a tiered, but distributive system of collective power roles and relations through which success and obligations were shared across the network cluster, (2) a focus on the active incorporation of other subjects within one's sphere of influence, and (3) a set of (inter)communally shared values, beliefs and practices geared towards mediation with and incorporation of other subjects, including other than human beings. Although these were not the only factors that shaped political networks during the late pre- and early colonial period, they were three highly important ones. It is no coincidence that these specific socio-political strategies co-evolved with the formation of the typically Antillean network of things, which was also present in the site assemblage of Kelbey's Ridge 2 (Chapter 6). The case-study in Chapter 8 will further explore these material counterparts of *cacical* networks.

---

19 Dr. Chanca (1992 [1493]), who accompanied Columbus on his second journey to the Caribbean, reports how a revered deity turned out to literally be the voice of political authority: an assistant of the leader communicated his will to his followers through a reed concealed in the back of the deity. Such charades were probably not common practice, but indicate how far leaders could go in order to ensnare spiritual politics within human politics.

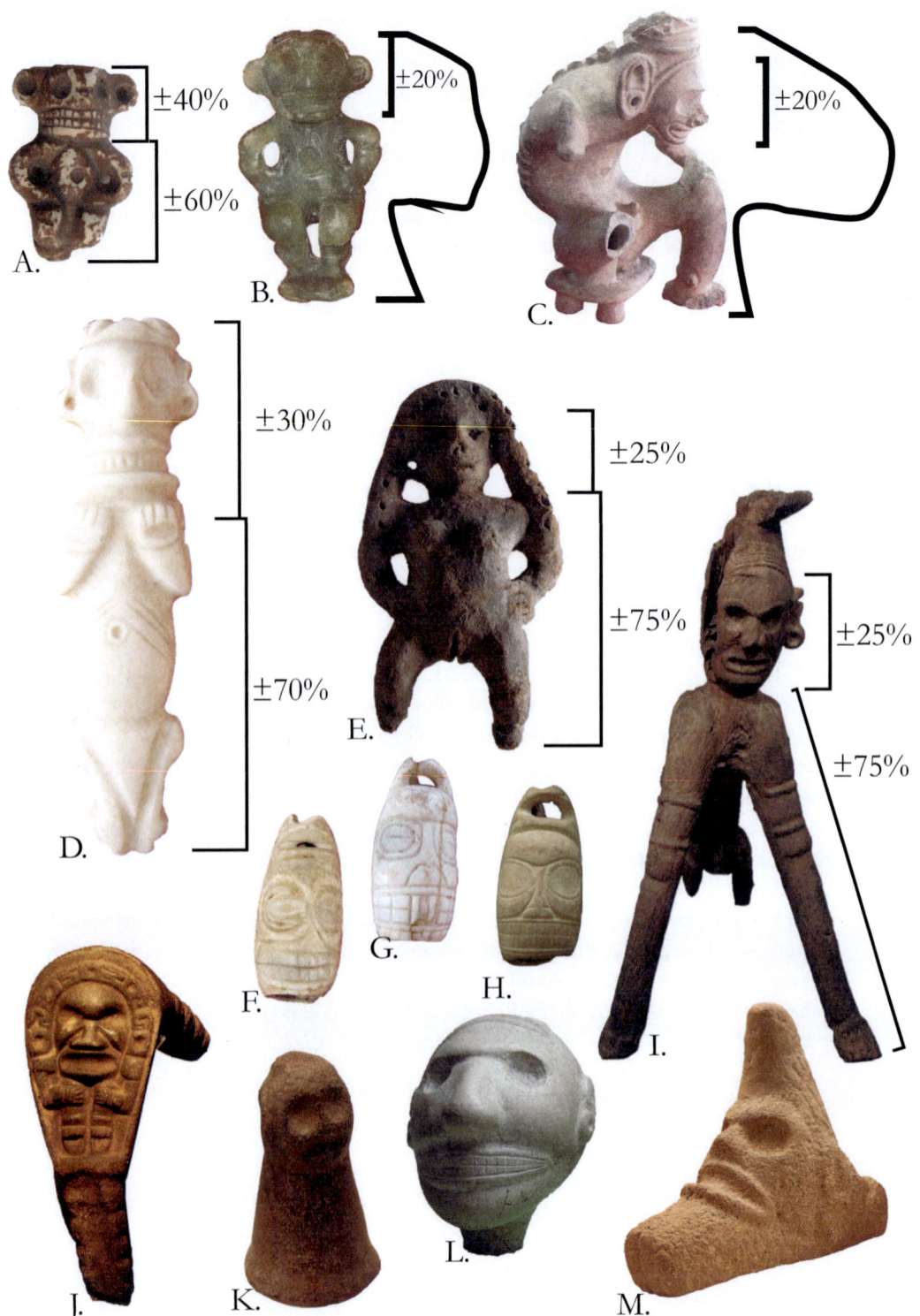

±40%

±20%

±20%

A.

B.

C.

±30%

±25%

±25%

±70%

±75%

±75%

D.

E.

±60%

F.

G.

H.

I.

J.

K.

L.

M.

Chapter 8

Familiar Faces: The Diverse Design of *Guaízas* and their Use as Gifts

[T]he result of this examination is: we see a complicated network of similarities overlapping and criss-crossing: sometimes overall similarities, sometimes similarities of detail. I can think of no better expression to characterize these similarities than 'family resemblances'; for the various resemblances between members of a family: build, features, colour of eyes, gait, temperament, etc. etc. overlap and criss-cross in the same way.

Ludwig Wittgenstein (1953) on "family resemblances"

This chapter will further investigate a set of late pre-colonial valuables that were identified as one of the focal points of the networks discussed in the previous chapters (see Figure 8.1).[1] The relatively strong interregional coherence of material culture assemblages, among other things attested by the close similarities between related Ostionoid assemblages, present a united façade (Bercht, *et al.* 1997; Rouse 1992). As discussed in the context of the ego-network of Kelbey's Ridge 2 (Chapter 6), the late pre-colonial period shows a similar widely shared valuation of these objects. After a period of declining interregional connections, material culture in the late pre-colonial Northeastern Caribbean once again became more similar. This is clear to such an extent that the material culture is said to represent an

Figure 8.1 (left): Various face-depicting artefacts from the Greater Antilles. The objects represented are not to scale. Those portraying entire bodies have skewed head to body ratios (h/b ratio). A: small, shell amulet from Jamaica with a 1:3 h/b ratio (Photo courtesy of the Institute of Jamaica); b: small, greenstone amulet with a 1:5 h/b ratio; c: Ceramic figurine of a behique with 1:5 h/b ratio; d: Small, shell figurine with a 3:10 h/b ratio; e: ceramic female figurine with a 1:4 h/b ratio; f and g: shell (Oliva spp.) hangers from Cuba; h: shell (Oliva spp.) hangers from the Dominican Republic (DR); i: Wooden statue from the DR, presumably depicting Opiyelguobirán, with a 1:4 h/b ratio; j: elbow stone from Puerto Rico, showing a head with a tightly compressed body; k: hammerstone with rudimentary head from the DR; l: "Macorix" head from the DR. M: Three-pointer from the DR.

---

1   This chapter is an extension of my previous research on shell faces as gifts in the late pre- and proto-contact Caribbean (see Mol 2007, 2011b).

overarching group of indigenous peoples that are often collectively referred to as the "Taíno" – or more recently as a regionally shared mode of identity referred to as "Taínoness" or *Tainidad* (Rodríguez Ramos 2010: 10).[2]

Ceremonial seats called *duhos,* for example, are found from Cuba and the Bahamas to Trinidad (Ostapkowicz 1997; Ostapkowicz, *et al.* 2011). However, when comparing these stools to those with similar use and comparable design we know from (ethnographic) contexts in the Lowlands of South America it would be possible to extend this group well into the Amazon Basin or even along the coasts or directly across the Caribbean to the Chibchan region. On the islands and mainland of the Caribbean Sea these seats can be joined to the distribution of a type of ceramic effigy, sometimes also constructed from other materials, that depicts a seated human figure that has been interpreted as a shaman (Arroyo, *et al.* 1999; García Arévalo 2001; Roe 1997). The same regional connections could be made with other categories of material culture such as the Greater Antillean bat winged-pendants – sometimes also in the form of bat winged vomit spatulas – of which the form is homologous to the *Klingelplatten* or shell pendants of the Venezuelan and Colombian coasts and interiors. The Greater Antillean *guaíza* shell faces (dealt with in greater detail below) similarly present us with either material or stylistic counterparts found from the Lake Valencia region up into Maya Belize.

On the other hand certain types of characteristically "Taínan" artefacts have a much more circumscribed distribution. The most iconic of the three-pointer *cemís* are contained to the small region of Hispaniola and Puerto Rico. In fact, such three-pointers have thus far not even been officially reported from the northern shore of Hispaniola (Ulloa Hung, personal communication 2010). There are far fewer examples from the Lesser Antilles, which are also less intricately carved, and next to none from the other Greater Antilles. The same goes for material culture that has been interpreted as being affiliated with the Greater Antillean ball game and the stone *macoris* heads (Walker 1993). Conversely, certain notable material culture expressions are absent from the traditional Taíno heartland. The east and south of Cuba is characterized by the preponderance of female ceramic statuettes (Portuondo Zúñiga 2002; Valcárcel Rojas 2002). They do not occur in the other Greater Antilles, but similar female figurines once again appear in the archaeological record of the Windward Islands and coasts of the mainland (Bright 2011). The island of Jamaica has a material cultural repertoire akin to the other Greater Antilles. Jamaican ceramics are part of the larger Ostionoid or Meillacoid series and we find the same form of pestles, *duhos*, statuettes and amulets, but in all those aspects Jamaican assemblages have very much their own character (Allsworth-Jones 2008; Atkinson 2006).

---

2   Nowadays this diverse range of objects embodies the most familiar face of indigenous heritage in the Northeastern Caribbean. It is often used in nationalist symbolism or as the emblem of indigenous revivalist groups (e.g. the neo-Taíno). The tourist industry has also tapped into their cultural and aesthetic appeal. As a result souvenirs and other accessories based on this indigenous design can be found from the Bahamas to the Windward Islands.

In short, "Taínan" material culture is as diverse as it is widespread. Certain objects at the core of this diverse yet connected group of material cultural repertoire are spread well beyond the area of Greater Antillean political and cultural influence (Hofman, Bright, *et al.* 2008). Other, supposedly prototypically "Tainan", artefacts are contained to a relatively small region (Oliver 2009). Seeing this diffuse pattern one cannot help but wonder if we are indeed speaking of a corpus of objects? Or is this diverse network of object designs and iconographies the result of unrelated, but convergent processes? More specifically, what are the relations in design between groups of objects that are referred to as "Taíno", but how do these stylistic connections relate to the structure and extents of pre-colonial social networks? I will argue that the answer to the first part of this question is quite straightforward, so much so that it literally stares one in the face: a particular type of facial iconography on a wide range of objects from a wide diversity of contexts (Mol 2007; Samson and Waller 2010). Aside from shamanic paraphernalia, the parallels in style, form and placement of faces is the one connecting factor in the diffuse, interregional material cultural repertoire of the late pre-colonial period.

I will explore the hypothesis that the patterns of homogeneity and diversity in "Taínan" material culture repertoires are not the result of converging group identities but rather are a "veneer" (cf. Keegan 2004). The case study will focus on face-depicting shells, also known as *guaízas*. The above hypotheses will be checked both by a discussion of their function as gifts as well as through a 2-mode network exploration of their design. In the latter case, I suggest that the "hidden" network structure of a "veneer" can be made more explicit by contrasting it to a model in which all objects have the same design, or in other words a perfectly dense affiliation network of objects to iconographic elements.

Depictions of the face in the pre-colonial Caribbean

Every single people on earth produces representations of the human face in some form or other, even if there are sometimes strong (religious) taboos against depicting the human form (Gell 1998: 96-154). Although *Homo sapiens* have not depicted faces during their entire evolutionary history, there nonetheless seems to be a deep socio-cognitive background to depictions of the human face (Guthrie 1993).[3] Among the plethora of face-depictions, we find quite a few societies that have been more focused on the human face than others, making it the centrepiece of much if not a majority of their material culture. The indigenous societies of the late pre-colonial Caribbean, especially those of the Antilles, are a case in point.

In the Caribbean in particular an extreme focus on the face is something that goes back to the period between 500 BC and AD 500. Much more so than previous cultural expressions, Saladoid material culture is rife with depictions of faces. Best-known are the ceramic adornos that functioned as lugs or were otherwise

---

3   The archaeological record suggests that face imagery has existed since at least the Upper Palaeolithic, for example in cave drawings or statuettes such as the famous Venus of Brassempouy. What is more, across the globe there seems to be a correlation between the development of a Neolithic way of life and the increasing representation of the human form.

part of the rims or walls of Saladoid ceramic vessels (Waldron 2010), but faces can be found in or on many other objects. Early Ceramic personal adornments often depict faces and ceramic masks are also found in Saladoid contexts. The few ritual effigies or figurines that have been found were often composed of highly contracted bodies with prominently displayed heads. It is impossible to precisely date the introduction of petroglyphs in the Antilles, but it seems that, from the introduction of Saladoid in the islands and onwards, images of faces in caves and other ritually charged places became more ubiquitous.

However we see variations in the depiction of faces during the early stages of the 1st millennium AD and the facial iconography of the first half of the 2nd millennium. The initial difference is that, while human beings are definitely part of the symbolic reservoir of the Saladoid and Huecoid ceramic using peoples, their representation is just one among many types of species. From the early to the late pre-colonial period an increasing anthropocentric material culture starts to develop. The amount of human versus animal iconography is difficult to quantify with any precise measure.[4] My own research has predominantly focused on amulets and other adornments. Here the shift is clear: from almost no human depiction independent of an overarching animal symbolism to a material cultural repertoire that mainly consists of anthropomorphic imagery.[5]

This is not just part of an anthropomorphization of the entire body, but it is concentrated on the face. For example, the face of zoomorphic bodies is often decidedly human in appearance. What is more, although there are clearly other body parts with important ideological connotations such as the navel and the joints, the face is the one element that is most distinctly present in the entire material cultural repertoire (Figure 8.1). In the course of my research I have found no depiction of an anthropomorphic body (part) that does not (also) depict an anthropomorphic face, with the possible exception of stylized motifs of the joints and the navel. In fact, the human face takes centre stage in any depiction of an anthropomorphic being. In two-dimensional or flat depictions it is always portrayed *en face* and even three-dimensional depiction of the body always strive to accentuate the face. This is apparent in the seated or squatting statuettes that extend their head in such a way that it is perpendicular with their knees. The carved three-pointer stones whose entire body almost completely consist of one or more faces (whereby sometimes the other corporeal elements are present in collapsed form) are another good case in point. *Duhos* of various types have one or more faces positioned in

---

4   Indeed, a complete change from other animals to human beings is less a matter of ceramic iconography, which still features quite a lot of partly stylized zoomorphic imagery. Nevertheless, in my view, if studied in-depth, increased anthropocentrism could probably also be found in this material category.

5   As discussed in Chapter 2, Amerindian metaphysical perspectives do not require beings to have one true natural form: a human being can be partly a dog or a frog and a frog or dog can be partly human, for example. Hence, the majority of the iconography of both periods is to some extent zoo-anthropomorphic, i.e. a depiction of a being with both human and animal aspects. Here too we see a shift: from mainly animals with human aspects to mainly humans with animal aspects (see Figure 8.1.i.).

such a way that would have stared at the person directly in front of the seated man or woman.

What is perhaps most revealing is that even when a figurine or amulet depicts an entire anthropomorphic body the head is out of proportion with the rest of the body. This is even the case with those objects that at first glance seem to be in the correct proportion (see Figures 8.1a to e and i). Where a head of a normal adult measures approx. 1/8 of the entire length of a body, late pre-colonial iconography has head to body ratios ranging from 1:6 to 1:3. The latter are roughly the body proportions of neonates. Either there was rampant pedomorphism in Caribbean pre-colonial times or this supersizing of the face was part of a widespread practice of accentuating the one body part that mattered most.

Faces were also central to interaction with the ancestors and other superhuman beings. Skulls and other skeletal features play an integral part: skulls were kept in a state of decomposition for a long time or were retrieved from burials for a new social life outside the grave (Hofman and Hoogland 2004). The well-known cotton *cemí*, built around the frontal of a skull (Ostapkowicz and Newsom 2012), is another example of how faces of literal ancestors remained a central part of life. The face was also important when socializing with beings other than ancestors. Across the Caribbean we see how stalactites and other cave phenomena were modified by carving eyes and mouths on them.

This also was the case with more mobile material culture as comes across clearly from the previously mentioned excerpt by Pané. In it the *behique* receives instructions on how a tree or rock wishes to be carved into a statue or something else (Pané 1999 [1571]: 25-26). Socializing a spirit, first and foremost entailed that the material to which they were connected would have facial features carved onto or crafted from it. In other words, the indigenous production of social partners from, what we consider to be, inanimate parts of social and natural landscapes would have focused on literally giving them a face.

Depictions of faces have two central elements: the eyes and the mouth. In many if not most of the faces there is a particularly large emphasis on the eyes. They would have been often inlayed, probably with a shiny, reflective material, and the eyes are generally large. Furthermore in iconographic motifs, such as the prototypic "Capá eye", are easily recognizable as eyes. It is known from animistic systems of the mainland that eyes are an important gateway for spirits to enter and exit the body. That vision, often enhanced by means of hallucinogenics, is central to the abilities of shamanic specialists. Nevertheless, while the importance of eyes in pre-colonial material culture is evident, scholarly discussions on the local cultural significance of eyes is non-existent and requires further research.

Mouth and teeth have been discussed more frequently. Like eyes, this motif should also be considered in the light of late pre-colonial worldview and shamanistic activities. Perhaps, its depiction was of central importance because this is the body orifice used when vomiting in order to purge oneself before inhaling the mind altering substances.[6] Moreover, the display of teeth has a more direct social significance, as well. José Arrom (1975), for example, explained the prominence of the mouth full of gritted teeth as a sign of aggression. However, recently Samson and Waller (2010) present an argument that focuses on the evolutionary context of the display of teeth: among all primates teeth are exposed in order to display pro-sociality rather than aggression.[7]

Faces would have been found on almost every form of material culture: from the ceramic eating bowl to the most sacred materialization of ancestors. All in all, it is clear that face-depicting objects occupy the central part of the pan-Antillean late pre-colonial material cultural repertoires. Thanks to their ubiquity things with faces were central in social networks, as well. This rings true for geographically extended, social networks between human beings, but also for the ritual network economies between human beings and other types of social actors such as spirits. In the following section I will delve deeper into the social networks based on the circulation of shell *guaízas*. This specific case-study deals with the way in which things with faces were critical nodes and ties in socio-material relations.

Guaízas as socio-cosmic nodes

Guaíza shell faces are shell discs or cones depicting anthropomorphic or zoo-anthropomorphic facial features. Their earliest appearances are in contexts from around AD 1000 and they were still in use during the first years of European contact. A database of Caribbean shell faces in archaeological sites and museums holds sixty-nine examples, with provenances from Cuba all the way to the tiny Île de Ronde (Grenadines), but many more are sure to exist in less accessible collections or as non-recorded finds (Figure 8.2 and Figure 8.6). The shell faces measure between 3 and 13 cm long and between 3 and 7 cm wide with the average *guaíza* measuring *c.*8 cm long and 4 cm wide. The majority have a face modelled on the flat lip or part of the body of the queen conch (*Lobatus gigas*). A number of shell faces are modelled on a milk conch (*Lobatus costatus*) or on a similar species. In these cases the face is not modelled two-dimensionally as seen from the front, but around the shell, more reminiscent of the actual shape of a human face.

These shell faces are quite well-known from the ethnohistoric documentation (Mol 2007). Although there are no ethnohistoric records that speak of actual shell faces, many speak of (shell) masks (de las Casas 1875: 477): "Columbus brought *guaycas*, which are faces made of fish bone in the manner of pearl with a great quantity of fine pieces of gold." [8] From this statement it seems that these shell faces

---

6   Another explanation is that the teeth are frequently depicted as clenched together due to a spasm of the face, caused by the hallucinogens.

7   Whether aggressive or benign, it is noteworthy to conclude that the display of a full row of teeth would not have been in line with everyday perception of the face: a Caribbean-wide dental anthropological study indicates that almost every person, from juvenile to older individuals, would have gone through life without several or even the majority of their teeth due to poor oral hygiene. The depictions of full rows of white teeth in statuettes and ornaments would thus have been a beautification of actual reality (Mickleburgh 2013).

8   "[Columbus l]levó ... guaycas, que eran unas carátulas hechas de pedrería de huesos de pescado, a manera puesto de aljófar con mucha cantidad y muestras de oro finísimo" (de las Casas 1875: 477).

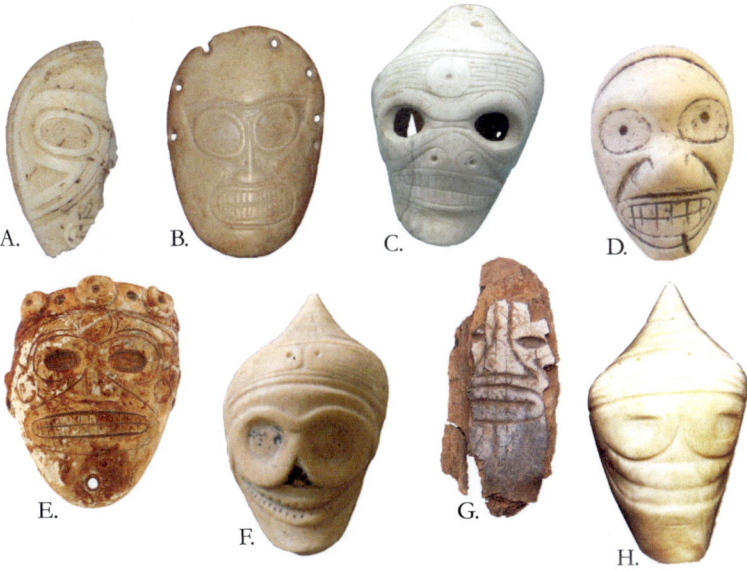

Figure 8.2: Examples of face-depicting shells or guaízas. The codes given in parentheses correspond to the node names in Figures 8.3 to 8.7. A: shell face from Cuba (CU9), length ±6 cm; b: shell face from Cuba (CU3), length ±6.5 cm; c: shell face from the Dominican Republic (HIS1), length ±9.5 cm; d: shell face from the El Cabo site, East Dominican Republic, length ±3.5 cm (photo courtesy of Menno Hoogland); e: shell face from Puerto Rico (PR1), length ±8 cm (photo courtesy of Reniel Rodríguez Ramos); f: shell face from Anguilla (ANG2), length ±10 cm (photo courtesy of Menno Hoogland); g: face of unknown material, perhaps fossilized wood, from Saint Lucia, length ±5 cm (photo courtesy of Menno Hoogland); h: shell face from Île de Ronde, the Grenadines, length ±9.5 cm.

were, in at least one of the Arawakan languages of the Greater Antilles, known as "*guayca*", or "*guaíza*". *Guaíza* has originally been translated by Granberry and Vescelius (2004) as "mask". However, actual masks large enough to cover the face are not found in collections or excavations.[9]

The term *guaíza* consists of two Arawakan morphemes (Arrom 1975; Oliver 2009). The core element -*íza* can also be found in "True Arawak" or Lokono *ísi(ba)* where it means "face" (de Goeje 2009 [1928]: §116). *Guaíza* also contains the prefix *wa-*, which is both the 1st person plural verb prefix and the 1st person plural possessive in Lokono (Eithne Carlin, personal communication 2013). A morpheme by morpheme analysis of *guaíza* thus results in the translation "our face". This broadens the concept of *guaíza* beyond the original identification as a mask. This is also indicated by another excerpt from the works of de las Casas (de las Casas 1992: Chapter 59) in which he links it to both masks and figurines.

---

9   Fewkes (Fewkes 1903/1904: 132) refers to a wooden mask kept in the "city of Haiti", presumably Port au Prince. Although illustrated in Cronau's (1892: 232) *Amerika*, it is impossible to determine its size from the illustration.

Fray Ramon Pané's Account of the Antiquities of the Indies (1999 [1571]: 18-19) has another reference to *guaízas* indicating they were not only masks.

> *"When a person is alive, they call his spirit goeíz, and when he is dead, they call it opía. They say this goeíz appears to them often, in a man's shape as well as a woman's, and they say there have been men who have wanted to do battle with it, and when such a man would lay his hands on it, it would disappear, and the man would put his arms elsewhere into some trees, and he would end up hanging from those trees."*

This reference seems to present an alternative indigenous understanding of the *guaíza*.[10] Opposed to *opía*, this *guaíza* is said to be the spirit of a living human being, therefore linking it directly to "humanness". According to this reconstruction, for the indigenous peoples of the proto-contact Greater Antilles their (human) face is also a spirit and a mask-like object. In line with the idea of Amerindian (object) perspectivism (Viveiros de Castro 1998). *guaízas* are thus a specific Hispaniolan, or perhaps Antillean, (element of a) multi-perspectivist subject.[11]

One of the above excerpts from the works of de las Casas speaks of *guaízas* as having "much quantity and pieces of fine gold". This corresponds closely to a number of other ethnohistoric descriptions of "masks" or mask-like objects, such as the one presented to Columbus by the *cacique* Guacanagarí on his second voyage (de Navarete 1922: 229). It has to be noted that in the Greater Antilles noble metals were particularly valued for a variety of reasons and their exchange takes a special place in the origin narratives recorded by Pané (Oliver 2000).[12]

In terms of their use, the perforations found in many shell faces are of interest. It is presumed they allowed for threads or strings to be attached to the *guaíza*, so that it could be worn as an ornament. However, another function for the perforations might have been to attach smaller ornaments, such as beads, small discs or feathers, to the *guaíza*. Often occurring perforations seen for example at the place of the ear could attest to this. Additional evidence can be found in a petroglyph from the Caguana ceremonial centre in Puerto Rico (Oliver 1998: 171). According to José Oliver the pendant serving as the centrepiece of the string of beads around the head is a *guaíza*. At both sides of the *guaíza* large discs are clearly visible. They symbolize accoutrements actually worn by real persons, such as the large ear discs, called *taguaguas* (Oliver 2000).

It seems that a number of these adornments have been internalized in the carvings on some of the *guaízas*, such as clearly visible discs in the ears, or a headband. Additionally, the suggestion of a string of beads on the petroglyph from

---

10　It is called *"goeíz"* in this quote, which is probably the result of an error made during the translation and transcription of the original document.

11　Although it would thus be possible to extend parts of the following analyses to masks and other types of faces depicting artefacts found in the islands, I will discuss *guaízas* only through the specific case of shell amulets. In this way it is possible to present a more focused account of the role of a certain group of things with faces in their respective networks.

12　Notably, in these narratives it serves primarily as a valuable that draws in previously "wild", i.e. unsocialized, people – Pané seems to speak of how the travelling hero Guahayona obtained a new set of affines together with acquisition of *guanín* (Pané 1999 [1571]; Vega 1980).

Caguana shows that the *guaíza* is most probably more than just a shell face; it is a carefully constructed signal consisting of a configuration of perishable and non-perishable material culture. Archaeologists only come across the non-perishable material, the shell *guaíza* faces, which have been removed from their configuration due to depositional processes or specific use in rituals. However as proposed by Oliver (*ibid.*) the interplay of white shell with materials of other colours could have caused the guaíza to become an aesthetically highly valued artefact during the Late Ceramic Age. It has to be noted that decorations added to the shell *guaíza* probably echoed the adornments of the individual who was supposed to wear it.

The Caguana petroglyph also presents us with a direct representation of how a *guaíza* should be worn: as a pendant. The perforations and the gully that can be seen on some of the artefacts point to exactly this way of wearing. However, we do find alternatives to how the *guaíza* could have been worn. For instance, on the forehead, as mentioned by Columbus when he speaks of the gift that the *cacique* Guacanagari presented to him (de Navarete 1922: 229).[13] Alternatively, *guaízas* were part of a configuration of a belt. These belts are mentioned in the Columbus Shipping List. A well-known example, dated to the contact period, survives to this day in the Vienna Museum für Völkerkunde (Bercht, *et al.* 1997: 159). The perforations on the edges of a number of *guaízas* could indicate that the artefact was to be sewn on cotton or was part of multiple strings of beads. The position the *guaíza* has on the body when part of a belt is not a coincidence, given that it is then positioned near or even exactly on the navel. The navel is anatomical phenomenon often stressed in Greater Antillean iconography, but more pointedly it was perceived as the mark that distinguished the living from the dead according to information presented by Pané (1999 [1571]: 19). The placement of the *guaíza* on or near the navel deftly harks back to what the *guaíza* actually is: a representation of the face of spirits of the living.[14]

Guaízas as gifts

Even though it was a highly valued adornment, part of an individual, and an inspirited thing, a *guaíza* was not a "sacred" object, hidden away from public life as an inalienable possession. Indeed, a shell face's final deposition was never in a ritualized context, such as a cache or a burial. The shell faces that have been recovered from an archaeological site or survey seem to have remained part of village life until their deposition: all have been found, either as a surface find or *in situ*, on or near habitation sites with an extended period of habitation. It is presumed that, when not worn, they were kept in storage within the village. A

---

13   Worn in this way the *guaíza* probably did not cover the entire face. It is therefore not literally a mask. It was, however, placed on top of the forehead, possibly in a headband configuration.
14   The catalogue presented by Bercht *et al*, (1997: 50) includes a statuette depicting an alternative way of wearing a *guaíza* belt: with the face positioned at the small of the back.

description, once again from the diary of Columbus, of "many, well-made shell heads", found together with many statuettes in a village hut near to the coast on Cuba, hints at this (de Navarete 1922: 50).[15]

Sites where *guaízas* are found always feature multiple lines of evidence for the presence of interactions with the wider region (Mol 2007: Chapter 7). The site of Punta Macao, known from ethnohistoric sources to be the seat of a *cacique* and located in the heart of the Mona Passage, has yielded one severely weathered shell face, for instance. Another example is the site of Potrero de El Mango, Banés region, Cuba. Here five of the twenty Cuban shell faces were recovered. This site was an extended habitation site with evidence for relatively large-scale agriculture around the river gully in its proximity and many other finely crafted shell, stone and bone ornaments (Valcárcel Rojas 1999). Archaeologists have marked the Banés region as one of the few areas in Cuba in which *cacicazgo*-like political constellations would have been present before contact (Valcárcel Rojas 1999, 2002). A similar argument has been made for the discovery of shell faces in Anguilla and the Guadeloupe archipelago (Crock 2000; de Waal 2006). The relative rarity of *guaízas* combined with their prevalence in relatively long-lived, large, and well-connected habitation sites would be an argument in favour of viewing the *guaíza* as a valuable that should be correlated with political actors who occupied a central position in political economies (Oliver 2009: 148-156).

The references to *guaízas* in the ethnohistorical record give the same impression. In the diary of the first voyage of Columbus, Columbus gives a quite detailed description about receiving a *guaíza* on December 26th, 1492, the day after his ship, the Santa María, ran aground. (de Navarete 1922: 129):

> "*They brought the Admiral a great face, which had large pieces of gold in its ears and eyes and other parts. They gave him this with other jewels and the King put it on his head and neck" The king who presents Columbus with this specific guaíza was the cacique Guacanagarí. This gift was part of a string of exchanges between Columbus and Guacanagarí. Indeed, during the second voyage Guacanagarí sent Columbus at least two more guaízas showing his dedication to their social bond*" (de Navarete 1922: 229).[16]

The use of *guaízas* in Equality Matching relations are also hinted at in a Shipping List that catalogued all the items presented by the indigenous peoples to Columbus (Alegría 1980). This list describes forty-five *guaízas* and six belts with faces (of which one contains two *guaízas*) in total. It is indeed, next to hammocks and skirts, the most frequently listed object (Mol 2008). Moreover, it is remarkable

---

15 "[M]uchas cabezas en manera de caratona muy bien labradas" (de Navarete 1922: 50). Other chroniclers report on houses containing valuables, too, although they were described as housing valuables in general and do not detail the express presence of *guaízas* (de las Casas 1875: vol. II, p.148). The El Cabo *guaíza* has been associated with a specific set of features. Samson (2010: 57 and 232-233) has argued that this *guaíza* was stored, together with other valuables found at the site, in a specially designated structure.

16 "Trujeron al Almirante una gran caratula, que tenía grandes pedazos de oro en las orejas y en los ojos en otras partes, la cual le dio con otras joyas de oro quel mismo Rey habia puesto al Almirante en la cabeza y al pescuezo […]"(de Navarete 1922: 129).

that on a later shipping list one of the few objects named are three *guaízas* (Mira Caballos 2000: 99-100). This indicates that the (inter-cultural) exchange of *guaízas* continued for a long time and that this item remained known under its indigenous name when referred to by the Spaniards.

The diary of the Columbus's first voyage holds another critical reference from which the reason for giving a *guaíza* can be deducted. Here, the context is as important as the exchange described. This event takes place on January 14th, after Columbus has founded the first Spanish settlement in the Americas, La Navidad. Here he leaves a group of men behind together with trade goods to then embark on the Niña. On January 13th, when the vessel was anchored in a bay somewhere on the Samaná peninsula, they came across a group of locals, carrying bows, their faces blackened with ash, who did not resemble any of the peoples they had met before and spoke another language or dialect than the local inhabitants they had so far interacted with on Hispaniola.

Columbus took the same approach as done before, attempting to exchange with them. He ordered his men to go ashore and barter trade goods for the bows the native men were carrying. According to Columbus they had exchanged two bows when the Spaniards were suddenly attacked and pursued. The Spaniards scattered the assailants but remained on guard the entire night, fearing they were cannibals. At dawn the situation was totally different. A mass had gathered on the beach, making gestures that indicated they had come in peace. Columbus firstly received gifts from one of the men who had attacked them the day before. Next their leader on the beach wished to visit Columbus on his ship. They shared food and, more importantly, Columbus received another *guaíza* as a present (de Navarete 1922: 154).

The *guaízas* presented by Guacanagarí and the behaviour of unnamed leader of the erstwhile hostile men are textbook examples of the peace-bringing gift (cf. Corbey 2006). Tellingly, the passage dealing with the first *guaíza* presented by Guacanagarí is also directly preceded by a passage in which the Europeans deliver an example of their power:

> *"The Admiral let [Guacanagarí] understand through signs that the Monarchs of Castile would order the destruction of the Caribs and have them all clapped in irons. The Admiral had a lombard and an espingarda fired and the king, seeing the force of the shot and its penetration, was amazed, and when his people heard the thunder of the explosion all fell to the ground"* (de Navarete 1922: 129).[17]

Both indigenous leaders tried to exchange with a social other that had just proven to be highly dangerous. Similarly, it is quite likely that the *guaízas* given by Guacanagarí during the Columbus's second sojourn in the Caribbean were meant to placate the Europeans following their discovery of the debacle at La Navidad. It is noteworthy that, after the first military expeditions into the interior, rather than

---

17   "El Almirante le dijo por señas que los Reyes de Castilla mandarian destruir à los caribes y que à todos se los mandarian traer las manos atadas. Mandó el Almirante tirar una lombarda y una espingarda, y viendo el efecto que su fuerza hacian y lo que penetraban, quedo maravillado. Y cuando su gente oyó los tiros cayeron todos en tierra" (de Navarete 1922: 129).

ceasing all diplomatic contacts, *guaíza* and other gifts presented by indigenous leaders only increased in quantity.

From a European diplomatic point of view, giving presents at this stage in the development of relations was like paying tribute, an Authority Ranking type of relations, which is how these gifts were literally referred to in the shipping list and other historical documents. Although their intentions were misconstrued by European chroniclers – for political purposes perhaps –, when *guaízas* were given Authority Ranking was likely not the dominant model of relations in these exchanges. Firstly, Columbus also gave various gifts to the caciques from which he received *guaízas*. This would make it an Equality Matching type of relations. This indicates that these gifts were not meant as an indication of submission by indigenous leaders just yet. Secondly, between 1492 and 1496 the European military hold on even the immediate surroundings of their settlement was tenuous at best and the larger battles were still to follow (Mol 2008). I suggest that these gifts should be viewed from an Amerindian point of view that stressed the personal life-forces contained in objects exchanged between multi-natural beings (Chapter 4; Oliver 2009). As discussed above, *guaízas* were infused with the most valued of personal and communal qualities. Following Lowland South American views on socio-material dynamics, the presentation of a *guaíza* would perhaps have served to internalize the (pro-social) qualities of the donor in one's exchange partner. In turn the recipient would perhaps give back an item to which his or her personal qualities were attributed.

This could well have served to render exchange partners more sociable.[18] Nevertheless it is not known if the indigenous leaders sending *guaízas* and other gifts to Columbus aimed at rendering the recipient more peaceful. They may have merely wished to socialize the newcomers in a more specific way, by drawing them into their own life-force networks without making him peaceable so they could still have them wreak havoc on their political rivals. If this transference between socio-cultural "strangers" is connected to the notion that *guaízas* are a representation of the spirit of the living, it seems that the gift of a *guaíza* is first and foremost an affirmation of the other's potential communality of "spirit". Thus, whatever the exact motive for the gift of a *guaíza* may be, the most important aspect of the give-and-take of things with faces was that it allowed both donor and recipient to materially transfer and incorporate aspects of the life-force of social others into the own sphere of influence. In this sense a *guaíza* gift thus cleverly mixes aspects of Communal Sharing, Authority Ranking and Equality Matching relations, with the latter as the dominant model in the case of the historically described exchanges between indigenous and Spanish leaders.

---

18   In this way the Waiwai utilized gifts of Western goods to "wild peoples" in the Guianas in order to make them less fierce (Vaughn Howard 2001).

Guaíza design as a network

Although early Spanish sources indicate that the *guaíza* was an important material node and social tie within networks in early contact-period Hispaniola, it would go too far to draw the same conclusion for all the shell faces found on the other islands. Such inferences extracted from ethnohistoric sources can perhaps be pushed back a few centuries or extended to neighbouring islands. Concluding from these sources that a village leader in 12th century Lavoutte, St. Lucia, transferred life-forces with a *cacique* from the Greater Antilles presumably overestimates the reach of the cultural and social influence of Hispaniolan *cacicazgos*. On the other hand, although their spatial and temporal distribution cannot be related to direct or even down-the-line exchange or control, shell faces dated from AD 1000-1500 seem to form a diffuse yet connected Pan-Antillean network.[19] This cohesiveness of this category of objects can be investigated further through a 2-mode network analysis of shell face design.

In these 2-mode network models we see the following nodes: (1) individual shell faces, coded with a unique number per island of archaeological provenance (e.g. HIS1 for a *guaíza* from Hispaniola) and (2) a range of facial features, shapes and motifs. Such a network does not directly represent or capture social reality. Rather, by drawing relations between individual shell faces and their iconographic motives one drafts their design as a network. In other words, what were the iconographic elements that connected a shell face to the other shell faces out there? What elements did a *guaíza* need to have to be a gift, an object that was exchangeable because it was broadly recognizable and individually valued at the same time? As a socio-politically important item of prestige, one can hypothesize that such a style network will be driven by aesthetic emulation, i.e. *guaízas* would refer formally and stylistically to themselves as part of but also in contrast to the wider array of shell faces out there.

From an initial view of its networked iconography it becomes clear that at the most basic level those who created them have drawn on a limited and shared set of ideas concerning the elements that constitute a *guaíza* (Figure 8.3). The first that springs to mind is the form of the object: most are more or less flat, white discs.[20] This is related to the material applied for crafting, although we also find a range of shell faces that is shaped around the shell, rather than on a plaque of shell.[21]

---

19   An advanced understanding of specific *guaíza* exchange networks is hampered by the following issues: (1) the amount of *guaízas* without secure archaeological contexts, (2) the absence of absolute dates correlated with those found in context, and (3) the difficulty with carrying out provenance studies on sea-shell (Eerkens *et al.* 2005; Mol 2011b).

20   It has to be noted that when the *Lobatus* shell is taken from the sea it is not completely white but rather has a quite attractive pink hue. When the shell is exposed to long periods of sunlight or undergoes chemical weathering processes in the soil, it gradually turns white. It could be the case that this whitening process was actually an important part of the artefact's narrative. Even the antiquity of an object could have been gauged in this way. This is impossible to substantiate archaeologically, however, and to my recollection none of the chroniclers go in-depth on the actual colour of the objects.

21   The database also includes one face from the Lavoutte site in St. Lucia. It was long thought to be made of shell, but according to Menno Hoogland (personal communication, 2009) is crafted from petrified wood. It is also white and has the same shape and design as other *guaízas*.

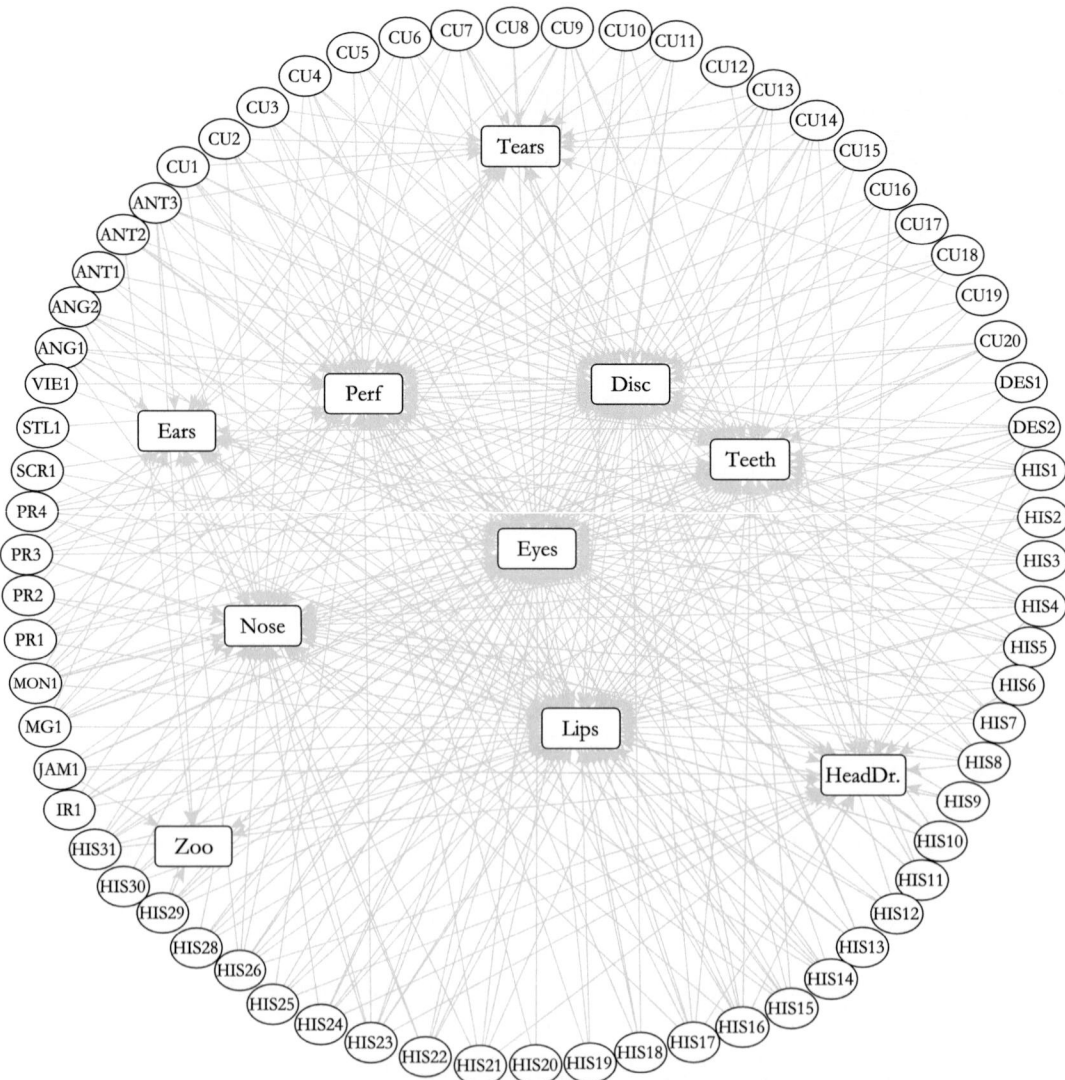

Figure 8.3: A 2-mode network of basic elements of shell faces. The idea here is not to represent what shell faces have which elements (see Mol 2007), but to visualize the degree, i.e. most often occurring traits, of shell faces. Aside from its placement in the inner part of the circle, the density of arrows around a "trait" node is a good indication of this phenomenon. This indicates that eyes are the most centrally occurring element of shell faces across the board, while headdresses or zoomorphic elements are found only on a few, recorded objects. Zoo = Zoomorphic elements present; HeadDr. = headdress present; Perf = perforations present; Disc = disc-shaped. These have been put affiliated with objects from these islands: Anguilla (ANG), Antigua (ANT), Cuba (CU), La Désirade (Guadeloupe, DES), Hispaniola (HIS), Île de Ronde (Grenadines, IR), Jamaica (JAM), Marie-Galante (Guadeloupe, MG), Montserrat (MON), Puerto Rico (PR), Saint Croix (U.S. Virgin Islands, SCR). Saint Lucia (STL), and Vieques (Puerto Rico, VIE).

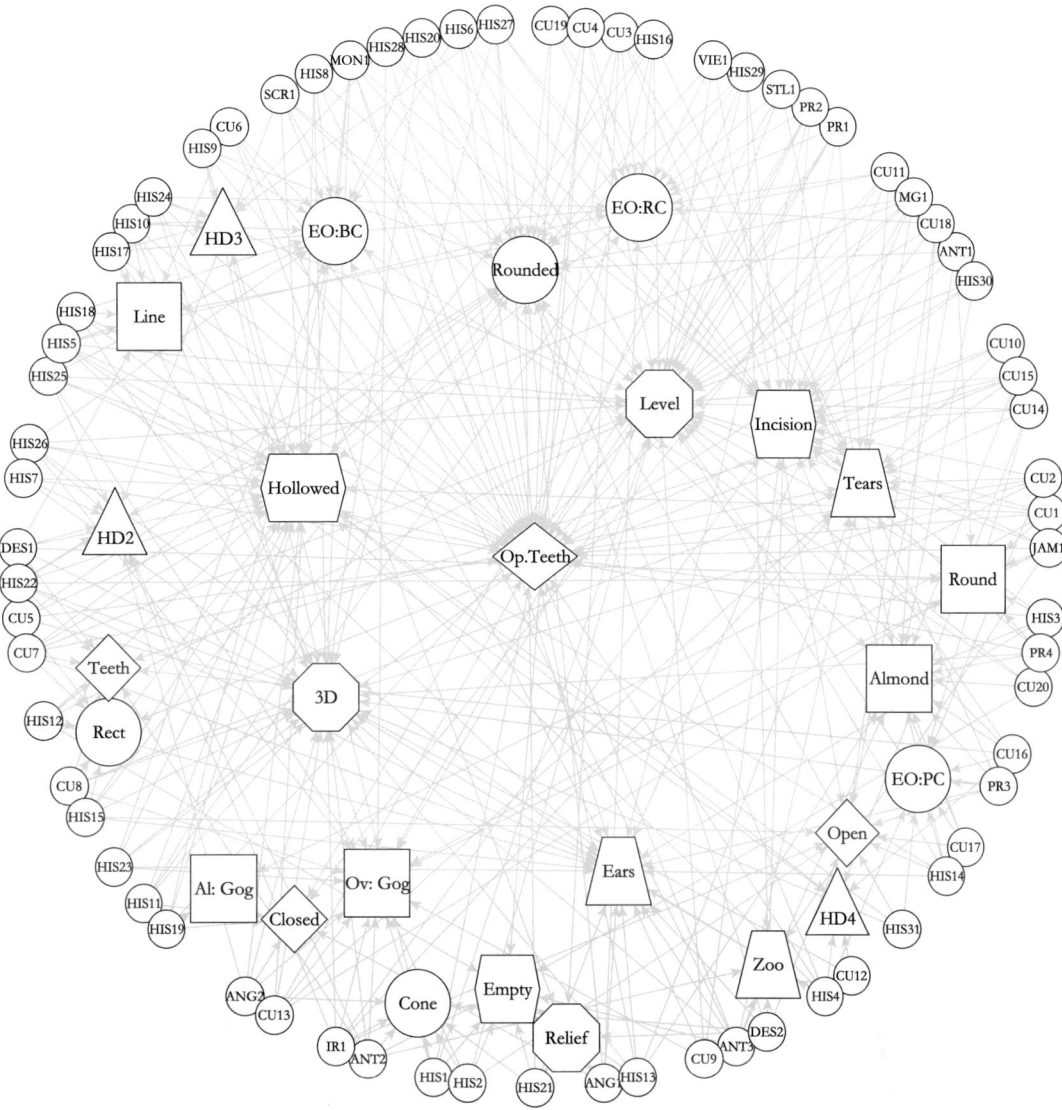

Figure 8.4: 2-mode network of detailed elements of shell faces. In contrast to Figure 8.3 the design elements of shell faces are broken down, revealing a much more varied picture. The idea here is not to represent which shell faces have which elements (see Mol 2007), but to visualize the degree of elements. Aside from its placement in the inner part of the circle, the density of arrows around a "trait" node is a good indication of this. The following design elements have been put into the 2-mode network: shape, perspective headdress, eye shape, carving of the eye, mouth and assorted elements. Shape refers to the shape of the shell face showing differences between Elongated Oval faces and Blunt Chins (EO:BC), Elongated Ovals and Pointed Chins (EO:PC), Elongated Ovals with Rounded Chins (EO:RC), Rounded refers to round discs, Rectangle to rectangular discs and Cone to faces modelled around shell cones rather than discs. Perspective relates how the face is modelled: relief faces have been carved deep into the shell, 3D designates the contour of the shell has been used to present a more three-dimensional face, and Level refers to a more or less two-dimensional carving on a flat disc. Eye shape falls into the categories of Almond shaped (Almond) and Almond shaped with Goggles (Al: Gog), Rounded (Oval) and Rounded with Goggles (Ov:Gog) and a simple line to indicate the presence of eyes (Line). The eye is carved in three ways: complete perforation of the shell (Empty), a hollowing of the eye socket without complete perforation (Hollowed), and simple incisions (Incision). Mouths come in four variants: Open with teeth, open without teeth, teeth only and completely closed. A more detailed description of these various motifs can be found in Mol (2007).

Regardless of the shell part or species used, all of them are (off-)white, although it is possible that it only turned completely white sometime after the shell was carved. In terms of motifs there a few central elements: firstly the depiction of eyes, followed by the lips. This might seem logical because a face is not a face without eyes and lips. However many shell faces lack other central elements of the face, such as a pronounced nose ($n= 38$) and ears ($n= 21$). Perforations and visibly displayed teeth, two other seemingly proto-typical elements of the shell faces, are also absent from numerous individual specimens.[22] Both are present in only forty-seven of the *guaízas* with no correlation between these features: only thirty-seven have teeth as well as perforations. In terms of similarities it seems that shell faces are best connected through their depiction of eyes and mouth.

Based on their specific appearance, these and other facial features can be divided into further design elements (see caption of Figure 8.4). In this analysis eye and teeth types are also distributed among the *guaíza* network. The same applies to other elements of shell face shapes and motifs as shown in the 2-mode network

Shape		Eye Shape	
EO:BC	15	Al: Gog	2
EO:PC	8	Almond	14
EO:RC	17	Ov:Gog	17
Cone	7	Oval	8
Rounded	25	Line	7
Rect	6	**Carving of the Eye**	
Perspective		Empty	10
Relief	5	Hollowed	29
3D	28	Incision	25
Level	34	**Mouth**	
Headdress		Open w/o teeth	39
HD2	10	Open	11
HD3	7	Teeth	8
HD4	6	Closed	6
Assorted elements			
Ears	21		
Tears	19		
Zoo(morphism)	6		

Table 8.1 The design elements of shell faces. This table shows the design elements grouped as larger categories and lists their prevalence among all shell faces. These traits and their ties to individual objects is visualized as a network in Figure 8.4.

---

22   It has to be said that the presence of perforations is difficult to establish when the object is broken.

of specific form and style elements (Figure 8.4). The membership, the indegree, of all groups is quite low (see Table 8.1). Only the "Op. Teeth"-group connects to more than 50% of the *guaízas*, an interesting result in the light of the pro-social qualities that are possibly attributed to such a display (Samson and Waller 2010). The shape of the eyes, the most central element in the other 2-mode network, is especially varied with a range of three different eye shapes, which are even further sub-divided by the pronounced "goggle-like" ring around the orbit. In addition, even within these relatively narrow categories we see many small iconographic motifs or variances in shape. In short, no shell face is alike.

This can be further analysed by means of an affiliation network of individual shell faces (carried out in UCInet 6.0, visualized in visone, Figure 8.5). This network connects individual specimens on the basis of a shared formal or stylistic element. Shell faces that look most alike will have the strongest ties. This is important in order to comprehend the shell faces as a network of (dis)similar design. The resulting network looks highly dense. However, the network is actually relatively sparse. With 1.920 ties in total, the binary density (i.e. nodes sharing at least one formal or stylistic element) of the network is roughly 42%.[23] If the fact that the ties are weighted is taken into account the density is much lower: only 18% of the total network capacity is put to use.[24] These seem like abstract figures, but compare this to the following counterexample. Suppose one would carry out a network analysis of the design of a certain manufactured good, say cans from the same brand of soft drink. In theory each can should be formally and stylistically identical. If we were to plot a graph of this, the network's density would be 1.0 or 100%. In other words, in terms of the stylistic and formal elements that were plotted, the total standardization of all shell faces in the database is only about 18%.[25]

There are two ways to interpret this lack of standardization. Firstly, to state that this network of things is not a network at all, but an artefact of archaeological categorization: there were really no cultural or social networks that co-evolved with the stylistic network of these objects. Secondly, to view this network of things as a collection with coarsely similar features. This connects a high individual diversity: a "shell face-veneer". (cf. Keegan 2004's "Saladoid veneer"). In this respect it is

---

23    $\dfrac{1920}{68 \times (68-1)} = 0.421$

24   Although Figure 8.4 shows twenty-eight formal or stylistic nodes they consist of nine categories that are mutually exclusive, so there are nine categories through which a *guaíza* might be related (Table 8.1). In other words the maximum strength of a tie is 9, i.e. when all of the plotted elements are shared implying that the potential maximum valued density of the network amounts to 9(68(68-1) = 41004. The actual total strength of all ties combined is 7526, therefore the weighted-tie network density equals $\dfrac{7526}{41004} = 0.183$.

25   Normally, various methods of 2-mode network analysis can serve to test patterning between members and groups, such as 2-mode cohesion and block modelling (Borgatti and Everett 1997; Newman 2010). Multiple iterations of core periphery block-modelling (In Ucinet 6.0, a measure based on a genetic algorithm) lead to only slightly better final fitness (around 0.35 instead of the starting fitness 0.339). This could be suggestive of high diversity of groups and members in the 2-mode network. I do not consider these results to be robust, because this 2-mode network has too many zeroes that are due to the fact that membership of one category precludes membership in another (e.g. disc-shaped shell faces cannot be cone-shaped shell faces).

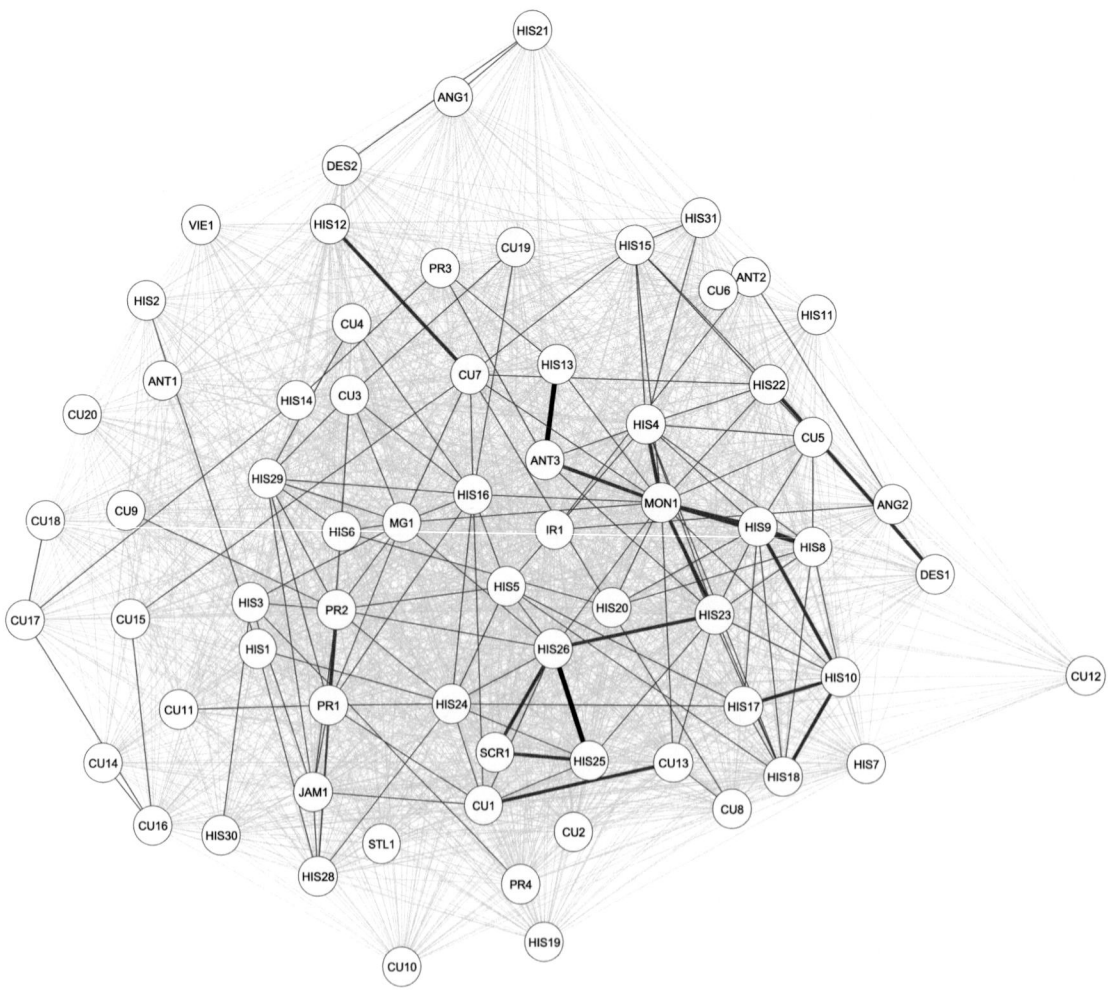

Figure 8.5: The dense affiliation network of shell face design based on the 2-mode network in Figure 8.4. The tie colour and size are related to the tie strength (from low to high = light to dark, thin to thick). Note how all shell faces have ties to numerous other shell faces. This shows that most shell faces share at least a number of design elements (also illustrated in Figure 8.3). Nonetheless, very few shell faces share the majority of their elements with other shell faces (the dark grey and black lines in the network). This indicates a very low amount of standardization across the entire, recorded shell face assemblage.

noteworthy that the absence of standardization among shell faces is not related to a total absence of stylistic standardization in the Antilles. Considering they were hand-crafted on irregularly shaped materials, face elements in other ornaments such as *colgantes* and dog teeth look very much alike to the point of being nearly as identical as two cans of cola drinks (e.g. Figure 8.1.f, g and h). In contrast, the elements of the *guaíza* face differ from object to object.

The differentiation of *guaízas* is not correlated with geographic incidence or, in other words, there do not seem to be more extensive relations with regard to the design of shell faces from the same geographic region. The best example hereof can be found when assessing the strength of connections of shell faces originating from the same archaeological region: the area of the municipalities of Holguín and Banes

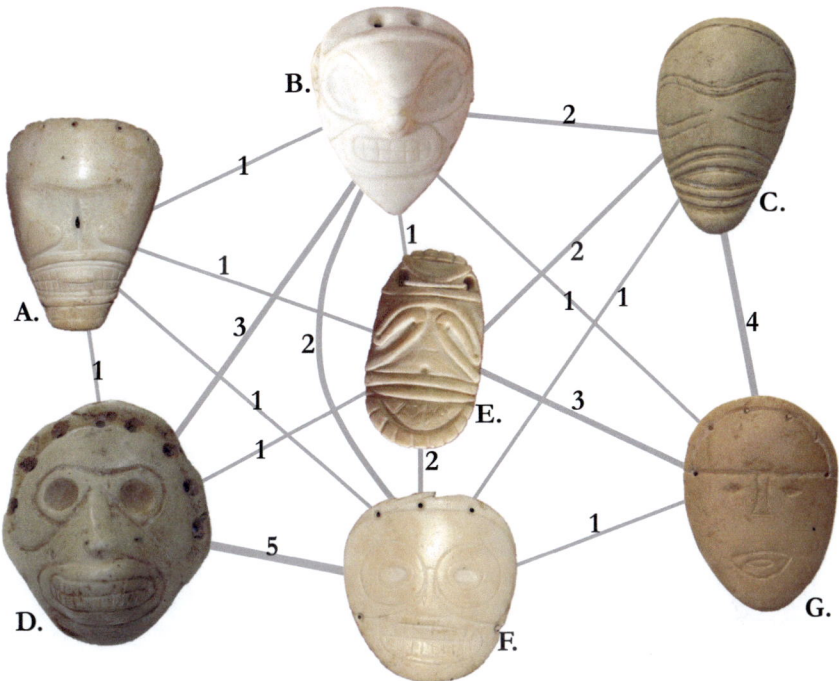

Figure 8.6: Affiliations in guaízas from Banés, Holguín province, Cuba. The tie strength is indicated by the depicted value (maximum strength is 6). These objects are from the Potrero de El Mango (A, B, D, F, G), Esterito (C) and Loma de Ochile (E) sites. The fact that these shell faces, which have all been found in the same region, share very few similarities is indicated by the tie strength and also illustrated by the highly varied appearance of the artefacts. Objects are not to scale. Photos of C, D and G are from casts of the original objects that were made by the CITMA/CISAT of Holguín.

in the Cuban province Holguín (Figure 8.6). These seven objects are only loosely connected. They form two cliques {CU1-CU2-CU6-CU11-CU13} and {CU1-CU2-CU11-CU17-CU18}, but they are not more strongly connected amongst each other than with the other nodes in the network. We find a tie strength average of 1.94 for the entries from Holguín province and 1.95 for the entire data set and a mean of 2 for both. This is even more remarkable when considering that five of these seven shell faces originate from the same site: the above-mentioned Potrero de El Mango site. However, with an average tie strength of 1.87, the formal and stylistic ties are less strong within this site than among all the shell faces from Holguín and beyond, although the dyad {CU1-CU13} is strongly connected (tie strength = 5).

The same can be said when referring to the shell faces found in the settings of smaller island archipelagos. The two specimens from La Désirade (DES1 and DES2), for example, are also highly distinct objects. In the network they are only connected through their ties to other shell faces, among which one from the nearby Marie Galante (MG1). Similarly, only two of the three examples from Antigua share stylistic or formal elements (three in total). Here, too, there are stronger relations between other shell faces within the wider region, such as the single specimen from Montserrat (MON1), than within the own island setting. This allows us to conclude that similarity in the appearance of shell faces was not strived for in the *habitus* of individual locales. In fact, there seems to have been a drive towards giving faces from the same locations a unique appearance.

This same phenomenon can be seen in the set of strongest connections across the network (Figure 8.7). Although we see some tentative regional patterns in iconography and form, such as the prevalence of the tear-motif on Cuba and headbands on Hispaniola, even within a single island region *guaíza* designs can be highly varied. This becomes evident when all but the strongest ties (5 and 6 shared formal or stylistic elements) in the affiliation network are removed. What is left is

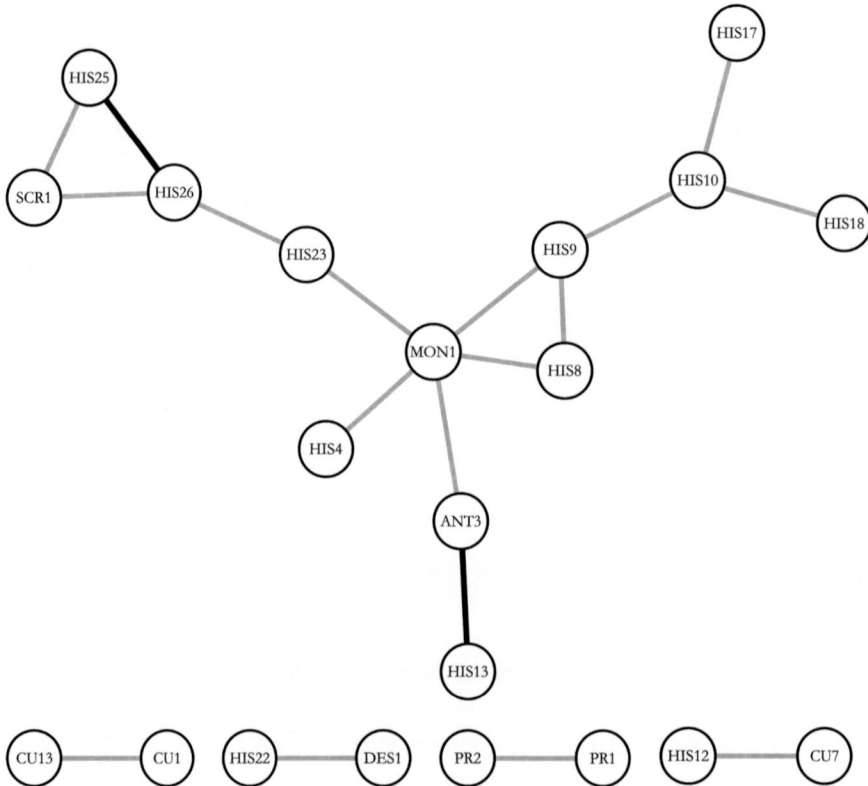

Figure 8.7: A network of the most strongly affiliated shell faces. This set of ties is "lifted" from the dense affiliation network in Figure 8.5 by removing all ties with strength 4 or less (maximum tie strength is 6). This close-up of the most similar shell faces shows that there is, in general, little correlation between geographical proximity and object similarity. It also shows that, while some shell faces are strongly similar to each other, there is no one larger group that is strongly similar, i.e. the only cliques, {HIS25- HIS26-SCR1} and HIS8-HIS9-MON1) have just three members. This network also illustrates that a shelf face from Montserrat (MON1), reported by Fred Olsen (1980), is the most "prototypical" of all the shell faces with the highest number (4) of strong similarity ties overall. This is also confirmed by the centrality of MON1 in the complete affiliation network (See Table 8.2).

one larger component consisting of thirteen nodes and eight nodes in four dyads. Two of the dyads connect shell faces from Puerto Rico, {PR1-PR2}, and we find the strong dyad from Potrero de El Mango: {CU1-CU13}. The other two connect Hispaniola and Cuba {CU7-HIS12} and Hispaniola and la Désirade, {DES1-HIS22}. The larger component is even more heterogeneous. The component consists of shell faces from Hispaniola (n= 10), St. Croix (SCR1), Antigua (ANT3) and Montserrat (MON1). Because the component is star-shaped these nodes do not all connect directly, falling apart in four or five separate paths (arms of the star) with a minimum distance of five ties between the farthest nodes in the subgraph. Most of the Hispaniolan shell faces would not be part of this strong-tie subgraph were it not for its hub: MON1.

This particular shell face is also well-connected in the whole of the affiliation network because of a high valued degree and betweenness centrality (Table 8.2). Realising it has the most similarities to other shell faces (degree) and ranks 4th in terms of connecting differently styled objects (betweenness), it can be considered the most prototypical of all the shell faces. This is noteworthy since this face was found in Montserrat (Olsen 1980), 680 km away as the crow flies from what could be termed the heartland of the shell face: Hispaniola, which has the highest number of shell faces in the database (n = 30). The other ten highest ranked faces also come from a variety of geographic locales. With its high overall presence in the database it is to be expected that the island of Hispaniola is well-represented. Remarkably Cuba is not featured in this Top 10 of most prototypical shell faces, suggesting that faces from the island form an even more heterogeneous collective

Rank	degree %	Node (dist.)	betw. %	Node (dist.)
1	2.21	MON1 (650)	2.83	HIS5 (0)
2	2.17	MG1 (800)	2.78	ANT3 (700)
3	2.09	HIS26 (0)	2.62	HIS4 (0)
4	2.05	HIS16 (0)	2.59	MON1 (650)
5	2.01	HIS4 (0)	2.55	MG1 (800)
6	1.91	HIS5 (0)	2.40	HIS26 (0)
7	1.91	PR2 (150-300)	2.39	HIS13 (0)
8	1.89	ANT3 (700)	2.34	HIS20 (0)
9	1.89	PR1 (150-300)	2.23	HIS16 (0)
10	1.87	HIS23 (0)	2.22	IR1 (1000)

Table 8.2 Top 10 of the best connected shell faces in the design affiliation network. The degree refers to the total amount of similarities an individual object shares with all others. Betweenness centrality (betw. %) can be taken as a reflection of the capacity of an individual object to connect shell faces that are most different in design. Distance (dist.) refers to roughly how far away from the so-called "Taíno" heartland (the Mona Passage) this particular shell face was found.

than the other faces. Of the thirteen objects in the list, four are from the Lesser Antilles, with a noteworthy position for IR1 in terms of betweenness. Even though this shell face is separated by means of the majority of the other nodes in term of geographic distance, it apparently connects relatively many formal and stylistic elements.

Let us return to the starting hypotheses that this corpus of "Taínan" objects represents a "veneer" (cf. Keegan 2004). This analysis of formal and stylistic elements in terms of subgraph formation and centrality measures tells the story of a heterogeneous collective. Each individual object has a unique design, its "own face", so to speak. On the other hand, a formal and stylistic network density of 18% also implies some similarity: when not belonging to one and the same corpus the network's density would be much closer to zero. Nevertheless these shared traits do not seem to be connected to geographic proximity. This is important in the light of their possible status as a unique thing-person that, if exchanged, carried a life-force of a specific person or community, not only in Hispaniola but perhaps even across their distribution range.[26]

Archaeologists have provided these shell faces with numerous names, but when doing so they have justly referred to the larger corpus of similar faces (Mol 2007). This grouping is in fact not that different from that which transpired in the past, when these faces were perhaps not known under the same name or part of identical sets of practices but were formally and stylistically related to each other over a large geographic range. How recognizable and recognizably unique an object is, is of consequence for their exchange value, especially in the case of shell valuables. Some shell valuables are highly recognizable and therefore seem very apt to hold a narrative (e.g. *kula* valuables, Malinowski 1992; the North-east American wampum, Graeber 2001). However other shell valuables are not highly recognizable and are seemingly less apt to hold an individual biographical narrative (e.g. *quirípa* bead strings; Gassón 2000). I would suggest that, in the wider context of inter-regional exchange networks, a broadly recognizable yet unique shell face would have served as a material aide-memoire with regard to specific life-force ties.

In this sense *guaízas* are themselves an aspect of the patterns of homogeneity and diversity in the Caribbean: it can hardly be argued that these shell faces form any sort of discrete category. In fact, a network of their design has a considerable amount of criss-crossing and overlapping similarities. The result is a mode of group recognition that Wittgenstein in the opening quote of this chapter referred to as "family resemblances" (1953: 31-38). He originally applied this term as an analogy in a larger analysis focusing on the pluriformity of language to show how in a family no single two members will look completely alike, but they still may be recognized

---

26 It is also possible that stylistic and formal references concerning other shell faces came about because of the networks of those who manufactured shell faces. These craftsmen or their patrons must have been intimately familiar with the appearance of other shell faces circulating in the direct proximity of their personal networks. Alternatively, shell facial iconography could have been connected by means of a larger network of ties with other face-depicting artefacts and that these were connected to a larger emphasis on the social power of faces. The answer to this question would necessitate examining the complete corpus of face-depicting artefacts in the Antilles and therefore goes way beyond the scope of the present chapter.

as belonging to a closely related group. This is because they have overlapping (physical) traits, rather than one or more defining traits in common.[27]

Shell faces can thus be said to form a similar family collective. On a large scale they repeat a few ingredients (shell, disc, pronounced eyes, mouth). On the other hand, when looking at detailed resemblances there is a fragmentation of overarching patterns of similarity in favour of smaller sets of relations at the level of formal and stylistic elements. This networked understanding of artefact traits is a new approach to conceiving of sets of objects, motifs, concepts, techniques or other archaeological (stylistic) groupings. Aside from this, the fact that shell face "family resemblances" are geographically contrasted, suggests that their similarity and diversity was also actively engaged with by their original creators.

Antillean political economies and face-depicting valuables

In the previous chapter the Antillean *cacicazgo* was defined as a political system built on the incorporation and interdependency of social others, mixing Communal Sharing and Equality Matching relations. In this chapter I have discussed a widespread focus on things with faces which were critical for interactions between social others. These two aspects of late pre-colonial social and material networks can be relatively straightforwardly connected by means of a socio-cognitive evolutionary perspective.

Faces are the most important visual clue of the presence and behaviour of social others from the moment we are born.[28] Babies realise that eye contact means instant attention. They can distinguish friendly from unfriendly faces and quickly learn to recognize faces of even marginal importance to them (Hrdy 2009). Later in life, faces and notably the eyes and mouth, indeed central elements of the shell faces, remain the focal point of the social person, essential for the recognition of identity, sex, race, age, emotional state, focus of attention, facial speech patterns, and attractiveness (Bruce and Young 2011; Calder, *et al.* 2011; see Samson and Waller 2010 for a Caribbean example). Human beings across the world often go to great length in order to extend the individual facial variance as a biological phenotype by means of facial decorations and other modifications, thereby increasing the ties of the face to an individual or group identity (Zebrowitz and Montepare 2008). This modification is also part of the shell faces in the Caribbean.

The point is that faces are the anchor of the individual person in human relations. This is also the reason why objects depicting faces are often highly individual: a portrait is perhaps the most personal manner of representation. However, things with faces are also highly recognizable: a portrait is meant to be seen and identified (with) by others. As discussed above the aspect of faces as being individuals in

---

27   The fact that the homogeneity and diversity in the *guaíza* design network was highly reminiscent of Wittgenstein's use of the concept of "family resemblances" was pointed out to me by Raymond Corbey.

28   This focus on facial expressions is not unique to human beings, but primates and especially Homo sapiens make more use of the face when interacting than any other species (Parr and Hecht 2011). Notably the innate reflexive cognitive competency of face recognition has been selected for in early human beings (McKone and Robbins 2011; Zebrowitz and Montepare 2008).

a larger family is also mimicked by means of the design of shell faces across the indigenous Antilles. The universal recognition of things with faces provided face-depicting material culture with a broad and relatively neutral sociability. This is why we find similarly styled faces in the late pre-colonial Northeastern Caribbean and further afield, far beyond the bounds of any stylistic, cultural, or political unit.

That face-depicting objects were (pro-)social factors is also apparent from their use in exchanges during the early contact period. From the perspective of the indigenous peoples, they were employed to bridge social and inter-cultural gaps. The link between objects with faces and their or their original owner's personhood is emphatically expressed in their function as gifts between social others. These exchanges were material manifestations of the ebb and flow of life-force between social others, a critical aspect of the social and political system that was discussed in Chapter 7. Moreover, as was discussed in Chapter 4 with the example of the *behique* interacting with a spirit in a tree, carving faces onto materials was also a way of activating other than human beings. Other engagements with the materialized faces of these spirit and ancestral beings were likely also perceived as a type of social relation. The ontological significance of faces may thus have added another layer of social relations to that which face-depicting objects naturally create between humans. In the Caribbean, materializations of the face of the self and others may have extended the presence of their social persons across time and space (see also Oliver 2009).

Unfortunately, the larger ontological status of the anthropomorphic face is currently poorly understood, perhaps because it is only hinted at in ethnohistorical documents (Samson and Waller 2010. Nevertheless, the importance of the face is indicated by archaeological evidence, such as the multi-perspective (and likely multi-perspectivist) adorno faces on pottery, the mortuary treatment and post-mortem manipulation of skulls, the incorporation of skulls in cotton objects, *etc.* (Hoogland and Hofman 2013; Ostapkowicz and Newsom 2012; Petersen and Crock 2007; Roe 2004; Samson and Waller 2010). This suggests that in the Antilles an already strong evolutionary link between sociality and (depictions of) human-like faces was strengthened further by a local development. Objects with (partly) anthropomorphic faces seem to have become increasingly central to objects and archaeological assemblages over time. Why this happened is unclear. Potentially, it is related to the absence of large, ideologically important predators in the islands in contrast to the coastal regions of the Caribbean mainland. As a result of this, humans may have filled key ontological roles that in Lowland South America were reserved for other animals (Roe 1982). However, in order to substantiate such claims and further explore the diverse yet connected facial iconography of the wider Caribbean more research is needed.

It is, however, clear that face-depicting objects became evermore central aspects of Antillean political economies. Based on the discussion in this and the previous chapter as well as other key publications on this subject (Boomert 2001a; Curet 1996, 2002, 2003; Hofman and Hoogland 2004; Keegan 2007; Oliver 2009; Siegel 1992, 2010), this suggests a co-evolutionary trajectory of objects and persons. In the early part of the first millennium AD, objects reflecting ties with exotic others were the ultimate means to differentiate oneself in a political system in which popular support was fickle and where egalitarian cliques had the tendency to equilibrate differentiations in power. In later times, as social and political networks continued to grow, it became increasingly important to show who controlled the political economy within the community. Materialized, publicly recognizable markers of control, for example, ornaments and statues representing deities, but also publicly built and managed architecture, became increasingly important to stabilize larger collectives. In the last phase before contact, political power started to become more distributed as its underlying networks gradually extended further and further beyond political, cultural, linguistic and cosmic boundaries. This is even more applicable to the earliest contact phase in which *caciques* and other socio-political actors tried to incorporate the new trans-Atlantic network within their local life-force networks. As the exchange of *guaízas* with Europeans indicates, their attempts to do so were based on pre-colonial ideas on sociality, in which objects with faces had gained a prominent position as nodes and ties of life-forces.

Pre-contact political economies were for an important part vested in the material expressions of the life-force of social others, especially in the material expressions of other than human subjects. Although they were powerful and potentially dangerous, giving faces to these beings socialized them. As a result ornaments, amulets, statuettes and other face-depicting things became a nexus of socio-material and socio-cosmic relations, interdependent with the communities and individuals to which they were tied. Yet whereas political constellations may have been volatile, objects endured and were in fact more easily manipulated than other political allies. Because they were relatively fixed and familiar aspects within wider Antillean value systems, items with faces would have served as socio-political anchors for communities. In other words, even if individual persons had never met and did not speak the same language, things with faces formed a familiar "family" of objects that were central to social relations across the board.

Let us imagine a visit of one *cacical* collective to another, for example in the case of an inter-communal feast. The political and economic negotiations included in this visit would have been supported by means of a material system replete with faces.[29] When visitors met face to face with the leader of the host community the latter was seated on a *duho* with a face as its centrepiece. The faces of ancestors and other superhuman beings were materialized in statues and personal ornaments in order to witness the procedures. Drinks and food were served in containers with faces. Whenever a social tie was established or renewed, one exchanged not only *guaízas*, but also many other face-depicting valuables. Finally, when returning to one's own community the life-force, the value, and narrative of exotic things would have been more easily recognized and integrated within the communal network. This was because things with faces at home were akin but not completely the same as the things with faces that were brought from exotic locales. Indeed, as long

---

29   See, for example, Alexandre (2003) for an ethnographic perspective on the importance of the face in Amazonian welcoming ceremonies.

as they remained in circulation, unique but broadly recognizable face-carrying artefacts would serve as *aide-memoires* with reference to a larger network of social partners. Objects with faces thus featured centrally in a myriad of Communal Sharing, Authority Ranking and Equality Matching relations. Things with faces, like the *kula* valuables that were discussed in Chapter 4, were a "total social material" fact of life in the Northeastern Caribbean.

Around the Caribbean seaboard we can observe a similar central role regarding facial imagery in many forms of socially valuable material culture: from Central American representations of anthropomorphic beings on tools, personal ornaments and monumental architecture to the Valencioid and other Venezuelan assemblages with their large-headed ceramic statuettes (e.g. Antczak and Antczak 2006; Hoopes 2007; Hoopes and Fonseca 2003). Although a far from complete knowledge on the archaeology of these regions on my part hinders any further substantiation of such a sweeping claim, it is at least possible to state that the focus on faces links the Northeastern Caribbean with other regions of the Antilles. This certainly applies to the rest of the Greater Antilles and Bahamas to the west and the Windward Islands to the south. On the face of it, the distribution of artefacts representing core icons of this interregional network may have been erratic – e.g. a snuff pipe in Saba, a *duho* in a cave in Dominica, a three-pointer with face in Guadeloupe, a *guaíza*-like shell face in Grenadines, *etc.* (Hofman, Bright, *et al.* 2008). Nevertheless, they can all be considered to be part of one larger family of objects due to their similar but unique faces. Even if cultural practices and socio-political affiliations differed from region to region, face-depicting valuables could have tapped into the local network of overarching Amerindian "political economies of life".

Chapter 9

Conclusion: Connecting the Caribbean

Whatever the twists and turns of a system of threads in space, one can always obtain an expression for the calculation of its dimensions, but this expression will be of little use in practice. The craftsman who fashions a braid, a net, or some knots will be concerned [...with] the manner in which the threads are interlaced.

Alexandre-Théophile Vandermonde (1771, quoted in Przytycki 1998)

The common thread of the previous eight chapters consisted of three sub-strands. The first theme was that of Northeastern Caribbean culture history and the dynamics of the (pan-)regional similarities and differences in the archaeological record of the region. Secondly, I also examined how network approaches can serve to abstract, explore, analyse and interpret archaeological relational data as networks. Thirdly, I have delved into the long-standing archaeological debate on how "pots" and "people", material culture and social life, are related. All three are distinct and highly complex problems. However, the aim of this work – and one could say of archaeology in general – has been to produce relevant social and cultural histories based on substantive *and* systemic studies of material culture. In order to do this I would argue that it is necessary to interlace these separate threads – even if at this point in time the yarn that can be spun will still be somewhat frayed.

A brief review

Chapter 1 started out with a characterization of the Caribbean pre-colonial archaeological record as typified by a complex pattern of homogeneity and diversity. Understanding how these patterns are created through a myriad of movements and interactions of people, objects and ideas is of key importance for understanding the history of the area. Yet traditional models have had tremendous difficulty with connecting archaeological evidence for (pan-)regional and inter-cultural connections to the large range of locally variable practices on the islands. My suggestion has been to approach the problem not by dividing site assemblages and other types of material cultural repertoires into separate categories. This often results in a monolithic view of history that focuses on the boundaries between rather than the connections of social and cultural groups. Instead I have studied them as networks and explored how these networks in material culture are reflections of social networks. As a result, ideas on what past networks looked like and how they functioned are widespread, even if the network theoretical status of such notions is not explicitly recognized as such. This has also led to a heuristic entanglement between networks of people and things, leading among other things to strong disavowals of the "pots as people" approach. Nevertheless, even in most recent studies the line between past networks of people and "pots" – relations between material culture in the archaeological record – is often blurred.

As was discussed in Chapter 2, there are many factors to be considered when discussing interaction and mobility in the pre-colonial Caribbean from a network perspective. Differential but analogous environments would have reinforced a mixed collective of socio-cultural practices. The geographic layout and the need for maritime voyaging would also have influenced the connections that can be reflected in the archaeological record. In this setting some of the "rules" on what constitute viable actors in traditional (social) network studies should be reconsidered. Amerindians generally have different ideas on what and who can be meaningfully interacted with.

From a bird's eye view the pre-colonial history of the Caribbean is exemplified by networks that expanded and contracted, merging and separating while doing so. Naturally, local network developments may have diverged from the larger developments that were discussed here. The main point is that what happened in certain points in time or in a certain place can be seen as part of a connected process and not as a unique or separate phenomenon (Keegan 2004). In the overview the Archaic-Saladoid-Huecoid interface period and the socio-political networks of the late pre-contact period were highlighted, but there are of course other timeframes, regions and themes that could benefit from archaeological studies incorporating network perspectives and analyses.

In Chapter 3 I outlined which network science methodologies, concepts and measures could serve as a starting point for such an undertaking. Subgraph and centrality analyses were the main focus, because introducing these first basic concepts into archaeological analysis and interpretation is a first necessary step and can already be quite insightful. Some better known network models were also discussed in order to show how various types of networks can potentially be influenced by similar systemic parameters.

However, as was discussed in Chapter 4, one problem with understanding such relations is that the material culture record has traditionally been primarily used as a proxy for social networks, without giving due thought to the impact of things on these networks. Recently, the insight that things are a contributing factor to and are not only indicative of human experience and society has led to a counter-movement, the "material cultural turn", in which anthropologists and archaeologists started to "take things seriously" (Olsen 2010). Studies on the "materiality" of things reveal how they impact an individual's place in the world and, on a larger scale, the fact that society and culture is materially embedded (Knappett 2005).

Nonetheless, although sometimes human relations with things can influence and even usurp other relations this does not imply that "pots" have the same status as people. While things are not people and people are not things, they are structurally integral to each other. This gives rise to new "socio-material" network dynamics. As post-Maussian (1923/1924) ethnography has shown, gifts, for example, are not only total social, but also material total social facts: they can function as gift because they make reference to persons as durable socio-material ties (Graeber 2001; Knappett 2011).

The importance of socio-material interdependence is succinctly and clearly illustrated by the example of the island Melanesian *kula*, arguably the most famous reciprocal exchange system. In the *Kula* ring, the "fame" – a measure of their success – of individual "players" and their clans are directly related to which valuables they own, have owned, and are likely to own in the future. Conversely, the value of individual armbands and necklaces is contingent upon who currently holds them, has owned them in the past and who they are promised to in the future. In this way in the *Kula* ring persons and things are part of a network loop that might continue *ad infinitum*, were it not for the intrusion of other social obligations and the lure of other types of (material) wealth.

Although it is very different from that of island Melanesia, an Amerindian perspective on the relations between things and people presents its own ontologically-grounded version of socio-material dynamics. From indigenous narratives and ethnographic accounts, for example, it becomes clear that Lowland South American things and persons are quite literally dependent on each other. Firstly, the state of human culture and society is the direct result of before-time exchanges (and thefts) of material culture and technical knowledge from non-human subjects. Furthermore, things are perceived as carrying over the life-forces of humans and thereby their circulation contributes to a "political economy of life". Conversely, things also require creative human energies in order to become active as subjects themselves (Santos-Granero 2009 a, b).

Building on the more theoretical and methodological discussion in the previous chapters, Chapters 5 to 8 presented four network explorations of archaeological and ethnohistorical case studies. These network explorations were contrasted to existing but "hidden" network models in Caribbean archaeological theories of culture continuity and change as well as socio-political organization and complexity. The diachronic discussion of lithic production and distribution in Chapter 5 indicated that network analysis holds promise for understanding the deep network history of the Caribbean. It illustrated how the Northeastern Caribbean had formed one network from the earliest moment that human presence can be detected even through to the end of the Archaic-Huecoid-Saladoid interface period, which was the cut-off point for the analysis. However, lithic networks did undergo profound changes between 3200 BC and AD 400. Through these phases of transition raw material sources as network nodes were constantly present. This was the case with Long Island flint before, during and after the Archaic-Early Ceramic Age interface period (800 – 200 BC). Additionally, the network models of Long Island distribution showed that the production, exchange and use of this stone material connected communities across time and perceived cultural boundaries.

Chapter 6 examined how archaeological networks can be understood from a multi-scalar perspective. The idea of ego-network models was introduced in order to investigate the socio-material interrelations of a site's assemblage. The ego-network of the 14th century site of Kelbey's Ridge 2 on the island of Saba showed that in the Northeastern Caribbean even the goings-on in communities on smaller islands impacted wider island networks. The ego-network furthermore illustrated that certain archaeologically visible features, house structures and shamanic paraphernalia in the case of Kelbey's Ridge 2, would have been central network nodes within the site's ego-network. A comparison between the ego-network of Kelbey's Ridge 2 and Spring Bay 3 also identified two dynamics, a network of "Taíno" objects with an interregional distribution and diachronic shifts in lithic distribution networks.

Other stone material exchange networks (such as those based on the production and exchange of Antiguan carnelian, St. Martin greenstone and Puerto Rican serpentinite) were part of new, emulative dynamics that evolved between 200 BC and AD 400. The creation of intercommunal Authority Ranking relations as indicated by – and presumably partly based on – lithic exchange, did not entail that the network became more segmented. On the contrary, network competition led to the development of increasingly stronger cliques of habitation sites.

The last case studies in Chapter 7 and 8 took a closer look at the connected phenomena of the *cacicazgo* and the distribution of a material cultural repertoire referred to as "Taíno" in the academic literature. To this end, the traditional, pyramid-shaped political model of the *cacicazgo* was contrasted to a *cacical* network collective in which power and obligations were distributed across multiple specialists. This late pre-colonial structure had developed from the more purely triadic political system of earlier times. These initial triadic dynamics of internal and external power relations developed into three, linked political economies: the communal, intercommunal and superhuman network economy. Rather than fragmenting the cultural map of the Caribbean along the territorial lines of emerging polities, a three-pronged and outward looking political system produced polity interdependence and widespread similarities in socio-politically valuable material repertoires. Things with faces were one of the more widespread and recognizable types of material culture during the last phase before contact. This family of objects formed important material counterparts of social networks in their capacity as medium of exchange or as "infrastructural" to intergroup and interpersonal dynamics.

Network approaches evaluated

One of the goals of this research was to show proof of the concept of network science approaches in archaeological cases. It is safe to conclude that the entirety of this study and specifically the four case studies indicate that a variety of data-driven network explorations can be implemented based on archaeological and ethnohistorical information. Furthermore these network models and their exploration brought new insights that either strengthened support for existing hypotheses or even challenged a number of standing theories. Given the success of archaeological network studies within other regions this is not surprising (see Brughmans 2013; Knappett 2013). Nevertheless, a great deal more can be done in order to advance network approaches in the field of archaeology and material culture studies. Below, I will discuss several strengths, weaknesses, potentials and pitfalls of applying a network approach for archaeological questions and case studies in greater detail.

First of all, it is clear that networks work in archaeology. Moreover, network approaches can provide new perspectives on existing problems or find new dynamics in archaeological data sets. Of course, archaeological relational data are not "perfect". The data sets from which networks have to be abstracted are sparse, fragmented, constrained by temporal and geographical parameters, and highly dependent upon data selection strategies. Nevertheless, this is the case for most if not all studies that abstract real-world networks into model networks for analysis (Brandes, *et al.* 2013; Prell 2012). What makes archaeological network approaches stand out from other network science disciplines is that the phenomena they are interested in (social and cultural systems) is one step extra removed from their source of data (assemblages of objects and associated material practices). My personal views on the strengths and weaknesses of network science approaches in archaeology, the promises they hold, and the threats they face will be discussed below.

There is a large range of spatial, temporal, artefactual – and in the Caribbean and many other regions also historical and ethnographical – sources of information that can serve to create, analyse and interpret past networks. If these sources are used properly and in conjunction, this is almost guaranteed to result in the discovery of new relational dynamics in archaeological studies. This is because, up till now, most archaeological methodologies are designed to compartmentalize parts of the archaeological record into distinct categories. In contrast, the type of network explorations that have been done here can be used in order to look at incidence relations and interdependencies of archaeological relational data. Naturally, "doing networks" is not a sure path to revolutionary breakthroughs. A network model may end-up supporting a previously established idea. However, even in these cases network approaches can yield valuable insights by pointing out the interdependencies in the system that is studied. In addition, they can connect the dynamics of these systems and serve to hypothesize network theories, which can sometimes be cross-checked with theories from other fields of network science (e.g. Golitko, *et al.* 2012; Mills, *et al.* 2013; Sindbæk 2007). Moreover, sometimes archaeological network studies can provide "surprising" insights, in the sense that they contradict standing theories (e.g. Graham 2006; Mizoguchi 2009; Mol and Mans 2013; Terrell 2010).

It is interesting to note that the networks in the case studies in Chapters 5 to 8 were all relatively small-scale, ranging between tens to a maximum of a few dozen nodes. Therefore the size and complexity of the data sets used in this study cannot be compared to the systems that network science can and very regularly deals with – i.e. networks of hundreds or thousands of nodes potentially related by hundreds of thousands of ties. Even in regards to a number of archaeological network studies the relational databases applied here were rather small (e.g. Brughmans 2013; Mills, *et al.* 2013; Sindbæk 2007). As a result of the small-scale of the database one may claim that the findings of the case studies were obvious from the data themselves and did not need abstraction, analysis and interpretation as networks. In other words, can new insight be acquired by studying relatively simple and small archaeological networks?

I would argue that they can. Several results of these relatively small and simple network analyses were "surprising" in the sense that they contradicted, supported or amended specific models of Caribbean socio-cultural and socio-political history: e.g. Kelbey's Ridge 2 was a strong, local but also diversely connected community during the 14th century Northern Lesser Antilles (cf. Hofman and Hoogland 2011); Hispaniola's political landscape presumably evolved from unstable, *cacical* collectives instead of ascribed status roles of divine *caciques* at the pinnacle of a class-based hierarchy (cf. Curet 2002, 2006; vs. Keegan 2006; Keegan, *et al.* 1998); lithic networks crossed perceived cultural boundaries during the Archaic up to Early Ceramic interface period (vs. Rouse 1992; cf. Rodríguez Ramos 2010); similarity in shell-face design was inversely correlated with regional distributions (vs. Mol 2007). Other conclusions on *cacical*, shell face, lithic distribution and Kelbey's Ridge 2 site-ego networks are too case-specific to re-iterate here. At any rate, it is clear that the network approach applied here provided (small) breakthroughs in longstanding and wide-ranging issues, albeit based on relatively small-scale and "simple" data.

Certain types of material networks can be relatively straightforwardly implemented with the use of existing network approaches. For example flows of goods in pre-colonial distribution networks are theoretically the same as flows of goods in modern networks. Measures and theories of spatial and cost-distance based networks can be the same for network archaeological and geographical studies. Several networks will be unique to archaeology. Indeed, certain network models and analyses the present study takes into account have, to the best of my knowledge, not previously been carried beyond the field of archaeology. Ego-network analysis of site assemblages and 2-mode network analyses of stylistic networks proved to be new and expedient ways of "doing networks".

Ego-networks may be a profitable addition to current archaeological studies (Brughmans 2012). Departing from a site's assemblage they do not necessarily privilege a certain scale of analysis, which is a weakness of existing regional network studies (Knappett 2011). They also allow for a combined network of multiple types of relational data set. Kelbey's Ridge 2 ego-network consisted of relations between house structures, burial assemblages, ceramic and stone provenance, *etc.* All these diverse features of the site assemblage were *a priori* treated as equally material for the identity of the community as a locally and regionally embedded community. Ego-networks are also somewhat less susceptible to sparse databases, since they model outward from a single site assemblage. In ego-network analysis the idea is not to model a full network of multiple site-nodes (or artefact-nodes), but the network of a single site. Fragmented, incomplete data will still be a threat because the ego-network model presupposes that the view of ties present between nodes is comprehensive. In the case of the ego-networks discussed here this hinges on the comparability of data collection, analysis and research strategies of the site with those of other sites within the network. Archaeological research on Saba has been quite exhaustive, but the majority of its relational databases are relatively comparable.

It is often difficult to identify dyads of the same type in archaeology and it is even harder to construct a network out of node incidents. It is very laborious to accurately pinpoint a node's dyadic partner based on, for example, artefact provenance data. Even if we see a tie entering *into* a node, an artefact in an assemblage that was locally exotic, we do not necessarily know where it came *from*. Even if we can establish a dyadic pair of sites this does not entail this can also be carried out with regard to other nodes in the network. The only reason that a 1-mode network of lithic distribution in Period D and E is relatively robust is because Caribbean lithic specialists have a comparatively clear view of raw material sources and workshop areas for Long Island flint, Puerto Rican serpentinite, Antiguan carnelian, St. Martin greenstone and red jasper from Martinique (Knippenberg 2007). Other types of provenance studies like ceramic (geo-chemical) analyses or isotopic provenance studies of individuals will be able to present less direction to their evidence of out-node, exotic ties (e.g. Isendoorn, *et al.* 2008; Laffoon 2012). It is always possible to apply such databases to model a range of 1-mode models based on probable areas of origin and the subsequent circulation of artefacts or even human beings. However, the range of possible provenances of most archaeologically recovered materials is generally quite high, particularly in the Caribbean (Laffoon 2012). One manner to alleviate this problem is to carry out more systematic analyses of site assemblages based on *chaîne operatoires* and artefact provenance. Casuistic studies of single sites reporting on intermittent exotic ties are not helpful for provenance-based network studies. In order to study "full" networks in archaeology we need to systematically study the complete range of sites within our network database. This requires an expansive archaeometrical programme and strict sampling and dating regime (Hofman, Mol, *et al.* 2011).

Two-mode networks side-step this directionality issue because they do not model direct ties between nodes but incidence ties of one type of node with another type of node. For example, it may not be known where an exotic trait or object found in a site assemblage originates from, but it is possible to connect various site assemblages to each other based on the presence of this trait. The networks presented in this study are by and large 2-mode ones. The hypothetical network of Chremanesia, the shell face style network, the majority of the lithic distribution networks and several parts of Saba's ego-network were based on membership of one type of nodes, such as sites or individual shell faces, to other types of nodes, e.g. presence of a stone material and iconographical facial elements.

It has to be noted that, because their matrix structure differs from 1-mode networks, 2-mode networks are a particular kind of network that are not in all ways as flexible or useful as 1-mode networks – e.g. they cannot be analysed by means of the majority of the measures applied on 1-mode networks (Borgatti, *et al.* 1997). Two-mode networks as such can be insightful. Affiliation networks provide a means to create 1-mode networks from 2-mode networks, allowing for 1-mode measures of 2-mode matrix rows or columns. All in all, I consider 2-mode networks to be of most immediate use to the field of archaeology in the future. It provides a way to connect nodes from interdependent but dissimilar relational data sets to each other. Of these archaeology has a large quantity: co-presence of certain artefact styles in multiple assemblages, house structures or middens and the presence of particular vessel types and shapes, burials and types of burial gifts, artefacts and their iconographic systems, *etc.*

If we shift the focus from the current strengths of network approaches to the future opportunities they may hold, it is clear there are many advances still to be made. In the Caribbean we could do more with existing GIS-models of site relations by modelling them as networks (cf. Torres 2012). The time and resources needed for additional and more advanced network based geographic models went beyond the scope of the present study. Nevertheless, albeit that PPA and MDN analyses of distances between island headlands provide a sound starting point, they are rather crude models of geographic relations. Intervisibility or cost-distance based network models could provide a much larger insight into spatio-cultural dynamics in the Northeastern Caribbean. It has yielded generally good results in other regions (e.g. Brughmans 2013; Knappett, *et al.* 2008). Several tools are already present – knowledge of spatio-temporal site patterning on various islands are quite complete. Travel cost-distance models and wind and current models for sea voyages that have already been tested are available (e.g. Callaghan 1990; Cooper 2008; Torres 2012). Hopefully future research will be able to advance GIS-based network models for the Northeastern and wider Caribbean.

The case-study networks only applied basic concepts and measures from graph theory. The implementation of more advanced models and measures was partly constrained by need. Subgraph and centrality measures sufficed to provide a better understanding of groupings in the case-study networks and point out structurally important nodes and ties. Perhaps even more so than archaeology, network science is an expansive field with many and varied interests and specialisms. This implies numerous opportunities for advancing archaeological network approaches based on the implementation of network models, methods and measures from the wider network sciences.

While the number of archaeological network studies is on the rise, they remain relatively marginal as both an archaeological and network science sub-discipline. Indeed, although they may be an innovation in (Caribbean) archaeology, the network case studies presented here are basic stuff as far as network science goes. The reason is that I have applied network science in an effort to better understand archaeological problems and not make advances in network science. The utilisation of more advanced network science was also inhibited as an archaeologist who has received only marginal training in network sciences. However, I can see many possibilities for employing more advanced network methods and concepts within the field of archaeology, such as block-modelling of networked site assemblages, multi-graph modelling of multiple lines of evidence, (Exponential) Random Graph Modelling or (E)RGM, genetic modelling of transitional phases in history, analyses of trade network embeddedness, longitudinal developments in distribution networks, autocatalytic networks of innovation spread, or multi-tie modelling of site assemblages and processes. These concepts, models and measures all stem from highly technical fields, which can probably not be fully grasped by non-network specialists.

Archaeology has a rich multi-disciplinary history in which specialists from various fields work together in order to operationalize a certain method or technique for the field of archaeology. We need to do the same with regards to the application of network science methods and techniques in archaeology. In order to incorporate more advanced network methods and theories in our discipline, archaeologists require assistance from network specialists (cf. Knappett, *et al.* 2008). Conversely archaeological networks have several traits – e.g. socio-material interdependencies, geographic and temporal constraints, multi-level networks, dissimilar relational data, longitudinal and evolutionary perspectives – which make them potentially challenging projects for network science specialists.

If we look at the mid-term future of network approaches within archaeology, it is clear that they are threatened in a number of ways. Firstly, they may be pushed towards the margins of archaeological practice because it is generally believed that a certain type of data context or structure is needed to carry out a network analysis. It is, for example, telling that network studies are currently most often found within island and coastal settings (Bright 2011; Broodbank 2000; Hofman, Mol, *et al.* 2011; Isaksen 2013; Knappett, *et al.* 2011; Malkin 2011; Mizoguchi 2009; Phillips 2011; Sindbæk 2007; Terrell 2008, 2010) – with some notable exceptions (Brughmans 2013; Mills, *et al.* 2013).[1] There is no reason why network approaches could not work equally well in landlocked as in maritime settings. Instead the selection of island settings for network studies may be underlain by the fact that the larger group of archaeologists out there does not fully understand the viability of network approaches, regardless of available sources of data and regional or temporal contexts.

That network approaches are primarily about abstracting, exploring, analysing and modelling patterns of relations in archaeological data sets and not (directly) about identifying social connections in the past should also be better communicated to the wider archaeological discipline. Moreover, the types of systems that archaeology looks at are of a very diverse kind, but at the moment network approaches emphasize (advanced) computer modelling studies. This approach coincides with the methods and aims of GIS, complex systems and

---

1   Although networks may be of great service within these contexts (Terrell 2008), an "island network archaeology" would continue a flawed scholarly tradition in which islands are seen as bounded, special environments that can therefore more easily be connected to other island nodes (Boomert and Bright 2007).

agent-based modelling studies. However, there is also a wide potential for network approaches to enhance other types of researches. The results of the case studies, for example, were based on basic measures and no modelling of relations in site assemblages, provenance, historic sources and iconographic analysis. Nevertheless, in combination with more substantive lines of evidence, these networks were able to provide new insights into the subject matter.

Another threat is that networks will continue to mainly serve as a metaphor, a buzz-word. Such an implementation of networks in archaeology will be stuck in a semantic discussion dealing with what it implies when referring to the relations we come across in the archaeological record as networks instead of as "webs", "meshes" or "entanglements". Furthermore, networks as key theoretical constructs are part of a wider relational movement in archaeology that comes and goes in waves. If the current wave of relational thinking subsides network approaches may be considered as a remarkable fad and then be discarded. This will perhaps be a small loss for network science as a whole, but a greater one for archaeology. It may entail a return to monolithic histories based on material culture categories and hidden assumptions concerning network structures, processes and dynamics determine interpretations of social and cultural processes and systems. This can be countered if archaeological relational theory is applied in conjunction with network science approaches.

In fact, network science approaches within archaeology will always need to be combined with archaeological theory if it is to be of any interpretive value. It needs to be clear what it entails when a part of the archaeological record is said to be a network. Why features in the record can be designated as a single node and how this node is connected to other, (dis)similar nodes is an issue that always needs to be expounded. We must thus examine on a case-by-case basis why taking a network approach is worthwhile and explain why it is applicable to the question at hand. This can be done by formulating archaeological problems or hypotheses in such a way that they can be explored by means of network approaches. If this is done, the limits of network science approaches are only defined by the inventiveness of archaeologists in recognizing systems of material culture assemblages and practices to be explored.

In any case, although the future of network approaches in archaeology is still unclear, I feel that, even if network as a metaphor will at some point become outmoded, an implementation of network science methods is bound to occur. Network science is a robust and growing discipline and, if developments from other humanities and social sciences can be taken as a sign, will likely become more influential in the future. At the same time, the questions and types of networks that can be modelled based on archaeological data are also gaining increasing attention within the network sciences. Longitudinal developments in networks is one example of this, as is network modelling based on data sets with a lot of "structural zeroes", the type of holes in data sets which are a given in archaeological research. By introducing more diverse set of network science approaches and emphatically coupling of network science method and theory with archaeological method and theory, this will lead to a development in which both disciplines will become increasingly more relevant for each other. So, network can be partly a theoretical perspective, but may be of most use when applied as a form of data analysis, a "relational statistics". The added benefit hereof is that, aside from being embedded in the discipline of archaeology, network approaches would also be part of an overarching network science discipline, presenting archaeology and archaeologists with a new field of researchers with which they can engage, cooperate, publish with, *etc*.

Socio-material networks: (Un)necessary dualism?

Many concepts in the archaeological and anthropological literature are closely analogous to the term "network": web, actor-network, fields, lines, meshes, flows, entanglements, systems, interaction, social and exchange spheres, *etc*. Although they have specific connotations and intellectual baggage, what they have in common is that they are all phenomena that are best understood relationally. However, even if they are intuitive, complex, and thought-provoking, these concepts remain attempts to capture through metaphor the complex relations they seek to understand. In contrast to this, network science is predicated on the conviction that these relations can be explored and explained – by abstracting, modelling and analysing them qualitatively *and* quantitatively as networks – and provides a strong methodology to back this claim up.

The use of the term "network" in this work was at first primarily for epistemological and methodological reasons. It stemmed from an interest to use network analysis of complex archaeological relational data to gain a better grasp on the variable patterns of interactions. Along the way I realized that the concept of network also entailed a specific way of looking at relations in systems. The realization that network approaches are not only methodologically functional but also present specific views on how these relations operated intrigued me. The idea of interdependency – i.e. that a (social) network does not stand on its own, but is impacted by the dynamics and processes of other "types" of networks – seems to me to be particularly interesting. It presents a new way of connecting the interfaces between material and social fields, a conceptual struggle that has been the subject of over a decade of discussion in both social and material culture studies.

The idea of network interdependence strikes close to what has been written about in (post-)Maussian theories concerning the gift. Gift theories present a framework in which we find mutually constitutive relations between persons and gifts objects, the one cannot really function without the other. To my mind this mutualism between persons and their things is not contained to reciprocal exchange or Equality Matching relations, which was the focus of the enquiry carried out by Mauss. The interdependency between people and their things can be extrapolated to Communal Sharing, Authority Ranking, and Market Pricing relational models, as well – or, in other words, to all forms of human to human relations.

In Chapter 4 I discussed the ideas by Thomas Hobbes and Jean-Jacques Rousseau on sociality in a "state of nature". These Enlightenment theories, on the origin of cooperation and the origin of innovation respectively, make clear that if we wish to start to understand our social natures it is imperative to understand our material culture and vice versa. Yet the fact that the things we make also make us and especially our connections to others has been an undervalued premise of much of social theory and even most archaeological theory (Olsen 2010; Webmoor 2007; Webmoor and Witmore 2008). As a reaction, certain theories have conceived of things in a similar way as human subjects or agents. Following Maussian theory, specifically the *Essai sur le don* and its reception (Graeber 2001; Mauss 1923/1924), I have argued how this extreme materialist position is based on a confusion that arises from the fact that humans and things are constituent part of each other's networks.

This confusion is to some extent also present in gift theory. Following a Maussian theory of reciprocity, among "archaic" peoples, social relations are maintained because there is an "active force" – based on the idea of the Maori *hau* – ,a spirit in the gift, that moves people to reciprocate the things they are presented with. The majority of ethnographies on gift giving that followed up on Mauss his original idea show that when social relations become material, a different dynamic is at play. One important constituent of that is the "fixity" that things lend to social networks. Social relations may be continuously (re-)negotiated and manipulated, but the exchange of things give such relations a much more irrevocable and immutable character. Through their interdependencies with objects, social relations become more "fixed". Paradoxically, as Mauss showed this fixity is often achieved through the circulation of objects. Through circulation or other ways of becoming part of multiple social relations, humans and objects become part of networks that are both social and material. As I have discussed in the example of the Melanesian *kula* exchange, it only takes a few exchanges to go from a gift relation to a wider socio-material network.

Although such ethnographic analogies can be highly insightful, an Antillean theory of socio-material interdependency can actually be more profitably based on the ontologies of Lowland South American peoples from today or the recent past. Although there is no one-to-one correlation, it is possible to project some of their ideas back into the pre-colonial past of the Antilles. This has been done here by looking at overlaps or contrasts between core ontological concepts as they can be understood from ethnographic studies and the study of artefacts and ethnohistorical documents. This indicates that many different types of dependencies between people and things were conceived of and seen as part and parcel of (social) life.

For example, wider exchange networks may have been created and sustained as part of an "economy of life-forces" in which interacting with others and their things literally provided new life to communities (Santos-Granero 2009a; Vaughn Howard 2001). What is more, being a human, spirit-thing or any other type of subject meant being part of a system of other subjects and all the cosmological, social and political constraints and possibilities that this entailed. Society and culture was thus created by exchanging or otherwise interacting with other subjects, often other than human beings that were sometimes materialized as things. Based on origin narratives such as those of the Warao or the Hispaniolan narratives documented by Pané, it seems that this is even how central values and concepts of society and culture had been created in "before-time". Important as they were as expressions of society, things as materializations of spirits and other subjects are also highly dependent on humans. For one the potential of things to act as subjects is often only activated through communication and interaction with humans. It can thus be said that the agency and the (pro-)social and cultural character of individuals and collectives, whether they are humans, spirits, animals, or other type of beings, is created and maintained by the material engagement with other subjects.

This provides a particular, Amerindian take on socio-material networks, which can be difficult to recover and interpret through archaeological means. For instance, it may be the case that a subjective engagement with raw materials and their sources as social partners was at the root of the longevity of Long Island flint production, exchange and use, but this remains speculation. It is, however, more clearly exemplified by the model of *cacical* collectives, in which a perspectivist view of the political economy will identify spirit-things as important nodes in the network. *Guaízas* are a particularly interesting example of such socio-material other than human beings. In their capacity as conspicuous, elite ornaments they were both an exchange valuable and a "face" of a living spirit-thing. Thereby they connected communal, intercommunal and ritual economies.

Interestingly, their stylistic network also illustrates that these shell faces can be seen as a loose collective in which highly individualized shell faces were presumably consciously set apart from other specimens. The case-study on *guaízas* also showed that the distribution of things with faces was a core factor behind the formation of late pre-colonial Caribbean patterns of homogeneity and diversity. In fact, if we look at the type of pre-colonial "indigenous art" either neo-Taíno, replica, or real that is most popular nowadays among indigenous revivalists, tourists and collectors, objects with faces still have the greatest appeal. Items acting as socio-material connectors in the past once again present a united face that is projected into the present.

Still, after so much focus has been put on the material side of society and the social side of materials, I feel the need to nuance this standpoint somewhat. The fact that social and material networks are interdependent does not entail that the only way society can exist is by means of material culture. In theory – yet rarely in practice – it would be perfectly conceivable for any social relation to take place in a space devoid of material culture. However, what this interdependency implies is that, given the chance, human beings find it more parsimonious to frame or "scaffold" social relations with things (Knappett 2006, 2011). Regardless of cultural context, individuals will tend to maintain or manipulate their relations with others and seek to produce new ties through the circulation of material culture (Graeber 2001). This also goes the other way around: the "material world" can indeed form systems without the constant presence of people. Imagine, for example, a food web, the nodes and ties of river deltas or a river bank overgrown with roots. Some (near-)present technologies can also bring about independent material networks, such as those based on auto-catalytic ties in self-governing computer networks or self-healing properties of certain types of ceramics and polymers. Still, in general the scope and complexity of material networks is limited without human intervention.

As soon as human beings become involved, however, materials become material culture and new types of material networks come into being.

In contrast to broader views on "materiality" and human engagement or "entanglement" within the world of things (Dant 2005; Hodder 2012; Ingold 2007b; Miller 2005), I would argue that it is specifically in socio-material networks that things and human beings have the greatest impact on one another. This is a concept that was already established in the essentially "socio-material" arm-chair theories of philosophers such as Hobbes, Rousseau and other important thinkers such as Smith and Marx. How the origins of societies and material cultures are in actuality based on the interaction of these two systems is difficult to answer. Despite new insights on this old issue (Coward and Gamble 2008; Dunbar, *et al.* 2010b; Hart and Terrell 2002; Malafouris 2010; Renfrew, *et al.* 2008; Shennan 2002), we still know very little of the deep-time, co-evolution of material culture and social networks. For now any attempt to find the "prime movers", the ultimate causal factors, of social and material networks will lead to a chasing of tails.

Perhaps the real question is whether the age-old differentiation between social and material nature and culture is not the result of a specific Western dichotomy? It could well be that the intricate dialectics of socio-material networks are based on an unnecessary conceptual schism founded on the Enlightenment, Cartesian dichotomy of a human mind reasoning about an external world of things (Corbey, personal communication 2013). Although I am not able to formulate an alternative to this, I perceive that the duality between the social and material states of human nature and culture is ultimately an unnecessary complication.[2] I am especially strengthened in this view after starting to understand more about Amerindian ontologies and the relative efficacy with which human and things are conceptualized as being part of a much larger constellation of subjects. Here, human society does not result from a dualistic social and material culture but from the rhythm of conflicts and coalitions between beings with different perspectival states, of which objects are an integral part. This proves that it may be very fruitful for archaeologists to look closely to and learn from alternative, non-Western conceptualizations of "social networks" and how they coalesce around specific "material" nodes and vice versa.

Culture History 2.0?

Aside from the more general challenges of using network approaches in archaeology, one of the specific criticisms that can be levelled against this work is that, in an attempt to explain the history of the Caribbean in terms of social and material networks, this study remains a thoroughly culture historical undertaking. The critique being here that in the Caribbean, as in many other regional disciplines,

---

2   This insight comes quite close to the perspective of Actor-Network-Theory of Latour (2005). The major difference between the approach advocated here and ANT is that the latter would deem it impossible or destructive to try and understand the subject matter of social and material interdependency through a systemic study of structure such as graph theory or other network analyses – which is why the name Actor-*Network*-Theory is actually very misleading.

culture historical archaeology is an outmoded theoretical and methodological framework that has failed to come up with relevant answers to the questions of today (Pestle, *et al.* 2013).

I have unfortunately never met Benjamin Irving Rouse in person; he had retired before I even started my studies. However, his phylogenetic, modal-based, culture historical research has shaped my embryonic career as a Caribbean archaeologist. The larger part of the Caribbean archaeological literature I read as an (under)graduate student was either written by Rouse or presented a reaction to his ideas. So, although Rouse was not the only one that made important advances in the study of pre-colonial culture history, he may be considered as the spokesman of a highly successful research programme.[3] Nevertheless, as discussed in Chapter 1, at the beginning of the new millennium it was felt that the regional discipline was in crisis and needed to break free from the culture historical project and specifically the ideas of Rouse if it was to overcome it. With the benefit of hindsight, I think this sense of crisis was misplaced (*pace* Fitzpatrick 2006; Keegan and Rodríguez Ramos 2004). Caribbean archaeology did not find itself in troubled waters as a result of 6 decades of Roussean culture historical archaeology in the Caribbean. The fact is there was never such a crisis to begin with.[4]

It is true that the two most recent decades have seen a huge development in theory and method, an expansion and re-interpretation of archaeological data sets, as well as the geographic and cultural refocusing of research to the Caribbean basin as a whole. This is reflected in the themes forming the basis of the network case studies: the Archaic-Saladoid-Huecoid interface, and the multi-scalar nature of site assemblages, the late pre-colonial socio-political system, and the idea of "veneers" in material cultural assemblages. New developments have not only affected these debates, but are also clear from numerous discussions not mentioned here or only referred to in passing (see Keegan, *et al.* 2013). Some of the results of recent research will neither stand the test of time nor that of falsification, but the face of Caribbean archaeology has already changed for good.

I am inclined to state that, despite these clear achievements, on an epistemological level the core tenets and interests of the discipline have not changed since the early 20th century. Caribbean archaeologists then and now are interested in the

---

3 One of the major achievements of culture historical archaeology in the Caribbean is the fact that it bundled the efforts of archaeologists from various different mainland and island territories and intellectual traditions into a single research programme. The aim was to understand the absence and presence of ties between groups of material culture and frame this within larger issues of cultural and social developments. This also allowed for cross-cultural analyses and debates, for example in the case of archaeologically observable migrations or the falsification of a cultural ecological theory of chiefdoms and tribes in the Antilles (Rouse 1953, 1986).

4 Unfortunately pre-colonial Caribbean archaeology finds itself in numerous other crises. Two important issues concern the relevancy of pre-colonial Caribbean archaeology for the people living in the region today and the rapid destruction of pre-colonial heritage. Less pressing questions are: how do we present the findings of Caribbean archaeology in such a way that they become more relevant to the academic community at large and how can we continue to cooperate between researchers and research groups, threading together the disparate island archaeological records, while the institutional context and international job market is set up for competition? See also the perspective on the future of Caribbean archaeology by Wilson (2013) and the edited volume on issues facing Caribbean heritage by Siegel and Righter (2011).

social, cultural and political history of the Caribbean seeking to understand these subjects by means of the study of (human) mobility and interaction (Hofman and Bright 2010; Mol 2013; Siegel 2013). In other words, the culture historical project of comprehending patterns of homogeneity and diversity in the Caribbean archaeological record in human and historical terms continues. This has always been and remains for the foreseeable future the overarching research programme that brings the various strands of Caribbean archaeological research together – including the gap between Caribbean pre-historical and historical archaeologies (Curet and Hauser 2011).

In actual fact, what has occurred during the past years is not a Kuhnian paradigmatic shift as the result of a scientific crisis (Kuhn 1962). It was instead a Lakatosian re-focusing of the outer body of Caribbean theory, method and data, leaving its inner core intact (Lakatos 1978). It would be good to remember that successive generations of archaeologists continue to build on the same core research programme, even if some of their particular standpoints are in complete contrast to those of previous generations. This does not entail that Caribbean archaeology is stuck in outmoded theories and methods until it can be advanced by means of a revolutionary crisis, but that new developments and discoveries serve as a scaffold for future work. In this way, new data, methods and ideas can provide increasingly better – not necessarily different – answers to the venerable and central questions on cultural change, similarity and variance in this mainland and island world. The continuation of this research project by professional and avocational archaeologists is in fact one of the great strengths of the regional discipline, rather than a drawback.

As an extension of this insight, my own research referring to networks within the Caribbean can indeed not be called "revolutionary". The archaeological network approach suggested here cannot provide all the answers or even completely new ones. However, there are minor breakthroughs to be made when applying network thinking and analysis to issues of culture history, particularly in the area of categorization. This is best exemplified by the case-study of the *guaíza* design network as consisting not of a discrete category but as group that shared "family resemblances" (cf. Wittgenstein 1958: 32). The idea that there may be only a few or no common denominators for a set of objects, while they can still form a group is something that can be extended to the larger corpus of face-depicting objects in the Caribbean with future study. Furthermore, if this is extrapolated to (Caribbean) stylistic studies as a whole, 2-mode and other types of network-based similarity studies may be used to strengthen or refute many other ideas of diffuse categories like the Saladoid as a "veneer" or the Caribbean as "cultural mosaic" (Keegan 2004, 2007; Wilson 1993).

The Connected Caribbean: first forays into 6000 years of networked histories

The primary aim of my research was to present a network-based exploration of the patterns of homogeneity and diversity in the archaeological record of the Caribbean. This partly arose from a renewed interest in Pan-Caribbean mobility and interactions of people, goods and ideas. It is thus a legitimate question if we can use the socio-material network approach developed here to explore the archaeological record of the pre-colonial Caribbean as whole (Hofman and Bright 2010; Hofman and Hoogland 2011; Rodríguez Ramos and Pagán Jiménez 2006). The answer is negative. Pan-Caribbean networks cannot be abstracted or studied at this point in time or in the foreseeable future. As explained above, this has nothing to do with an incompatibility of network approaches with archaeological theory, method or data. Comprehending the patterns of homogeneity and diversity in *the* Caribbean in terms of socio-material network is impossible because (1) the geographic and temporal span of Caribbean networks is simply too large and (2) the archaeological coverage is too spotty. As I have shown here, it is possible to understand certain aspects of this immense social and cultural system by abstracting and exploring smaller networks from archaeological and historical cases. With more studies of this kind it would even be possible to link "separate" networks together, as they would have been in the past – e.g. study the overlaps between mainland and island lithic production and distribution networks. However, at this point in time we lack the databases as well as the perspective to model networks at the pan-regional level, let alone to grasp the social and cultural mechanisms and motivations behind them.

One of the contributions of the pan-Caribbean theory has been to take a new look at the possibility of long-distance, cross-Caribbean exchange networks that may have been at the basis of cross-regional socio-cultural patterns (Hofman and Bright 2011; Rodríguez Ramos 2010). The problem is that the majority of evidence for such extremely long-distance interactions is tentative or episodic. On the other hand as has become clear it only requires a single tie to connect two previously unconnected regions and even many smaller itinerant steps will finally fuse local networks into one pan-regional network. In other words the pervasiveness and impact of pan-Caribbean networks is an open-ended question in which we should be careful not to consider absence of evidence as evidence for absence. It is simply too early to close the book on this issue (*versus* Fitzpatrick 2013a).

It is better to change our way of thinking regarding this issue and accept it is likely that a constellation of pan-Caribbean social networks existed from the moment the islands and mainlands were inhabited. The question nonetheless remains what its impact has been on daily life on the one hand and culture historical processes on the other? It is specifically this issue concerning the micro- and macro-scale impacts of cross-Caribbean or other interregional ties that cannot be adequately dealt with at the moment, because it would for a start have depended on the frequency of interactions and the diameter of the pre-colonial social network. Can we estimate how many "handshakes" a fisherman from a pre-colonial village on Saba would have been removed from a Mayan king? No. Of course this is an absurd question to begin with, but it illustrates that at present the impact of pan-regional interactions cannot be systematically assessed by means of a network approach.

For now it is therefore much more feasible and fruitful to discuss specific social and material cultural networks, compare these to Caribbean networks of other types or similar ones from other regions, and perhaps draw general inferences from this, instead of theorizing on the impact of literally immeasurable pan-Caribbean systems. In this way we may at some point better understand how single systems fuse into societal and (material) cultural systems of a pan-regional scale and possibly beyond. In the process this will advance our knowledge of the history of the wider region to the point that we will understand how societal and cultural processes are connected and dynamic instead of monolithic. The case studies in Chapters 5 to 8 represent only some of the first steps in this direction.

At the moment the nature of the available data also affects the possibility of applying (popular) network models, such as the small-world or scale-free model, in order to characterize and explain the formation and evolution of networks that can be abstracted from archaeological assemblages. I do not reject the possibility that it may be feasible to observe small-world, scale-free or other network models in some archaeological data sets. Still, the type of networks I abstracted from the data at hand did not show any correlation with any of the network science models discussed in Chapter 1 – with the exception of the lattice-shaped geographic layout of the Northeastern Caribbean islands. Admittedly, the relational database and type of networks were far from ideal or even typical of such an undertaking. Regardless, as dealt with in Chapter 5, when referring to the tentative sequential growth, preferential attachment and fitness of the lithic distribution networks, applying specific models to archaeological cases without a clear idea of their diachronic and contextual dynamics will not bring the interpretation of a data-driven network any further. It even risks replicating the model's inherent assumptions. In other words, they may be popular, highly cited examples of network models, it remains to be seen if they are best suited for understanding most archaeological cases (cf. Brughmans 2013). Before this topic can be addressed any further we need to have a better base-line understanding of network models as they pertain to archaeological cases.

Based on the case studies it also remains difficult to conclude that a certain model of relation dominated during specific moments in time (Fiske 1991). However, it is feasible to positively identify certain models of relation such as Authority Ranking and Equality Matching in certain periods of the lithic distribution network (e.g. Period C, D and E). Furthermore, in combination with substantive lines of evidence it should be clear that the Caribbean must have seen its fair share of Communal Sharing (see also Mol 2010). For example, Kelbey's Ridge 2's archaeological record presents a set of intense and exclusively communal relations (Chapter 6), while the information on the arrival of Columbus is indicative of a Greater Antillean and perhaps even Pan-Antillean network in which useful bits of information were freely shared (Mol 2011a). Beyond the ethnohistoric accounts of barter the presence of Market Pricing relational models is difficult to substantiate at present. A future diachronic exploration of Market Pricing and Communal Sharing models in the archaeological record will lead to new and interesting lines of research, especially with regard to the prevalence of such relational models in the early contact period. Irrespective of specific cases, this base-line model opens up traditional notions concerning the limited presence of social economies beyond redistributive, prestige good or gift exchange to include all forms of human social relations.

The networks in Chapters 5 to 8 did allow for many case-specific insights. I shall reiterate some thought-provoking ones here. For example, in Period E (AD 100-400) not more than six "handshakes", or exchanges of stone materials, separated an inhabitant of the village of Maisabel in Puerto Rico from a member of the community of Brighton Beach on St. Vincent. What is more, a longitudinal view of this distribution network shows that material cultural practices and assemblages and the peoples they represent can be connected from the first peopling of the North-east Caribbean to late pre-colonial communities such as those at Kelbey's Ridge 2 on Saba. The ego-network also indicated that even in late pre-historic times smaller communities located in assumedly frontier regions were seated at the heart of multi-levelled interaction networks, in strategic locations with access to important local and regional resources and tapped into a pan-Antillean system of valuables. Stylistic network analysis can show that these valuables had similar yet unique designs, such as a *guaíza* from the Eastern Dominican Republic that had more in common with a shell face from La Désirade (Guadeloupe) than with any other shell face. It can also point out that a group of geographically proximal, shell faces in the Cuban region of Banés had actually little in common with each other. Other lines of evidence can illustrate how *guaíza*s and other valuables were strategically used in flexible, interdependent political economies. This can be combined with an ethnohistorically informed view of *cacique*s and their networked collectives. This suggests that, with regard to their success, *cacical* collectives were critically reliant on other power figures than the *cacique*, or chief, whether they were other humans or inspirited socio-material beings, like *guaíza*s.

If we connect individual insights such as these and thread them together, it becomes possible to start putting Northeastern Caribbean pre-colonial networks into perspective. One aspect that has become clear from all lines of evidence discussed in the present study is that the networks of the indigenous peoples of the Caribbean were essentially robust, inclusive and outward-looking systems. If we further take into account other lines of evidence for extensive toing and froing within archipelagos and the sometimes extreme (1000 km or more) long-distance procurement of goods, one could even say that throughout history these peoples linked a keen, even entrepreneurial interest in exotic contacts and material culture with strong local traditions.

Such qualifications seem to contradict the stereotyped view of indigenous Caribbean peoples as somewhat naïve, pastoral or barbaric "islanders" which they gained as a result of colonial representations. Yet even when close-reading the primary historic sources it is clear that this stereotype does not do justice to the two-sidedness of early contact situations such as between Guacanagarí and Columbus discussed in Chapter 4. As was the case with the interactions between these two men from very different parts of the world, before contact wider inter-island networks seem to have been set up in such a way that individuals, communities and their things could interact and wander across various cultural, ethnic and linguistic borders with relative ease, without losing their particular character. Indeed, as seen from the scope of their networks, instead of characterizing them as "islanders" it may be more apt to refer to the indigenous peoples of the Northeastern Caribbean as "archipelagists" – the type of people that mixes a strong local character with an outward-looking attitude.

Although these early contact networks that emerged from the encounters between indigenous and European (and later African) peoples were not a main theme of this work, as a final remark I wish to point out that the deep history of the Caribbean should not be separated from the upheaval of the colonial period. In fact, because they are part of unbroken chains of interaction, pre-colonial networks can even inform us of how the "network society" of our time came to be. Albeit that extensive research has been carried out on the global network that emerged after the first sustained contacts between the Old and the New World, we as yet know very little of the ways in which indigenous Caribbean social and cultural systems contributed to this process. This glaring lapse in our knowledge, underlain by a continued disregard for the value and particularities of alternative histories of non-Western peoples, has served to obscure the impact that indigenous peoples and their networks had on world history. The application of network approaches by means of archaeological and historic sources has a huge potential to connect the history of the pre-colonial and the contemporary Caribbean to that of the rest of the world.[5]

---

5   This challenge will be undertaken as part of a synergy programme set up by Leiden University (prof. dr. Hofman and prof. dr. Willems) the Free University of Amsterdam (prof. dr. Davies) and Konstanz University (prof. dr. Brandes). This research project, called *Nexus 1492*, is funded by the European Research Council. Having commenced in September 2013, it seeks to establish a new understanding of the role Caribbean indigenous people played in the global transformations that began with the first contacts between them and Europeans in 1492. I will collaborate with other researchers from archaeology and the network sciences in order to continue the line of research explored here as part of a post-doctoral research project.

Acknowledgements

Every science is the product of collective work

Marcel Mauss 1998: 30

Marcel Mauss, to my mind one of the great scholars of the 20th century, has it right. Every science *is* the product of collective work. This is definitely true for archaeology, in which so many people and things need to come together in the production of a scholarly work. It is therefore no exaggeration to say that this thesis owes much of its existence to the following collective of people.

First of all, I would like to thank my *promotor* Prof Dr. Corinne L. Hofman and my *co-promotor* Prof. Dr. Raymond Corbey for the supervision of my PhD project. More than that, I would like to thank both of them for the opportunities, advice, and faith they have extended to me in the course of my PhD studies, often going above and beyond their duties as supervisors. They allowed me to expand my interests and skills into fields that are increasingly critical for becoming a successful, young academic, such as teaching, fieldwork, (research) management, writing of grant proposals, paper presentations and publications, and transdisciplinary research and collaboration.

This work is the result of the *Communicating Communities in the Circum-Caribbean* research project, funded as a Dutch NWO-VICI research programme and headed by Prof. Dr. Hofman. Furthermore, Corinne L. Hofman and Menno L. P. Hoogland were at the cradle of one of the other essential ingredients for my PhD research: Leiden University's Caribbean Research Group. They and all the other members of the Caribbean Research Group with whom I studied and worked with from 2005 (the start of my Master studies) onwards are thanked for jointly creating a vibrant, stimulating and collegial academic environment. This thesis is only one of the many outcomes of the NWO-VICI project mentioned above and in many ways this study has been critically reliant on the overall and specific results of this project. In fact, I would not even have been able to start asking and answering the broad questions that are discussed here if it were not for the more specific thematic and methodological interests of other members of the Caribbean Research Group. I would also like to thank the members of the new *Nexus 1492* (ERC Synergy), *Caribbean Connections* (HERA) and *Island Networks* (NWO) projects. Although new lines of research on the study of the transformations in indigenous societies and cultures of the pre-colonial and early colonial Caribbean have not yet been incorporated in this work, their novel insights have already given me many new things to think about and explore in future work.

I would like to extend a word of gratitude to the wider Caribbean archaeological community, whose studies also provided critical groundwork for my own. This thesis is just one example of how one product is rooted in the work of a collective of Caribbean local and non-local, professional and avocational archaeologists. In particular, I would like to express my profound thanks to the following individuals for their assistance and companionship during my travels in the region from 2006 to 2013 (ordered chronologically): Roberto Valcárcel Rojas, his wife Hidalmis, his son Lino, other members of his family and his colleagues at the CITMA in Holguín (Cuba), Reg Murphy (Antigua), Lennox Honychurch (Dominica), Gerry Aird and his family (Dominica), Eduardo Herrera (IVIC, Venezuela), Rodrigo Navarete (Universidad Central, Venezuela), Rafael Gassón (IVIC, Venezuela), Franz Scaramelli (IVIC, Venezuela), Kay Tarble (IVIC, Venezuela), Andrzej and Marlena Antczak and their family (Universidad Simón Bolívar, Venezuela), Lilliam Arvélo (IVIC, Venezuela), Jorge Ulloa, his wife Jypsis, son Enmanuel, and the other members of his family, Harold Olsen (Museo del Hombre Dominicano), Lou Jacobs, Yann Hoogland, Marc Bautil and family (Doña Elvira, Dominican Republic), Lesley Gail-Atkinson (JNHT, Jamaica), George Lechler (Jamaica), Paul Banks (Jamaica), Kathy Martin, Rachel Moses and co-workers (SVG National Trust, St. Vincent), Jay Haviser (SIMARC, St. Maarten), Grant Gilmore III (SECAR, St. Eustatius), and Ryan Espersen (SABARC, Saba).

A special word of thanks goes out to Dr. Arie Boomert. He has been invaluable both as a mentor and travelling companion. In addition, he supervised my MA thesis, which is expanded on in Chapter 8, as well as proofread, edited and commented on Chapter 2. I would also like to thank Sebastiaan Knippenberg, Reniel Rodríguez Ramos and Corinne Hofman for our joint work on a paper presented at the IACA in 2011, of which Chapter 5 provides an in-depth discussion of the network explorations undertaken there. Menno Hoogland and Corinne Hofman are thanked for the discussions and information provided on the study of the ego-networks of Saba (Chapter 6). I am grateful to Jimmy Mans for co-authoring a chapter on "Old Boys in the Indigenous Caribbean" with me, which featured an incipient version of the ethnohistorical study on socio-political organization in Chapter 7. My warmest regards go out to Peter Richardus for his excellent and efficient editing of the thesis manuscript.

I would like to thank all the participants of the "Re-connecting the Past" Forum at the 2013 SAA in Honolulu and in particular my co-organizer Mark Golitko. The Forum's lively discussion on the strengths, weaknesses, opportunities and threats that face network approaches in archaeology, allowed me to better formulate my own ideas about this topic, as reflected in Chapter 9. The organizers and tutors of the 2009 POLNET summer course, in particular Prof. Dr. Ulrik Brandes, are thanked for my first introduction in the world of network theory and method. My early and continuing discussions with John Terrell on the topics of networks in archaeology (and beyond) not only served to strengthen my conviction that network approaches could be used to further Caribbean archaeological questions, but that this interest was shared by archaeologists and anthropologists from many other regions. José Oliver is thanked for our discussions on *cemís, guaízas* and other things as well as for the many brilliant stories of Caribbean archaeological explorations and larger than life characters. I would like to acknowledge Peter Siegel for his course on socio-political organization, which he taught as part of his Fulbright scholarship at Leiden. The discussions during these classes helped to further shape my arguments in Chapter 7. Jago Cooper, William Keegan and Antonio Curet are thanked for their continued interactions and discussions with me and other members of the Caribbean Research Group, among other occasions as part of "Leiden in the Caribbean" conferences. I am also grateful to Eithne Carlin (Faculties of the Humanities, Leiden University): thanks to our joint teaching of a Graduate course on "Amerindian Ontologies", my own thinking and knowledge on this topic has been greatly advanced.

Institutional co-workers too often remain unmentioned in academic acknowledgements. Therefore I wish to explicitly voice my gratitude to all my other colleagues at the Faculty of Archaeology. Of course this refers to the community of researchers and teachers, but also entails the supporting staff members. Together they provide an extremely fertile and friendly ground for archaeological research and education in a stimulatingly large range of thematic and geographical areas. Specifically, I would like to thank Dr. Roswitha Manning, secretary of the Graduate School with whom I also co-organized several Graduate School Workshops, my fellow Archaeological Forum-committee members, Adam Jagich, Alice Samson, Bleda Düring, and Eleanor Croxall, as well as the members of the Mesoamerican Research Group headed by Prof. Dr. Jansen. I would also like to acknowledge the Graduate School of the Faculty of Archaeology for their financial support in publishing this work. In addition, I have also enjoyed interacting with and learned much from the students that took part in courses I taught on *Mobility and Exchange* and *Shamanism and Cosmovision in Archaeology* as well as the Leiden University *Honours College.*

I feel privileged in that I do not only have great friends but great groups of old and new friends both within and outside of the archaeological profession. There are simply too many to mention them all. In particular I would like to thank my current and previous hockey teammates. The "three halves" of our Sunday hockey match have been and will remain an important and highly enjoyable non-academic outlet for me. I would also like to thank the "nerds who shall not be named and shamed" for engaging with me in some badly needed Monday night escapism.

I express my deepest thanks to Alice, Alistair, Anne, Daan, Eva, Jason, Jimmy, Joost, Jorge and Roberto, for their continued inspiration as scholars and friends. Some of you, together with other epicureans like Maarten, Tim and Peppie always know how to replenish my morale during our regular end of the week *curryworst* fests. I express my gratitude to Laura, Marije and Noortje for lending out their guys to me every other Friday and, of course, for being good friends. These friendships and those with others from the *Entre Nous* group helped me through some of the more difficult moments in my life, especially after the sudden death of my father which happened when I had just started my PhD research.

Stefan, Karim, Evert, nothing I can say here would express how grateful I am for a friendship that has already lasted (more than) half our lives. During that period much has changed, but my admiration and affection for you as friends, intellectuals and *bon vivants* has only deepened. Lex, my kind and greathearted friend, I miss you still. Nevertheless, I am glad for getting to know your wonderful parents, Peter and Hanneke, much better over the last ten years.

Like every science is the product of collective work, every prospective career "scientist" is the product of a collective labor of love. I have only ever felt love, support, trust and respect from and for my uncles, aunts, great uncles and great aunts. Being the eldest cousin in our family and so the first to start studying, it is great to see all my cousins now do at least equally well in their lives, studies and careers. They and I owe much to my grandparents, even if they have now long gone from our lives. Their love and enthusiasm gave me an early boost in self-confidence and positive thinking, something which any prospective PhD will need ample amounts of. This tradition is continued by my sisters, Annedith and Annick. When writing about "family resemblances" in Chapter 8, I was continuously reminded of my bond with you. You are wonderful, one of a kind, persons who I still resemble and relate to in all ways that matter. Fortunately, the same can be said for the partners you share your lives with. Most of all, I consider myself to be an extremely fortunate son to have a mother like Anja Mol-Verkade. Mama, not only because of my upbringing, but also through your continued support and love can I be the person that I am today. Any *gouden stapelbed* that I happen to encounter in my archaeological work has your name on it.

When people ask what I do for a living and I tell them I am a Caribbean archaeologist, they are often intrigued or sometimes jealous. When I add to that: "So is my girlfriend," they often are less enthusiastic, asking: "Does that not get boring if your partner is working in the same place on the same things?" If they ask this, they clearly have not met Hayley Mickleburgh. The last thing I would say that you bring to my life is boredom. For one, even if this is not always clear for outsiders, we work in the same region but on vastly different topics, using completely different approaches and can hold very contrasting opinions on matters large and small. Granted, it has sometimes been difficult to work on our PhDs at the same time – if going camping is considered a good way to test if your relationship is future-proof, try simultaneously finishing your PhD theses. Yet even during the most stressful times you and I were able to strike a balance between work and normal life, even when our work is also our passion. I thank you for paving the way, having my back *and* being at my side during these years. We make for a dynamic duo that I wouldn't change for the world.

Finally, I thank my father for his love and support as well as the wisdom he has imparted on me throughout and by his life. My father, a long-time sailor and all-time dreamer, was too oriented on living in the present and thinking about the future to have a passion for or even take a deeper interest in studies of the past. Still, I feel that our outlook on life is ultimately not that different. It can be defined by a curiosity that drives one to try and peer beyond the horizon to what is not yet or, in my case, no longer visible. Furthermore, there is a shared love for the repeating patterns of the Caribbean, he for those of its waves and sea, I for those of its islands and past. I write this sitting behind his old desk that now stands in my home office, which is only one of the many ways I continue to feel his presence in my life. I dedicate this book to his memory.

Bibliography

Agorsah, E. Kofi

    1993   An Objective Chronological Scheme for Caribbean History and Archaeology. *Social and Economic Studies* 42(1): 119-147.

Alegría, Ricardo E.

    1980   *Cristóbal Columbus y el Tesoro de los Indios Taínos de Española*. Ediciones Fundación García Arévalo, Santo Domingo, Dominican Republic.

Allaire, Louis

    1977   Later Prehistory in Martinique and the Island Caribs: Problems in Ethnic Identification. Unpublished PhD thesis, Graduate School, Yale University, New Haven.

    1990   Prehistoric Taino Interaction with the Lesser Antilles. Paper presented at the 55th congress of the Society for American Archaeology, Las Vegas, Nevada.

Allsworth-Jones, Philip

    2008   *Pre-Columbian Jamaica*. University of Alabama Press, Tuscaloosa, Alabama.

Anderson, Benedict

    1991   *Imagined Communities*. Verso Books, London.

Antczak, María Magdalena and Andrzej Antczak

    2006   *Los Ídolos de las Islas Prometidas*. Editorial Equinoccio, Caracas, Venezuela.

Appadurai, Arjun

    1986   Introduction: Commodities and the Politics of Value. In *The Social Life of Things: Commodities in Cultural Perspective*, edited by Arjun Appadurai, pp. 3-63. Cambridge University Press, Cambridge, United Kingdom.

Århem, Kaj

    1996   The Cosmic Food Web: Human-Nature Relatedness in the Northwest Amazon. In *Nature and Society: Anthropological Perspectives*, edited by Philippe Descola and Gísli Pálson. Routledge, London.

Arrom, José J.

    1975   *Mitología y Artes Prehispánicas de las Antillas*. Siglo veintiuno editors, Mexico D.F., Mexico.

Arroyo, Miguel, Lourdes Blanco and Erika Wagner (editors)

    1999   *El Arte Prehispánico De Venezuela*. Fundación Galería de Arte Nacional, Caracas, Venezuela.

Atkinson, Lesley-Gail (editor)

    2006   *The Earliest Inhabitants: The Dynamics of the Jamaican Taíno*. University of the West Indies Press, Kingston, Jamaica.

Axelrod, Robert M.

    1997   *The Complexity of Cooperation: Agent-Based Models of Competition and Collaboration*. Princeton University Press, Princeton, New Jersey.

Axelrod, Robert M. and William D. Hamilton

    1981   The Evolution of Cooperation. *Science* 211(4489): 1390.

Benítez Rojo, Antonio

    1998   *La Isla Que Se Repite*. Editorial Casiopea, Barcelona, Spain.

Bentley, R. Alexander and Herbert D. G. Maschner

    2003   *Complex Systems and Archaeology: Empirical and Theoretical Applications*. University of Utah Press, Salt Lake City, Utah.

Bentley, R. Alexander and Stephen J. Shennan

    2003   Cultural Transmission and Stochastic Network Growth. *American Antiquity*: 459-485.

Bérard, Benoit

    2004   *Les Premieres Occupations Agricoles de l'Arc Antillais, Migrations et Insularite: le Cas de l'Occupation Saladoïde Ancienne de la Martinique*. Archaeopress, Oxford, United Kingdom

    2013   The Saladoid. In *The Oxford Handbook of Caribbean Archaeology*, edited by William F. Keegan, Corinne L. Hofman and Reniel Rodríguez Ramos, pp. 184-198. Oxford University Press, Oxford, United Kingdom.

Bérard, Benoit, Jean-Yves Billard and Bruno Ramstein

    2011   Ioumoúlicou: "Koumoúlicou Nhányem Amonchéentium Oúbao," the Caribs from the Other Islands Are People from Our Nation. *Proceedings of the 23rd Congress of the International Association for Caribbean Archaeology*: 577-589. Antigua.

Bercht, Fatima, Estrellita Brodsky, John A. Farmer and Dicey Taylor (editors)

    1997   *Taíno: Pre-Columbian Art and Culture from the Caribbean*. The Monacelli Press/El Museo del Barrio, New York.

Bérnaldez, Andres

    1992   Memoirs of the Catholic Sovereigns' Reign. In *Christopher Columbus's Discoveries in the Testimonials of Diego Alvarez Chanca and Andres Bernáldez*, edited by Anna Unali, pp. 63-203. Istituto Poligrafico e Zecca dello Stato and Libreria dello Stato, Rome.

Billard, Jean-Yves, Benoit Bérard and Bruno Ramstein

    2009   Apport de l'Hydrostatique à l'Archéologie Expérimentale: Etude d'une Pirogue de Haute Mer (Kanawa). Paper presented at the 19th Congrès Français de Mécanique, Marseille.

Blancaneaux, Annabelle F.

    2009   Contribution à l'Étude de la Disparition de la Culture Saladoïde aux Petites Antilles. Corrélation Préhistorique Possible Entre Climat et Culture. Unpublished PhD thesis, Université des Antilles et de la Guyane and Université Paris I, Panteón Sorbonne.

Blanton, Richard E., Gary M. Feinman, Stephen A. Kowalewski and Peter N. Peregrine

    1996   A Dual-Processual Theory for the Evolution of Mesoamerican Civilization. *Current Anthropology* 37(1): 1-14.

Bond, Gloria

    2006   *Sons of Yocahu: A Saga of the Tainos' Devastation on Hispaniola*. S & S Press, Clayton, New York.

Bonnissent, Dominique

    2008   Archéologie Précolombienne de l'Île de Saint-Martin, Petites Antilles: (3300 BC - 1600 AD). Unpublished PhD thesis, Civilisations et Humanités, Université Aix-Marseille, Marseille.

2013 *Les Gisements Précolombiens de la Baie Orientale: Campements du Mésoindien et du Néoindien sur l'île de Saint-Martin (Petites Antilles)*. Maison des Sciences de l'Homme, Paris.

Boomert, Arie

1986 The Cayo Complex of St. Vincent: Ethnohistorical and Archaeological Aspects of the Island Carib Problem. *Antropológica* 67: 33-54.

1987 Gifts of the Amazons: "Green Stone" Pendants and Beads as Items of Ceremonial Exchange in Amazonia and the Caribbean. *Antropológica* 67: 33-54.

2000 *Trinidad, Tobago and the Lower Orinoco Interaction Sphere: An Archaeological/ Ethnohistorical Study*. Cairi Publications, Alkmaar, Netherlands.

2001a Saladoid Sociopolitical Organization. *Proceedings of the 18th International Congress for Caribbean Archaeology*: 1-21. St. George, Grenada.

2001b Names for Tobago. *Journal de la Societé des Américanistes* 87: 339-349.

2001c Raptorial Birds as Icons of Shamanism in the Prehistoric Caribbean and Amazonia. *Proceedings of the 19th International Congress for Caribbean Archaeology*: 1-4&1-33. Aruba.

2009 Between the Mainland and the Islands: The Amerindian Cultural Geography of Trinidad. *Bulletin of the Peabody Museum of Natural History* 50(1): 63-73.

2011 From Cayo to *Kalinago*. In *Communities in Contact: Essays in Archaeology, Ethnohistory and Ethnography of the Amerindian Circum-Caribbean*, edited by Corinne L. Hofman and Anne van Duijvenbode, pp. 291-306. Sidestone Press, Leiden, the Netherlands.

Boomert, Arie and Alistair J. Bright

2007 Island Archaeology: In Search of a New Horizon. *Island Studies Journal* 2(1): 3-26.

Borgatti, Stephen P. and Martin G. Everett

1997 Network Analysis of 2-Mode Data. *Social Networks* 19: 243-269.

Borgatti, Stephen P., Ajay Mehra, Daniel J. Brass and Giuseppe Labianca

2009 Network Analysis in the Social Sciences. *Science* 323(5916): 892-895.

Bourdieu, Pierre

1977 *Outline of a Theory of Practice*. Cambridge University Press, Cambridge, United Kingdom.

1984 *Distinction: A Social Critique of the Judgement of Taste*. Translated by Richard Nice. Harvard University Press, Cambridge, Massachussets.

1997 Marginalia: Some Additional Notes on the Gift. In *The Logic of the Gift: Toward an Ethic of Generosity*, edited by Alan D. Schrift, pp. 231-245. Routledge, London.

Brandes, Ulrik and Thomas Erlebach (editors)

2005 *Network Analysis: Methodological Foundations*. Springer Verlag, Berlin.

Brandes, Ulrik, Linton C. Freeman and Dorothea Wagner

2012 Social Networks. In *Handbook of Graph Drawing and Visualization*, edited by Roberto Tamassia, pp. 803-837. CRC Press, Boca Raton, Florida.

Brandes, Ulrik, Garry Robins, Ann McCranie and Stanley Wasserman

2013 What Is Network Science? *Network Science* 1(1): 1-15.

Brandes, Ulrik and Dorothea Wagner

2004 Analysis and Visualization of Social Networks. In *Graph Drawing Software*, edited by Michael Jünger and Petra Mutzel, pp. 321-340. Springer Verlag, Berlin.

Breton, Père Raymond

    1999 [1665]   *Dictionnaire Caraïbe-Francais*. Éditions Karthala et IRD, Paris.

Breukel, Thomas W.

    2013   Threepointers on Trial: A Biographical Study of Amerindian Ritual Artefacts from the Pre-Columbian Caribbean. Unpublished MA thesis, Faculty of Archaeology, Leiden University, Leiden, the Netherlands.

Bright, Alistair J.

    2011   *Blood Is Thicker Than Water: Amerindian Intra- and Inter-Insular Relationships and Social Organizaton in the Pre-Colonial Windward Islands*. Sidestone Press, Leiden, the Netherlands.

Brink, Stefan and Neil Price

    2008   *The Viking World*. Routledge, New York.

Broodbank, Cyrprian

    2000   *An Island Archaeology of the Early Cyclades*. Cambridge University Press, Cambridge, United Kingdom.

Brughmans, Tom

    2012   Facebooking the Past: A Critical Social Network Analysis Approach for Archaeology. *In Thinking Beyond the Tool: Archaeological Computing and the Interpretive Process*, edited by Angelika Chrysanthi, Patricia M. Flores, & Constantinos Papadopoulos, pp. 191-203. Archaeopress, Oxford, United Kingdom.

    2013   Thinking through Networks: A Review of Formal Network Methods in Archaeology. *Journal of Archaeological Method and Theory*: 1-40.

    in press   The Roots and Shoots of Archaeological Network Analysis: A Citation Analysis and Review of the Archaeological Use of Formal Network Methods. *Archaeological Review from Cambridge* 29(1).

Bruijn, Iris

    2009   *Ship's Surgeons of the Dutch East India Company: Commerce and the Progress of Medicine in the Eighteenth Century*. Amsterdam University Press, Amsterdam.

Bullen, Ripley P. and Adelaide K. Bullen

    1975   Culture Areas and Climaxes in Antillean Prehistory. *Proceedings of the 6th International Congress for the Study of Pre-Columbian Cultures of the Lesser Antilles*: 1 t/m 10. Guadeloupe.

Caldwell, Joseph R. (editor)

    1964   *Interaction Spheres in Prehistory*. Illionois State Museum, Springfield, Illinois.

Callaghan, Richard T.

    1990   Mainland Origins of the Preceramic Cultures of the Greater Antilles. Unpublished PhD thesis, University of Calgary, Canada.

    1993   Passage to the Greater Antilles: An Analysis of Watercraft and the Marine Environment. *Proceedings of the 14th Congress of the International Association for Caribbean Archaeology*, pp. 65-71, Barbados.

    2001   Ceramic Age Seafaring and Interaction Potential in the Antilles: A Computer Simulation. *Current Anthropology* 42: 308-313.

    2010   Crossing the Guadeloupe Passage in the Archaic Age. *Island Shores, Distant Pasts: Archaeological and Biological Approaches to the pre-Columbian Settlement of the Caribbean*, edited by Scott M. Fitzpatrick and Ann Ross, pp. 127-147, University of Florida Press, Florida.

2013 Archaeological Views of Caribbean Seafaring. In *The Oxford Handbook of Caribbean Archaeology*, edited by William F. Keegan, Corinne L. Hofman and Reniel Rodríguez Ramos, pp. 283-295. Oxford University Press, Oxford, United Kingdom.

Callaghan, Richard T. and Stephanie J. Schwabe

2001 Watercraft of the Islands. *Proceedings of the 18th Congress of the International Association for Caribbean Archaeology* 1999: 231-242. St. Georges, Grenada.

Campbell, Shirley F.

2002 *The Art of Kula*. Berg, Oxford, United Kingdom.

Carlin, Eithne B.

2004 *A Grammar of Trio: A Cariban Language of Suriname*. Peter Lang, Frankfurt Am Main, Germany.

Carlson, Elizabeth

1993 Strings of Command: Manufacture and Utilization of Shell Beads among the Taino Indians of the West Indies. Unpublished MA thesis, University of Florida, Gainesville.

Castells, Manuel

2011 *The Rise of the Network Society: The Information Age: Economy, Society, and Culture* 1. Wiley-Blackwell, Chichester, United Kingdom.

Chacon, Richard J. and David H. Dye

2007 Introduction to Human Trophy Taking: An Ancient and Widespread Practice. In *The Taking and Displaying of Human Body Parts as Trophies by Amerindians*, edited by Richard J. Chacon and David H. Dye, pp. 5-31. Springer, New York.

Chanca, Diego Alvarez

1992 [1493] "Letter" to the Mayor of Seville. In *Christopher Columbus's Discoveries in the Testimonials of Diego Alvarez Chanca and Andres Bernáldez*, edited by Anna Unali, pp. 11-59. Istituto Poligrafico e Zecca dello Stato and Libreria dello Stato, Rome.

Chanlatte Baik, Luis A.

1984 *Arqueología De Vieques*. Editora Corripio, Santo Domingo, República Dominicana.

2013 Huecoid Culture and the Antillean Agroalfarero. In *The Oxford Handbook of Caribbean Archaeology*, edited by William F. Keegan, Corinne L. Hofman and Reniel Rodríguez Ramos, pp. 171-183. Oxford University Press, Oxford, United Kingdom.

Chanlatte Baik, Luis A. and Yvonne M. Narganes Storde

1990 *La Nueva Arqueología de Puerto Rico: Su Proyección en las Antillas*. Editora Taller, Santo Domingo, Dominican Republic.

2005 *Cultura la Hueca*. Museo de Historia, Antropología y Arte, San Juan, Puerto Rico.

Chapman, John and Bisserka Gaydarska

2007 *Parts and Wholes: Fragmentation in Prehistoric Context*. Oxbow Books, Oxford, United Kingdom.

Chapman, Robert

2003 *Archaeologies of Complexity*. Routledge, London.

Cheal, David

1996 'Showing Them You Love Them': Gift Giving and the Dialectic of Intimacy. In *The Gift: An Interdisciplinary Perspective*, edited by Aafke Komter, pp. 95-107. Amsterdam University Press, Amsterdam.

Cherry, John F., Krysta Ryzewski, Thomas P. Leppard and & Emanuela Bocancea

    2012   The Earliest Phase of Settlement in the Eastern Caribbean: New evidence from Montserrat. *Antiquity* 86(333): 1-5.

Churampi Ramírez, Adrianan

    2007   Caizcimu: el Cacicazgo Oriental Escenario de la Tristemente Célebre Bahía de las Flechas y de las Feroces Guerras de Higüey. *Caribe Arqueológico* 10: 165-172.

Cody, Ann K.

    1990   Prehistoric Patterns of Exchange in the Lesser Antilles: Materials, Models and Observations. Unpublished MA thesis, Department of Anthropology, San Diego State University, San Diego.

Coleman, Simon

    2004   The Charismatic Gift. *Journal of the Royal Anthropological Institute* 10(2): 421-442.

Collar, Anna

    2007   Network Theory and Religious Innovation. *Mediterranean Historical Review* 22(1): 149-162.

Conrad, Geoffrey W., Charles D. Beeker, Christophe Descantes, John W. Foster and Michael D. Glascock

    2008   Compositional Analysis of Ceramics from La Aleta, Dominican Republic: Implications for Site Function and Organisation. *Journal of Caribbean Archaeology* special issue #2: 57-68.

Conrad, Geoffrey W., John W. Foster and Charles D. Beeker

    2001   Organic Artefacts from the Manantial de la Aleta, Dominican Republic: Preliminary Observations and Interpretations. *Journal of Caribbean Archaeology* 2: 1-20.

Cooper, Jago

    2007   Island Interaction in the Prehistoric Caribbean: An Archaeological Case Study from Northern Cuba. Unpublished PhD thesis, University College London, London.

    2013   The Climatic Context for Pre-Columbian Archaeology in the Caribbean. In *The Oxford Handbook of Caribbean Archaeology*, edited by William F. Keegan, Corinne L. Hofman and Reniel Rodríguez Ramos, pp. 47-58. Oxford University Press, Oxford, United Kingdom.

Cooper, Jago and Richard Boothroyd

    2011   Living Islands of the Caribbean: A View of Relative Sea Level Change from the Waters Edge. In *Communities in Contact: Essays in Archaeology, Ethnohistory and Ethnography of the Amerindian Circum-Caribbean*, edited by Corinne L. Hofman and Anne van Duijvenbode, pp. 393-406. Sidestone Press, Leiden, the Netherlands.

Cooper, Jago, Marcos Martinón-Torres and Roberto Valcárcel Rojas

    2008   American Gold and European Brass: Metal Objects and Indigenous Values in the Cemetary of El Chorro de Maíta, Cuba. In *Crossing the Borders: New Methods and Techniques in the Study of Archaeological Materials from the Caribbean*, edited by Corinne L Hofman, Menno L. P. Hoogland and Annelou L. van Gijn. Alabama University Press, Tuscaloosa, Alabama.

Copeman, Jacob

    2005   Veinglory: Exploring Processes of Blood Transfer between Persons. *Journal of the Royal Anthropological Institute* 11(3): 465-485.

Corbey, Raymond H. A.

2000   On Becoming Human: Mauss, the Gift and Social Origins. In *Gifts and Interests*, edited by Antoon Vandevelde, pp. 157-174. Peeters, Leuven, Belgium.

2006   Laying Aside the Spear: Hobbesian Warre and the Maussian Gift. In *Warfare and Society: Archaeological and Social Anthropological Perspectives*, edited by Ton Otto, Henrik Thrane and Helle Vandkilde, pp. 29-36. Aarhus University Press, Aarhus, Denmark.

2008   Marcel Mauss. *Het Kritisch Denkers Lexicon* 40(April): 1-15.

Corbey, Raymond H. A. and Angus A. A. Mol

2012   'By Weapons Made Worthy': A Darwinian Perspective on Beowulf. In *Creating Consilience: Issues and Case Studies in the Integration of the Sciences and Humanities*, edited by Mark Collard and Edward Slingerland. Oxford University Press, Oxford, United Kingdom.

Coward, Fiona

2010   Small Worlds, Material Culture and Ancient near Eastern Social Networks. *Proceedings of the British Academy* 158: 453-484.

Coward, Fiona and Clive Gamble

2008   Big Brains, Small Worlds: Material Culture and the Evolution of the Mind. *Philosophical Transactions of the Royal Society B: Biological Sciences* 363(1499): 1969-1979.

Crock, John G.

2000   Interisland Interaction and the Development of Chiefdoms in the Eastern Caribbean. Unpublished PhD thesis, Graduate Faculty of Arts and Sciences, University of Pittsburgh, Pittsburgh, Kansas.

Crock, John G., Birgit F. Morse, Christophe Descantes, James B. Petersen and Michael D. Glascock

2008   Preliminary Interpretations of Ceramic Composistional Analysis from Late Ceramic Age Sites in Anguilla and the Salt River Site in St. Croix. *Journal of Caribbean Archaeology* special issue #2: 45-56.

Crock, John G. and James B. Petersen

2004   Inter-Island Exchange, Settlement Hierarchy, and a Taíno-Related Chiefdom on the Anguilla Bank, Northern Lesser Antilles. In *Late Ceramic Age Societies in the Eastern Caribbean*, edited by André Delpuech and Corinne L. Hofman, pp. 139-158. Archaeopress, Oxford, United Kingdom.

Crock, John G., James B. Petersen and Nik Douglas

1995   Preceramic Anguilla: A View from the Whitehead's Bluff Site. *Proceedings of the 15th International Congress for the Study of Pre-Columbian Cultures of the Lesser Antilles*: 283-292. San Juan, Puerto Rico.

Cronau, Rudolf

1892   *Amerika: Die Geschichte Seiner Entdeckung Von Der Ältesten Bis Auf Die Neueste Zeit, Erster Band*. Abel and Müller, Leipzig, Germany.

Crosby, Alfred W.

2003   *The Columbian Exchange: Biological and Cultural Consequences of 1492*. Praeger, Westport, Connecticut.

Curet, L. Antonio

1992   The Development of Chiefdoms in the Greater Antilles: A Regional Study of the
        Valley of Maunabo, Puerto Rico. Unpublished PhD thesis, Arizona State University,
        Phoenix, Arizona.

1996   Ideology, Chiefly Power and Material Culture: An Example from the Greater
        Antilles. *Latin American Antiquity* 7(2): 114-131.

2002   The Chief Is Dead, Long Live... Who? Descent and Succession in the Protohistoric
        Chiefdoms of the Greater Antilles. *Ethnohistory* 49(2): 259-280.

2003   Issues on the Diversity and Emergence of Middle-Range Societies of the Ancient
        Caribbean: A Critique. *Journal of Archaeological Research* 11(1): 1-42.

2005   *Caribbean Paleodemography: Population, Culture History, and Sociopolitical Processes
        in Ancient Puerto Rico.* University of Alabama Press, Tuscaloosa, Alabama.

2006   Missing the Point and an Illuminating Example: A Response to Keegan's Comments.
        Ethnohistory 53(2): 393-398.

2011   Irving Rouse's Contribution to American Archaeology: The Case of Migration.
        In *Islands at the Crossroads: Migration, Seafaring, and Interaction in the Caribbean*,
        edited by L. Antonio Curet and Mark W. Hauser, pp. 13-21. University of Alabama
        Press, Tuscaloosa, Alabama.

Curet, L. Antonio and Mark W. Hauser (editors)

2011   *Islands at the Crossroads: Migration, Seafaring, and Interaction in the Caribbean.*
        University of Alabama Press, Tuscaloosa, Alabama.

Curet, L. Antonio and William J. Pestle

2010   Identifying High-Status Foods in the Archeological Record. *Journal of Anthropological
        Archaeology* 29(4): 413–431.

Curet, L. Antonio and Lisa M. Stringer

2010   *Tibes: People, Power, and Ritual at the Centre of the Cosmos.* The University of
        Alabama Press, Tuscaloosa, Alabama.

Damon, Frederick H.

1980   The Kula and Generalised Exchange: Considering Some Unconsidered Aspects of
        the Elementary Structures of Kinship. *Man* 15(2): 267-292.

2002   Kula Valuables: The Problem of Value and the Production of Names. *L'Homme*
        162(2): 107-136.

Daniels, Inge

2009   The 'Social Death' of Unused Gifts: Surplus and Value in Contemporary Japan.
        Journal of Material Culture 14(3): 385-408.

Dant, Tim

2005   *Materiality and Society.* Open University Press, New York.

Davis, Dave D.

2000   *Jolly Beach and the Preceramic Occupation of Antigua, West Indies.* Yale University
        Press, New Haven, Connecticut.

de Goeje, Claudius H.

2009 [1928]   *The Arawak Language of Guiana.* Cambridge Library Collection. Cambridge
               University Press, Cambridge, United Kingdom.

de Hostos, Adolfo

1923   Three-Pointed Stone Zemi or Idols from the West Indies: An Interpretation.
        American Anthropologist 25(1): 56-71.

de Josselin de Jong, Jan P.B.

    1947   *Archaeological Material from Saba and St. Eustatius, Lesser Antilles*. Mededelingen Van Het Rijkmuseum Voor Volkenkunde 1. E.J. Brill, Leiden, the Netherlands.

de la Borde, The Sieur

    1684   Relation de l'Origine, Mœurs, Costumes, Religion, Guerres et Voyages des Caraïbes Sauvages des Isles Antilles de l'Amerique. In *Recueil de Divers Voyages, Faits en Afrique et en l'Amerique*, edited by Henry Justel. Louis Billaine, Paris.

de las Casas, Bartolomé

    1875   *Historia de las Indias: Tomo I*. Imprente de Miguel Ginesta, Madrid.

    1909   *Apologética Historia De Indias*. Ediciones Serrano y Sanchez, Madrid.

    1992   *Apologética Historia Sumaria*. Allianza, Madrid.

    1992 [1542]   *A Short Account of the Destruction of the Indies*. Translated by Nigel Griffin. Penguin Books, London.

de Montaigne, Michel

    1958 [1580]   Of Cannibals. In *The Complete Essays*, pp. 105-119. Translated by John M. Cohen, London.

de Navarete, M. Fernandéz

    1922   *Viajes de Cristóbal Columbus*. Calpe, Madrid.

de Oviedo y Valdés, Gonzalo Fernandez

    1851   *Historia General y Natural de las Indias, Islas y Tierra-Firme del Mar Océano*. La Real Academia de la Historia, Madrid.

de Waal, Maaike

    2006   Pre-Columbian Social Organisation and Interaction Interpreted through the Study of Settlement Patterns: An Archaeological Case-Study of the Pointe des Châteaux, la Désirade and les Îles de la Petite Terre Micro-Region, Guadeloupe, F.W.I. Unpublished PhD thesis, Faculty of Archaeology, Leiden University, Leiden, the Netherlands.

Deagan, Kathleen

    2004   Reconsidering Taíno Social Dynamics after Spanish Conquest: Gender and Class in Culture Contact Studies. *American Antiquity* 69(4): 597-626.

Deagan, Kathleen and José M. Cruxent

    2002   *Columbus's Outpost among the Taínos: Spain and America at La Isabela, 1493-1498*. Yale University Press, New Haven, Connecticut.

DeFrance, Susan D.

    2013   Zooarchaeology in the Pre-Columbian Caribbean: Current Research and Future Prospects. In *The Oxford Handbook of Caribbean Archaeology*, edited by William F. Keegan, Corinne L. Hofman and Reniel Rodriguez Ramos, pp. 378-390. Oxford University Press, Oxford, United Kingdom.

DeFrance, Susan D., Carla S. Hadden, Michelle J. LeFebvre and Geoffrey DuChemin

    2010   Animal Use at the Tibes Ceremonial Centre. In *Tibes: People, Power, and Ritual at the Centre of the Cosmos*, edited by L. Antonio Curet and Lisa M. Stringer, pp. 115-151. The University of Alabama Press, Tuscaloosa, Alabama.

Delpuech, André

    2004   Espaces Naturels et Territoires Amérindiens dans la Caribe Orientale. In *Late Ceramic Age Societies in the Eastern Caribbean*, edited by André Delpuech and Corinne L. Hofman, pp. 3-16. Archaeopress, Oxford, United Kingdom.

Delpuech, André and Corinne L. Hofman (editors)

    2004   *Late Ceramic Age Societies in the Caribbean*. Archaeopress, Oxford, United Kingdom.

Descola, Philippe

    1996   Constructing Natures: Symbolic Ecology and Social Practice. In *Nature and Society: Anthropological Perspectives*, edited by Philippe Descola and Gísli Pálson. Routledge, London.

Dobres, Marcia-Anne and John E. Robb

    2005   "Doing" Agency: Introductory Remarks on Methodology. *Journal of Archaeological Method & Theory* 12(3): 159-166.

Draper, Grenville, Trevor A. Jackson and Stephen K. Donovan

    1994   Geologic Provinces of the Caribbean Region. In *Caribbean Geology: An Introduction*, edited by Trevor A. Jackson and Stephen K. Donovan, pp. 3-12. UWI Publishers' Association, Kingston, Jamaica.

Dumont, Louis

    1970   *Homo Hierarchicus: An Essay on the Caste System*. University of Chicago Press, Chicago.

Dunbar, Robin

    1988   *Primate Social Systems*. Yale University Press, New Haven, Connecticut.

    2003   The Social Brain: Mind, Language, and Society in Evolutionary Perspective. *Annual Review of Anthropology*: 163-181.

Dunbar, Robin, Clive Gamble and John Gowlett

    2010a   The Social Brain and Its Distributed Mind. In *Social Brain, Distributed Mind*, edited by Robin Dunbar, Clive Gamble and John Gowlett, pp. 3-16. Oxford University Press, Oxford, United Kingdom.

    2010b   *Social Brain, Distributed Mind*. Oxford University Press, Oxford, United Kingdom.

Durkheim, Émile

    1897   *Le Suicide: Étude De Sociologie*. Les Presses Universitaires de France, Paris.

    1982 [1895]   *The Rules of the Sociological Method*. Free Press, New York.

Dyke, Ruth M. Van and Susan E. Alcock (editors)

    2003   *Archaeologies of Memory*. Blackwell Publishing, Malden, Massachusetts.

Ensor, Bradley E.

    2013   Kinship and Social Organization in the Pre-Hispanic. In *The Oxford Handbook of Caribbean Archaeology*, edited by William F. Keegan, Corinne L. Hofman and Reniel Rodriguez Ramos, pp. 84-96. Oxford University Press, Oxford, United Kingdom.

Evans, Tim S., Ray J. Rivers and Carl Knappett

    2012   Interaction in Space for Archaeological Models. *Advances in Complex Systems* 15(1 and 2): 1-17.

Fewkes, Jesse W.

    1896   Pacific Coast Shells from Prehistoric Tusayan Pueblos. *American Anthropologist* 9(11): 359-368.

    1903/1904   *The Aborigines of Puerto Rico*. Annual Report of the Bureau of American Ethnology 25. Government Printing Office, Washington.

1912/1913   *A Prehistoric Island Culture Area of America*. Annual Report of the Bureau of American Ethnology 34. Government Printing Office, Washington.

Figueredo, Alfredo E.

1978   The Virgin Islands as an Historical Frontier between the Tainos and the Caribs. *Revista/Review Interamericana* 8(3): 393-399.

Firth, Raymond

1959 [1929]   *Economics of the New Zealand Maori*. R.E. Owen, Wellington, New Zealand.

Fiske, Alan Page

1991   *Structures of Social Life: The Four Elementary Forms of Human Relations: Communal Sharing, Authority Ranking, Equality Matching, Market Pricing*. Free Press, New York.

Fitzpatrick, Scott M.

2004   *Quo Vadis* Caribbean Archaeology?: The Future of the Discipline in an International Forum. *Caribbean Journal of Science* 40(3): 281-290.

2006   A Critical Approach to 14C Dating in the Caribbean: Using Chronometric Hygiene to Evaluate Chronological Control and Prehistoric Settlement. *Latin American Antiquity* 17(4): 389-418.

2013a   Seafaring Capabilities in the Pre-Columbian Caribbean. *Journal of Maritime Archaeology* 8(1): 101-138.

2013b   The Southward Route Hypothesis. In *The Oxford Handbook of Caribbean Archaeology*, edited by William F. Keegan, Corinne L. Hofman and Reniel Rodríguez Ramos, pp. 198-205. Oxford University Press, Oxford, United Kingdom.

Fitzpatrick, Scott M., Michiel Kappers, Quetta Kaye, Christina M. Giovas, Michelle J. LeFebvre, Mary Hill Harris, Scott Burnett, Jennifer A. Pavia, Kathleen Marsaglia, James Feathers

2009   Precolumbian Settlements on Carriacou, West Indies. *Journal of Field Archaeology* 34(3): 247-266.

Fitzpatrick, Scott M., Quetta Kaye, James Feathers, Jennifer A. Carstensen and Kathleen M. Marsaglia

2008   Evidence for Inter-Island Transport of Heirlooms? Luminescence Dating and Petrographic Analysis of Ceramic Inhaling Bowls from Carriacou, West Indies. *Journal of Archaeological Science* 36(3): 596-606.

Fitzpatrick, Scott M. and Ann H. Ross

2010   *Island Shores, Distant Pasts: Archaeological and Biological Approaches to the Pre-Columbian Settlement of the Caribbean*. University of Florida Press, Gainesville, Florida.

Flannery, Kent V. (editor)

1976   *The Early Mesoamerican Village*. Academic Press, New York.

Fournier, Marcel

2006   *Marcel Mauss: A Biography*. Translated by Jane Marie Todd. Princetion University Press, Princeton, New Jersey.

Freeman, Linton C.

1982   Centred Graphs and the Structure of Ego Networks. *Mathematical Social Sciences* 3(3): 291-304.

Fry, Douglas P.

2006   *The Human Potential for Peace: An Anthropological Challenge to Assumptions About War and Violence*. Oxford University Press, Oxford, United Kingdom.

Gamble, Clive, John Gowlett and Robin Dunbar

    2011   The Social Brain and the Shape of the Palaeolithic. *Cambridge Archaeological Journal* 21(1): 115-136.

Garcia-Casco, Antonio, Sebastiaan Knippenberg, Reniel Rodríguez Ramos, George E. Harlow, Corinne L. Hofman, José Carlos Pomo and Idael F. Blanco-Quintero

    2013   Pre-Columbian Jadeitite Artefacts from the Golden Rock Site, St. Eustatius, Lesser Antilles, with Special Reference to Jadeitite Artefacts from Elliot's, Antigua: Implications for Potential Source Regions and Long-Distance Exchange Networks in the Greater Caribbean. *Journal of Archaeological Science* 40(8): 3153-3169.

García Arévalo, Manuel. A.

    1997   The Bat and the Owl: Nocturnal Images of Death. In *Taíno: Pre-Columbian Art and Culture from the Caribbean*, edited by Fatima Bercht, Estrellita Brodsky, John A. Farmer and Dicey Taylor, pp. 112-123. The Monacelli Press, New York.

    2001   El Ayuno del Behique y el Simbolismo del Esqueleto. *Proceedings of the 19th International Congress For Caribbean Archaeology*: 56-69. Aruba.

Gassón, Rafael A.

    2000   Quirípas and Mostacillas: The Evolution of Shell Beads as a Medium of Exchange in Northern South America. *Ethnohistory* 47(3/4): 581-609.

Gell, Alfred

    1998   *Art and Agency: An Anthropological Theory*. Clarendon Press, Oxford, United Kingdom.

Geurds, Alexander

    2011   The Social in the Circum-Caribbean: Toward a Transcontextual Order. In *Communities in Contact: Essays in Archaeology, Ethnohistory and Ethnography of the Amerindian Circum-Caribbean*, edited by Corinne L. Hofman and Anne van Duijvenbode, pp. 45-60. Sidestone Press, Leiden, the Netherlands.

Geurds, Alexander and Laura N. K. van Broekhoven

    2010   The Similarity Trap: Engineering the Greater-Caribbean, a Perspective from the Isthmo-Colombian Area. *Journal of Caribbean Archaeology* special publication #3: 52-75.

Gintis, Herbert

    2000   Strong Reciprocity and Human Sociality. *Journal of Theoretical Biology* 206(2): 169-179.

Gintis, Herbert, Samuel Bowles, Robert Boyd and Ernst Fehr (editors)

    2005   *Moral Sentiments and Material Interests: The Foundations of Cooperation in Economic Life*. MIT Press, Cambridge, Massachussets.

Godelier, Maurice

    1999   *The Enigma of the Gift*. Translated by Nora Scott. University of Chicago Press, Chicago, Illinois.

Godelier, Maurice and Marilyn Strathern

    1991   *Big Men and Great Men: Personifications of Power in Melanesia*. Cambridge University Press, Cambridge, United Kingdom.

Gofman, Alexander

    1998   The Total Social Fact: A Vague but Suggestive Concept. In *Marcel Mauss: A Centenary*, edited by Wendy James and N.J. Allen, pp. 63-70. Berghahn, Oxford, United Kingdom.

Golitko, Mark, James Meierhoff, Gary M. Feinman and Patrick Ryan Williams

    2012   Complexities of Collapse: The Evidence of Maya Obsidian as Revealed by Social Network Graphical Analysis. *Antiquity* 86: 507-523.

Goodman, Nelson

    1978   *Ways of Worldmaking*. Hackett Publishing Company, Indianapolis, Indiana.

Gosden, Chris

    2004   *Archaeology and Colonialism: Cultural Contact from 5000 BC to the Present*. Cambridge University Press, Cambridge, United Kingdom.

    2005   What Do Objects Want? *Journal of Archaeological Method and Theory* 12(3): 193-211.

Graeber, David

    2001   *Toward an Anthropological Theory of Value: The False Coin of Our Own Dreams*. Palgrave, New York.

    2011   *Debt: The First Five Thousand Years*. Melville House, New York.

Graham, Shawn

    2006   *Ex Figlinis: The Network Dynamics of the Tiber Valley Brick Industry in the Hinterland of Rome* 1486. Archaeopress, Oxford, United Kingdom.

Granberry, Julian

    2013   Indigenous Languages of the Caribbean. In *The Oxford Handbook of Caribbean Archaeology*, edited by William F. Keegan, Corinne L. Hofman and Reniel Rodríguez Ramos, pp. 61-69. Oxford University Press, Oxford, United Kingdom.

Granberry, Julian and Gary S. Vescelius

    2004   *Languages of the Pre-Columbian Antilles*. The University of Alabama Press, Tuscaloosa, Alabama.

Gregory, Chris A.

    1982   *Gifts and Commodities*. Academic Press, London.

Grouard, Sandrine

    2001   Subsistance, Systèmes Techniques et Gestion Territoriale en Milieu Insulaire Antillais Précolombien. Exploitation des Vertébrés et des Crustacés aux Époques Saladoïdes et Troumassoïdes de Guadeloupe (400 av. J.-C. à 1 500 ap. J.-C.). Unpublished PhD thesis, U.F.R. Sciences Sociales et Administration, Université Paris X, Paris.

Grove, Matt

    2011   An Archaeological Signature of Multi-Level Social Systems: The Case of the Irish Bronze Age. *Journal of Anthropological Archaeology* 30(1): 44-61.

Guthrie, Stewart

    1993   *Faces in the Clouds: A New Theory of Religion*. Oxford University Press, Oxford, United Kingdom.

Hage, Per and Frank Harary

    1991   *Exchange in Oceania: A Graph Theoretic Analysis*. Clarendon Press, Oxford, United Kingdom.

    2006   *Island Networks: Communication, Kinship, and Classification Structures in Oceania*. Cambridge University Press, Cambridge, United Kingdom.

Harary, Frank

    1969   *Graph Theory*. Addison–Wesley, Reading, Massachusetts.

Hardy, Meredith D.

  2008   Saladoid Economy and Complexity on the Arawakan Frontier. Unpublished PhD thesis, Department of Anthropology, Florida State University, Tallahassee, Florida.

Harlow, George E., A. Reg Murphy, David J. Hozjan, Christy N. de Mille and Alfred A. Levinson

  2006   Pre-Columbian Jadeite Axes from Antigua, West Indies: Description and Possible Sources. *Canadian Mineralogist* 44(2): 305-321.

Harrison, Simon

  2008   War Mementos and the Souls of Missing Soldiers: Returning Effects of the Battlefield Dead. *Journal of the Royal Anthropological Institute* 14(4): 774-790.

Hart, John P. and John E. Terrell (editors)

  2002   *Darwin and Archaeology: A Handbook of Key Concepts.* Bergin and Garvey, Westport, Connecticut.

Haslam, Nick

  2004   Research on the Relational Models: An Overview. In *Relational Models Theory: A Contemporary Overview*, edited by Nick Haslam, pp. 27-57. Lawrence Erlbaum Associates, London.

Haviser, Jay B.

  1985   An Archaeological Survey of Saba, Netherlands Antilles. Phase I Report. Reports of the Institute of Archaeology and Anthropology of the Netherlands Antilles, no. 3: 41.

  1991   Development of a Prehistoric Interaction Sphere in the Northern Lesser Antilles. *New West Indian Guide/Nieuwe West-Indische Gids* 65(3): 129.

Heckenberger, Michael J.

  2005   *The Ecology of Power: Culture, Place, and Personhood in the Southern Amazon, A.D. 1000-2000.* Routledge, New York.

  2013   The Arawak Diaspora: Perspectives from South America. In *The Oxford Handbook of Caribbean Archaeology*, edited by William F. Keegan, Corinne L. Hofman and Reniel Rodríguez Ramos, pp. 111-126. Oxford University Press, Oxford, United Kingdom.

Helms, Mary W.

  1987   Art Styles and Interaction Spheres in Central America and the Caribbean: Polished Black Wood in the Greater Antilles. In *Chiefdoms in the Americas*, edited by Robert D. Drennan, pp. 67-84. University Press of America, Lanham, Maryland.

  1988   *Ulysses' Sail: An Ethnographic Odyssey of Power, Knowledge, and Geographical Distance.* Princeton University Press, Princeton, New Jersey.

  1995   *Creations of the Rainbow Serpent.* University of New Mexico Press, Alberquerque.

Henare, Amiria, Martin Holbraad and Sari Wastell (editors)

  2007   *Thinking through Things.* Routledge, London.

Herrmann, Gretchen M.

  1997   Gift or Commodity: What Changes Hands in the U. S. Garage Sale? *American Ethnologist* 24(4): 910-930.

Hicks, Dan

  2010   The Material-Cultural Turn: Event and Effect. In *The Oxford Handbook of Material Culture Studies*, edited by Dan Hicks and Mary C. Beaudry, pp. 25-99. Oxford University Press, Oxford, United Kingdom.

Hillier, Bill and Julienne Hanson

1984   *The Social Logic of Space*. Cambridge University Press, Cambridge, United Kingdom.

Hobbes, Thomas

1929 [1651]   *Leviathan*. Oxford University Press, Oxford, United Kingdom.

Hodder, Ian

2012   *Entangled: An Archaeology of the Relationships between Humans and Things*. Wiley-Blackwell, Malden, Massachusetts.

Hofman, Corinne L.

1993   In Search of the Native Population of Pre-Columbian Saba (400-1450 AD): Part One, Pottery Styles and Their Interpretations. Unpublished PhD thesis, Institute for Prehistory, Leiden University, Leiden.

1995   Inferring Inter-Island Relationships from Ceramic Style: A View from the Leeward Islands. *Proceedings of the 15th Congress for Caribbean Archaeology*: 1-6 and 1-17. San Juan, Puerto Rico.

2013   The Post-Saladoid in the Lesser Antilles (AD 600/800-1492). In *The Oxford Handbook of Caribbean Archaeology*, edited by William F. Keegan, Corinne L. Hofman and Reniel Rodríguez Ramos, pp. 205-220. Oxford University Press, Oxford, United Kingdom.

Hofman, Corinne L., Arie Boomert, Alistair J. Bright, Menno L. P. Hoogland, Sebastiaan Knippenberg and Alice V. M. Samson

2011   Ties with the 'Homelands': Archipelagic Interaction and the Enduring Role of the Continental American Mainland in the Precolumbian Lesser Antilles. In *Islands at the Crossroads: Migration, Seafaring, and Interaction in the Caribbean*, edited by L. Antonio Curet and Mark W. Hauser, pp. 73-85. University of Alabama Press, Tuscaloosa, Alabama.

Hofman, Corinne L. and Alistair Bright

2010   Towards a Pan-Caribbean Perspective of Pre-Colonial Mobility and Exchange: Preface to a Special Volume of the Journal of Caribbean Archaeology. *Journal of Caribbean Archaeology* special publication #3: i-iii.

Hofman, Corinne L., Alistair Bright, Menno L. P. Hoogland and William F. Keegan

2008   Attractive Ideas, Desirable Goods: Examining the Late Ceramic Age Relationships between Greater and Lesser Antillean Societies. *Journal of Island and Coastal Archaeology* 3: 17–34.

Hofman, Corinne L., Alistair J. Bright, Arie Boomert and Sebastiaan Knippenberg

2007   Island Rhythms: The Web of Social Relationships and Interaction Networks in the Lesser Antillean Archipelago between 400 BC and AD 1492. *Latin American Antiquity* 18(3): 243-268.

Hofman, Corinne L., Alistair J. Bright and Menno L. P. Hoogland

2006   Archipelagic Resource Procurement and Mobility in the Northern Lesser Antilles: The View from a 3000-Year-Old Tropical Forest Campsite on Saba. *The Journal of Island and Coastal Archaeology* 1(2): 145-164.

Hofman, Corinne L. and Eithne B. Carlin

2010   The Ever-Dynamic Caribbean: Exploring New Approaches to Unraveling Social Networks in the Pre-Colonial and Early Colonial Periods In *Linguistics and Archaeology in the Americas: The Historization of Language and Society*, edited by Eithnee B. Carlin, and Simon van de Kerke, pp. 107-122. Brill, Leiden, the Netherlands.

Hofman, Corinne L., André Delpuech, Menno L. P. Hoogland and Maaike S. de Waal

2004   Late Ceramic Age Survey of the Northeastern Islands of the Guadeloupean Archipelago. In *Late Ceramic Age Societies in the Eastern Caribbean*, edited by André Delpuech and Corinne L. Hofman, pp. 159-182. Archaeopress, Oxford, United Kingdom.

Hofman, Corinne L. and Menno L. P. Hoogland

1991   Ceramic Developments on Saba, N.A. (650-1400 A.D.). *Proceedings of the 14th International Congress for Caribbean Archaeology*: 1-6. Barbados.

1999   *Archaeological Investigations on St. Martin (Lesser Antilles): The Sites of Norman Estate, Anse des Pères and Hope Estate with a Contribution to the 'La Hueca Problem'*. Leiden University Press, Leiden, the Netherlands.

2003   Plum Piece: Evidence for Archaic Seasonal Occupation on Saba, Northern Lesser Antilles around 3300 BP. *Journal of Caribbean Archaeology* 4: 12-27.

2004   Social Dynamics and Change in the Northern Lesser Antilles. In *Late Ceramic Age Societies in the Eastern Caribbean*, edited by André Delpuech and Corinne L Hofman, pp. 47-59. Archaeopress, Oxford, United Kingdom.

2011   Unravelling the Multi-Scale Networks of Mobility and Exchange in the Pre-Colonial Circum-Caribbean. In *Communities in Contact: Essays in Archaeology, Ethnohistory and Ethnography of the Amerindian Circum-Caribbean*, edited by Corinne L. Hofman and Anne van Duijvenbode, pp. 14-44. Sidestone Press, Leiden, the Netherlands.

2012   Caribbean Encounters: Rescue Excavations at the Early Colonial Island Carib Site of Argyle, St. Vincent In *Analecta Praehistoria Leidensia 43/44: The End of Our Fifth Decade*, edited by Corrie Bakels and Hans Kamermans, pp. 63-76. Leiden University Press, Leiden, the Netherlands.

Hofman, Corinne L., Menno L. P. Hoogland and Annelou L. van Gijn (editors)

2008   *Crossing the Borders: New Methods and Techniques in the Study of Archaeological Materials from the Caribbean*. Alabama University Press, Tuscaloosa, Alabama.

Hofman, Corinne L., A. J. Daan Isendoorn, Mathijs A. Booden and Lou F. H. C. Jacobs

2008   In Tuneful Threefold: Combining Conventional Archaeological Methods, Geochemical Analysis and Ethnoarchaeological Research in the Study of Pre-Columbian Pottery of the Caribbean. In *Crossing the Borders: New Methods and Techniques in the Study of Archaeological Materials from the Caribbean*, edited by Corinne L Hofman, Menno L. P. Hoogland and Annelou L. van Gijn, pp. 21-33. Alabama University Press, Tuscaloosa, Alabama.

Hofman, Corinne L., A. J. Daan Isendoorn and Mathijs A. Booden

2005   Clays Collected: Towards an Identification of Source Areas for Clays Used in the Production of Pre-Columbian Pottery in the Northern Lesser Antilles. *Leiden Journal of Pottery Studies* 21: 9-26.

Hofman, Corinne L., Angus A. A. Mol, Sebastiaan Knippenberg and Reniel Rodríguez Ramos

2011   Networks Set in Stone: Archaic-Ceramic Interaction in the Early Prehistoric Northeastern Caribbean. Paper presented at the 24th Congress of the International Association of Caribbean Archaeology, Martinique.

Hofman, Corinne L., Jorge Ulloa Hung and Lou F. H. C. Jacobs

2007   Juntando las Piezas del Rompecabezas: Dándole Sentido a la Cronología Cerámica del Este de la República Dominicana. *Caribe Arqueológico* 10: 104-115.

Hofman, Corinne L. and Anne van Duijvenbode (editors)

2011   *Communities in Contact: Essays in Archaeology, Ethnohistory and Ethnography of the Amerindian Circum-Caribbean*. Sidestone Press, Leiden, the Netherlands.

Honychurch, Lennox

2000   *Carib to Creole: A History of Contact and Culture Exchange*. The Dominica Institute, Rousseau, Dominica.

Hoogland, Menno L. P.

1996   In Search of the Native Population of Pre-Columbian Saba (400-1450 AD): Part Two: Settlements in Their Natural and Social Environment. Unpublished PhD thesis, Institute of Prehistory, Leiden University, Leiden.

1999   Settlement Structure of a Taino Site on Saba, Netherlands Antilles. *Proceedings of the 16th International Congress for Caribbean Archaeology* 2: 146-155. Guadeloupe.

Hoogland, Menno L. P. and Corinne L. Hofman

1991   A 14th Century Taino Settlement on Saba, Netherlands Antilles. *Proceedings of the 14th International Congress for Caribbean Archaeology*: 1-23. Barbados.

1993   Kelbey's Ridge 2, a 14th Century Taíno Settlement on Saba, Netherlands Antilles. In *The End of Our Third Decade. Papers Written on the Occasion of the 30th Anniversary of the Institute of Prehistory*, edited by Corrie Bakels, pp. 163-181. Analecta Praehistorica Leidensia, Leiden, the Netherlands.

1999   Expansion of the Taíno Cacicazgos Towards the Lesser Antilles. *Journal de la Société des Américanistes* 85: 93-113.

2013   From Corpse Taphonomy to Mortuary Behaviour in the Caribbean: A Case Study from the Lesser Antilles. In *The Oxford Handbook of Caribbean Archaeology*, edited by William F. Keegan, Corinne L. Hofman and Reniel Rodríguez Ramos, pp. 452-469. Oxford University Press, Oxford, United Kingdom.

Hoopes, John W.

2007   Sorcery and the Taking of Trophy Heads in Ancient Costa Rica. In *The Taking and Displaying of Human Body Parts as Trophies by Amerindians*, edited by Richard J. Chacon and David H. Dye, pp. 444-480. Springer, New York.

Hoopes, John W. and Oscar M. Fonseca

2003   Goldwork and Chibchan Identity: Endogenous Change and Diffuse Unity in the Isthmo-Columbian Area, pp. 49-91. Dumbarton Oaks, Washington, D.C.

Hopkins, Brian and Robin J. Wilson

2004   The Truth About Königsberg. *The College Mathematics Journal* 35(3): 198-207.

Hornborg, A., R. Gasson, M. Heckenberger, J. D. Hill, E. G. Neves, F. Santos-Granero and A. Hornborg

2005   Discussion: Ethnogenesis, Regional Integration, and Ecology in Prehistoric Amazonia. *Current Anthropology* 46(4): 589-620.

Hornborg, Alf

2005   Ethnogenesis, Regional Integration, and Ecology in Prehistoric Amazonia. *Current Anthropology* 46(4): 589-620.

Hrdy, Sarah B.

2009   *Mothers and Others: The Evolutionary Origins of Mutual Understanding*. The Belknap Press of Harvard University Press, Cambridge, Massachussets.

Hulme, Peter

1993   Making Sense of the Native Caribbean. *New West Indian Guide/Nieuwe West-Indische Gids* 67(3/4): 189-220.

Humphrey, Caroline and Stephen Hugh-Jones

1992   *Barter, Exchange and Value: An Anthropological Approach*. Cambridge University Press, Cambridge, United Kingdom.

Ingold, Tim

2007a   *Lines: A Brief History*. Routledge, New York.

2007b   Materials against Materiality. *Archaeological Dialogues* 14(01): 1-16.

International Hydrographic Organization

1953   *Limits of Oceans and Seas: 3rd Edition*. International Hydrographic Organization, Monaco.

Isaksen, Leif

2013   'O What a Tangled Web We Weave': Towards a Practice That Does Not Deceive. In *Network Analysis in Archaeology: New Approaches to Regional Interaction*, edited by Carl Knappett, pp. 43-67. Oxford University Press, Oxford, United Kingdom.

Isendoorn, A. J. Daan , Corinne L. Hofman and Mathijs A. Booden

2008   Back to the Source: Provenance Areas of Clay and Temper Materials of Pre-Columbian Ceramics. *Journal of Caribbean Archaeology* special publication #2: 15-24.

Jackson, Trevor A

2002   *Caribbean Geology: Into the Third Millenium: Transactions of the Fifteenth Caribbean Geological Conference*. University of West Indies Press, Kingston, Jamaica.

Kandler, Anne and Kevin N. Laland

2009   An Investigation of the Relationship between Innovation and Cultural Diversity. *Theoretical Population Biology* 76(1): 59-67.

Keane, Webb

2006   Subjects and Objects. In *Handbook of Material Culture*, edited by Christopher Tilley, Webb Keane, Susanne Küchler, Mike Rowlands and Patricia Spyer, pp. 197-202. Sage Publications, London.

Keegan, William F.

1995   Modeling Dispersal in the Prehistoric West Indies. *World Archaeology* 26(3): 400-420.

1997   "No Man (or Woman) Is an Island": Elements of Taíno Social Organization. In *The Indigenous peoples of the Caribbean*, edited by Samuel M. Wilson, pp. 109-117. University Press of Florida, Gainesville, Florida.

2004   Islands of Chaos. In *Late Ceramic Age Societies in the Eastern Caribbean*, edited by André Delpuech and Corinne L Hofman, pp. 33-44. Archaeopress, Oxford, United Kingdom.

2006   All in the Family: Descent and Succession in the Protohistoric Chiefdoms of the Greater Antilles - a Comment on Curet. *Ethnohistory* 53(2): 383-392.

2007   *Taíno Indian Myth and Practice: The Arrival of the Stranger King*. University of Florida Press, Gainesville.

2009   The Synergism of Biology and Culture. *The Journal of Island and Coastal Archaeology* 4(2): 240 - 248.

2010   Island Shores and "Long Pauses". In *Island Shores, Distant Pasts: Archaeological and Biological Perspectives on the Pre-Columbian Settlement of the Caribbean*, edited by Scott M. Fitzpatrick and Ann H. Ross, pp. 11-20. University Press of Florida, Gainesville, Florida.

Keegan, William F., Scott Fitzpatrick, Kathleen Sullivan Sealey, Michelle LeFebvre and Peter Sinelli

2008   The Role of Small Islands in Marine Subsistence Strategies: Case Studies from the Caribbean. *Human Ecology* 36(5): 635-654.

Keegan, William F., Corinne L. Hofman and Reniel Rodríguez Ramos

    2013   *The Oxford Handbook of Caribbean Archaeology*. Oxford University Press, Oxford, United Kingdom.

Keegan, William F., Morgan D. Machlachlan and Bryan Byrne

    1998   Social Foundations of Taíno Caciques. In *Chiefdoms and Chieftaincy in the Americas*, edited by Elsa M. Redmond, pp. 215-244. University Press of Florida,, Gainesville, Florida.

Keegan, William F. and Reniel Rodríguez Ramos

    2004   Sin Rodeos. *Caribe Arqueológico* 8: 8-14.

Keehnen, Floris W. M.

    2011   Conflicting Cosmologies: The Exchange of Brilliant Objects between the Taíno of Hispaniola and the Spanish. In *Communities in Contact: Essays in Archaeology, Ethnohistory and Ethnography of the Amerindian Circum-Caribbean*, edited by Corinne L. Hofman and Anne van Duijvenbode, pp. 253-268. Sidestone Press, Leiden, the Netherlands.

Keeley, Lawrence H.

    1996   *War before Civilization: The Myth of the Peaceful Savage*. Oxford University Press, Oxford, United Kingdom.

Kendall, David G.

    1970   A Mathematical Approach to Seriation. *Philosophical Transactions of the Royal Society of London. Series A, Mathematical and Physical Sciences* 269(1193): 125-134.

Kerchache, Jacques

    1994   *L'Art des Sculpteurs Taïnos: Chefs-d'œuvres Des Grandes Antilles Précolombiennes*. Paris Musées, Paris.

Kineman, John J.

    2011   Relational Science: A Synthesis. *Axiomathes* 21(3): 393-437.

Kirch, Patrick V.

    1997   *The Lapita Peoples: Ancestors of the Oceanic World*. Blackwell Publishing, Malden, Massachussets.

Kline, Anthony S. (translator)

    2008   The Stone Beloved. In *Dante Rime*. Found at http://www.poetryintranslation.com/klineasdanterime.htm, accessed on 9-12-2013.

Knappett, Carl

    2005   *Thinking through Material Culture: An Interdisciplinary Perspective*. University of Pennsylvania Press, Philadelphia.

    2011   *An Archaeology of Interaction: Network Perspectives on Material Culture and Society*. Oxford University Press, Oxford, United Kingdom.

    2013   *Network Analysis in Archaeology: New Approaches to Regional Interaction*. Oxford University Press, Oxford, United Kingdom.

Knappett, Carl, Tim Evans and Ray Rivers

    2008   Modelling Maritime Interaction in the Aegean Bronze Age. *Antiquity* 82: 1009-1024.

Knappett, Carl and Lambros Malafouris

    2008   *Material and Nonhuman Agency: An Introduction*. Material Agency: Towards a Non-Anthropocentric Approach. Springer, New York.

Knappett, Carl, Ray J. Rivers and Tim S. Evans

    2011   The Theran Eruption and Minoan Palatial Collapse: New Interpretations Gained from Modelling the Maritime Network *Antiquity* 85(329): 1008-1023.

Knight, Franklin W.

    2011   *The Caribbean: The Genesis of a Fragmented Nationalism*. Oxford University Press, Oxford, United Kingdom.

Knippenberg, Sebastiaan

    2007   *Stone Artefact Production and Exchange among the Northern Lesser Antilles*. Archaeological Studies Leiden University 13. Leiden University Press, Leiden.

Komter, Aafke E.

    2005   *Social Solidarity and the Gift*. Cambridge University Press, Cambridge, United Kingdom.

Kopytoff, Igor

    1986   The Cultural Biography of Things: Commoditization as Process. In *The Social Life of Things: Commodities in Cultural Perspective*, edited by Arjun Appadurai, pp. 64-95. Cambridge University Press, Cambridge, United Kingdom.

Kosub, Sven

    2005   Local Density. In *Network Analysis: Methodological Foundations*, edited by Ulrik Brandes and Thomas Erlebach, pp. 112-142. Springer Verlag, Berlin.

Kozlowski, Janusz K.

    1974   *Preceramic Cultures in the Caribbean*. Panstwowe Wydawn, Krakow.

Krackhardt, David

    1999   The Ties That Torture: Simmelian Tie Analysis in Organizations. *Research in the Sociology of Organizations* 16: 183-210.

Kropotkin, Petr A.

    1907   *Mutual Aid: A Factor of Evolution*. W. Heinemann, London.

Kuhn, Thomas S.

    1962   *The Structure of Scientific Revolutions*. The University of Chicago Press, Chicago.

Labat, Jean-Baptiste

    1979 [1722]   *Voyage Aux Îles de l'Amérique: Antilles, 1693-1705*. Seghers, Paris.

LaBianca, Øystein S. and Sandra Arnold Scham

    2006   Introduction: Ancient Network Societies. In *Connectivity in Antiquity: Globalization as Long-Term Historical Process*, edited by Oystein Sakala LaBianca and Sandra Arnold Scham, pp. 1-5. Equinox, London.

Laffoon, Jason E.

    2012   Patterns of Paleomobility in the Ancient Antilles: An Isotopic Approach. Unpublished PhD thesis, Faculty of Archaeology, Leiden University, Leiden, the Netherlands.

Laffoon, Jason E. and Bart de Vos

    2011   Diverse Origins, Similar Diets: An Integrated Isotopic Perspective from Anse À La Gourde, Guadeloupe. In *Communities in Contact: Essays in Archaeology, Ethnohistory and Ethnography of the Amerindian Circum-Caribbean*, edited by Corinne L. Hofman and Anne van Duijvenbode, pp. 187-203. Sidestone Press, Leiden, the Netherlands.

Laffoon, Jason E., Esther Plomp, Gareth R. Davies, Menno L. P. Hoogland, and Corinne L. Hofman.

in press   The Movement and Exchange of Dogs in the Prehistoric Caribbean: An Isotopic Investigation. *International Journal of Osteoarchaeology*.

Lakatos, Imre

1978   *The Methodology of Scientific Research Programmes*. Cambridge University Press, Cambridge, United Kingdom.

Lammers-Keijsers, Yvonne M. J.

2007   *Tracing traces from present to past: a functional analysis of pre-Columbian shell and stone artefacts from Anse à la Gourde and Morel, Guadeloupe, FWI*. Leiden University Press, Leiden, the Netherlands.

Latour, Bruno

2005   *Reassembling the Social: An Introduction to Actor-Network Theory*. Oxford University Press, Oxford, United Kingdom.

Leach, Jerry W. and Edmund R. Leach

1983   Introduction. In *The Kula: New Perspectives on Massim Exchange*, edited by Jerry W. Leach and Edmund R. Leach, pp. 1-26. Cambridge University Press, Cambridge.

Lévi-Strauss, Claude

1943   Guerre et Commerce chez les Indiens de l'Amérique du Sud. *Renaissance* 1(1): 122-139.

1949   *Les Structures Élémentaires de la Parenté*. Presses Universitaires, Paris.

1969   *The Raw and the Cooked: Introduction to a Science of Mythology Volume 1*. Translated by John Weigthman and Doreen Weigthman. Harper & Row, New York.

1997   Introduction to the Works of Marcel Mauss. In *The Logic of the Gift: Toward an Ethic of Generosity*, edited by Alan D. Schrift, pp. 45-70. Routledge, London.

Levinson, Stephen C.

2006   On the Human Interaction Engine. In *Roots of Human Sociality: Culture, Cognition and Interaction*, edited by Stephen C Levinson and Nicholas J. Enfield, pp. 39-70. Berg Publishers, Oxford, United Kingdom.

Lieberman, Erez, Christoph Hauert and Martin A. Nowak

2005   Evolutionary Dynamics on Graphs. *Nature* 433(7023): 312-316.

Liep, John

1991   Great Man, Big Man, Chief: A Triangulation of the Massim. In *Big Men and Great Men: Personifications of Power in Melanesia*, edited by Maurice Godelier and Marilyn Strathern, pp. 29-47. Cambridge University Press, Cambridge, United Kingdom.

Liiv, Innar

2010   Seriation and Matrix Reordering Methods: An Historical Overview. *Statistical analysis and data mining* 3(2): 70-91.

Lincoln, Jennifer M. and Devin L. Lucas

2010   Occupational Fatalities in the United States Commercial Fishing Industry, 2000–2009. *Journal of Agromedicine* 15(4): 343-350.

Lovén, Sven

1935   *The Origins of Tainan Culture, West Indies*. Elanders Bokfryekeri Aktiebolag, Göteborg, Denmark.

Machlachlan, Morgan and William F. Keegan

    1990   Archaeology and the Ethno-Tyrannies. *American Antrhopologist* 92(4): 1011-1013.

Malafouris, Lambros

    2010   The Brain-Artefact Interface (Bai): A Challenge for Archaeology and Cultural Neuroscience. *Social Cognitive and Affective Neuroscience* 5(2-3): 264-273.

Malinowski, Bronisław

    1922   *Argonauts of the Western Pacific*. Waveland Press, Prospect Heights, Illionois.

Malkin, Irad

    2011   *A Small Greek World: Networks in the Ancient Mediterranean*. Oxford University Press, Oxford, United Kingdom.

Mans, Jimmy L. J. A.

    2011   Trio Movements and the Amotopoan Flux In *Communities in Contact: Essays in Archaeology, Ethnohistory and Ethnography of the Amerindian Circum-Caribbean*, edited by Corinne L. Hofman and Anne Duijvenbode, pp. 205-224. Sidestone Press, Leiden, the Netherlands.

Martyr D'Anghera, Piedro

    1912   *De Orbe Novo*. Translated by Francis Augustus Macnutt. Knickerbocker Press, London.

Marx, Karl

    1893   *Das Kapital, Kritik der Politischen Oekonomie Buch 2: Der Cirkulationsprocess Kapitals*. Verlag von Otto Meissner, Hamburg, Germany.

Marx, Karl and Friedrick Engels

    1970 [1845-1846]   *The German Ideology*. Translated by Christopher J. Arthure. International Publishers, New York.

Mauss, Marcel

    1914   Les Origines de la Notion de Monnaie. *Comptes-rendus des séances* 2(1): 14-19.

    1923/1924   Essai sur le Don: Forme et Raison de l'Échange dans les Sociétés Archaïques. *L'Année Sociologique (nouvelle serie)* 1: 30-186.

    1998   An Intellectual Self-Portrait. In *Marcel Mauss: A Centenary*, edited by Wendy James, & Nicholas J. Allen. Berghahn, Oxford, United Kingdom.

    1990   *The Gift: The Form and Reason for Exchange in Archaic Societies*. Translated by W.D. Halls. Routledge, London and New York.

McGinnis, Shirley A.

    1997   Ideographic Expression in the Precolumbian Caribbean. Unpublished PhD thesis, University of Texas, Austin.

McGuire, Randall H.

    2002   *A Marxist Archaeology*. Percheron Press, New York.

McGuire, Randall H. and Rodrigo Navarrete

    2005   Between Motorcycles and Rifles: Anglo-American and Latin American Radical Archaeologies. In *Global Archaeological Theory*, pp. 309-336. Springer, New York.

McKone, Elinor and Rachel Robbins

    2011   Are Faces Special? In *Oxford Handbook of Face Perception*, edited by Andy Calder, Gillian Rhodes, Mark Johnson and Jim Haxby, pp. 149-176. Oxford University Press, Oxford, United Kingdom.

McKusick, Marshall B.

    1970   *Aboriginal Canoes in the West Indies*. Yale University, New Haven, Connecticut.

Michener, James A.

1989   *The Caribbean: A Novel.* Random House, New York.

Mickleburgh, Hayley L.

2013   Reading the Dental Record: A Dental Anthropological Approach to Foodways, Health and Disease, and Crafting in the Pre-Columbian Caribbean. Unpublished PhD thesis, Faculty of Archaeology, Leiden University, Leiden.

Mickleburgh, Hayley L. and Jaime R Pagán-Jiménez

2012   New Insights into the Consumption of Maize and Other Food Plants in the Pre-Columbian Caribbean from Starch Grains Trapped in Human Dental Calculus. *Journal of Archaeological Science* 39(7): 2468-2478.

Miller, Daniel

1987   *Mass Consumption and Material Culture.* Blackwell Publishing, Oxford, United Kingdom.

2005   *Materiality.* Duke University Press, Durham, United Kingdom.

Mills, Barbara J. (editor)

2000   *Alternative Leadership Strategies in the Prehispanic Southwest.* The University of Arizona Press, Tucson, Arizona.

Mills, Barbara J., Jeffery J. Clark, Matthew A. Peeples, W. R. Haas, John M. Roberts, J. Brett Hill, Deborah L. Huntley, Lewis Borck, Ronald L. Breiger, Aaron Clauset and M. Steven Shackley

2013   Transformation of Social Networks in the Late Pre-Hispanic US Southwest. *Proceedings of the National Academy of Sciences* 110(15): 5785-5790.

Mills, Barbara J. and William H. Walker (editors)

2008   *Memory Work: Archaeologies of Material Practices.* School for Advanced Research Press, Santa Fe, New Mexico.

Mizoguchi, Koji

2009   Nodes and Edges: A Network Approach to Hierarchisation and State Formation in Japan. *Journal of Anthropological Archaeology* 28(1): 14-26.

Mol, Angus A. A.

2007   *Costly Giving, Giving Guaízas: Towards an Organic Model of the Exchange of Social Valuables in the Late Ceramic Age Caribbean.* Sidestone Press, Leiden, the Netherlands.

2008   Universos Socio-Cósmicos en Colisión: Descripciones Etnohistóricas de Situaciones de Intercambio en las Antillas Mayores durante el Perodo De Proto-Contacto *Caribe Arqueológico* 10: 13-22.

2009   The Dark Side of the Shaman: The Evidence for Sorcery in the Antilles. Paper presented at the 23rd Congress of the International Association for Caribbean Archaeology, Antigua.

2010   Something for Nothing: Exploring the Importance of Strong Reciprocity in the Greater Caribbean. *Journal of Caribbean Archaeology* special publication #3: 76-92.

2011a   Bringing Interaction into Higher Spheres: Social Distance in the Late Ceramic Age Greater Antilles as Seen through Ethnohistorical Accounts and the Distribution of Social Valuables. In *Communities in Contact: Essays in Archaeology, Ethnohistory and Ethnography of the Amerindian Circum-Caribbean*, edited by Corinne L. Hofman and Anne van Duijvenbode, pp. 61-86. Sidestone Press, Leiden, the Netherlands.

2011b   The Gift of the Face of the Living: Shell Faces as Social Valuables in the Late Ceramic Age Caribbean. *Journal de la Societé des Américanistes* 97(2): 7-44.

2013   Studying Pre-Columbian Interaction Networks: Mobility and Exchange. In *The Oxford Handbook of Caribbean Archaeology*, edited by William F. Keegan, Corinne L. Hofman and Reniel Rodríguez Ramos, pp. 329-347. Oxford University Press, Oxford, United Kingdom.

in press.   Play-Things and the Origins of Online Networks: Virtual Material Culture in Multi-Player Games. *Archaeological Review from Cambridge* 29(1).

Mol, Angus A. A. and Jimmy L. J. A. Mans

2013   Old Boy Networks in the Indigenous Caribbean. In *Network Analysis in Archaeology: New Approaches to Regional Interaction*, edited by Carl Knappett, pp. 307-335. Oxford University Press, Oxford, United Kingdom.

Mol, Eva

2012   *Hidden Complexities of the Frankish Castle: Social Aspects of Space in the Configurational Architecture of Frankish Castles in the Holy Land, 1099-1291*. Leiden University Press, Leiden.

Morsink, Joost

2012   The Power of Salt: A Holistic Approach to Salt in the Prehistoric Circum-Caribbean Region. Unpublished PhD thesis, Department of Anthropology, University of Florida, Gainesville, Florida.

Moscoso, Fransisco

1977   Tributo y Formación de Clases en la Sociedad de los Taínos de las Antillas. *Proceedings of the 7th International Congress for the Study of Pre-Columbian cultures in the Lesser Antilles*: 306-323. Caracas, Venezuela.

1999   *Sociedad y Economía de los Taínos*. Editorial Edil, Río Piedras, Puerto Rico.

Munn, Nancy D.

1986   *The Fame of Gawa: A Symbolic Study of Value Transformation in a Massim (Papua New Guinea) Society*. Duke University Press, Durham, United Kingdom.

Murphy, A. Reg, David Hozjan, Christy N. de Mille and Alfred Levinson

2000   Pre-Columbian Gems and Ornamental Materials from Antigua, West Indies. *Gems & Gemology* 36(3): 234-245.

Nadal, Joaquín

2004   *Palinología De Punta Macao*. Unpublished report of the Museo del Hombre Dominicano, Santo Domingo, República Dominicana.

Narganes Storde, Yvonne M.

1995   La Lapidaria de la Hueca, Vieques, Puerto Rico. *Proceedings of the 15th International Congress for Caribbean Archaeology*: 144-155. San Juan, Puerto Rico.

Newman, Mark

2010   *Networks: An Introduction*. Oxford University Press, Oxford, United Kingdom.

Newsom, Lee A.

1993   Native West Indian Plant Use. Unpublished PhD Thesis, University of Florida, Gainesville, Florida.

Newsom, Lee A. and Deborah M. Pearsall

2003   Trends in Caribbean Island Archaeobotany. In *Plants and People in Ancient Eastern North America*, edited by Paul E. Minnus, pp. 347-412. Smithsonian Books, Washington, D.C.

Newsom, Lee A. and Elizabeth S. Wing

2004   *On Land and Sea: Native American Uses of Biological Resources in the West Indies.* University of Alabama Press, Tuscaloosa, Alabama.

Nicholson, Desmond V.

1994   *The Archaeology of Antigua and Barbuda.* Museum of Antigua and Barbuda, Antigua.

Oaksford, Mike and Nick Chater

2001   The Probabilistic Approach to Human Reasoning. *Trends in Cognitive Sciences* 5(8): 349-357.

Oliver, José R.

1997   The Taíno Cosmos. In *The Indigenous peoples of the Caribbean*, edited by Samuel M. Wilson, pp. 140-153. University Press of Florida, Gainesville, Florida.

1998   *El Centro Ceremonial de Caguana, Puerto Rico: Simbolismo Iconográfico, Cosmovisión y el Poderío Caciquil Taíno de Borinquen.* British Archaeological Report International Series. Archaeopress, Oxford, United Kingdom.

1999   The 'La Hueca Problem' in Puerto Rico and the Caribbean: Old Problems, New Perpectives, Possible Solutions. In *Archaeological Investigations on St. Martin (Lesse Antilles). The Site of Norman Estate, Anse des Peres and Hop Estate with a Contribution to the La Hueca Problem.*, pp. 253 t/m 297. Leiden University Press, Leiden, the Netherlands.

2000   Gold Symbolism among Caribbean Chiefdoms: Of Feathers, Cibas, and Guanín Power among Taíno Elites. In *Precolumbian Gold. Technology, Style and Iconograph*, edited by Colin McEwan, pp. 198- 219. British Museum Press, London.

2009   *Caciques and Cemí Idols: The Web Spun by Taíno Rulers between Hispaniola and Puerto Rico.* Caribbean Archaeology and Ethnohistory. University of Alabama Press, Tuscaloosa, Alabama.

Oliver, José R., Colin McEwan and Anna Casas Gilberga (editors)

2008   *El Caribe Precolombino: Fray Ramón Pané y el Universo Taíno.* Comgrafic, S.A., Barcelona.

Oliver, José R. and Yvonne M. Narganes Storde

2003   The Zooarchaeological Remains from Juan Miguel Cave and Finca De Doña Rosa, Barrio Caguana, Puerto Rico: Ritual Edibles or Quotidian Meals? *Proceedings of the 20th International Congress for Caribbean Archaeology*: 227-242. Santo Domingo, Dominican Republic.

Olsen, Bjørnar

2010   *In Defense of Things: Archaeology and the Ontology of Objects.* AltaMira Press, Plymouth, United Kingdom.

Olsen Bogaert, Harold

2008   *Investigaciones Arqueológicas Punta Macao.* Unpublished report of the Museo del Hombre Dominicano, Santo Domingo, Dominican Republic.

Olsen, Fred

1980   The Arawaks: Their Art, Religion, and Science. *Proceedings of the 8th International Congress for the Study of the pre-Columbian cultures of the Lesser Antilles*: 3-24.

Olson, David M., Eric Dinerstein, Eric D. Wikramanayake, Neil D. Burgess, George V. N. Powell, Emma C. Underwood, Jennifer A. D'amico, Illanga Itoua, Holly E. Strand and John C. Morrison

    2001   Terrestrial Ecoregions of the World: A New Map of Life on Earth: A New Global Map of Terrestrial Ecoregions Provides an Innovative Tool for Conserving Biodiversity. *BioScience* 51(11): 933-938.

Ortega, Elpidio J.

    1978   Informe sobre Investigaciones Arqueológicas Realizadas en la Región Este del País, Zona de Costera desde Macao a Punta Espada. *Boletín del Museo del Hombre Dominicano* 11: 77-105.

    2005   *Los Objetos de Conchas de la Prehistoria de Santo Domingo*. Fundación Ortega Alavarez, Santo Domingo, Dominican Republic.

Ostapkowicz, Joanna

    1997   To Be Seated with "Great Courtesy and Veneration": Contextual Aspects of the Taíno Duho. In *Taíno: Pre-Columbian Art and Culture from the Caribbean*, edited by Fatima Bercht, Estrellita Brodsky, John A. Farmer and Dicey Taylor, pp. 56-68. The Monacelli Press, New York.

    1998   Taíno Wooden Sculpture: Duhos, Rulership and the Visual Arts in the 12th-16th Century Caribbean, Unpublished PhD thesis, University of East Anglia, Norwich, United Kingdom.

Ostapkowicz, Joanna, Christopher Bronk Ramsey, Alex Wiedenhoeft, Fiona Brock, Tom Higham and Samuel Wilson

    2011   'This Relic of Antiquity': 5th-15th Century Wood Carvings from the Southern Lesser Antilles. In *Communities in Contact: Essays in Archaeology, Ethnohistory and Ethnography of the Amerindian Circum-Caribbean*, edited by Corinne L. Hofman and Anne van Duijvenbode, pp. 137-170. Sidestone Press, Leiden, the Netherlands.

Ostapkowicz, Joanna and Lee Newsom

    2012   "Gods... Adorned with the Embroiderer's Needle": The Materials, Making and Meaning of a Taino Cotton Reliquary. *Latin American Antiquity* 23(3): 300-326.

Overing, Joanna

    1990   The Shaman as a Maker of Worlds: Nelson Goodman in the Amazon. *Man* 25(4): 602-619.

Oyuela-Caycedo, Augusto

    2001   The Rise of Religious Routinization: The Study of Changes from Shaman to Priestly Elite. In *Mortuary Practices and Ritual Associations: Shamanic Elements in Prehistoric Funerary Contexts in South America*, edited by John E. Staller and Elizabeth J. Currie, pp. 5-19. British Archaeological Report International Series. Archaeopress, Oxford, United Kingdom.

Padgett, John F. and Walter W. Powell

    2012   *The Emergence of Organizations and Markets*. Princeton University Press, Princeton, New Jersey.

Pagán Jiménez, Jaime

    2011   Early Phytocultural Processes in the Pre-Colonial Antilles: A Pan-Caribbean Survey for an Ongoing Starch Grain Research. In *Communities in Contact: Essays in Archaeology, Ethnohistory and Ethnography of the Amerindian Circum-Caribbean*, edited by Corinne L. Hofman and Anne van Duijvenbode, pp. 87-117. Sidestone Press, Leiden, the Netherlands.

2013   Human-Plant Dynamics in the Precolonial Antilles: A Synthetic Update. In *The Oxford Handbook of Caribbean Archaeology*, edited by William F. Keegan, Corinne L. Hofman and Reniel Rodríguez Ramos, pp. 391-406. Oxford University Press, Oxford, United Kingdom.

Pagán Jiménez, Jaime and Reniel Rodríguez Ramos

2007   Sobre los Orígenes de la Agricultura en las Antillas. *Proceedings of the 21ˢᵗ International Congress for Caribbean Archaeology*: 252-259. University of the West Indies, Trinidad and Tobago.

Paleček, Martin and Mark Risjord

2013   Relativism and the Ontological Turn within Anthropology. *Philosophy of the Social Sciences* 43(1): 3-23.

Pané, Fray Ramón

1999 [1571]   *An Account of the Antiquities of the Indians*. 1999 edition with an introductory study, notes, and appendixes by José Juan Arrom ed. Translated by Susan C. Griswold. Duke University Press, Durham, United Kingdom.

Pantel, A. Gus

1988   Precolumbian Flaked Stone Assemblages in the West Indies. Unpublished PhD thesis, University of Tennessee, Knoxville, Tennessee.

Parr, Lisa A. and Erin E. Hecht

2011   Face Perception in Non-Human Primates In *Oxford Handbook of Face Perception*, edited by Andy Calder, Gillian Rhodes, Mark Johnson and Jim Haxby, pp. 149-176. Oxford University Press, Oxford, United Kingdom.

Parry, Jonathan P.

1986   The Gift, the Indian Gift and the 'Indian Gift'. *Man* 21(3): 453-473.

Parry, Jonathan P. and Maurice Bloch

1989   *Money and the Morality of Exchange*. Cambridge University Press, Cambridge, United Kingdom.

Pauketat, Timothy R.

2001   Practice and History in Archaeology. *Anthropological Theory* 1(1): 73-98.

2008   *Chiefdoms and Other Archaeological Delusions*. Altamira Press, Lanham, Maryland.

Peeples, Matthew A. and John M. Roberts Jr.

2013   To Binarize or Not to Binarize: Relational Data and the Construction of Archaeological Networks. *Journal of Archaeological Science* 40(7): 3001-3010.

Pels, Peter J.

2005   The Spirit of Matter: On Fetish, Rarity, Fact and Fancy. In *Border Fetishisms. Material Objects in Unstable Spaces*, edited by Patricia Spyer, pp. 91-121. Routledge, London.

2010   Magical Things: On Fetishes, Commodities, and Computers. In *The Oxford Handbook of Material Culture Studies*, edited by Dan Hicks and Mary C. Beaudry, pp. 613-633. Oxford University Press, Oxford, United Kingdom.

Pestle, William, L. Antonio Curet, Reniel Rodríguez Ramos and Miguel Rodríguez López

2013   New Questions and Old Paradigms: Reexamining Caribbean Culture History. *Latin American Antiquity* 24(3): 243-261.

Petersen, James B.

    1997   Taino, Island Carib, and Prehistoric Amerindian Economics in the West Indies: Tropical Forest Adaptations to Island Environments. In *The Indigenous peoples of the Caribbean*, edited by Samuel M. Wilson, pp. 118-130. University Press of Florida, Gainesville, Florida.

Petersen, James B. and John G. Crock

    2007   Handsome Death: The Taking, Displaying and Consumption of Human Remains in the Insular Caribbean and Greater Amazonia. In *The Taking and Displaying of Human Body Parts as Trophies by Amerindians*, edited by Richard J. Chacon and David H. Dye, pp. 547-574. Springer, New York.

Petersen, James B., Corinne L. Hofman and L. Antonio Curet

    2004   Time and Culture: Chronology and Taxonomy in the Eastern Caribbean and the Guianas. In *Late Ceramic Age Societies in the Eastern Caribbean*, edited by André Delpuech and Corinne L. Hofman, pp. 17-33. British Archaeological Reports, Oxford, United Kingdom.

Petitjean-Roget, Henry

    1997   Notes on Caribbean Art and Mythology. In *The Indigenous Peoples of the Caribbean*, edited by Samuel M. Wilson, pp. 100-108. University Press of Florida, Gainesville, Florida.

Petitjean Roget, Henry

    1993   Les Pierres à Trois Pointes des Antilles: Essai d'Interprétation. *Revue Internationale de Sciences Humaines et Sociales* 1: 7-26.

Petrie, W. M. Flinders

    1899   Sequences in Prehistoric Remains. *Journal of the Anthropological Institute of Great Britain and Ireland* 29(3/4): 295-301.

Pfeiffer, Thomas, Claudia Rutte, Timothy Killingback, Michael Taborsky and Sebastian Bonhoeffer

    2005   Evolution of Cooperation by Generalized Reciprocity. *Proceedings of the Royal Society B: Biological Sciences* 272(1568): 1115-1120.

Phillips, Stephen

    2011   Networked Glass: Lithic Raw Material Consumption and Social Networks in the Kuril Islands, Far Eastern Russia. Unpublished PhD thesis, University of Washington, Seattle, Washington.

Pinchon, Rev. Robert

    1961   The Different Forms of Pottery in the Arawak Civilisation. *Proceedings of the 1st congress for the study of the Pre-columbian Civilisations of the Lesser Antilles*. Martinique.

Pindell, James L. and Stephen F. Barrett

    1990   Geological Evolution of the Caribbean Region: A Plate Tectonic Perspective. In *The Caribbean Region*, pp. 405-432. Geological Society of America, Boulder, Colorado.

Pinker, Steven

    2011   *The Better Angels of Our Nature: Why Violence Has Declined.* Penguin Books, London.

Pitt-Rivers, Lt-Gen. A. Lane-Fox

    1906   *The Evolution of Culture and Other Essays.* Clarendon Press, Oxford, United Kingdom.

Plomp, Esther

2013   Dogs on the Move. Unpublished MA thesis, Faculty of Archaology Leiden University, Leiden, the Netherlands.

Polanyi, Karl

1957   The Economy as Instituted Process. In *Trade and Market in the Early Empires*, edited by Karl Polanyi, Conrad M. Arensberg and Harry W. Pearson, pp. 243-270. Free Press, Glencoe, Illinois.

1963   Ports of Trade in Early Societies. *The Journal of Economic History* 23(1): 30-45.

Portuondo Zúñiga, Olga

2002   *La Virgen de la Caridad del Cobre: Símbolo de Cubanía*. Editorial Oriente, Havana, Cuba.

Prell, Christina

2011   *Social Network Analysis: History, Theory and Methodology*. Sage Publications Limited, London.

Preucel, Robert W.

2008   *Archaeological Semiotics*. Blackwell Publishing, Malden, Massachusetts.

Przytycki, Józef H.

1998   Classical Roots of Knot Theory. *Chaos, Solitons and Fractals* 9(4): 531-545.

Rafinesque, Constantine S.

1836   *The American Nations; or Outlines of Their General History, Ancient and Modern: Including the Whole History of the Earth and Mankind in the Western Hemisphere; the Philosophy of American History; the Annals, Traditions, Civilization, Languages, &C., of All the American Nations, Tribes, Empires and States*. F. Turner, Philadelphia, Pennsylvania.

Rainey, Froelich G.

1935   A New Prehistoric Culture in Puerto Rico. *Proceedings of the National Academy of Sciences* 21: 12-16.

1952   *Porto Rican Prehistory*. New York Academy of Sciences, New York.

Redmond, Elsa. M.

1998   The Dynamics of Chieftaincy and the Development of Chiefdoms. In *Chiefdoms and Chieftaincy in the Americas*, edited by Elsa M. Redmond, pp. 215-244. University Press of Florida, Gainesville, Florida.

Reed, Jessica A. and James B. Petersen

2001   A Comparison of Huecan and Cedrosan Saladoid Ceramics at the Trants Site, Montserrat. *Proceedings of the 18th International Congress for Caribbean Archaeology* 2: 253-268. Grenada.

Regional Museum of Archaeology Altos de Chavon

1991   *Quincentennial Commemorative Catalogue*. Fundación Centro Cultural Altos de Chavón, La Romana, Dominican Republic.

Renfrew, Colin

1977   Alternative Models for Exchange and Spatial Distribution. In *Exchange Systems in Prehistory*, edited by Timothy K. Earle and Jonathon E. Ericson, pp. 71-90. Academic Press, New York.

1986   Varna and the Emergence of Wealth in Prehistoric Europe. In *The Social Life of Things: Commodities in Cultural Perspective*, edited by Arjun Appadurai, pp. 169-194. Cambridge University Press, Cambridge, United Kingdom.

Renfrew, Colin, Chris Frith and Lambros Malafouris

2008   Introduction. The Sapient Mind: Archaeology Meets Neuroscience. *Philosophical Transactions of the Royal Society B: Biological Sciences* 363(1499): 1935-1938.

Richerson, Peter J. and Robert Boyd

2004   *Not by Genes Alone: How Culture Transformed Human Evolution*. Chicago University Press, Chicago, Illinois.

Ritzer, George and Pamela Gindoff

1992   Methodological Relationism: Lessons for and from Social Psychology. *Social Psychology Quarterly* 55(2): 128-140.

Rivière, Peter

1984   *Individual and Society in Guiana: A Comparative Study of Amerindian Social Organization*. Cambridge University Press Cambridge, United Kingdom.

Rodríguez Ramos, Reniel

2005   The Crab-Shell Dichotomy Revisited: The Lithics Speak Out. In *Ancient Borinquen: Archaeology and Ethnohistory of Native Puerto Rico. University of Alabama Press, Tuscaloosa*, edited by Peter E. Siegel, pp. 1-54. University of Alabama Press, Tuscaloosa, Alabama.

2010a   *Rethinking Puerto Rican Precolonial History*. Alabama University Press, Tuscaloosa, Alabama.

2010b   What Is the Caribbean?: An Archaeological Perspective. *Journal of Caribbean Archaeology* special publication #3: 19-51.

2011   The Circulation of Jadeitite across the Caribbeanscape. In *Communities in Contact: Essays in Archaeology, Ethnohistory and Ethnography of the Amerindian Circum-Caribbean*, edited by Corinne L. Hofman and Anne van Duijvenbode, pp. 117-136. Sidestone Press, Leiden, the Netherlands.

Rodríguez Ramos, Reniel, Elvis Babilonia, L. Antonio Curet and Jorge Ulloa Hung

2008   The Pre-Arawak Pottery Horizon in the Antilles: A New Approximation. *Latin American Antiquity* 19(1): 47-63.

Rodríguez Ramos, Reniel and Jaime Pagán Jiménez

2006   Interacciones Multivectoriales en el Circum-Caribe Precolonial: Un Vistazo desde las Antillas. *Caribbean Studies* 34(2): 103-143.

Rodríguez Ramos, Reniel, Jaime Pagán Jiménez and Corinne L. Hofman

2013   The Humanization of the Insular Caribbean. In *The Oxford Handbook of Caribbean Archaeology*, edited by William F. Keegan, Corinne L. Hofman and Reniel Rodríguez Ramos, pp. 126-140. Oxford University Press, Oxford, United Kingdom.

Rodríguez Ramos, Reniel, Joshua M. Torres and José R. Oliver

2010   Rethinking Time in Caribbean Archaeology: The Puerto Rican Case Study. In *In Island Shores Distant Pasts: Archaeological and Biological Approaches to the Pre-Columbian Settlement of the Caribbean*, edited by Scott M. Fitzpatrick and Ann H. Ross, pp. 21-53. University of Florida Press, Gainesville, Florida.

Roe, Peter G.

1982   *The Cosmic Zygote: Cosmology in the Amazon Basin*. Rutgers University Press, New Brunswick, New Jersey.

1997   Just Wasting Away: Taíno Shamanism and Concepts of Fertility. In *Taíno: Pre-Columbian Art and Culture from the Caribbean*, edited by Fatima Bercht, Estrellita Brodsky, John A. Farmer and Dicey Taylor, pp. 124-157. The Monacelli Press, New York.

2004   The Ghost in the Machine. In *Embedded Symmetries: Natural and Cultural*, edited by Dorothy K. Washburn, pp. 95-134. University of New Mexico Press, Albuquerque, New Mexico.

Roscoe, Paul

2009   Social Signaling and the Organization of Small-Scale Society: The Case of Contact-Era New Guinea. *Journal of Archaeological Method and Theory*.

Rosman, Abraham and Paula G. Rubel

1986   *Feasting with Mine Enemy: Rank and Exchange among Northwest Coast Societies.* Waveland Press, Prospect Heights, Illinois.

Roth, Walter E.

1915   *An Inquiry into the Animism and Folk-Lore of the Guiana Indians.* Government Printing Office, Washington, D.C.

Rouse, Irving B.

1939   *Prehistory in Haiti: A Study in Method.* Yale University Press, New Haven, Connecticut.

1948a   The Arawak. In *Handbook of South American Indians Vol. 4: The Circum-Caribbean Tribes*, edited by Julian H. Steward, pp. 507-546. Smithsonian Institution, Washington, D.C.

1948b   The Carib. In *Handbook of South American Indians Vol. 4: The Circum-Caribbean Tribes*, edited by Julian H. Steward, pp. 547-565. Smithsonian Institution, Washington, D.C.

1948c   The Ciboney. In *Handbook of South American Indians Vol. 4: The Circum-Caribbean Tribes*, edited by Julian H. Steward, pp. 497-506. Smithsonian Institution, Washington, D.C.

1953   The Circum-Caribbean Theory, an Archeological Test. *American Anthropologist* 55(2): 188-200.

1977   Pattern and Process in West Indian Archaeology. *World Archaeology* 9(1): 1-11.

1986   *Migrations in Prehistory: Inferring Population Movement from Cultural Remains.* Yale University Press, New Haven, Connecticut.

1992   *The Taínos: Rise and Decline of the People Who Greeted Columbus.* Yale University Press, New Haven and London.

Rouse, Irving B. and Ricardo E. Alegría

1990   *Excavations at María de la Cruz Cave and Hacienda Grande Village Site, Loiza, Puerto Rico.* Yale University Press, New Haven, Connecticut.

Rouse, Irving B. and José M. Cruxent

1963   *Venezuelan Archaeology.* Yale University Press, New Haven, Connecticut.

Rousseau, Jean-Jacques

1966 [1762]   *Du Contrat Social.* Garnier-Flammarion, Paris.

2012 [1754]   Discourse on the Origin and Foundations of Inequality among Men. In *The Basic Political Writings: Discourse on the Sciences and the Arts, Discourse on the Origin and Foundations of Inequality among Men, Discourse on Political Economy, on the Social Contract*, edited by David Wootton, pp. 27-121. Translated by Donald A. Cress. Hackett Publishing Company Incorporated, Indianapolis, Indiana.

Rozenberg, Guillaume

2004   How Giving Sanctifies: The Birthday of Thamanya Hsayadaw in Burma. *Journal of the Royal Anthropological Institute* 10(3): 495-515.

Sahlins, Marshall D.

　　1963　　Poor Man, Rich Man, Big-Man, Chief: Political Types in Melanesia and Polynesia. *Comparative Studies in Society and History* 5(3): 285-303.

　　1975　　*Islands of History*. Unversity of Chicago Press, Chicago, Illinois.

Sahlins, Marshalll

　　1972　　*Stone Age Economics*. Routledge, London and New York.

Samson, Alice V. M.

　　2010　　*Renewing the House: Trajectories of Social Life in the Yucayeque (Community) of El Cabo, Higüey, Dominican Republic, AD 800 to 1504*. Sidestone Press, Leiden, the Netherlands.

Samson, Alice V. M. and Bridget M. Waller

　　2010　　Not Growling but Smiling: New Interpretations of the Bared Teeth Motif in the Precolumbian Caribbean. *Current Anthropology* 51(3): 425-433.

Sanoja, Mario

　　2007　　*Memorias Para La Integración*. Monte Ávila Editores Latinoamericana, Caracas, Venezuela.

Santos-Granero, Fernando

　　2007　　Of Fear and Friendship: Amazonian Sociality Beyond Kinship and Affinity. *Journal of the Royal Anthropological Institute* 13(1): 1-18.

　　2009a　　*The Occult Life of Things: Native Amazonian Theories of Materiality and Personhood*. The University of Arizona Press, Tucson, Arizona.

　　2009b　　*Vital Enemies: Slavery, Predation and the Amerindian Political Economy of Life*. University of Texas Press, Austin, Texas.

Sauer, Carl O.

　　1966　　*The Early Spanish Main*. University of California Press, Berkeley, California.

Schiffer, Michael B.

　　1999　　*The Material Life of Human Beings: Artefacts, Behavior and Communication*. Routledge, London.

Schortman, Edward M. and Wendy Ashmore

　　2012　　History, Networks, and the Quest for Power: Ancient Political Competition in the Lower Motagua Valley, Guatemala. *Journal of the Royal Anthropological Institute* 18(1): 1-21.

Scott, John

　　2000　　*Social Network Analysis: A Handbook.*. Sage, London.

Service, Elman R.

　　1962　　*Primitive Social Organization*. Random House, New York.

Sheller, Mimi

　　2003　　*Consuming the Caribbean: From Arawaks to Zombies*. Routledge, London.

Siegel, Peter E.

　　1992　　Ideology, Power and Social Complexity in Puerto Rico. Unpublished PhD thesis, State University of New York, Bighamton, New York.

　　1996a　　An Interview with Irving Rouse. *Current Anthropology* 37(4): 671-689.

　　1996b　　Ideology and Culture Change in Prehistoric Puerto Rico: A View from the Community. *Journal of Field Archaeology* 23(3): 313-333.

1997   Ancestor Worship and Cosmology among the Taino. In *Taíno: Pre-Columbian Art and Culture from the Caribbean*, edited by Fatima Bercht, Estrellita Brodsky, John A. Farmer and Dicey Taylor, pp. 106-111. The Monacelli Press, New York.

1999   Contested Places and Places of Contest: The Evolution of Social Power and Ceremonial Space in Prehistoric Puerto Rico. *Latin American Antiquity* 10(3): 209-238.

2004   What Happened after Ad 600 in Puerto Rico?: Corporate Groups, Population Restructuring, and Post-Saladoid Changes. In *Late Ceramic Age Societies in the Eastern Caribbean*, edited by André Delpuech and Corinne L. Hofman, pp. 87-101. Archaeopress, Oxford, United Kingdom.

2010   Continuity and Change in the Evolution of Religion and Political Organization on Pre-Columbian Puerto Rico. *Journal of Anthropological Archaeology* 29(3): 302-326.

2013   Caribbean Archaeology in Historical Perspective. In *The Oxford Handbook of Caribbean Archaeology*, edited by William F. Keegan, Corinne L. Hofman and Reniel Rodríguez Ramos, pp. 21-47. Oxford University Press, Oxford, United Kingdom.

Siegel, Peter E., Renzo Duin and Jimmy L. Mans

2013   Down-the-Line Encounters: Processes of Exchange, Post-Colonial Experiences, and Globalization in the Island of Guiana on the South American Continent. Paper presented at the Society for American Archaeology Annual Congress, Honolulu, Hawaii.

Siegel, Peter E. and Elizabeth Righter (editors)

2011   *Protecting Heritage in the Caribbean*. University of Alabama Press, Tuscaloosa, Alabama.

Sigaud, Lygia

2003   The Vicissitudes of the Gift. *Social Anthropology* 10(03): 335-358.

Sillitoe, Paul

1979   *Give and Take: Exchange in Wola Society*. Australian National University Press, Canberra, Australia.

2006   Why Spheres of Exchange? *Ethnology* 45(1): 1-23.

Simmel, Georg

1950   *The Sociology of Georg Simmel*. Translated by Kurt H. Wolff. The Free Press, Glencoe, Illinois.

Simpson, Bob

2004   Impossible Gifts: Bodies, Buddhism and Bioethics in Contemporary Sri Lanka. *Journal of the Royal Anthropological Institute* 10(4): 839-859.

Sindbæk, Søren M.

2007   The Small World of the Vikings: Networks in Early Medieval Communication and Exchange. *Norwegian Archaeological Review* 40(1): 59-74.

Skrbina, David

2005   *Panpsychism in the West*. The MIT Press, Cambridge, Massachusetts.

Smith, Adam

2009 [1776]   *An Inquiry into the Nature and Causes of the Wealth of Nations*. Cosimo, Inc., New York.

Smith, Erminnie A.

1883   Myths of the Iroquis. In *Second Annual Report of the Bureau of American Ethnology for the Years 1880-1881*, pp. 47-116. Government Printing Office, Washington D.C.

Sober, Elliot and David S. Wilson

1998   *Unto Others: The Evolution and Psychology of Unselfish Behavior*. Harvard University Press, Cambridge, Massachussets.

Spencer, Charles S. and Elsa M. Redmond

1992   Prehispanic Chiefdoms of the Western Venezuelan Llanos. *World Archaeology* 24(1): 134-157.

Spielmann, Katherine A.

2002   Feasting, Craft Specialization, and the Ritual Mode of Production in Small-Scale Societies. *American Anthropologist* 104(1): 195-207.

Spriggs, Matthew

2008   Ethnographic Parallels and the Denial of History. *World Archaeology* 40(4): 538-552.

Ssorin-Chaikov, Nikolai

2006   On Heterochrony: Birthday Gifts to Stalin, 1949. *Journal of the Royal Anthropological Institute* 12(2): 355-375.

Steele, James, Claudia Glatz and Anne Kandler

2010   Ceramic Diversity, Random Copying, and Tests for Selectivity in Ceramic Production. *Journal of Archaeological Science* 37(6): 1348-1358.

Stevens-Arroyo, Antonio M.

2006   *Cave of the Jagua: The Mythological World of the Taínos*. University of Scranton Press, Scranton, United Kingdom.

Steward, Julian H.

1948   *Handbook of South American Indians Volume 4: The Circum-Caribbean Tribes*. Smithsonian Institution, Washington, D.C.

Strathern, Andrew

1971   *The Rope of Moka: Big-Men and Ceremonial Exchange in Mount Hagen, New Guinea*. Cambridge University Press, Cambridge, United Kingdom.

Strathern, Marilyn

1996   Cutting the Network. *The Journal of the Royal Anthropological Institute* 2(3): 517-535.

Stumpf, Michael P. H. and Mason A. Porter

2012   Critical Truths About Power Laws. *Science* 335(6069): 665-666.

Surrallés, Alexandre

2003   Face to Face: Meaning, Feeling and Perception in Amazonian Welcoming Ceremonies. *Royal Anthropological Institute* 9(4): 775-791.

Sverdrup, Harald U., Martin W. Johnson and Richard H. Fleming

1942   *The Oceans: Their Physics, Chemistry, and General Biology*. Prentice-Hall, New York.

Sykes, Karen

2005   *Arguing with Anthropology: An Introduction to Critical Theories of the Gift*. Routledge, London.

Tavárez María, Clenis and Ferdinand L. Calderón

2005   Estudios De Antropología Fisica del Cementerio De Macao, República Dominicana. *Proceedings of the 21st Congress of the International Association of Caribbean Archaeologists*: 92-101. Trinidad and Tobago.

Taylor, Douglas

1938   The Caribs of Dominica. *Bulletin of the Smithsonian Institution* 119: 103-160.

Tero, Atsushi, Seiji Takagi, Tetsu Saigusa, Kentaro Ito, Dan P. Bebber, Mark D. Fricker, Kenji Yumiki, Ryo Kobayashi and Toshiyuki Nakagaki

2010   Rules for Biologically Inspired Adaptive Network Design. *Science* 327(5964): 439-442.

Terrell, John E.

1977   Human Biogeography in the Solomon Islands. *Fieldiana Anthropology* 68(1): 1-47.

2008   Islands and the Average Joe. *The Journal of Island and Coastal Archaeology* 3(1): 77-82.

2010   Language and Material Culture on the Sepik Coast of Papua New Guinea: Using Social Network Analysis to Simulate, Graph, Identify, and Analyse Social and Cultural Boundaries between Communities. *Journal of Island and Coastal Archaeology* 5(3): 3-32.

Thomas, Nicholas

1991   *Entangled Objects: Exchange, Material Culture, and Colonialism in the Pacific*. Harvard University Press, Cambridge, Massachusetts/London.

Thurnwald, Richard

1932   *Economics in Primitive Communities*. Oxford University Press, Oxford, United Kingdom.

Tilley, Christopher

1996   *An Ethnography of the Neolithic: Early Prehistoric Societies in Southern Scandinavia*. Cambridge University Press, Cambridge, United Kingdom.

1999   *Metaphor and Material Culture*. Blackwell Publishers, Oxford, United Kingdom.

Tilley, Christopher, Webb Keane, Susanne Küchler, Mike Rowlands and Patricia Spyer (editors)

2006   *Handbook of Material Culture*. Sage Publications, London.

Torres Etayo, Daniel

2004   La Arqueología Cubana en la Encrucijada: La Teoría o la Empiria. *Caribe Arqueológico* 8: 2-7.

Torres, Joshua M.

2005   Deconstructing the Polity: Communities and Social Landscapes of the Ceramic-Age Peoples of South Central Puerto Rico. In *Ancient Borinquen: Archaeology and Ethnohistory of Native Puerto Rico*, edited by Peter E. Siegel, pp. 202-229. University of Alabama Press, Tuscaloosa, Alabama.

2010   Complex Socialities and the Construction of Communities in the Ancient Caribbean. Paper presented at the The SAA 75th Anniversary Meeting, St. Louis, Missouri.

2012   The Social Construction of Community, Polity, and Place in Ancient Puerto Rico (AD 600-AD 1200). Unpublished PhD thesis, University of Florida, Gainesville.

Torres, Joshua M. and Reniel Rodríguez Ramos

2008   The Caribbean: A Continent Divided by Water. In *Archaeology and Geoinformatics: Case studies from the Caribbean*, edited by Basil A. Reid, pp. 13-29. the University of Alabama Press, Tuscaloosa, Alabama.

Torres Santiago, Osvaldo

2009   *El Pueblo Taíno, los Hijos de Atabeyra*. Lulu.com, Raleigh, North Carolina.

Trigger, Bruce G.

2006   *A History of Archaeological Thought*. Cambridge University Press, Cambridge, United Kingdom.

Trivers, Robert L.

1971   The Evolution of Reciprocal Altruism. *The Quarterly Review of Biology* 46(1): 35.

Tylor, Edward B.

1871   *Primitive Cultures Volume 1: Researches into the Development of Mythology, Philosophy, Religion, Art, and Custom*. John Murray, London.

Ulloa Hung, Jorge

2008   La Alferería del Yacimiento Macao en el Contexto de la Arqueología Dominicana. *Bolétin del Museo del Hombre Dominicano* 40: 289-305.

2013   Arqueología en la Línea Noroeste de la Española: Paisajes, Cerámicas e Interacctiones. Unpublished PhD thesis, Faculty of Archaeology, Leiden University, Leiden.

Ulloa Hung, Jorge and Julio Corbea Calzado (editors)

2011   *José Juan Arrom: La Búsqueda de Nuestras Raíces*. Fundación García Arévalo, Santo Domingo, Dominican Republic.

Ulloa Hung, Jorge and Roberto Valcárcel Rojas

2002   *Cerámica Temprana en el Centro del Oriente de Cuba*. Impresos Viewgraph, Santo Domingo, Dominican Republic.

2013   Archaeological Practice, Archaic Presence, and Interactions in Indigenous Societies in Cuba. In *The Oxford Handbook of Caribbean Archaeology*, edited by William F. Keegan, Corinne L. Hofman and Reniel Rodríguez Ramos, pp. 232-249. Oxford University Press, Oxford, United Kingdom.

Valcárcel Rojas, Roberto

1999   Banes Precolombino. Jerarquía y Sociedad. *Caribe Arqueológico* 5.

2002   *Banes Precolombino. La Ocupación Agricultora*. Edicones Holguín, Holguín, Cuba.

2012   Interacción Colonial En Un Pueblo De Indios Encomendados: El Chorro De Maíta, Cuba. Unpublished PhD thesis, Faculty of Archaeology, Leiden University, Leiden.

Valéry, Paul

1920   Le cimetière marin. Émile-Paul Frères, Paris.

van As, Abraham, Lou F. H. C. Jacobs and Corinne L. Hofman

2008   In Search of Potential Clay Sources Used for the Manufacture of the Pre-Columbian Pottery of El Cabo, Eastern Dominican Republic. *Leiden Journal of Pottery Studies* (24): 55-74.

van Rossenberg, Erik

2012   Cultural Landscapes, Social Networks and Historical Trajectories. Unpublished PhD thesis, Faculty of Archaeology, Leiden University, Leiden.

Vargas Arenas, Iraida

    1985   Modo De Vida: Categoría de las Mediaciones entre Formación Social y Cultura. *Boletín de antropología americana* 12: 5-16.

    1989   Teorías eobre el Cacicazgo como Modo de Vida: El Caso del Caribe. *Boletín de Antropología Americana* 20: 19-30.

Vaughn Howard, Catherine

    2001   Wrought Identities: The Waiwai Expeditions in Search of the "Unseen Tribes" of Northern Amazonia. Unpublished PhD thesis, Department of Anthropology, University of Chicago, Chicago, Illinois.

Veloz Maggiolo, Marcio

    1972   *Arqueología Prehistorica De Santo Domingo*. McGraw-Hill Eastern Publishers, Singapore.

    2001   Los Agricultores Tempranos en la Isla de Santo Domingo. In *Culturas Aborigenes del Caribe*, edited by Ramon H. Seiffe, pp. 199-201. Publicaciones del Banco Central de la Republica Dominicana, Santo Domingo.

Veloz Maggiolo, Marcio and Elpidio J. Ortega

    1972   Excavaciones en Macao, República Dominicana. *Boletín del Museo del Hombre Dominicano* 2: 157-175.

Veloz Maggiolo, Marcio, Elpidio Ortega, and Angel Caba Fuentes

    1981   *Los Modos de Vida Meillacoides y sus Posibles Origenes*. Museo del Hombre Dominicano, Santo Domingo, Dominican Republic.

Viveiros de Castro, Eduardo

    1998   Cosmological Deixis and Amerindian Perspectivism. *The Journal of the Royal Anthropological Institute* 4(3): 469-488.

    2004   Exchanging Perspectives: The Transformation of Objects into Subjects in Amerindian Ontologies. *Common Knowledge* 10(3): 463-484.

Waldron, Lawrence

    2010   Like Turtles, Islands Float Away: Emergent Distinctions in the Zoomorphic Iconography of Saladoid Ceramics of the Lesser Antilles, 250 Bce to 650 Ce, City University of New York, New York.

Walker, Jeffrey B.

    1993   Stone Collars, Elbow Stones, and Three-Pointers and the Nature of Taíno Ritual and Myths. Unpublished PhD thesis, Department of Anthropology, Washington State University, Pullman.

Waters, Michael R.

    1992   *Principles of Geoarchaeology: A North-American Perspective*. University of Arizona Press, Tucson, Arizona.

Watters, David R.

    1982   Relating Oceanography to Antillean Archaeology: Implications from Oceania. *Journal of New World Archaeology* 5(2): 3-12.

    1997   Maritime Trade in the Prehistoric Eastern Caribbean. In *The Indigenous peoples of the Caribbean*, edited by Samuel M. Wilson, pp. 88-99. University Press of Florida, Gainesville, Florida.

Watters, David R. and Richard Scaglion

    1994   Beads and Pendants from Trants, Montserrat: Implications for the Prehistoric Lapidary Industry of the Caribbean. *Annals of Carnegie Museum* 63(3): 215-237.

Watts, Duncan J.

    1999   *Small Worlds: The Dynamic of Networks between Order and Randomness*. Princeton University Press, Princeton, New Jersey.

    2003   *Six Degrees: The Science of a Connected Age*. Vintage Books, London.

Webmoor, Timothy

    2007   What About 'One More Turn after the Social' in Archaeological Reasoning? Taking Things Seriously. *World Archaeology* 39(4): 563-578.

Webmoor, Timothy and Christopher L. Witmore

    2008   Things Are Us! A Commentary on Human/Things Relations under the Banner of a 'Social' Archaeology. *Norwegian Archaeological Review* 41(1): 53-70.

Weiner, Annette B.

    1987   *The Trobrianders of Papua New Guinea*. Wadsworth Group/Thomson Learning, Belmont, California.

    1992   *Inalienable Possessions: The Paradox of Keeping-While-Giving*. University of California Press, Berkeley, California.

Welsch, Robert L., John E. Terrell and John A. Nadolski

    1992   Language and Culture on the North Coast of New Guinea. *American Anthropologist* 94(3): 568-600.

West, S. A., A. S. Griffin and A. Gardner

    2007   Social Semantics: Altruism, Cooperation, Mutualism, Strong Reciprocity and Group Selection. *Journal of Evolutionary Biology* 20(2): 415-432.

Weston, Darlene A.

    2010   Human Skeletal Report: Kelbey's Ridge 2 and Spring Bay 1c, Saba. Paper presented at the Barge's Antropologica, Departement of Anatomy and Embryology, Leiden University Medical Centre, Leiden, The Netherlands.

Whitehead, Neil L.

    1995   Introduction: The Island Carib as Anthropological Icon. In *Wolves from the Sea: Readings in the Anthropology of the Native Caribbean*, edited by Neil L. Whitehead. KITLV Press, Leiden, the Netherlands.

    2011   *Of Cannibals and Kings: Primal Anthropology in the Americas*. Pennsylvania State University Pres, University Park, Pennsylvania.

Wilbert, Johannes

    1970   *Folk Literature of the Warao Indians: Narrative Material and Motif Content*. Latin American Centre of the University of California, Los Angeles, California.

    1993   *Mystic Endowment: Religious Ethnography of the Warao Indians*. Harvard University Press, Cambridge, Massachussets.

Wilk, Richard R. and Lisa C. Cliggett

    2007   *Economies and Cultures: Foundations of Economic Anthropology*. Westview Press, Boulder, Colorado.

Willerslev, Rane

    2011   Frazer Strikes Back from the Armchair: A New Search for the Animist Soul. *Journal of the Royal Anthropological Institute* 17(3): 504-526.

Wilson, Samuel M.

    1990   *Hispaniola: Caribbean Chiefdoms in the Age of Columbus*. University of Alabama Press, Tuscaloosa, Alabama.

1993   The Cultural Mosaic of the Indigenous Caribbean. *Proceedings of the British Academy* 81: 37-66.

2007   *The Archaeology of the Caribbean.* Cambridge University Press, Cambridge, United Kingdom.

2013   Caribbean Archaeology in the Next 50 Years. In *The Oxford Handbook of Caribbean Archaeology*, edited by William F. Keegan, Corinne L. Hofman and Reniel Rodríguez Ramos, pp. 568-578. Oxford University Press, Oxford, United Kingdom.

Wittgenstein, Ludwig
1953   *Philosophical Investigations.* Translated by Gertrude E. M. Anscombe. Basil Blackwell Publishing, Oxford, United Kingdom.

Zebrowitz, Leslie A. and Joann M. Montepare
2008   Social Psychological Face Perception: Why Appearance Matters. *Social and Personality Psychology Compass* 2(3): 1497-1517.

Zucchi, Alberta
1984   Nueva Evidencia sobre la Penetración de Grupos Cerámicos a las Antillas Mayores. In *Relaciones Prehispánicas De Venezuela*, edited by Erika Wagner, pp. 35-50. Asociación Venezolana para el Avance de la Ciencia, Caracas, Venezuela.

1991   Prehispanic Connections between the Orinoco, the Amazon, and the Caribbean Area. *Proceedings of the 13th Congress of the International Association of Caribbean Archaeology* 1: 202-220.

Dutch summary

Een Verbonden Verleden: Een socio-materiële netwerkbenadering van de patronen van homogeniteit en diversiteit in de pre-koloniale Cariben

Deze dissertatie presenteert een nieuwe benadering om sociale en culturele diversiteit en homogeniteit in de pre-koloniale periode van het Caribische gebied te bestuderen. Het hiervoor ontwikkelde theoretische en methodologische raamwerk is ten dele ontleend aan het domein van de netwerkwetenschappen. Hiernaast concentreert deze benadering zich specifiek op de kruisverbanden tussen materiële culturele en sociale relaties. In andere woorden, hoe kan het exploreren van systemen van archeologische voorwerpen inzicht geven in sociale netwerken tussen mensen in het verleden en *vice versa*. Deze benadering wordt getest in vier "proof of concept" case studies, welke inspelen op bestaande vraagstukken in de Caribische archeologie. De twee overkoepelende thema's in deze case studies richten zich op recente discussies rond de verbanden en interacties tussen cultureel verschillende gemeenschappen en de structuur en dynamiek van pre-koloniale socio-politieke organisatievormen.

Reeds sinds de eerste regionale studies is het duidelijk dat de pre-koloniale periode van het Caribisch gebied gekarakteriseerd kan worden door twee tegengestelde processen. Aan de ene kant vindt men er een grote lokale verscheidenheid in de praktijken omtrent en het repertoire aan materiële cultuur van de oorspronkelijke bewoners. Aan de andere kant bevat het archeologische bestand van deze regio aanwijzingen voor overkoepelende relaties tussen de samenlevingen en culturen van dit gebied. Het samenspel tussen de twee tegengestelde patronen van homogeniteit en diversiteit is wat het Caribisch gebied toen, maar ook vandaag de dag nog, zijn unieke karakter geeft. Archeologen die zich specialiseren in de pre-koloniale, inheemse geschiedenis hebben dit unieke regionale karakter al op vele manieren proberen te vatten. De Caribische archeologische literatuur grossiert dan ook in metaforen om dit fenomeen van eenheid in diversiteit te beschrijven, met benamingen als "mozaïek", "caleidoscoop", "(cultureel) vernis", "chaos" en "eiland ritmes."

Deze patronen in het archeologische bodemarchief zijn een weerspiegeling van een lange mobiliteits- en interactiegeschiedenis van mensen, dieren, goederen en ideeën, waardoor de regio al ver voor de komst van de Europeanen een complex, verbonden geheel vormde. Het is dus niet verwonderlijk dat onderzoek naar de ontwikkeling van mobiliteit en interactie door middel van het bestuderen van veranderingen in materiële cultuur altijd een van de kernpunten van de Caribische archeologie heeft gevormd. Dit type onderzoek kan worden samengepakt onder de noemer "cultuurhistorie". Traditionele, cultuurhistorische benaderingen, waaronder de "*modal approach*" van Irving B. Rouse het meest wijdverspreid en bekend is, zijn te vergelijken met de taxonomische systemen uit de biologie, gecombineerd met klassieke ideeën over culturele verspreiding, specifiek door middel van volksmigratie (Figuur 1.2). Methodologisch concentreren cultuurhistorische benaderingen zich op het categoriseren van groepen voorwerpen en het volgen van deze groepen in de geografische ruimte en door de tijd heen. Uitingen van materiële cultuur, met name aardewerk, worden op basis van een reeks (decoratieve) kenmerken binnen de een of de andere groep geclassificeerd. De theorie is dat deze materiële cultuurgroepen correleren met de culturele en sociale organisatie en mobiliteit van menselijke gemeenschappen. De uitkomsten van deze lijn van onderzoek wezen op sterke verbanden tussen de culturen en samenlevingen van de Caribische eilanden met het gebied rond de Orinoco en Oost Venezuela.

Sinds het einde van de vorige eeuw kwam er echter een reeks aan archeologische vondsten en studies die dit idee weerspraken. Deze wezen op een grotere interne verscheidenheid van Caribische samenlevingen en culturen als ook die van hun wortels buiten de regio. Veel van de nieuwe opgedane inzichten conflicteerden met het monolithische karakter van traditionele cultuurhistorische theorieën. Het gevolg van deze nieuwe studies was een verandering in het denken over sociale en culturele verbanden in de Cariben en hoe deze het beste bestudeerd kunnen worden. Nieuwe ontdekkingen kwamen samen met een gevoel van "crisis" over de methodes van de traditionele cultuurhistorische benaderingen. De hierdoor ontstane omwenteling in de Caribische archeologie werd op de voet gevolgd door een hernieuwde focus op mobiliteit, uitwisseling en contacten tussen groepen, met daarin extra aandacht voor relaties tussen de eilanden en het vasteland van het gebied (ook wel de "Pan-Caribische theorie" genoemd).

Deze studie presenteert een nieuwe aanpak die de mogelijkheid geeft zowel de diversiteit en homogeniteit van Caribische, pre-koloniale culturen en samenlevingen in ogenschouw te nemen door middel van een netwerkwetenschappelijke exploratie van archeologische en etnohistorische informatiebronnen. Dit wordt gedaan door deze bronnen van informatie te "abstraheren" als netwerken (d.w.z. er wordt een op data gebouwd model van gemaakt; Figuur 3.2 en 3.3). Deze netwerken kunnen dan verder verkend worden met behulp van netwerkwetenschappelijke concepten en metingen. Vanwege het vaak onvolledige karakter van de gebruikte datasets en de prille staat van dit type onderzoek in de (Caribische) archeologie is het nog niet mogelijk om een "zuivere" netwerktheorie (d.w.z. een theoretisch model uit de netwerkwetenschappen) te gebruiken om met de op data gebaseerde modellen te vergelijken. In plaats daarvan is er hier voor gekozen in de case studies traditionele Caribische archeologische theorieën over cultureel contact en socio-politieke organisatie als het ware te vertalen naar een ideaal netwerkmodel (Figuur 1.3 en 1.4). De op archeologische en historische informatie gebaseerde netwerken kunnen dan worden gebruikt om de bestaande archeologische theorie te weerspreken of juist te onderbouwen.

Voor de verdere interpretatie van deze netwerken is het noodzakelijk om een goede grip te hebben op de rol van objecten in sociale systemen en hoe dit beïnvloed wordt door de relaties tussen personen. Omdat zij traditioneel gericht zijn op waargenomen relaties tussen (groepen) mensen, voorzien de netwerkwetenschappen echter niet in theorieën of concepten waarmee archeologische netwerken kunnen worden geïnterpreteerd. De oplossing hiervoor wordt in dit werk gevonden in een combinatie van archeologische, antropologische en Amerindiaans "ontologische" (d.w.z. gericht op de beleving van de originele bewoners) theorieën. Deze kaders hebben veel bij te dragen aan het denken over de onderlinge afhankelijkheid van voorwerpen en personen of, op een grotere schaal, van de materiële culturen en samenlevingen van de oorspronkelijke bewoners van het Caribisch gebied. De focus in deze studie ligt dus niet op de exploratie en analyse van traditionele sociale netwerken, maar op de ontwikkelingen en dynamiek in zogenaamde socio-materiële netwerken. Deze netwerken laten zich typeren als heterogeen (bestaande uit meerdere typen actoren), multiscalair (functionerend over meerdere schalen, bvb. lokaal, regionaal, interregionaal), temporeel overgankelijk (geplaatst in de tijd en gericht op processen), en onderling afhankelijk (ontwikkelingen in het ene netwerk hebben effect op het andere netwerk en vice versa).

De context van pre-koloniale netwerken

Het maken van een "Facebook" van het verleden is echter geen sinecure. Ten eerste is bij het interpreteren van de resultaten van netwerk studies de context altijd van groot belang. De reden hiervoor is dat netwerkmodellen qua structuur en dynamieken vergelijkbaar kunnen zijn, maar dat dit niets hoeft te zeggen over de reflectie van een netwerk in de realiteit. De structuur van mijn Facebook netwerk mag vergelijkbaar zijn met het netwerk van een metrostelsel, computers, voedselketens of het archeologisch bestand, maar in termen van wat deze netwerken doen en voorstellen zijn zij natuurlijk niet direct vergelijkbaar. Studies van "echte" netwerken vinden dus nooit in een vacuüm plaats. Wat dat betreft is het dus belangrijk om de context van deze studie, het Caribisch gebied en haar pre-koloniale culturen en samenlevingen, goed te doorgronden. Deze bezitten een aantal specifieke, dynamische en complexe contextuele parameters. Aan de andere kant zijn juist dit de factoren die een netwerkstudie in dit gebied en van deze periode bijzonder interessant maken.

Ten eerste is er de vraag hoe men het Caribisch gebied als geografische eenheid moet zien vanuit een netwerkperspectief. Sommige ideeën van de oorspronkelijke bewoners over de geografie van dit gebied zijn aan ons overgedragen in de vorm van historische documenten van Spaanse en andere Europese ontdekkingsreizigers, missionarissen, handelsreizigers, en geschiedschrijvers. Geen van deze bronnen of die uit de archeologie geven echter blijk van een inheems geografisch concept dat overeenkomt met ons beeld van het Caribisch gebied als geopolitieke of geoculturele entiteit. Dé Cariben zijn dus een "uitvinding" die stamt uit de vroeg-koloniale periode. Het via de grenzen van interactie en mobiliteitsnetwerken verder bepalen van de grenzen van het Caribisch gebied biedt geen uitkomst. Het is waarschijnlijk dat bewoners van de Caribische eilanden via een klein aantal stappen in een netwerk in contact stond met gemeenschappen ver voorbij de kusten van de Caribische Zee. Net zoals gewoon is bij andere archeologische studies, is het dus noodzakelijk om in een studie als deze de uiterste geografische (of andere vorm van) begrenzingen van de netwerken vooraf duidelijk te omschrijven. Deze studie focust zich specifiek op de Noordoostelijke Cariben (het gebied van de oostelijke Grote Antillen tot aan de Leeward Islands; Figuur 2.1).

Een eerste PPA (*Proximal Point Analysis*) netwerk van de eilandgeografie geeft een beeld van een archipel waarin de verschillende eilanden op gelijkwaardige en opeenvolgende wijze verbonden zijn (Figuur X). Met andere woorden, gebaseerd op de geografie zijn er weinig verschillen in hoe centraal eilandgebieden gelegen zijn en is het PPA-netwerk te vergelijken met de connecties zoals men die kan vinden in het een "*lattice*" netwerk (Figuur 2.2 zie ook Figuur 6.1). Dit gebied wordt echter wel gekenmerkt door een grote geologische en ecologische variatie. Omdat dit effect heeft op het type en de hoeveelheid van materiaal- en voedselbronnen, zijn er toch gedifferentieerde relaties tussen de eilandgemeenschappen te verwachten.

Om gebruik te kunnen maken van het volledige scala aan natuurlijke rijkdommen waren overzeese reizen met peddelkano's tussen de eilanden van groot belang. Wat betreft deze reizen is het duidelijk dat maritieme mobiliteit aan de ene kant grote logistieke voordelen biedt boven die van landreizen en dat factoren zoals zichtbaarheid tussen eilanden en gunstige wind- en stromingsrichtingen lange afstandsreizen zeker mogelijk maakten. Hierdoor is er een beeld ontstaan van connectiviteit tussen eilanden waarbij de Caribische Zee functioneerde als een "watersnelweg". Aan de andere kant hebben wij een onvolledig beeld van de culturele en sociale beleving van zeereizen in de pre-koloniale periode. Verder zijn de gesuggereerde sterftecijfers ten onrechte als laag gekwalificeerd. In andere woorden, de bestaande maritieme en navigatie-studies en modellen geven een uiteenlopend beeld van de mogelijkheden en moeilijkheden van zeereizen. Experimentele archeologische kanoreizen, zoals recentelijk ontplooid in het Martiniquese *Ioumoúlicou* project, en studies naar culturele en sociale factoren en ervaringen van zeereizen, kunnen in de toekomst grote mogelijkheden bieden om de maritieme connectiviteit in de regio beter te doorgronden.

In vogelvlucht laat de culturele en sociale geschiedenis van de pre-koloniale noordoostelijke Cariben zich kenmerken door de samenkomst, groei, krimp en wederopbouw van (inter)regionale interactienetwerken. De eeste kolonisatie van het gebied, vanaf zesduizend jaar geleden, vond plaats vanuit twee richtingen. Vanuit Midden Amerika naar Cuba en verder westwaarts en vanuit het laagland van Zuid Amerika naar Trinidad en verder noordwaarts. Rond 2000 BC kwamen deze twee kolonisatiestromen bijeen in de noordelijke Kleine Antillen. Na een lange periode waarin contact tussen de eilandregio's en het vasteland aanwezig maar wel summier was, ontstond er rond 200 BC een situatie waarin sociale en culturele interactienetwerken zich over een veel groter gebied gingen uitstrekken, vanuit alle kusten van het vasteland en de eilanden zien wij een diffuus en complex web van relaties tussen de verschillende archeologische assemblages. Deze periode staat daarnaast bekend om de relatief plotselinge opkomst van nieuwe vormen van materiële cultuur in de noordoostelijke Cariben, zoals het Saladoïde en Huecoïde aardewerk als ook persoonlijke decoratie en ceremoniële gebruiken en voorwerpen. Vaak werden deze gelinkt aan de eerder besproken migraties, maar nieuwe vondsten laten zien dat er veel overlap bestond tussen de culturen en samenlevingen van de oorspronkelijke bewoners en mogelijke nieuwkomers.

Vanaf 500 AD vond er een tegengestelde ontwikkeling plaats. Contactnetwerken krompen en er was een steeds grotere diversiteit aan lokale materiële cultuurrepertoires en praktijken. Dit komt samen met belangrijke concentratie van de sociale en politieke structuur van de gemeenschappen in de regio. De uitkomst van dit proces mondde uit in de zogenaamde *cacicazgos*, grotere politieke collectieven onder leiding van een *cacique* of "chief". Archeologisch blijft het hoe en waarom van deze ontwikkeling moeilijk vast te stellen. Op dit moment kennen wij de *cacicazgos* het beste vanuit de historische bronnen die vanaf 1492 via de eerste Europeanen in de regio beschikbaar zijn. Wel kunnen we vaststellen dat reeds ver voor contact met Europa de interactienetwerken in de regio zich echter weer in kwantiteit en complexiteit aan het uitbreiden waren. Vanaf AD 1000-1200 waren er weer meer contacten in en tussen de Grote Antillen en oostelijke Kleine Antillen. Het resultaat van deze lange geschiedenis van pre-koloniale ontmoetingen betekent dat rond de tijd van contact de Cariben een hoog diverse culturele, linguïstische en etnische samenstelling had.

De sociale netwerken van een gemiddeld persoon bestonden dus uit een keur aan mensen met verschillende achtergronden, talen en gebruiken, wat een zekere flexibiliteit in omgangsvormen gevraagd moet hebben. Om deze netwerken tussen mensen te begrijpen is het essentieel om te zien hoe vanuit de beleving van de oorspronkelijke bewoners hun dagelijkse interacties verweven waren met grotere "socio-cosmische" netwerken. Deze netwerken bestonden uit dieren, geesten, voorouders en andere "niet menselijke" wezens. Door vergelijkingen met etnografische studies van het tropisch laagland van Zuid Amerika te trekken en deze te verbinden met de materiële cultuur en de overgeleverde verhalen van de oorspronkelijke bewoners van het Caribisch gebied kunnen we een inzicht krijgen in hoe men dacht over deze socio-cosmische partners.

Een groot verschil tussen hedendaagse, Westerse samenlevingen en die van het pre-koloniale Caribisch gebied is dat men zich niet meer zondermeer verheven voelde boven of ondergeschikt aan "niet menselijke" wezens. Volgens deze zienswijze delen mensen, dieren, geesten en anderen misschien niet eenzelfde uiterlijk maar wel een overeenkomstige innerlijk met daarbij behorend gedrag en "cultuur". In het bijzonder shamanen (*behiques*) hadden de mogelijkheid om door de uiterlijke verschijning van niet-mensen heen te zien en met deze wezens in contact te treden – een menselijke shamaan zou dus op bezoek kunnen gaan in het dorp van de schildpadden, daar schildpaddendansen doen en dronken worden van schildpaddenbier en omgekeerd zou een "schildpaddenshamaan" hetzelfde kunnen doen in een mensendorp. In deze ontologie of wereldbeleving, die door de antropoloog Viveiros de Castro "Amerindiaans perspectivisme" is genoemd, was het een kwestie van het aftasten van relaties en de bedoelingen begrijpen achter de acties van dieren, geesten, voorouders en goden. Er bestond dus een veel grotere mogelijke constellatie aan relaties met grillige en soms gevaarlijke wezens. In andere woorden, de dynamiek van pre-koloniale sociale netwerken was totaal anders dan wij heden ten dage gewend zijn. Dit is niet enkel een uitdaging voor de archeologische interpretatie van de sociale en culturele diversiteit in het gebied, maar bovenal voor hoe men dit type relaties via de netwerkwetenschappen zou moeten kwalificeren én kwantificeren of op andere wijze inzichtelijk maken.

Netwerkbenaderingen toegepast op de archeologie

Waar de archeologische en antropologische theorie kunnen bijdragen aan het begrijpen van de context en de socio-culturele praktijk van interactie en mobiliteit in het gebied, zijn de netwerkwetenschappen juist bij uitstek geschikt om de structuur van de vaak complexe en diffuse patronen in het archeologisch bestand te kunnen karteren, exploreren en analyseren. Vooral de laatste paar jaar zijn er meer en meer archeologische studies bijgekomen die benaderingen toepassen uit de netwerkwetenschappen. Netwerkstudies in de archeologie zijn echter verre van nieuw. Ten eerste is er het veelvoorkomend gebruik van het begrip "netwerk" als metafoor voor handel, uitwisseling of andere vermoede sociale relaties in het verleden. Verder is er al sinds het begin van de archeologie als wetenschap de tendens om objecten en andere archeologische kenmerken in netwerk-achtige systemen te plaatsen (Figuur 3.1). Een goed voorbeeld is de typo-chronologie, waarin men aardewerk en andere materiële cultuur uitingen verbindt op basis van uiterlijke kenmerken en in de tijd rangschikt. Daarnaast komen er al sinds de jaren '70 bij tijd en wijlen archeologische studies uit die zich meer uitdrukkelijk verbinden met netwerkbenaderingen.

Niettemin kunnen de netwerkwetenschappen nog veel bijdragen aan archeologische studies. Ondanks dat de netwerkwetenschappen een stevige wiskundige basis hebben in de statistiek, topologie en met name de grafentheorie, is het in eerste instantie niet strikt noodzakelijk om van deze disciplines een diep specialistische kennis in huis te hebben om het toe te kunnen passen op archeologische netwerken. Van groot voordeel hierbij is de recente ontwikkeling van en grote keuze aan software die specifiek gebouwd is om netwerken te kunnen abstraheren, visualiseren, analyseren en modelleren. In deze studie is voornamelijk gebruik gemaakt van *visone*, gratis beschikbare software die zich specialiseert in het visualiseren en intuïtief onderzoeken van verbanden in allerlei verschillende typen relationele data. In deze studies worden de verzamelde data gepresenteerd als afbeeldingen met "*nodes*" (cirkels of andere symbolen) verbonden met "*ties*" (banden of relaties). Achter deze afbeeldingen houden zich echter matrices (tabellen met op de kruisingen van de rijen en kolommen de waarde of "kracht" van de *ties*) schuil die gebruikt kunnen worden om aspecten van het netwerk te meten.

De case studies richten zich vooral op drie meetbare aspecten van netwerken. Ten eerste zijn daar de metingen van het netwerk als geheel, zoals "dichtheid" en "afstanden". Let wel dat deze termen binnen de netwerkwetenschap ene specifieke betekenis hebben. Afstanden worden bijvoorbeeld niet gemeten in geografische eenheden, maar in stappen in een netwerk (van een *node* naar een andere *node*). Een voorbeeld hiervan is bijvoorbeeld de populaire misvatting dat een willekeurig persoon slechts "zes handdrukken" of stappen in het mondiale sociaal netwerk van elkaar verwijderd is. Een tweede focus in de case studies ligt op het onderzoeken van verschillende vormen subgroepen in netwerken, zoals netwerk componenten waarin alle nodes slechts via paden met alle andere *nodes* zijn verbonden (bijv. "ik ken haar niet persoonlijk, maar wel via via"), de totaal verbonden *cliques* (bijv. "wij zijn allen bekenden van elkaar"), of *n-cliques* (bijv. in een 2-clique "een bekende van een bekende behoort nog steeds tot de groep"; Figuur 3.2, 3.3 en Tabel 3.1). Een derde nadruk ligt hier op de "positionele analyse", ook wel bekend als metingen van centraliteit in het netwerk, waarbij men kan berekenen hoeveel controle een individuele *node* heeft over andere *nodes* (Figuur 3.2, 3.3 en Tabel 3.2). Het is belangrijk om bij positionele analyses te onthouden dat men niet direct zaken zoals "macht" of "populariteit" meet, maar dat men deze kan afleiden uit de structurele positie van een *node*. *Degree* is het meest basale voorbeeld hiervan en telt simpelweg de hoeveelheid inkomende en uitgaande *ties* (bijv. "ik heb n kennissen"). Andere metingen, zoals bijvoorbeeld *betweenness*, richten zich op een meer strategische positie van *nodes* in een netwerk, waarbij er gekeken wordt op welke paden in een netwerk een *node* zich bevindt (bijv. "kennissen en anderen in mijn bredere netwerk zijn onderling niet in contact en moeten dit via mij laten verlopen"). Nog een ander voorbeeld van positionele analyse is de *status* centraliteit wat de positie van een *node* bepaalt aan de hand van de *ties* tussen andere nodes (bijv. "ik heb n kennissen, die zelf weer n kennissen hebben").

Verbindende materie en materïele verbanden

Het in samenhang gebruiken van de bovenstaande metingen en in de context van de Caribische pre-koloniale periode vormt de basis van de netwerkbenaderingen in de case studies. Context en kwantificatie zijn echter niet voldoende om inzicht te krijgen in de kruisverbanden tussen het type netwerken waar archeologen normaliter mee werken (netwerken tussen voorwerpen) en het type netwerken waarin zij geïnteresseerd zijn (sociale netwerken in het verleden). In veel van de traditionele archeologie bestaat een loskoppeling tussen deze twee aspecten. De vorm van en strategieën in sociale netwerken in het verleden worden behandeld in archeologische theorie, waar de archeologische methodologie zich buigt over hoe objecten en andere archeologische kenmerken zich verhouden tot elkaar, in de ruimte en in de tijd.

Aan de andere kant zijn er al vele boekenkasten volgeschreven over de vraag hoe onze sociale relaties zich verhouden tot de "wereld der dingen" of, op breder vlak, hoe een samenleving zich verhoudt tot haar (materiële) cultuur. Naast de bekendere (sociaal en moreel) economische theorieën van grootheden als Karl Marx en Adam Smith, zijn de "contract theorieën" van de verlichtingsfilosofen Thomas Hobbes en Jean-Jacques Rousseau een goed voorbeeld hiervan. Hun ideeën zijn hier specifiek van interesse omdat zij zich richten op een gedachte-experiment wat gebaseerd was op de ervaringen van Europeanen met de volkeren van de Nieuwe Wereld. Beiden gaan ervan uit dat mensen in een "originele natuurstaat" (zoals men aannam in de Cariben aangetroffen te hebben) het "contract" tussen staat en bevolking mist. Dat wil zeggen dat allen in deze natuurstaat buiten een samenleving leefden. Het hebben van een samenleving was niet mogelijk vanwege individuele conflicten door schaarste (Hobbes) of omdat men hier geen strikte behoefte aan had vanwege vrijelijk beschikbare, natuurlijke rijkdommen (Rousseau). Wat opvalt is dat er in deze natuurstaat echter ook een afwezigheid is van enige type bezittingen en (materiële) cultuur. Zowel Hobbes als Rousseau plaatsten de wil van mensen om materiële middelen te bezitten als een drijfveer om samen te komen in een samenleving.

Opmerkelijk genoeg, vinden we een soortgelijk idee terug bij de oorspronkelijke bewoners van het Caribisch gebied, maar dan verpakt in hun eigen ontologie. Zaken zoals vuur, riten, gereedschap en ornamenten waren vaak in een oer- of "voortijd" verkregen of geroofd van niet-menselijke wezens door voorouders van de eerste mensen. De daden van deze voorouders hadden hun weerslag op de relaties tussen mensen en tussen mensen en niet-menselijke wezens in het heden – luipaarden zijn bijvoorbeeld in continue oorlog met mensen van nu omdat zij in het verleden beroofd zijn van hun vuur. Het verkrijgen van (materiële) cultuur in een voortijd was dus gekoppeld aan het de dynamiek van de perspectivistische "samenleving" in het heden.

Natuurlijk is er geen direct verband tussen deze hypothetische natuurstaat en de oorspronkelijke bevolking van het Caribisch gebied. Niettemin kan dit gedachte-experiment wel gebruikt worden om inzicht te krijgen in hoe de eerste contacten tussen Europeanen en de oorspronkelijke bevolking tot stand kwamen. Vanwege de vroegheid van dit contact kunnen deze ontmoetingen als een extensie beschouwd worden van (laat) pre-koloniale sociale en culturele praktijken. Wat opvalt is dat, in de afwezigheid van een bestaande taal of eerder bepaalde sociale structuren, de uitwisseling van voorwerpen een centrale rol speelde in de totstandkoming van sociale netwerken tussen deze personen en groepen met totaal verschillende achtergronden. Van specifieke interesse hier zijn het over en weer geven van al dan niet waardevolle voorwerpen tussen belangrijke figuren, zoals Columbus en inheemse *caciques*.

Ook in andere tijden en gebieden speelt materiële cultuur en specifiek het geven en terug geven van cadeaus een essentiële rol. Marcel Mauss, een Frans socioloog en etnograaf, heeft over dit fenomeen in de jaren '20 van de vorige eeuw een belangrijk essay geschreven wat diende als een uitgangspunt voor een studieveld dat zich specialiseerde op de totstandkoming en instandhouding van sociale relaties door middel van giften. Zich baserend op onder meer Maori uitwisselingssystemen, concentreerde Mauss zich in zijn essay op de aanwezigheid van een "geest", d.w.z. een magische kracht, die ervoor zorgde dat cadeaus die gegeven waren ook gereciproceerd werden. Deze mystificatie van een sociaal feit leverde Mauss aanvankelijk veel kritiek op. Dit idee van een bepaalde (onverklaarbare) vorm van subjectiviteit in materiële cultuur keert echter recentelijk weer terug in nieuwe archeologische en materiële cultuurtheorie over de *agency of objects* (het idee dat objecten een sturende invloed hebben op menselijk gedrag).

Veel van de (etnografische) studies die er aan de hand van Mauss zijn originele studie gedaan zijn concentreerden zich echter niet op het idee van het object als subject, maar op de rol die de uitwisselingen van voorwerpen spelen in het creëren en behouden van sociale relaties tussen personen en *vice versa*. Aan de hand van deze rijke literatuur is het mogelijk om vast te stellen dat het bij de kruisverbanden tussen voorwerpen en mensen niet zozeer draait om voorwerpen als menselijk of subject te behandelen, maar hoe de relaties tussen een persoon en zijn of haar voorwerpen zich reflecteert in zijn of haar relaties met anderen. Verder kijkend naar voorbeelden van uitwisselingssystemen zoals de Melanesische *kula*, waarin schelpen armbanden en kettingen tegen elkaar uitgeruild worden in een eeuwigdurende strijd om prestige, is het ook duidelijk hoe dit individuele kruisverband tussen hoe voorwerpen en personen snel kan uitgroeien naar een "socio-materieel netwerk" (Figuur 4.1).

Hiermee wordt een systeem bedoeld waarin juist het samenspel tussen sociale en materiële factoren de structuur en dynamiek van het netwerk bepalen. Mensen geven beweging en (inter)actie aan systemen van objecten, zichtbaar in de archeologie aan de hand van exotische objecten in archeologische assemblages of verschuivingen in materiële cultuur. Bekeken vanuit een Maussiaans perspectief geeft materiële cultuur de mogelijkheid sociale netwerken te "materialiseren" en zodoende interpersoonlijke of groepsrelaties onder meer publiekelijk te manifesteren, te manipuleren, te erkennen, of te herinneren.

Dit Maussiaanse perspectief vindt ook aansluiting in Amerindiaanse ideeën hierover. Het eerder besproken idee van Amerindiaans perspectivisme is namelijk niet slechts van toepassing op de relaties van mensen tot wat wij ook als levende wezens zouden beschouwen, maar ook op de relaties van mensen met de wereld der voorwerpen. Anders dan het resultaat van een "magische band" of vagelijk geconceptualiseerde objecten als subjecten was het volstrekt realistisch om te interacteren met voorwerpen zelf. Sterker nog, als we hedendaagse verhalen uit het tropisch laagland bekijken en deze vergelijken met wat Europeanen gerapporteerd hebben over het wereldbeeld van de oorspronkelijke bewoners van het Caribisch gebied, zien we dat dit type interacties zeer relevant was voor zowel sociale als socio-cosmische netwerken. Hierdoor konden individuen en groepen de hulp van bovenmenselijk wezens inroepen. Daarentegen kregn kregen deze gematerialiseerde geestwezens door hun interactie met mensen de mogelijkheid tot het manifesteren van hun eigen wil. Het resultaat hiervan was dat sommigen van hen pragmatische eisen ging stellen als een woning, voedsel, en eerbewijzen. Het onderhouden van netwerken tussen mensen en bovenmenselijke wezens die gematerialiseerd waren als beeldjes, amuletten en andere typen voorwerpen was dus verre van onproblematisch. Toch zien wij dat door de tijd heen deze gematerialiseerde, socio-cosmische counterparts een steeds belangrijker rol gingen spelen in menselijke verhoudingen. Een dynamiek en proces wat ook sterk naar voren komt in de case studies.

Een hart van steen: netwerken tussen 3200 BC en AD 400

De eerste case study gaat dieper in op de bestaande ideeën rond de veranderingen in de culturen en samenlevingen in de periode van 3200 BC tot AD 400, met daarbij de focus op de periode waarin voor het eerst gemeenschappen opkwamen die Saladoïde en Huecoïde aardewerk gebruikten. De bestaande theorieën hierover ondersteunen het beeld van een netwerk waarin cultureel superieure migranten de positie innemen van de autochtone bevolking zonder daarbij met hen in contact te treden (Figuur 1.4.a). Dit traditionele beeld wordt aan de kaak gesteld door een exploratie van de aanwezigheid van steenmateriaal afkomstig uit de Noordoostelijke Antillen in archeologische sites (Figuur 5.1 en 5.2). Eerdere studies hiervan hebben uitgewezen dat deze werden verspreid in de regio via directe verwerving en uitwisselingsnetwerken. Om het verloop van de exploitatie van en handel rond deze stenen bronnen in de tijd te kunnen volgen is deze langere periode opgedeeld in 5 kortere periodes.

Periode A (3200-2000 BC; Figuur 5.3) betreft de vroegste bewoning van de regio, bestaande uit kleine, rondtrekkende families die er waarschijnlijk opportunistische exploitatiestrategieën op na hielden. Vanwege de slechte archeologische zichtbaarheid is het moeilijk om iets met zekerheid vast te stellen over de contacten en mobiliteit van deze vroege bewoners. Wel is duidelijk dat vuursteen, het belangrijkste materiaal voor de vervaardiging van gereedschappen, betrokken wordt uit de directe regio. Periode B (2000-800 BC; Figuur 5.4) laat een soortgelijk, weinig helder beeld zien. Wel is er een grote groei in het aantal sites en worden de gebruikte vuursteenbronnen meer divers, terwijl de manieren van vervaardiging van vuurstenen gereedschappen juist minder divers worden. Eén bron springt boven de anderen uit: Long Island Flint, afkomstig van een klein eiland voor de kust van Antigua. De gemeenschappen die hier gebruik van maken vormen een duidelijke *clique*, maar zijn echter vooral geconcentreerd in de noordelijke Kleine Antillen. Er is een kleine mogelijkheid dat dit materiaal zich rond die tijd al een weg had gevonden naar Puerto Rico.

Dit is veel duidelijker in Periode C (800-200 BC; Figuur 5.5 en 5.6), waarin er duidelijk bewijs is voor de aanwezigheid van Long Island Flint voorbij de eilanden die zich het dichtst bij deze bron bevinden. Dit speelt op een grotere mate van connectiviteit in de regio, maar hoe deze precies is vormgegeven (via directe verwerving of via uitwisselingsnetwerken) is nog moeilijk te zeggen. Aan het einde van deze periode zien wij ook de opkomst van de eerste Saladoïde en Huecoïde aardewerk gebruikende gemeenschappen in de regio. De opkomst van deze aardewerkstijlen bracht ook een verschuiving in de steenassemblages en gebruik in de regio. Vanaf nu was er naast het gebruik van steen voor werktuigen ook een veel grotere rol weggelegd voor het decoratief gebruik van dit materiaal. Hoewel dit waarschijnlijk ook een verschuiving betekende in de sociale strategieën en relaties rond steengebruik is dit nog niet met zekerheid te stellen. Wel is het duidelijk dat er ondanks materiële cultuurverschillen tussen de vroegere gemeenschappen en de mogelijke nieuwkomers ook verbintenissen tussen hen waren. Beiden maakten gebruik van dezelfde vuursteenbronnen, met een prominent plaats voor Long Island Flint. Dit maakt het waarschijnlijk dat autochtone inwoners en nieuwkomers, ondanks eerdere ideeën over migratiegolven en culturele dominantie, toch onderdeel namen aan dezelfde interactienetwerken.

Dit patroon zet zich voort in Periode D (200 BC-AD 100; Figuur 5.7-5.9). Hier is voor het eerst sprake van een uitwisselingsnetwerk dat zich uitstrekte van Martinique tot aan Puerto Rico. In dit netwerk werden niet enkel grondstoffen voor gereedschappen uitgewisseld, maar ook rijk bewerkte ornamenten van Puerto Ricaans serpentiniet en kornalijn uit Antigua. Niettemin bleef Long Island Flint in deze periode het meest wijd verspreidde materiaal, waardoor het gemeenschappen van verschillende achtergronden in *cliques* en *2-cliques* verbond. In Periode E (AD 100-400; Figuur 5.9-5.13) werd deze verbindende rol van Long Island Flint nog verder versterkt. Een positionele analyse laat zien dat het juist de gemeenschappen waren die toegang hadden tot de grondstofbron van Long Island Flint die de beste strategische (*betweenness*) positie had in het netwerk. Het gaat te ver om hierin sociale ongelijkheid en de aanwezigheid van grotere groepsorganisatievormen te zien, maar men zou kunnen zeggen dat het juist deze uitwisselingsnetwerken waren tussen cultureel verschillende gemeenschappen, hier belicht vanuit de distributie van lokaal steen tussen gemeenschappen met hun eigen aardewerkrepertoires, die aan de basis stonden van de latere patronen van diversiteit en homogeniteit in de regio (Figuur 5.14).

Verreweg niet lokaal: de interactienetwerken van Kelbey's Ridge 2

De tweede casus concentreert zich op een gemeenschap aan de andere kant van het prehistorische spectrum, het 14[de] eeuwse Kelbey's Ridge 2. Dit was een kleine gemeenschap op het eveneens kleine eiland Saba, in de noordelijke Kleine Antillen. Het bijzondere aan deze archeologische site is echter dat het veel bewijs laat zien voor interactienetwerken binnen en buiten de eilandregio. Om beter inzicht te krijgen in wat voor type site Kelbey's Ridge 2 was is het mogelijk om, aan de hand van deze informatie, een zogenaamd ego-netwerk te construeren. Een ego-netwerk, ook wel een gecentraliseerd netwerk genoemd, is een specifiek type netwerkmodel dat zich focust op hoe de relaties van een *ego-node*, in dit geval de site Kelbey's Ridge 2, met en tussen andere *nodes* verschillende aspecten van *ego* kan bepalen. Het klassieke voorbeeld van een ego-netwerk stamt uit de sociologie en is een populaire toepassing van netwerkanalyse voor leken die bijvoorbeeld de structuur van hun eigen Facebook-netwerk willen bestuderen. Het idee is dat de relaties tussen de *ego* en tussen de *nodes* waarmee *ego* een relatie heeft iets zegt over de mogelijkheden die *ego* heeft om controle uit te oefenen op zijn of haar netwerk of juist gecontroleerd te worden door anderen (Figuur 3.5).

In de archeologie is het gebruik van ego-netwerken natuurlijk gecompliceerder, maar het kan niettemin gebruikt worden om een "schaalvrije" of multi-scalair perspectief te verkrijgen van de interactienetwerken waarin een gemeenschap participeerde – i.t.t. bijvoorbeeld de eerste case study waarin de analyse zich op het niveau van gemeenschappen in de regio bevond. De verschillende lijnen van bewijs in Kelbey's Ridge 2 bestaan bijvoorbeeld niet enkel uit uitwisselingsrelaties van producten en grondstoffen met andere eilanden, maar ook op relaties binnen de site zelf. Een voorbeeld hiervan is de relaties die de bewoners van de site gehad moeten hebben met hun voorouders: overledenen bleven geïntegreerd in het leven van alle dag doordat zij begraven werden in (open) putten en hun botten werden herhaaldelijk verplaatst of op andere manieren gemanipuleerd. Verder laat de vondst van ceremoniële artefacten – zogeheten "driepunters" en een snuifpijpje, gebruikt om hallucinogene middelen te inhaleren – zien dat de bewoners van Kelbey's Ridge 2 onderdeel waren van de reeds besproken socio-cosmische netwerken (Figuur 6.2). Voorbij de grenzen van het dorp had Kelbey's Ridge 2 een impact op de wijdere regio doordat het toegang had tot de rijke visgronden van de Saba bank en omdat het zich op het snijpunt bevond van uitwisselingsnetwerken van de noordelijke en meer zuidelijk gelegen Kleine Antillen. Deze strategische ligging biedt misschien ook een verklaring voor de interregionale contacten van Kelbey's Ridge 2 met de Grote Antillen, waarvan de daar gelegen *cacicazgos* een steeds belangrijkere culturele en waarschijnlijk ook politieke invloed gingen uitoefenen op dit gebied. Alles bijeen genomen karakteriseert Kelbey's Ridge zich in zijn ego-netwerk (Figuur 6.3), ondanks de geringe grootte van de gemeenschap en het eiland waarop deze gelegen was, als een belangrijke en zelfstandige speler in de complexe culturele en sociale netwerken van de 14de eeuw.

Caciques en hun collectieven: leiderschap in de pre- en vroeg koloniale Grote Antillen

De derde casus gaat specifiek over deze *cacicazgos* zoals zij beschreven werden door de Europeanen aan het eind van de 15de eeuw. Ondanks een lange en rijke traditie van archeologisch onderzoek in onder meer Puerto Rico en Oost Hispaniola (de Dominicaanse Republiek), is het zeer moeilijk om archeologisch vat te krijgen op de mogelijke structuur en dynamiek van de politieke netwerken in de regio. Dit is problematisch aangezien *cacicazgos* en hun leiders, de *caciques*, vaak verkeerd worden gerepresenteerd als koninkrijken en koningen door de vroeg-koloniale kronieken enerzijds en anderzijds als een typisch voorbeeld van chiefdommen in de antropologische literatuur. Aan de hand van een etnohistorische studie beargumenteer ik dat *caciques* noch koningen of autocratische chiefs aan de top van de politieke piramide waren (Figuur 7.1).

In plaats daarvan moeten wij de *cacicazgos* zien als bestaande uit een collectief van belanghebbenden. Voorbeelden hiervan zijn de *cacica*, de vrouw van de *cacique*, die vanwege de matrilineaire familieverbanden de eigenlijke controle had over de gemeenschappelijke rijkdommen en de nauwste (bloed)banden met de lokale bevolking. *Nitaínos* waren ook bondgenoten van de *cacique*, zij verzorgden onder meer de relaties met andere leiders en hoogwaardigheidsbekleders. *Behiques* (shamaanachtige, rituele specialisten) waren degenen die de politieke netwerken van mensen verbonden met die van de geesteswereld. Zoals reeds eerder besproken waren deze socio-cosmische netwerken ook van grote invloed op het leven van alledag en zeker in de machtsverhoudingen tussen *cacicazgos*. Samen vormden deze politieke actoren een collectief waarin het succes van de een afhing van het succes van de ander. Een analyse van status centraliteit in een geïdealiseerd model geeft deze onderlinge afhankelijkheid goed weer (Figuur 7.3).

Aan het hoofd van dit collectief stond wel degelijk de *cacique*, maar zijn daadwerkelijke macht en de daar bijkomende verantwoordelijkheden was verdeeld in zijn collectief. Om precies te zijn was het grotere politieke netwerk onderverdeeld in politieke economieën waarin specialisten hun eigen rol te spelen hadden: de rituele economie, de interne gemeenschapseconomie en de externe gemeenschapseconomie. Doordat deze economieën communicerende vaten waren, had een onbalans in de een echter ook negatieve invloed op de status van de andere. Een verder kenmerk van dit systeem was een afhankelijkheid van de continue aanwas van (relaties met) menselijke en niet-menselijke wezen van buiten. De gezondheid van een cacicazgo kon dus niet zozeer afgelezen worden aan zijn materiële rijkdom, maar aan het succes van zijn "HR management".

Terugkijkend in de tijd houden deze elementen van de laat pre-koloniale *cacicazgos* waarschijnlijk verband met de ontwikkeling van leiderschap en politieke organisatievormen in een veel vroegere periode, besproken in de eerste case study. Door instabiele interpersoonlijke verbanden hadden de leiders die de voorlopers waren van de latere *cacique* moeite om een blijvende politieke eenheid te smeden. Vanuit een netwerkperspectief waren deze leiders als het ware "manusjes van alles" en moesten zij continu schipperen tussen de politieke verhoudingen binnen de eigen groep en die met andere groepen en individuen van menselijke en niet-menselijke wezens. Het resultaat hiervan was dat na de dood of het falen van één leider de groep makkelijk uit elkaar kon vallen – de reden dat in de vroege periode nog geen grotere politieke eenheden zichtbaar zijn in de archeologie van de regio. Het is waarschijnlijk dat de succesvollere leiders en gemeenschappen juist diegenen waren die macht en verantwoordelijkheid deelden. Dit is ook weerspiegeld in de overgangsperiode tussen AD 500 en 1000 waarin er een verschuiving is van het verkrijgen van persoonlijke status naar die van het verankeren van de status van een gemeenschap of andere type collectief. Eens te meer speelde materiële cultuur hierbij een grote rol, enerzijds in het smeden van politieke allianties en anderzijds als materialisatie van potentieel machtige maar beïnvloedbare bondgenoten uit de geesteswereld.

Facebook van het verleden: de sociale en stilistische relaties van schelpen gezichten

Op deze laatste twee aspecten wordt uitgebreid ingegaan in de laatste netwerkstudie. Deze richt zich op de diversiteit en homogeniteit in het repertoire van voorwerpen dat bekend staat onder de noemer "Taíno". Deze term wordt dikwijls verbonden aan de volkeren die in de Grote Antillen leefden in de eeuwen voor en tijdens het eerste contact met Europeanen: de "Taíno". Omdat geen van de volkeren van de Grote Antillen zichzelf echter aanduidde als "Taíno" zou het eigenlijk juister zijn om dit begrip te verbinden aan een breed gedeelde materiële cultuur waaronder een grote variabiliteit schuil gaat, door de archeoloog William Keegan ook wel een "vernis" genoemd (i.v.m. eenzelfde eenheid in diversiteit in het eerder besproken Saladoïde aardewerk). Maar wat betekent het precies als een cultuuruiting aangeduid wordt als "vernis" en welke sociale en culturele relaties liggen hieraan ten grondslag?

Naast studies naar andere typen objecten, kan de studie naar gezicht-afbeeldende schelpen amuletten en ornamenten, ook wel bekend als *guaízas*, hier inzicht in geven (Figuur 8.2). De gezichten lijken allen op elkaar maar zijn echter ook allen uniek. Deze paradox laat zich ten eerste uitleggen door het gebruik van dit type voorwerpen als giften. Deze uniciteit en tegelijkertijd herkenbaarheid van deze objecten zorgden ervoor dat zij bij uitstek geschikt waren om gegeven te worden aan bezoekende leiders en andere hooggeplaatste gasten. Dit wordt ondersteund door de beschrijvingen van ontmoetingen tussen Europeanen en *caciques* waarin het schenken van *guaízas* een veel gebruikte uitwisselingsstrategie vormde.

Het is mogelijk om dit idee verder uit te diepen door een netwerk van de uiterlijke stijlkenmerken van deze voorwerpen te maken, als het ware creëert dit letterlijk een Facebook van schelpen ornamenten (Figuur 8.3 en 8.4. Hieruit komen twee patronen naar voren. Ten eerste delen alle voorwerpen een paar elementen met andere in het netwerk. Desalniettemin delen zij zelden een merendeel van hun uiterlijke kenmerken met een ander object. De dichtheid of *density* (de hoeveelheid aanwezige *ties* t.o.v. de maximaal mogelijke hoeveelheid *ties*) van het stilistisch netwerk is dus erg laag (rond de 18%; Figuur 8.5). Dit lijkt een abstract gegeven, maar als men de dichtheid zou meten bij een reeks voorwerpen waarvan het ontwerp en de fabricage gestandaardiseerd is, bijvoorbeeld een modern frisdrankblikje, zou zo'n stilistisch netwerk een dichtheid hebben van (tegen de) 100%. Uniekheid was dus wel degelijk van belang bij het ontwerp van deze voorwerpen. Sterker nog, een tweede patroon in het netwerk laat zien dat er een omgekeerde correlatie is tussen objecten die dichtbij elkaar terug gevonden zijn en hun uiterlijke gelijkenissen. In andere woorden, voorwerpen uit dezelfde regio lijken juist minder op elkaar (Figuur 8.6 en 8.7). Dit is een andere aanwijzing dat deze voorwerpen met opzet uniek gemaakt werden. Bij dit type "Taíno" materiële cultuur kan men dus inderdaad spreken van een vernis of, in deze context misschien toepasselijker, een familiegelijkenis. Net zoals een familie van mensen waren de patronen van gelijkenissen van dit type voorwerpen zodanig dat men wel over een homogeen verband kan spreken, maar bij nadere inspectie blijken de *nodes* in deze groepen toch unieke individuen te zijn.

Het was wel belangrijk voor het succes van deze objecten als geschenken dat zij een brede esthetische en sociale waarde bleven houden. Hier valt een vergelijking te trekken met veel van de andere laat pre-koloniale materiële cultuur en zeker in het type objecten wat een grotere rol zou spelen in sociale, politieke en socio-cosmische netwerken (Figuur 8.1). De grote gemene deler van al deze objecten is een focus op het gezicht en specifiek de mond en ogen. Als wij ons een bezoek van de ene aan de andere *cacique* zouden voorstellen, zou dit gepaard gaan met het gebruik van een grote hoeveelheid aan gezicht-afbeeldende voorwerpen: men dronk en at uit aardewerk met gezichten als handvaten, men zat op ceremoniële stoelen met hoofden die uit het zitvlak staken, beelden met uitvergrote hoofden sloegen de onderhandelingen gade, en men wisselde ornamenten en amuletten uit die ook voor het thuisfront een bekend gezicht waren. Op deze manier was de circulatie en diffusie van gezicht-afbeeldende materiële cultuur dus van groot belang voor het voortbestaan van sociale netwerken en lagen zij ook ten dele ten grondslag aan de patronen van homogeniteit en diversiteit van de pre-koloniale periode.

Conclusie: Caribische verbanden

Deze dissertatie rijgt drie archeologische thema's aan elkaar die in het verleden vaak als losse strengen werden gezien: culturele homogeniteit en diversiteit, archeologische netwerkbenaderingen en de kruisverbanden tussen socialiteit en materialiteit. Dit is gedaan door de ontwikkeling van een raamwerk aan netwerk concepten en antropologische theorieën die verder zijn geoperationaliseerd in de hierboven besproken casussen. Een van de doelen is hiermee zeker bereikt: de mogelijkheid om dit type studie in de Caribische archeologie uit te voeren is aangetoond. De hier ontwikkelde aanpak en de uitwerking in de casussen is slechts een eerste verkenning van de mogelijkheden. Toch laten de case studies al duidelijk zien waar dit type aanpak voordelen heeft boven meer traditionele cultuurhistorische benaderingen. Hier moet de kanttekening bij geplaatst worden dat de hier voorgestane benadering zich niet zozeer distantieert van de traditionele en succesvolle cultuurhistorische benaderingen in de Caribische archeologie, zoals sommige recente studies, maar deze juist probeert te vernieuwen.

Een archeologische netwerk aanpak geeft de mogelijkheid om voorbij het monolithische denken te gaan, door zowel de overkoepelende diversiteit en homogeniteit van de pre-koloniale Cariben in ogenschouw te nemen. Dit biedt nieuwe mogelijkheden in de archeologische methodologie van classificatie en categorisering maar ook binnen de ideeën over de sociale geschiedenissen van samenlevingen. Verder plaatst het de archeologie binnen een bredere stroom aan sociale, economische en natuurwetenschappelijke disciplines die zich allen verbonden zien in de studie van netwerken.

Archeologie en netwerkwetenschappen hebben elkaar veel te brengen, maar hierbij moet wel oog blijven voor de specifieke vragen, methodes en doelstellingen van beide vakgebieden. Een heikele kwestie hierin blijft hoe men de netwerkwetenschappelijke benaderingen kan verbinden met zowel de archeologische geschiedschrijving over mensen gebaseerd op studies naar objecten als ook de perceptie van de sociale realiteit in het verleden. Antropologische en archeologische theorieën die de sociale, materiële en cosmische dynamieken van relaties en samenlevingen aan elkaar verbinden bieden hier uitkomst.

Ten laatste is het belangrijk om de studie van netwerken in het Caribisch gebied binnen een breder kader te plaatsen. Ten eerste weerspreekt deze en soortgelijke studies de karakterisering van de oorspronkelijke bewoners van het Caribisch gebied als vreedzame, niet materialistische naïevelingen, een nog steeds populaire stereotypering die ontstaan is door Europese koloniale representatie. Uit deze en andere studies blijkt dat dit beeld vervangen moet worden door een waarin deze samenlevingen en culturen eerder getypeerd worden door hun culturele flexibiliteit, insluitende sociale strategieën en een zeker oog voor ondernemerschap. Een verdere (v)erkenning van Caribisch inheemse netwerken is ook van grote waarde voor als we de fundamenten van de hedendaagse, globaliserende netwerken beter willen begrijpen. Het is hiervoor noodzakelijk dat we voorbij de grenzen van de Caribische pre-koloniale periode kijken naar de invloed van de oorspronkelijke bevolking op de trans-Atlantische netwerken van de koloniale periode. Wanner we dit zouden doen zou het goed mogelijk zijn dat, ondanks dat zij tot een verre en voor ons exotische geschiedenis lijken te behoren, onze eigen complexe en diverse netwerken voor een gedeelte hun wortels en weerklank vinden in de netwerken van het Caribische verleden.

Curriculum Vitae

Angus Mol was born in Rotterdam on June 15, 1984. After his secondary education at the Johan de Witt Gymnasium in Dordrecht (1996-2002), he studied archaeology at Leiden University (2002-2007), obtaining a BA degree (with extra-curricular courses in philosophy and intercultural studies) and an MPhil *cum laude* in archaeology, with a specialisation on Religion and Society in Native America. He participated in a number of archaeological field projects in the Netherlands and the Caribbean in the course of his study. For his MPhil thesis he undertook collection research in Cuba and the Dominican Republic. The resulting work, *Costly Giving, Giving Guaízas*, was published by Sidestone Press.

After his graduation he worked as a part-time bridge keeper, gave several guest lectures, participated in a Leiden University survey on the island of Dominica and co-authored a chapter on evolutionary dynamics in *the Beowulf* with Raymond Corbey (in *Creating Consilience*, Oxford University Press).

In 2008 he obtained a four-year PhD research position at Leiden University's Faculty of Archaeology to partake in the NWO-VICI funded research project *Communicating Communities in the Circum-Caribbean*, led by Prof. dr. Hofman. During the course of his PhD he taught courses and guest lectures, organized several conferences and was a member of the Faculty of Archaeology's research committee. He undertook collection research in Jamaica, Cuba, the Dominican Republic and the Lesser Antilles as well as participated in fieldwork by Leiden University in the Dominican Republic, St. Vincent and St. Eustatius. Together with Arie Boomert he undertook excavations of the site of Brighton Beach in St. Vincent. He also published a number of single authored and co-authored papers and book chapters, among which in *The Oxford Handbook of Caribbean Archaeology* and *Network Analysis in Archaeology* (Oxford University Press).

In 2011 he was offered a position as coordinator of the Faculty of Archaeology's Honours College. In 2013 this was followed up with a position to teach BA and MA-level courses in Caribbean archaeology.

Since September 2013 Angus takes part as a post-doc in two research projects: *Nexus 1492* (ERC synergy grant) and *Island Networks* (NWO programmatic research grant). His role in these projects is to investigate the networks that arose as a result of the indigenous-European encounters in the early colonial period. He focuses on embedding network science concepts and methods in archaeological heuristics. For this he is working together with researchers from both Leiden and Konstanz University (Germany).